VISIONS AND VOICES

ACKNOWLEDGEMENTS

The realization of this book has been a trek, from the original conception to the present, more than three decades later. That it finally happened is truly amazing. But fate has a way of pulling off some really remarkable twists. Were it not for an invitation from a long-time dear friend, Ms. Marcia Bullock-Jobson, to a dinner party at her former home in Kendall, Florida, in 1999, I would not have met Professor Kwame Dawes. By that time, I had pretty much given up trying to get these interviews published.

As it was, Professor Dawes was in town for the Miami International Book Fair, and along with some other Caribbean writers – among them the Jamaican novelist, Colin Channer, and the poet Shara McCallum – was in attendance at Ms. Bullock-Jobson's home. That evening, we talked about Caribbean writers and Caribbean writing. I had not been in such a setting for many years, since the days when I lived New York and such discussions were a regular part of my life. During the evening, I was asked to say a little about myself. In passing, I mentioned that I had a manuscript which comprised some fourteen interviews with English-speaking Caribbean playwrights. At the end of my little chatter, Professor Dawes expressed interest in seeing the manuscript. That was the new beginning of the journey of this book.

As such, my humblest appreciation and thanks goes out to Kwame Dawes for possessing a keen eye and diligence in seeing this project through.

Tremendous thanks goes to Ms. Marcia Bullock-Jobson for having the thoughtfulness for inviting me to her home at the time when she did, for without meeting Kwame Dawes this book would never have happened.

Also, my thanks and appreciation goes to my agent, Claudia Menza, who stuck with me all the way.

My thanks and appreciation also extends to the staff at Peepal Tree Press: Hannah Bannister, Emma Smith and Jeremy Poynting.

Thank you all for making this book become a reality.

– O.S.

VISIONS AND VOICES

INTERVIEWS WITH CARIBBEAN PLAYWRIGHTS

WITH

OLIVIER STEPHENSON

PREFACE BY KWAME DAWES

PEEPAL TREE

First published in Great Britain in 2013
Peepal Tree Press Ltd
17 King's Avenue
Leeds, LS6 1QS
UK

ISBN: 9781845231736

Supported by
ARTS COUNCIL
ENGLAND

CONTENTS

To Aldwyn, Josepha and Erik

KWAME DAWES

PREFACE

If there was a decade during which Caribbean theatre began to be unselfconscious (in the sense that it no longer felt it needed to make excuses for itself), but wilful (in the sense of being goal-driven) and skilled at presenting a poetics that was wholly West Indian, and confidently so, it was during the 1970s. It was a decade when Caribbean people, more assuredly then than since, threw off the vestiges of colonialism and looked hard at what knowledge and experience had been gained during the long colonial years. It was a decade of impatience with the halting postcolonial agenda of many of the newly independent governments, and an intense ideological idealism about the possibilities of real sovereignty and deep concern about the encroachments of American imperialism, which took overt cultural forms and was involved in covert political subversion. It was an uneasy time for those reasons, but it was also the time when the West Indies was becoming the greatest cricket team in history and Bob Marley was striding the universe with his reggae revolution. Theatre seemed an exciting part of that enterprise of cultural nationalism – populist, serious and increasingly professional.

In 1970, events at the Creative Arts Centre at the University of the West Indies in Mona (Jamaica) gave evidence of the urge to nationalistic correction and the complications of its effects on the Jamaican theatre world. Activists occupied the Centre for a term, shutting down all productions. The complaint was that the theatre was still inscribed in a colonialist agenda. It was a flawed quarrel, one spurred unfairly by the fact that at the time the relatively new drama tutor who had replaced the obviously black Errol Hill was a white Jamaican, the veteran and gifted theatre director Noel Vaz. It did not matter that in his short term as tutor Vaz had mounted productions of plays by Wole Soyinka including *The Road*; it was his acclaimed production of Chekhov's *The Cherry Orchard* and Weiss's *Marat/Sade* that did not endear him to the activists.

Vaz chose to direct no more plays at the theatre. He assisted other directors, but a change was taking place and that defining moment represented two critical developments: the growing desire for a theatre that proactively sought to articulate an aesthetic that was Caribbean (albeit one largely defined by an Afrocentric bias) and a growing shift away from the privileging of European plays and European or Europe-trained playwrights directors and actors. In Jamaica, in the 1970s, the School of Drama was established with a mandate that seemed to respond positively to the spirit of the occupation: a theatre of the Caribbean led by internationally and classically trained Caribbean theatre practitioners such as Carroll Dawes and Dennis Scott.

What came before is glimpsed in several of the interviews. Alwin Bully, for instance, speaks of his beginnings writing and directing plays in Dominica in the early 1970s in an environment when local theatre meant variety performances and skits, when groups might come together to put on what was usually an English play, and then disperse. Even in Trinidad, where a Caribbean theatre had much earlier beginnings (c1950s), the precursors that Errol Hill and Errol John describe were very much the same. One of the important topics discussed by many of the interviewees was the challenge and the need to create an audience for a Caribbean theatre that demanded more of its viewers than the comedy double act or the brief satirical skit. Whilst the issue of how to build an audience – or indeed who that audience was supposed to be – continued to demand the attention of the playwrights interviewed, at least from the late sixties onwards, the political ferment of independence had created an environment in which audiences could be supposed to expect to see Caribbean subject matter and language at the theatre.

This is the world that defined the careers of the playwrights interviewed by Olivier Stephenson in this remarkable collection, because even when the playwrights were making theatre outside of the Caribbean, they did so in the same spirit of quest for a legitimate and authentic aesthetic.

This gathering of interviews reminds us of what was gained and what has been lost. It reminds us, especially, that much has been lost in terms of the perpetuation of a growing tradition, and a critical reading of the interviews begins to suggest some of the intrinsic reasons for that loss. Stephenson, in many ways, was a man in a unique position. At the time, he may not have fully understood the significance of the moment, but his decision to take advantage of the unique access that he had to these writers in full flight cannot be said to be fortuitous. For years he was pursuing a career in a place, New York, that enabled him to give an account of a growing, Caribbean-wide tradition, an account that subsequent playwrights and playmakers have not had the same access to. Even at the time that Stephenson was conducting these interviews, you sense that the region's playwrights only caught glimpses if what their peers were doing, and more often than not were inclined to believe that they were inventing a tradition on their own. For those who came later, this lack of mutual awareness became even more marked. It is evident, for instance, that there were four fairly distinct centres of theatre in the Anglophone Caribbean: in Jamaica, in Trinidad, in a loose South-Eastern Caribbean network (that included Dominica, St Lucia, Barbados and Antigua), and in Guyana – with little mutual interconnection. As Olivier Stephenson argues, there was certainly a desire amongst at least some of the playwrights to know about each other's work, but there are also many admissions of ignorance in the interviews. One wonders, for instance, how much some of the Trinidadian, Port of Spain-based interviewees actually knew about the theatre groups in the south of Trinidad around San Fernando. They are mentioned, but almost as if they exist on another island. Perhaps, just as London in the 1950s and 1960s had been the place where writers from the West Indies discovered that they were writing West Indian fiction, New York was the place where a Caribbean theatre could be found. Our good fortune is that Olivier Stephenson's New York was one of the hubs around which Caribbean theatre converged.

There are very important indications in these interviews of some of the directions which Caribbean theatre has taken over the last three decades, and one of the most striking is the centrality of financial considerations in many of the decisions made and framings of ideas that were constructed. Already the tension between a commercial theatre and a theatre committed to artistic aspirations was apparent. Errol Hill's ungracious broadside against Trevor Rhone's work is a case in point. He accuses Rhone of being an untalented playwright whose commercial ambitions were producing a crass, populist form of theatre. Time has shown that Rhone's plays are far better works of theatrical art than Hill gave him credit for, but it is clear that Hill was somewhat panicked about what he saw as a terrible trend taking over the Caribbean theatre. Rhone's own reported fixation on money would not have helped.

What the contribution of Rhone to this gathering of interviews does show is that he was preoccupied with the idea of a commercial and popular theatre, and, even though he does not state this explicitly, Hill appears ambivalent about and suspicious of commercial success in theatre. He does want the theatre to be popular but not at the expense of artistic merit. Rhone evidently believed that a commercially viable artistic theatre was possible. Ironically, Rhone lived to see his brand of popular theatre branded as highbrow and artistic by an even more commercially-driven theatre in Jamaica. Indeed, as other interviews make evident, the distinction was not simply between the "serious" artistic theatre and the commercially driven theatre, but between what Alwin Bully described as the "Holy" or "pure" theatre and the "Bacchanalian" theatre. For him it was a debate that centred around the poetic dramas of Derek Walcott with their literary demands on audiences, and various forms of "folk" or "calypso" theatre, concerning which Bully uses the example of the Trinidadian dramatist and director

Freddie Kissoon. The point is that these interviews help us to understand the present state of theatre better, though it is a pity that there is no reference to the theatre in Guyana in the collection. There the issue of audience and the divergences between the artistic and the commercial, the folk and the literary, the popular theatre and the theatre of the "cultivated" middle class was on clear display. In the same physical space, the National Cultural Centre in Georgetown, two very different kinds of theatre were presented. As Al Creighton once reported, either the car park was full and the theatre half empty, or the theatre was full and the car park empty. In other words, there was a close connection between theatre with artistic ambitions and the small Guyanese middle class, and a populist theatre which often featured a broadly satirical take on current events which had working-class Georgetown support. Frank Thomasson's chronicle cum-compendium of reviews, *A History of the Guyanese Theatre*, though lacking in analysis, is a useful record of how those choices between "art" and "commerce" lay at the heart of debates within Guyana's most proficient, mostly amateur (and mostly middle class) repertory group, the Theatre Guild.

Hill's broadside against Rhone was not insignificant given his long-standing position as one of the "gatekeepers" of what would constitute genuine Caribbean or West Indiān drama, in his capacity as the series editor of the Extra Mural Plays series and in his role as a director and a respected authority on West Indian theatre. One is, of course, fascinated to read the strong views held by Hill on what he clearly viewed as the crass commercialism of Rhone's, quite urban, and largely "un-folksy" theatre. Rhone was obviously not writing *Echo in the Bone*, or, for that matter *Man Better Man*, and Rhone, to what would seem Hill's chagrin, was cashing in just fine, thank you. The Hill and Rhone interviews, I believe, present us with an instance of a generational fissure, a fissure shaped by the shift from a strong anti-colonial agenda in the drama to what could best be called a postcolonial agenda – all the elements that were coming to define West Indian literature in general. This generational fissure is nicely (and generously) picked up in Abdur Rahman Slade Hopkinson's interview, where he acknowledges Hill's immense importance, and what was owed to him, his "importance as somebody who taught us in the beginning and with whom we have grown to disagree..." Another, later, generational shift is picked up in the interview with Mustapha Matura where he talks of his one-time perception of the 1950's generation as "has-beens" and "no influence at all." How far there has been, in reality, influence from, reaction to or just sheer ignorance of the work of previous generations is a question for future historians of Caribbean theatre. Has there been a growing theatrical culture, or has each generation felt that it was beginning from scratch again? It's amusing to note that a little later in Matura's interview, he speaks of the debt he thinks the new generation of Black British writers of the 1980s owed to the cultural politics pioneered by his 1960's generation.

Instructive, too, is what the interview with Hill shows us about the forcefulness of his views about what constituted good theatre, and we can't help but wonder what might have been different for the legacy of Caribbean drama, or at least the way that legacy has been represented, had Hill's views been a little more inclusive. This is a point made by Dennis Scott in his interview where he welcomes the diversity of the Jamaican theatre in the early 1980s – from the experimental plays at the School of Drama (including, no doubt, some that "befuddled" Trevor Rhone) to the immensely popular LTM annual pantomimes – because, with such a variety of theatre, "at least the options are kept open".

These interviews demonstrate another striking feature in the development of Caribbean theatre. At the time of the interviews, Stephenson implicitly classifies all of the playwrights, some of whom regarded themselves as outside the Caribbean dramatic tradition, as Caribbean. This may be explained by his own evolving immigrant status at a time when he was trying to establish a base in the US while still remaining connected to Jamaica. The theatre company, CART (Caribbean American Repertory Theatre), he and his friends formed in New York, emerged out of the frustration of immigrant writers and actors who were finding it impossible to get gainful employment in the American theatre, black or white. In many ways Stephenson and the visiting playwrights from across the region found affinity because of this need; he was meeting these playwrights because he was in search of plays for his company. It is clear that some of those who were interviewed saw themselves as primarily as national writers (Jamaican, Trinidadian), others as primarily located in their place of settlement (Abbensetts in the UK, Edgar White in the USA). However, under Stephenson's questioning, all acknowledge their Caribbean heritage, though in interestingly diverse ways.

Given Olivier Stephenson's own Jamaican background, it would not be unreasonable to suspect a bias in this sample of playwrights in favour of Jamaica. In fact, Trinidad is equally well represented. Of the playwrights interviewed, Tipling, Scott, Rhone and Harrison are all Jamaicans and Brown, Hill, John, Matura, and by location Derek Walcott are Trinidadian; there is no-one from Barbados and the rest are scattered throughout the smaller islands in the east (Bully, Roderick Walcott and, only by birth, Edgar White). Actually, in terms of the population distribution of the region, and the testimony of almost all the interviewees that Jamaica has had (and continues to have) the most active theatre environment, it could be argued that Jamaica is underrepresented. That said, it is a shame not to see more representation of the Guyanese theatre during that period. Whilst

Abbensetts originated from Guyana, his theatre is almost wholly focused on a Black British experience developed in the UK. Guyanese playwrights such as Harold Bascom, Michael Gilkes, Francis Farrier, Ken Corsbie and Sheik Sadeek are missing.

Even so, the geographical distribution of the interviewees and what they have to say both makes it possible to speak of a Caribbean theatre with some common points of focus, *and* cautions against seeing that theatre as having any kind of unitary existence. My view is that, for the best of motives, Olivier Stephenson overstates the degree of unity. It is clear, for instance, that playwrights such as Abbensetts, Lennox Brown, Mustapha Matura and Edgar White, whose careers developed in the UK or North America, wrote in very different sociocultural and racial contexts and for different kinds of audiences than those writing in the Caribbean itself. It is equally clear that whilst all those in the Caribbean were responding to similar tides of radical political ideas (the February 1970 Black Power Uprising in Trinidad; Manley's socialist phase in Jamaica; the agitation that culminated in the New Jewel Movement seizure of power in Grenada), playwrights in different parts of the Caribbean began from very different material and cultural-historical bases. This is something that Alwin Bully's interview, in particular, makes clear when he talks – concerning his own work and those of his peers in St Vincent, Antigua and Montserrat – of there being so little to build on. The fragility of institutional survival in small island states such as St Lucia is corroborated in Roderick Walcott's interview: how the dynamic existence of the Creative Arts Guild in the 1950s (led by the Walcott brothers) had dwindled by the 1970s because of their absence abroad.

The most serious absence in this collection are those of the women playwrights who were already important or were emerging at the time of the interviews. In the first category was Sylvia Wynter, whose first play, *Under the Sun*, was performed by the Royal Court in London as early as 1958, but whose most influential work was with the Jamaican pantomime, giving it a cultural and political pertinence in plays such as *Rockstone Anancy* (1970) and *Maskarade* (1973). Of those emerging, the most significant included Pat Cumper (*The Rapist* (1977), *Rufus* (1978) and *Coming of Age* (1983)); Gloria Lannnaman (*Stanley, Faye, Pularchie and P* (1974)); Marina Omowale Maxwell (*Play Mas* and *Hounsi Kanzo* (1976)), who, though from Trinidad, founded "Yard Theatre" in Jamaica; and Honor Ford Smith with the Sistren collective. By the period of the interviews, Sistren had performed *Down Pression Get a Blow* (1977), *Bellywoman Bangarang* (1978) and *Domestick* (1982).

Though Carmen Tipling is interviewed, the absence of other women tends to mean that issues of gender, which were emerging powerfully in other Caribbean literary forms, are overlooked here. How issues of gender connected to the collective forms of theatre developed by Maxwell and Sistren would have been worth exploring, in addition to questioning how far male Caribbean theatre was telling women's stories at any level, or indeed questioning how the female characters in male plays were actually being written.

It would be easy to say that the overwhelming male centredness of these interviews is merely a product of the times – few women were writing plays, men were making plays, and Stephenson could not be blamed. But we are not speaking here of the dark ages; Stephenson himself admits that his most credible excuse for this imbalance lay in the way that the project unfolded. He interviewed the people he associated with, first of all, and secondly, the people he really admired and regarded as giants. It would be fair to say that there were, at the time, no female playwrights with the kind of reputation and productivity that Hill, Walcott, Scott, or White, for instance, could boast of. But Stephenson included some quite fledgling voices, and it is here that one suspects his own contemporary biases of association and value may have been located. I imagine that Stephenson might honestly say that he felt, *at the time*, no compulsion to include more women. In the region, we were, after all, only just starting to think of proactive gestures in the matter of gender equality. One cannot help noticing, in almost all of the interviews, an assumption in the use of pronouns that writers were male and – more unforgivably – that audiences were male. It is significant that the only really insightful comment on the innovative theatre of Honor Ford Smith and Sistren comes from Carmen Tipling, the only woman interviewed. Errol Hill expresses his interest in what the group were doing, but expresses more forcefully his reservations about their methodology of collective improvisation. We should, perhaps, except from the general absence of gender consciousness amongst the male interviewees Dennis Scott's perceptive comments on Carmen Tipling's work, which locates her concerns within a jointly male-female world. Indeed, on the evidence of Scott's generous, sometimes tough but always honest comments on his peers, we might wish we had access to more of his writing on the theatre.

That said, it is still fair for us to speculate on just what the inclusion of female voices might have done to round off the historical telling that this book represents. Interviews with Honor Ford Smith, Pat Cumper or Omowale Maxwell would have been both fitting and revelatory in so many ways. Clearly, the challenges that these women faced, and their ideas about gender and politics and race would have offered us so much more knowledge about the theatre of the time. I think of the work Cumper had been doing for popular radio drama and the way that translated into an innovative and powerful theatrical practice, of her airing of very controversial subjects on a stage that had remained fairly conservative for decades. Again, I think that the transformative work of Honor Ford Smith and the Sistren Theatre Collective may have had as significant an impact on future Caribbean theatrical practice as Ntosake Shange's *for colored girls who have considered suicide/ when the rainbow is enuf* had on American theatre in the late seventies.

The other absence, perhaps inevitable, is of the theatre of Indo-Caribbeans in Trinidad and Guyana, both in terms of traditional dramatic forms such as the Ram Lila cycles, described by Derek Walcott in his *The Antilles: Fragments of Epic Memory* (1993), and of practising playwrights such as Ralph Maraj in Trinidad and Sheik Sadeek in Guyana. There is the interview with Mustapha Matura, of course, but as he makes clear, he does not write from an Indo-Caribbean cultural experience or sensibility.

It is noticeable in some interviews, such as that with Errol Hill, that the markers of what was regarded as authentic Caribbean theatre ("a recognisable indigenous theatre") were all Afro-Creole. This from a Trinidadian dramatist was a very partial view of theatre's potential cultural resources. The ethnocentricity of Hill's views are more clearly seen in contrast with those of fellow Trinidadian Lennox Brown, who talks about the wealth of cultural influences – African, Indian, Chinese – available to Trinidadian writers. Derek Walcott makes the same point in setting out what the Trinidadian needs to know to understand the composite culture of the island.

Of course, such absences are easily explained by the way this book came together. Stephenson never set out to interview a regionally representative sample of playwrights. He was guided more by who he felt was influential and perhaps hot at the time. Above all, most of his interviews were done in New York and happened because these playwrights were in the city.

And while it is incorrect to assume that all the important work being done in the Caribbean theatre had somehow to find its way, whether in stagings or in the ambition to stage, to New York, there is something valuable about considering the work of playwrights sufficiently committed to a professional career in theatre and sufficiently ambitious in vision to believe their work relevant to a world stage. These interviews reveal some of the implications, not all of them positive, of such an ambition. In some instances the playwrights are dismissive of work being done in the Caribbean by artists with a more nationalistic bent, artists interested in creating a Caribbean theatre for Caribbean people. Others, if not dismissive of such work, are simply ignorant of it and certainly do not regard those projects as consistent with their own. Stephenson's interviews grant us ample insights into both the aesthetic goals of many of these playwrights, but also the way that the pragmatics of material resource limitations, or the desire for commercial success, were constantly affecting the style and thematic focus of the work being produced both inside and outside the region.

The interviews tell us much, too, about the zeitgeist – and the diverse range of perspectives – of the time. One can scarcely imagine a contemporary playwright passing through the same kind of philosophical/cultural journey as Edgar White reveals in a fascinating interview, if curiously dated in its language. Read beyond the "hip" phraseology of the period, though, and a rewarding account of the intellectual development of one of the Caribbean's most interesting, but now neglected, playwrights, emerges. The contrast with Derek Walcott's brief account of his intellectual making is instructive.

Perhaps, though, the most valuable thing about these interviews is what they reveal, sometimes implicitly, about the failure of institutional forms of theatre (with all that implies in terms of stability and continuity of development) to take root. The interviews record for us the level of thought, imagination and effort that these artists were putting into the theatre and into their own art at a time when support for this work was limited. While it is true that some Caribbean governments in the 1970s were offering a little support for theatre, for the most part these theatre makers were working with very limited resources. They were working in an industry that demanded that any individual with ambitions to make plays would have to assume multiple hats to do so. There were more than a handful of quite brilliant directors working in theatre in the Caribbean at the time. These included Carroll Dawes, Dennis Scott, Michael Gilkes, Noel Vaz, Errol Hill, Barry Reckord, Yvonne Brewster, Earl Warner and Eugene Williams to name a few – most clustered in Jamaica – but few were responsible for managing theatres or had the opportunity to mount seasons of plays. At the same time, given the limited funds that most plays generated, it became obvious to many playwrights that if they managed all aspects of the production, including acting, producing, designing, marketing and directing, they would stand a better chance of making some money. Sadly, this approach undermined the capacity for institutional development, and the sad legacy of the work documented in these interviews is that apart from Trinidad's Theatre Workshop, run for years by Derek Walcott and then by others who shared his vision, there exists no consistently successful national theatre committed to producing the work of Caribbean playwrights in the region today. Indeed, there are few if any equivalents to the National Dance Theatre of Jamaica that are committed to drama.

Contemporary Caribbean theatre is largely either commercial or educational. A few national schools of drama or theatre are able to function in the embryo role of national theatres, but, inevitably, they are designed around amateur performance and teaching, and not around the idea of producing a defining professional theatre for the region. Commercial theatre largely pursues what it believes will draw audiences, whether this be broad comedy or increasing sexual explicitness, but it rarely leaves any legacy or the scope for playwrights to develop distinctive voices.

A commitment to developing a distinctiveness of style, a way of seeing and to dramatic structures that express that uniqueness is very much present in the playwrights interviewed in this book. The hustle, energy and drive evident in these interviews is quite exciting to encounter because, for the most part, it is characterized by optimism, ambition and a sense of possibility. However, it is already evident in some of the more mature playwrights, that the grind of producing plays in an environment that was not supportive of the artist, was taking its toll. It is one of the points that Lennox Brown makes when he talks about the pressure on Derek Walcott as a writer, who had also to function as a business manager, director and publicity agent for the Trinidad Theatre Workshop. And it is one of the fascinating things about this book that it offers not only Derek Walcott's own perception of those years, but also of those of Abdur Rahman Slade Hopkinson, who was involved as an actor in the TTW.

Visions and Voices is a necessary reassessment of the history and development of the idea of Caribbean theatre. In Wycliffe Bennett's long awaited book, *The Jamaican Theatre* (2011), a lively and largely upbeat sense of the energy and drive of the theatre is given. But the story told grows thin during the last twenty years. More significantly, Bennett's accounting does not try to gauge the mood, reflections and attitudes of the practitioners themselves to the theatre environment on the island. Stephenson's book offers a sobering and revealing balance.

One can conclude by noting that theatre is alive and doggedly present in the Caribbean. Small and large halls, sheds and theatres are staging plays to small and large audiences night after night. Some are actually making a decent living from the theatre. A number of actors have become celebrities in the region and in the immigrant Caribbean communities in the major cities of the UK, the US and Canada. The "roots" theatre spoken of in several of these interviews has evolved from the vision of a homegrown, folk-based theatre, which seems to characterize the perception of the "roots" form in the interviews, to a highly commercial form of comic theatre that is tremendously popular, but which employs production practices that scrimp on professional values (sets, costumes, staging, rehearsal time – and in the writing), in favour of speed and high box-office returns. And unlike the parallel popular form of dancehall music, the roots theatre does not have as solid a "publishing" system as the recording industry has developed over the years. As a result, the work produced is fleeting, disposable and entirely dependent on the unreliable memories of its practitioners to create a context for growth and development. A number of companies have developed a CD/video industry around these plays, which is reminiscent of the Chitlin drama circuit of Black America, or the Nollywood maverick juggernaut in Nigeria, but these productions are almost exclusively comic and do not pretend to be anything other than commercial dramas.

At the end of the day, without the legacy of published plays and works that chart the history of Caribbean drama as this collection does, Caribbean drama will continue to struggle to build on its rich history. For instance, one cannot read the remarkably fertile interview with Lennox Brown (spoken of by many of his contemporaries as an hugely gifted playwright) without lamenting that his work has disappeared from view. For this reason we are deeply indebted to Olivier Stephenson for his remarkable work in bringing to us the voices of these important makers of Caribbean theatre.

EVERYTHING TO BE MADE: SOME THOUGHTS ON CARIBBEAN THEATRE

Colonials, we began with this malarial enervation: that nothing could ever be built among these rotting shacks, barefooted back yards, and moulting shingles; that being poor, we already had the theatre of our lives. So the self-inflicted role of martyr came naturally, the melodramatic belief that one was message bearer for the millennium, that inflamed ego was enacting their will. In that simple schizophrenic boyhood one could lead two lives: the interior life of poetry, the outward life of action and dialect. Yet the writers of my generation were natural assimilators. We knew literature of empires, Greek, Roman, British, through their essential classics; and both the patois of the street and the language of the classroom hid the elation of discovery. If there was nothing, there was everything to be made. With this prodigious ambition one began.

— Derek Walcott, *What the Twilight Says*

Caribbean theatre, whether Anglophone, Francophone, Hispanic or Dutch-speaking, whether in the region or in its diasporas, is very much alive in its various forms – from popular farce to serious verse drama – and continuing to develop and grow. This book does not attempt to survey that vast range in time and place; it focuses on the reflections of Anglophone playwrights whose work was appearing between the 1950s and the 1980s. The continuing significance of the interviews recorded in this volume is that they were conducted during some of the most defining years of what was then referred to as West Indian theatre.

For whilst as early as the 1970s, the term "Caribbean Theatre" was being used by those who had for various reasons developed a more pan-Caribbean, multinational, multilingual and multicultural view of the region's culture and art, nonetheless, for the English-speaking Caribbean, the term "West Indian" still dominated, and it certainly shaped the thinking of many of the playwrights interviewed for this project. The interviews showcase dramatists who were at the forefront of this West Indian literary movement, and their insights and frameworks remain extremely relevant to anyone interested in understanding how Caribbean drama has evolved. With that context in mind I am confident that this book will become a valuable work of reference and hope that the words of the playwrights interviewed will provide a continuing stimulus to the ambitions of the writers and directors who are engaged in Caribbean theatre's continuing development.

The interviews were conducted between the mid 1970s and the early 1980s. Most of the playwrights and theatre practitioners interviewed here could be fairly described as among the most important dramatists of the postcolonial era, though the fact that most of the interviews took place in the USA meant that some more locally based playwrights – island and Guyanese – are missing from the tally. However, the book attempts to provide some documentation of these figures in the footnotes to the interviews, when names are mentioned. Readers will also quickly identify a dearth of women dramatists interviewed, an issue addressed below.

The Interviews

When I conducted these interviews, I was still very new to theatre, and possessed an idealistic, wide-eyed curiosity not only about the craft of dramatic writing, but an intense intellectual interest in the arts of the Caribbean, Africa and African-America as a whole. That curiosity has not changed.

The genesis for this book goes back to 1975, in New York City. It was the summer of that year when the Caribbean American Repertory Theatre (CART) was formed at my former apartment on West 88th St. and Amsterdam Ave. in Manhattan by a group of disgruntled Caribbean actors who had difficulty being accepted by either black or white theatre groups in New York at the time.

Apart from myself, the original founding members of CART included Basil Wallace, the company's first artistic director (Jamaica); Lou Ferguson, Arlene Quiyou, Lennox Brown, Pat Bynoe, Cheryl Byron, Neville Richen (all from Trinidad); Edgar White (Montserrat); Martha Gonsalves (Guyana); Anna Maria Horsford (American of Caribbean parents); and Yves Rene (Haiti). Rodney Douglas (Grenada) would later become a member and at one point artistic director along with his wife, Olive Douglas (Trinidad).

During the early meetings of the company, it occurred to me that within our midst were two fairly well-established playwrights in Edgar White and Lennox Brown. While I was elected as the group's executive director, I was also a freelance journalist and still neophyte actor who had performed a year earlier in White's play, *Lament for Rastafari*. I decided to write an article on these two playwrights. I interviewed White on 8 January, 1976 in his then

Lower Eastside apartment in Manhattan, and I interviewed Brown at his then Lefrak City apartment almost a month later on 1 February, 1976.

Because of the administrative demands of running this fledgling company, the actual writing of an article on these writers was sidelined. However, I remained committed to the idea of producing something about them, especially because of the extensive and insightful ideas that came out of the interviews. It would take another year before I returned to the project.

Meanwhile, in an effort to raise funding for the company, CART made its premier in the New York Off-Off Broadway theatre world with the mounting of two one-act plays by Lennox Brown, *The Trinity of Four* and *Fog Drifts in the Spring,* at the Impossible Ragtime Theatre (IRT) in Manhattan in the Fall theatre season of 1975-1976. Another production of the plays was later presented at the Billie Holiday Theatre in Bedford-Stuyvesant, Brooklyn, in February 1976.

Over the next year I began to pay close attention to the work of other playwrights from the Caribbean who were advancing a distinctive and dynamic movement of drama. While the idea for this book had not yet taken shape, I was certainly taking note of playwrights who I thought might be worth more extensive examination. I was also on the look out for playwrights whose work might be an interesting fit for the New York stage.

That same year, Stafford Harrison (his later name Stafford Ashani had not yet taken root) came to my attention with his play *The Quickie*, which had a fairly successful run at The Barn Theatre in Kingston, Jamaica. What distinguished Harrison was that he was the first Rastafarian playwright of note to have his work produced professionally. The play was directed by actor-director, Munair Zacca. I later met Stafford Ashani, Dennis Scott and Slade Hopkinson at an after-party for *Summer Dread* (the original title was *The Long Vacation*), a play by Hopkinson, which was directed by Scott. Ashani had an acting role in the production. I later went to meet Hopkinson at his home in Kingston not so much to conduct an interview but more to see if I could obtain a copy of his *Summer Dread* playscript for a possible CART production in New York. I managed to get a copy and returned to New York excited that we had a wonderful play we might produce.

I returned to Jamaica in December of that year, just after the re-election of Michael Manley. I met with Harrison on January 4, 1977, having decided to interview him for a possible feature article, though the idea for a book had not yet been formalised.

I interviewed him again three years later when he moved to New York to study videography at New York University and was living in an apartment on First Avenue on the Lower Eastside of Manhattan on 17 October, 1980. By this time he had changed his surname to "Ashani", which was not necessarily an African name but had an African *sounding* flavour. It was an amalgam of his given birth names of "Arthur Stafford

Harrison" and the "ani" which gave it the "Africanised" implication – this according to his friend and former working partner, Diane Gurwitz.

But that was three years later. Things were picking up with CART during its first two years. For the 1976-77 theatre season CART produced Michael Abbensetts' play, *Sweet Talk,* at the Riverside Church Theater in New York City, where it had a relatively successful two-weekend showcase run. The play was first presented in New York in the 1974-1975 theatre season at the New York Shakespeare Festival's Public Theater.

CART was then gaining a stronger organizational and financial footing. It was being funded by grants from two sources, the New York State Council on the Arts and the Brooklyn Cultural Arts Council, and the company was not just producing plays but was also offering acting and movement workshops. It was during this time that I and two other co-founding members of the company, Arlene Quiyou and Neville Richen, came in contact with Derek Walcott who had just then quit his post as the artistic director of the Trinidad Theatre Workshop, which he had founded in 1959. Richen, who had been in contact with Walcott, learnt that he had a comedy which he would like CART to produce, called *Beef, No Chicken*. The prospect of staging a Walcott play was, for an up-and-coming theatre company, very encouraging. And given Walcott's position as a major Caribbean writer, I thought that besides producing one of his plays, I would also want to interview him. It was at this time that the idea for a book of interviews with English-speaking Caribbean playwrights began to form.

I met and interviewed Derek Walcott at the famous Hotel Chelsea at 222 W. 23rd St. in Manhattan on 29 August, 1977. We met for another session at the Chelsea on 12 September, 1977, and a third one at the home of his friend, the Russian poet and Nobel Laureate, the late Joseph Brodsky, on Morton Street, Greenwich Village, on 10 February, 1981. It was Walcott who recommended, during our first interview, that I interview Errol John who was also staying at the Hotel Chelsea at the same time.

When I met Errol John I found him to be quite polite and welcoming. He was a dark, handsome man with penetrating eyes; his voice was that of a trained actor's – and British in tone, without a trace of Trinidad in it. The interview lasted about an hour. He seemed to me, at the time, to be a decidedly angry man, miffed by his inability to be better recognised as a writer; he found it ironic that he got more recognition as an actor than as a writer. Unfortunately, the interview published here does not contain any of his thoughts on those subjects since the second tape, which contained that part of our conversation, was lost, probably when I moved from my apartment in Manhattan. I was unable to get another interview with John.

At this point I was on the lookout for more interesting playwrights for the project, even though its shape and objectives had not been clearly defined in my own mind. Finding the various writers was more one of a catch-as-catch-can approach than anything else. There was no set method to the process. I had no master list of writers to include. I simply added to the list when I came across a playwright who was willing to give me the time of day to conduct an extensive interview.

For instance, I first met Alwin Bully at the Eugene O'Neill Theatre Center Playwrights' Conference in Waterford, Connecticut, in the summer of 1980. He was there to workshop one of his plays. He agreed to be interviewed and so we conducted the interview in New York City on 14 August of that year.

I had heard of Carmen Tipling and her play *Straight Man* through Stafford Harrison, who starred in it in Jamaica. I also learnt that she worked as a public relations account executive at Peter Martin Associates in Manhattan, where she handled the account of the Jamaica Tourist Board. *Straight Man,* a play about undocumented Jamaican residents in the USA, had received critical acclaim in Jamaica in 1974. Up until that time I had not managed to interview any female Caribbean playwrights and Tipling's residence nearby made it possible for me to correct this. I made contact with her and we agreed to meet at her apartment on East 86th Street in Manhattan on 11 May, 1981. It was fortunate I caught her when I did because she had just resigned from Peter Martin Associates and was preparing to return to Jamaica.

In the fall of 1981, a friend invited me to Kitchener, Ontario. Before heading there, I contacted Slade Hopkinson who lived in Toronto and told him of my intended visit. We spoke on the phone about his play, *The Long Vacation* (aka *Summer Dread*) and he asked me if I had a copy of the script since he hadn't. He described our reconnection as "providential" since he had given up hope of ever getting a copy of his play. As when we first met in Kingston five years earlier, he was on his personal dialysis machine, given him by the Guyanese government some years before. He told me that each time he had to go on the machine it affected his memory. Bad for a writer, he noted. He had to have dialysis three times weekly. I interviewed him at his home on 28 September, 1981. The interview lasted about an hour and as he began to tire, with an apology, he had to end the conversation.

Later that year, I contacted Errol Hill about interviewing him. From the first, when I spoke to him on the telephone about the project, he warmed to the idea. I spent an entire day at his home in Hanover, New Hampshire, where the interview was conducted on 8 November, 1981. Having arrived at his home on a snowy morning, Hill and his wife, Grace, invited me not only to breakfast, but lunch and dinner as well. He showed me his work area and capacious library. I found both he and his wife to be very warm, genteel people. From then on, I stayed in touch with him intermittently over the following years. In 1999, I contacted him requesting photos of himself and of his plays, which he responded to forthwith, including photographs from other Caribbean plays. He, in turn, asked me to provide information on myself and CART for a book he was coauthoring with James V. Hatch titled, *A History of African American Theatre,* which I did.

After having met Dennis Scott for the first time in Kingston in early 1976, I later met him in New York where he was directing Edgar Nkosi White's play, *The Defense*, at the Henry Street Settlement's New Federal Theatre in the 1976-1977 theatre season. I finally got to interview him at his home in Kingston on 9 February, 1982.

While I was in Kingston, I had already made arrangements to meet with Trevor Rhone on the following day. When I arrived at the Way Out Theatre, which was then located on the ground floor of the Pegasus Hotel, where he was directing a production of *Two Can Play*, I was about fifteen minutes late for our appointment. He was on his way out when I arrived, and he made a distinct point of letting me know I was late. He said he could no longer stay to do the interview and that he wasn't feeling well as he was coming down with a cold. I explained to him where I was staying and that the taxi had arrived late in picking me up in Stony Hill. He asked how much time I would need; I told him at least fifteen minutes or so. He thought about it and said it was okay and we went back inside the theatre. As I quickly shot questions at him I could see him warming up to the interrogation. He became most engaged when I said that some people regarded Derek Walcott as "the Caribbean's Shakespeare". He responded that "Shakespeare wrote for the man down the road, and I write for the man down the road." The interview was concluded about an hour later. After telling him a little about myself, he asked when was I returning to States. He then invited me to his home and showed me all of his theatre paraphernalia – awards, posters, etc. As the playwright who was, up until then, regarded as the most commercially successful in the English-speaking Caribbean, he told me that if I ever planned to return to Jamaica, he would show me how to make money in the theatre there.

The first time I met Michael Abbensetts was in the fall theatre season of 1974-1975 when he came to New York to see a production of his first play, *Sweet Talk*, which was being produced at the New York Shakespeare Festival's Public Theater in Manhattan. I found him to be a very funny, softly-spoken, self-effacing man with a distinct British accent. I did not interview him until a year after he had returned to the USA in 1981, while he was a visiting professor at Carnegie Mellon University in Pittsburgh, Pennsylvania. The interview was conducted at a friend's home in New York City on 17 May, 1982.

Later that year, I managed to contact Roderick Walcott, who was living in Montreal at that time. Prior to meeting him in person we had a number of telephone conversations, but I had no idea what he looked like. I had read his work, heard a lot about him, but never seen any photos of him. When we finally did meet at his apartment in Montreal, I unavoidably found myself comparing him to his twin brother, Derek. I found him to be slimmer and slightly shorter than his brother. I also found his speaking voice to be less formal, and his demeanour a bit more earthy than his brother's. Coincidentally, Derek Walcott was giving a poetry reading at McGill University on 28 October, 1982, the same day as the interview with "Roddy" – as he was more familiarly called. We started early in the day with intermittent breaks, but he kept eyeing the time, constantly reminding me that he wanted to get to the university in time for his brother's reading. His adoration for Derek was obvious.

Mustapha Matura was the fourteenth and final playwright I interviewed for the project. Our interview took place in 1983 five years after I first became aware of his work. CART co-founder Neville Richen told me about Matura while he was preparing to play the principal role in Matura's *Play Mas'* at the late Vinnette Carrolle's Urban Arts Corp Theater on West 23rd St. in Manhattan in 1976, directed by Carolle. Matura's other play, *Rum an' Coca Cola,* which was produced at the Brooklyn Academy of Music Theater that same year, starred another CART co-founder, Lou Ferguson. It was during the run of *Rum an' Coca Cola* that I had the opportunity to meet Mustapha when he came to New York to see the production. We first met at the home of his friend and fellow playwright, Steve Carter. We met again in the spring of 1983 when his play *Welcome Home Jacko* was being presented in midtown Manhattan as part of a cultural venture presented by the City of New York called "New York Salutes Britain". The interview included here was conducted on 17 May, 1983 at the home of the New Dramatists, one of America's leading playwright centres, and nationally recognised new play laboratories, located at 424 West 44th Street in Manhattan.

In retrospect, a more organized and deliberate project would have sought greater representation in terms of gender and region, and much else. But as should be clear from this description of how the project evolved, I relied on the serendipity of meetings with writers and their availability to conduct the interviews. I did not begin with a book contract or any effort to secure a publisher for the project. I simply had a sense that I was living during an important time in Caribbean theatre and a strong impulse made me want to record these developments. I recognise, though, there was a considerable misjudgement on my part in not interviewing a number of highly talented Caribbean female playwrights for this collection, women such as Honor Ford-Smith, Sylvia Wynter, Pat Cumper, Gloria Lannaman, Cicely Waite-Smith, Barbara Gloudon, Marina Omowale Maxwell and others from around the region. I would like to correct this in the near future, if possible. A similar thing can be said for other male Caribbean playwrights.

That said, I believe that this list of playwrights is an impressive and important one. Of especial value is the fact that most of them were being interviewed at a time when they would not have had a sense of the extent of their importance to the development of Caribbean theatre. The fact that most of these playwrights were interviewed in New York or outside the Caribbean indicates that most of them were set on gaining international reputations as Caribbean artists. Like CART, they were seeking ways to bring the energy and distinctiveness of Caribbean theatre to the New York stage. (And it is worth noting that CART, led by the driving force of the Guyanese-born actor, Rudolph Shaw, has continued for the past two decades to make a contribution to the New York theatre.) Whilst for many of them this was not the *raison d'etre* of their art, committed as they were to the Caribbean and its aesthetics, as our conversations reveal, the challenge of placing their work on the world stage played an important role in helping them to define their own aesthetics.

These interviews sought to explore the thinking of Caribbean theatre artists about their work. I asked them about their experiences as artists living and working in the Caribbean and, beyond that, about how they regarded their work vis-à-vis the work of other playwrights throughout the world. We also talked a great deal about their feelings concerning the socio-political climate in the Caribbean as it related to the arts. It is clear that these conversations became a space for these artists to talk about how they were starting to define and practice a Caribbean theatre aesthetic.

While this selection of playwrights cannot be said to be a comprehensive reflection of all Caribbean theatre at the time, I would argue that the prominence of many of these playwrights makes the selection significant enough to at least engage some discussion of the trends dominating Caribbean theatre at the time. Stylistically, these playwrights tend to lean strongly toward a theatre that incorporates familiar popular and traditional aspects of Caribbean culture in the use of ritual, dance, music, local vernacular, popular music, folkways and folklore. This can be seen in the work of Lennox Brown (*A Ballet Behind the Bridge, Devil Mas'*); Edgar Nkosi White (*Lament for Rastafari*); Derek Walcott (*Dream on Monkey Mountain, Joker of Seville*); Dennis Scott (*Dog, Echo in the Bone*); Stafford Ashani (*Masqueraders, Anancy and the Unsung Heroes Out West*); Errol Hill (*Ping Pong, Dance Bongo* and *Man Better Man*), Trevor Rhone (*Old Story Time*), Alwin Bully (*The Nite Box*); Roderick Walcott (*The Banjo Man, The Harrowing of Benjy*). For these writers, the quest to formulate a theatre aesthetic by employing elements of Caribbean culture is reflective of their desire to practice a theatre that is distinctive to the region. It is also clear that despite the challenges of communication between the islands, at least some of these playwrights were familiar with the work of others. How far they were being influenced by each other is a more difficult question. Directors produced the works of the same playwrights, and they also shared many of the actors. This kind of cross-fertilization has not been replicated since that period. While local theatre has continued to grow in the region, it is no longer the case that playwrights from various islands have any such familiarity with each other.

This is why I think it fair to argue that a close examination of the ideas and the works of the artists of this period offers us the best chance to see what a Caribbean theatre might look like, at least in the context of the English-speaking Caribbean. This project was driven by my conviction that without a willingness to study the work of the great artists of the past, much of what will emerge in the future will be in some way crippled and incomplete. The problem, of course, is that we are dealing with an artistic form that is notorious for not leaving a record of its most brilliant moments for others to study. This is especially the case in the Caribbean where most productions are not recorded and most plays will never be published. Consequently, the best record of these productions remains in the oral history of the practitioners. The playwrights collected here were uniquely fortunate to have emerged at a time when a monumental effort had been undertaken to maintain some record of the work being produced by the playwrights of the 1950s and 1960s. The publishing enterprise devised and executed by Errol Hill generated a body of work in print that to this day remains the most valuable resource of Caribbean plays. The Extra-Mural series from the University of the West Indies, in St Augustine, Trinidad, became the means whereby playwrights from different parts of the Caribbean could learn about the work being produced on other islands. High schools and colleges throughout the region routinely mounted productions of these plays, and many of the young actors learned something about writing plays for a Caribbean audience through their experience in these productions.

Since the cessation of the series, there has been no sustained publication of Caribbean plays in the region. My hope is that this volume will begin to fill a gap in our collective memory and might also lead to a publishing enterprise that brought back some of the great plays written by these playwrights, and offer a venue of exchange for those playwrights who are working in some isolation today.

It is hard to miss a consistent commitment towards the development of theatre in the Caribbean in the words of the playwrights interviewed here. All sought a theatre with a signature style, not unlike the music of the region, which would replace the colonial style of theatre with one possessing its own unique postcolonial voice. Without exception, these playwrights were engaged artists and their work never lost sight of the sociopolitical dynamics of the region. For this reason, their words offer us a way to understand, at least in part, the role of the playwright in Caribbean society. I sincerely believe that a lot of what was said in the interviews still holds true to the present time.

Finally, I should make a brief comment on the approach these interviews took. As the project developed, I decided that rather than conduct interviews that bore no relation to each other, I would pose similar questions to all the playwrights to try to create a kind of symposium, as if all these writers were in one room discussing particular subjects, responding to particular ideas. I hope it worked.

— Olivier Stephenson, Margate, Florida,
December 30, 2012

PUBLISHER'S NOTE ON THE TRANSCRIPTION OF THE INTERVIEWS

Initially these taped interviews were transcribed verbatim. In returning to them the opportunity has been taken to edit discreetly, to cut repetitions, "throat clearing", periods of occasional "rambling" and errors of naming. To clarify or pin-down vague references some additional material has been placed in square brackets within the text. These are editorial additions. Material in round brackets represents an attempt to punctuate verbatim speech. Efforts were made to check names and titles mentioned by interviewees, and these have in some instances been corrected. Inevitably some names and dates will have been misremembered.

Because they were speaking to a fellow theatre person, interviewees tended to assume a good deal of shared reference. In a good many cases, we felt that at this distance of time a new generation interested in Caribbean theatre would not necessarily know who or what was being referenced. Accordingly, some amplifications, explanations and guidance to further information have been added as end-notes. We do not claim that the original interviewees would have necessarily agreed with these additions. Two books in particular need to be acknowledged as sources of information: *The Cambridge Guide to African and Caribbean Theatre*, Edited by Martin Banham, Errol Hill and George Woodyard (Cambridge: CUP, 1994) and Judy S. J. Stone, *Theatre: Studies in West Indian Literature* (London and Basingstoke: Macmillan, 1994).

MICHAEL ABBENSETTS (1938-)

Born in British Guiana, Abbensetts became a naturalized British citizen in 1974. He attended Queen's College, in Guyana from 1952-56; Stanstead College, Quebec; Sir George Williams University, Montreal, 1960-61. He worked as a security attendant at the Tower of London, 1963-67; was a staff member at the Sir John Sloane Museum, London, 1968-71; was resident playwright at the Royal Court Theatre, London, 1974; the visiting professor of drama at Carnegie Mellon University, Pittsburgh, 1981. He was the recipient of the George Devine Award, 1973; received an Arts Council bursary in 1977. He has been presented with scores of awards for his lifetime artistic accomplishments in the area of television drama writing, and in 1979, received an award for an "Outstanding Contribution To Literature" by a black writer living in England.

A good deal of Abbensetts' dramatic work has dealt with issues concerning race and power. He has, though, not wished to be regarded as a solely issue-based dramatist, but one who is concerned with the "development and growth of character".

His work thrived at a time when there was very little drama on British television which focused on the lives of black Britons, and his television plays offered new perspectives to British viewers.

His first play, *Sweet Talk*, premiered at the Royal Court in 1973, with another production at the New York Shakespeare Festival's Public in the fall season of 1974, starring Al Freeman Jr., Anna Maria Horsford and a young Trinidad-born actress, Arlene Quiyou, in a supporting role. It was also performed by CART at the Riverside Church Theatre in New York. It was last performed as a staged reading at the Tricycle Theatre in London on 9 December, 2012.

Abbensetts' first television play, *The Museum Attendant,* directed by Stephen Frears, was broadcast in 1973 on BBC2. It was a play based on his own early experiences as a security guard at the Tower of London.

Other productions followed: *Inner City Blues* (1975), *Crime and Passion* (1976), *Black Christmas* (BBC, 1977, starring Carmen Munroe and Norman Beaton), *Alterations* (1978 in a CART production in Brooklyn), *Samba* (1980), *The Dark Horse* (1981); *In The Mood* (1981); *Easy Money* (1982); *Outlaw* (1983) and *El Dorado* (1984) *Big George Is Dead* (1987) and *Living Together* (1988).

Inner City Blues, Crime and Passion, Roadrunner (1977) and *Fallen Angel* were produced on television.

Abbensetts wrote the script for British television's first black soap opera, *Empire Road,* which ran for two series from 1978-79. Set in Handsworth, Birmingham, it featured Norman Beaton as Everton Bennett and Corinne Skinner-Carter as his long-suffering screen wife. The late Norman Beaton said, "It is perhaps the best TV series I have been in."

His radio plays include *Home Again* (1975); *The Sunny Side of the Street* (1977); *Brothers of the Sword* (1978); *The Fast Lane* (1980); *The Dark Horse* (1981); *Summer Passions* (1985).

Norman Beaton continued to star in many of Abbensetts' later television productions including *Easy Money* (1981), *Big George Is Dead* and *Little Napoleons* (1994/Channel 4). *Little Napoleons* was a four-part comic-drama depicting the rivalry between two solicitors, played by Saeed Jaffrey and Norman Beaton. It focused on such themes as the price of power, the relationship between West Indian and Asian communities in Britain and the internal workings of political institutions.

The play *Sweet Talk* was published in 1976 in London by Eyre Methuen. Other published plays include *Samba* (Eyre Methuen, 1980); *Living Together* (Heinemann (1988) and *Four Plays – Sweet Talk, Alterations, In the Mood, El Dorado* (Oberon Books, 2001). Abbensetts also wrote a novel, *Empire Road* (Panther, 1979) based on the television series.

Comments on his work include, "Abbensetts an Example", by Suzan Leavy, *Television Today* (London, 19 May 1994) and Margaret Walters, "Taking Race for Granted", *New Society* (London, 16 November 1978).

MICHAEL ABBENSETTS
17 May 1982

Q: When did you first start writing?

MICHAEL ABBENSETTS: Well, the truth is I've been writing since my teens, but I wasn't writing plays, at that time I was writing short stories. I was trying to write a book, even a novel, but mainly I was concentrating on short stories, or at least telling myself that I was going to write short stories. But I found that I was copying the styles of the people I read and liked. I'd write a mishmash of their work, their styles. A good writer – my idea of a good writer – is a writer who has his own voice, who has his own *style* of writing, a guy that you can read a few pages of his work and say right away: "I know who wrote this", and that to me is what makes a successful and a good writer, a serious writer. Just in the same way I feel about a singer, that whether you like a certain singer or not, if you can hear his voice, you just say I know who's singing that; that is usually the guy that people know because he's got a style, and I think that is the secret to writing as well.

Q: A unique voice.

MA: Yes. And then, when I got older, I began to go to plays and I suddenly thought I'd like to write plays. But at that time I didn't even know how to read plays because I never really liked plays, so when I first decided I wanted to write plays I actually had to learn to *read* them because I think that it's harder to read a play, especially if you're more accustomed to reading novels. I had to learn to read all that dialogue. I didn't know that much about plays other than the plays I had done at school like Shakespeare, and I never liked Shakespeare. Shakespeare, as far as I was concerned, was just a course I had to pass so that I could some day get some certificate.

Q: Who were some of your early influences?

MA: I liked Edward Albee's plays. I liked plays like *A Raisin in the Sun*... [Lorraine Hansberry, 1959]. I also liked Osborne's *Look Back in Anger* [1956] as a play that really was exciting to watch and even to read. When I first started, I think that there were certain black plays... but there wasn't a body of plays... – but even now I think one of the problems that black playwrights have – people are always complaining that it's hard for a black playwright to get a play on – but I think that even when he has a play that may make a success, the harder part is for him to continue to be successful. There are black plays that I liked and that influenced me in certain ways, but in general black playwrights were never *allowed* to have a number of plays, enough plays. I read some of Derek Walcott's early plays, but it is only now that he's really been allowed to build up a reputation. Even now, I find playwrights that I meet here in America, black playwrights, who complain that they do one hit, but when they try with a second play they have as much trouble getting that second play on as they had with their first. Because people will say: "Well, we had a play from you, let's look for a new black playwright."

Q: Is it like that in London?

MA: I think it might be to some extent. I can only speak for myself, but I didn't have quite that much of a problem because I decided from the start that… if there was any problem about getting on a new stage play… and because I began to realize that even though I had somewhat of a success with *Sweet Talk* [1973], there wasn't enough money, I decided I would go into television so that I could live. And I think that made more scope for me – I could do both.

Q: Was *Empire Road* [1978-79] the first TV thing that you wrote?

MA: No. I'd written a one-off TV play before that. It came out the same week that *Sweet Talk* opened at the Royal Court Theatre, so that I had two things opening, and that also helped with publicity because people were interested in the fact that I had a television play *and* a stage play opening at the same time. The reason that happened was that when I first wrote *Sweet Talk* – this all happened in June 1973 – my agent showed *Sweet Talk* to a producer at the BBC who really liked it and said, "We like this play, perhaps we can get Michael to write a new television play for us."

Q: What was the name of the television play?

MA: *The Museum Attendant* [1973], and that came about because I had this job working in a museum in England – of all places it was at the Tower of London. But it was a good job in that it allowed me to do a little writing as well, because I used to carry around a little notebook while I was working. The job was basically like a sort of security attendant and I'd keep an eye on people. But I'd be jotting down things while I was on duty; sometimes people would come and complain and so I'd have to put it away; I would be pretty good for a few days then I would go back to doing it again.

Q: Complain?

MA: Well, we're talking about me being a sort of security attendant while the room was full of people who might have touched and tried to steal things – although they are pretty heavy, they couldn't actually steal them, but they could touch them, break them. So I'm talking about the head security attendant coming by and saying, "Michael would you put that away, please." The interesting thing is when my television play came out – and by then I had left that job – the same head attendant saw it and he just said that he had seen the play and he said no more about it, in other words he didn't care for it that much, but the boss of the whole museum, he wrote me a letter saying how much he liked the play and said, "I'm glad you didn't waste your time when you were working here." (*Laughs*)

Q: *Sweet Talk* was never done for television?

MA: I never wanted it done for television. I think I might have sold it for television at some point, but I always felt, if I did that, that might have killed it as a stage play. I mean, even now, last year it was done in Trinidad and it was also done in Pittsburgh where I have been teaching, at Carnegie-Mellon University, so *Sweet Talk* is a play that has always been in some little production somewhere. I felt that if I let it be done as a television play it would have killed it, shortened its life.

Q: How was the Pittsburgh production?

MA: We had Oz Scott who directed it – the director who did *For Colored Girls…* [Ntozake Shange, *For Colored Girls Who Have Considered Suicide/When the Rainbow Is Enuf*, 1975] on Broadway, and he also did it recently on PBS television. Having Oz Scott was very good. And I had Carl Lumley, a professional stage actor, who was very good as well; so that went down pretty well. The only thing was that it was a mixed production in the sense that we also had to use students from the university and they were just too young… Some of the life that I was trying to talk about in *Sweet Talk* – about a woman who is married and who has a miscarriage – they don't really know, they haven't really gone through that life to even have any real idea of what I was talking about. Some actors and actresses felt, well, why didn't I ask them, why weren't they called. Some of the students complained about the fact that we brought in *one* professional; they felt we shouldn't have brought in anybody, and we had a bit of a problem with that.

Q: A fellow contemporary playwright said of *Sweet Talk* that he wasn't sure whether you were really writing comedy or a social drama, or whether you were attempting to write a social drama and were pulled towards writing comedy.

MA: Well, that's how I see life. No, I wanted it to be exactly that. I mean, you put two, three black people together, you get comedy, but yet behind that comedy they're usually saying that life is hard for them, but usually they say it in a funny manner. You never hear black people *just* say that life is hard, they usually have some humour as well and I was trying to get the humour *and* the tragic side together.

Q: How did you conceive the idea for that play? I remember you told me some years ago that it was based on some relative of yours.

MA: Yes, a relative of mine who was very much into horses, yeah. The interesting thing is that now he has given up the horses, though I'm not sure if he is as happy as he used to be when he was crazy with the horses. He made hi-fi record players and hi-fi sets. What he would do is put on a bet and then he would work for a while, then he would rush out to check at the betting shop how the horse had done, put on another bet, come back in and continue to work. But he was very good at his job; he was so good that he could still be faster than anybody else, so nobody minded.

Q: You also said that your relative did not recognize himself in the play.

MA: I don't know if he ever recognized himself; he never said too much about it. What was interesting was there were some *other* guys who used to tell people it was about them. I've had people rush up to me and say, "Hey, that's my life, man, you've put my life down on the stage!" I was at a little party and this guy, some East Indian West Indian, came up to me and said, "You're the guy who wrote *Sweet Talk*? That's *my* life you've put on the stage there, man. That's exactly how I've lived in England." And I do believe that those people, especially in England, develop a sort of protective humour and that's the thing that I try to capture, that humour, the joke about things and behind the joke the seriousness. You know, one of the things that every production I have seen of *Sweet Talk* depended on was getting an actor who could handle that part. One of the best productions was seeing Al Freeman Jr. do that play. Also, getting a woman who balances him. When people tell me about the play, I sometimes wonder, well, where did they see it; it's been done in Jamaica, in Trinidad, in certain parts of Africa and they ain't gonna be quite as good as Al Freeman, Jr., doing it at the Public Theatre. And, I think, Carl Lumley, too, when he did it, did a pretty good job, but he didn't have a strong enough balancing woman, so that play looked like it's all a one-sided, one-man show.

Q: *Sweet Talk* is your best known play worldwide, is it not?

MA: Yes. But in England, really, people know *Empire Road* more, the television series, because that was watched by more people.

Q: How did the *Empire Road* series come about?

MA: Well, again, because I had written another television play... called *Black Christmas* [1977], and when we were filming that in Birmingham [in the Midlands] – I began to see how England, how certain areas had changed, especially outside of London. The difference between

London and certain other cities is that in London you have areas which are all West Indian areas, then this might be an Indian area and this Pakistani, that sort of thing. When I was in Birmingham I began to see streets where you'd have a mixture of people, so you would have some Indians, some West Indians, even some English people all living on one street. And I tried to write a series about a man, a West Indian, who lived on that sort of street and he was like the godfather of that street, not in a criminal sense at all, but he was the most successful on that street. And they, particularly the West Indians, would come to him if they had problems; he owned a few houses, he was their landlord, he was a lot of things in their lives; and if there were problems with the police or someone needed a job – he was like a head man in that area, someone that they would come to for advice. But, again, it was also a funny thing; all of my plays have comedy – I call them "comedy-dramas" or "dramas with comedy." And I think that series was pretty funny.

Q: How long did it run?

MA: Fifteen episodes, with two series. People say now it could have run longer if there had been other writers. I wrote every one of the episodes and by the end of that I was just burnt out. It had, also, a sort of Romeo and Juliet love affair between the son of this West Indian man and the daughter of an Indian who rented one of his houses, and the Indian man didn't want his daughter to have anything to do with the West Indians, and that went on throughout the series until it ended with them getting married. But I was trying to make the point that I think that immigrants in England – non-whites in England – should start getting together with each other instead of looking down at each other. Because West Indians have a tendency to sometimes look down on the Indians and the Indians have tendency to look down on the West Indians and the whites look down on both of them; so instead of them getting together they divide among themselves.

Q: Is that changing?

MA: Well, I think it has changed to some degree, but when *Empire Road* was on, for example, and that's not that long ago, we had letters from Indians saying, "We don't like this sort of thing." They would complain to the BBC: "Stop it. Our daughters would never marry West Indians." The point is, some of the younger Indians are now getting together with West Indians. Since I think Indian fathers are still pretty strong in their families, it's going to take a bit more time.

Q: Was *Empire Road* shown throughout Britain? What was the response?

MA: Yes. It was shown on the BBC 2 station, which is shown throughout Britain, and it had a good response. The thing about BBC 2 is that it is a less popular channel, but in the *ratings* it did quite well. I'm still most known as the creator of *Empire Road*. It made some impact.

Q: You said you are working on another TV project.

MA: Yes. I had a play that was put on in England last year at the Hampstead Theatre called *In The Mood* [1981], and the commercial television channel approached me to write a series based on the characters of this play. So what I have got to write now is the pilot, and if we both agree on the pilot then I'll write some more episodes.

Q: So how many plays have you written so far?

MA: Well, from *Sweet Talk* to now, I have written four stage plays plus I've just written a new one, which I have only just shown to my agent, plus about six television plays plus fifteen episodes of *Empire Road*, plus about eight radio plays. That's been the output since *Sweet Talk* to now. And I think *In The Mood* will be done here on Off-Broadway, later on this year – we'll see.

Q: How often do you write?

MA: I try to write every day. I mean, sometimes I don't write every day and then I get very edgy.

Q: Are you one of those people who has to have something to write down, even if it is nothing of any particular importance, but just to have something on paper?

MA: Well, I think that when I finish a play, I need to take a little rest, but pretty soon I'm looking around: "What am I going to write next?" I always want to do a certain amount of writing or else I feel I'm not being productive. You see, I think that this word "playwright" is something that a lot of people use. I look at myself as a man who makes his *living* selling plays, and writing plays that on the whole – practically ever play I ever wrote is a play that I wanted to write. I mean no one came up to me and said, "Here's a suggestion, you must write this sort of play." When I first decided to write a television series, people said the BBC is not going to put on a black television series, forget it; so it wasn't that the BBC approached me. But anyway, I see myself as a professional who lives by his plays, so if I don't write my plays, I don't eat. – unless I get work like I've done this past year as a playwright-in-residence at a university.

Q: How was that experience for you?

MA: It was pretty good; I mean, I think I also learnt a lot as a writer. I was a writer who taught myself to write – in England there are very few places where you can actually get a *degree* in playwriting, I never heard of anything like *this*, really – what I was doing was teaching playwriting and I would bring in my own plays. I've just written a new play called – tentatively, working title – *Indian Summer* [This may have been broadcast on BBC Afternoon Radio, 24.7. 1983, but no recording survives]. Now what I would do is write some of that play and then I would bring it in to my class and I got them to read it and let them criticize it the same way that I would criticize their plays. What I most learnt, I think, was to be more structured as a playwright. While I taught myself to write plays, at the university playwriting is something they actually feel they can teach to the students – certain things, like about conflict and climaxes. And I began to realize that a play can have a tight structure – I mean, I always knew it *should* have a tight structure – but in the sense of that right from the start; now, I think more of characters with problems. What, I also think, though, is, if you're not a real good playwright yourself, going to a drama department ain't gonna make a playwright out of you. At the end of it you're still going to be a mediocre playwright because I think playwrights are born; you can't make them. Some people came in on a C average, and as far as I am concerned, they go out at the end of the year with a C average. While I think that you don't have to have talent to be an accountant, if you have a love for maths, people can make an accountant out of you. But just having a love for being a playwright, for plays, for the theatre, ain't gonna make you a playwright no matter how much technique people teach you. I used to get into arguments with people because some people think that because they *feel* that they are playwrights, because they love plays, therefore that makes them playwrights – even some of the students I've got there; it's very hard to explain to them… it's only when they *see* their plays in production that they suddenly see that what they *thought* they were saying in the plays ain't coming through. Another thing you cannot teach a young playwright is *what* he should write about; I can think of at least one of the students I had in my class this year – he wrote a play about a writer writing a play. Well, this is a guy in his twenties, and I said to him, "You know, you shouldn't be writing about that, you don't know enough about being a writer to write a play about a writer." So what he wrote is he's a writer writing a play about a writer writing a play – there's no life in it. The truth is that many of them have not *lived* enough, haven't had any experiences to write about.

Q: It seems a lot of young writers tend to be caught up with style rather than dealing with what they are trying to say. I read an article where the interviewer asked Isaac Bashevis Singer what was the secret to his art, and he said, "The secret is simply to tell a story."

MA: Yeah, but I still think that you must tell the story in your own unique way. That's what I meant by saying you should have your own voice; I don't mean that you should just have style with no content. I mean that, as a serious playwright, you have *something* to say, some *theme*, but it's saying it in your own way – how no one else could say it. I would maintain that whatever the faults of *Sweet Talk*, I do not believe that any other writer could have written it in quite the way that I wrote it; he might write it more of a tragedy or more of a comedy, but I feel that my style is blending the two together.

Q: When do you find that you write best?

MA: In the mornings. I tell you, this is how I normally write: I get up early in the morning and I wash my face and brush my teeth and then I go straight to the desk. I do *not* change my clothes, I do *not* cook food, I do not read the newspaper, I go straight to the desk and I work for a certain number of hours. Then I stop to eat, then I change my clothes – though I still don't go out even then to buy a newspaper. I will sit down again at my desk and work some more; and then about lunchtime or after lunch I will go out and I will buy a paper. Then if, say, I'm doing a television play or something that I am commissioned to do, I will actually come back and write some more. After I've finished the play, that's when I need to relax and just totally recharge my batteries; I find then I sleep a lot.

My plan is to work a certain number of hours every day. I never try to work day and night, day and night until I drop. If I do enough every day, I never need to do that. I think when you've got to do that is usually when you've not been doing... you've left it to the last minute. When I used to have *Empire Road* to write, sometimes I would almost write a whole episode in a weekend. On Fridays or so, I would be thinking, "What am I going to do? I haven't got anything down on paper, I need to do an episode for Monday morning." And here I am on Friday night, I've got nothing on paper yet and I'd be going crackers. I'd be phoning people and annoying people – not really annoying them but just phoning – but they knew that I was getting into that state. Sometimes even by Saturday morning I would get up and I'm still not quite sure, and then suddenly I would begin to write. And I would write Saturday night, sleep for a little bit, then get up early Sunday morning and write most of Sunday and some Sunday night, so by Monday morning I would have a play. But that was when I was writing for a series where I knew all the characters, but I had to have different stories every week. But on the whole, whenever I'm working, I do work every morning – religiously.

Q: Lennox Brown told me that once he was so taken up with his work that he worked for eighteen hours at one sitting.

MA: No, as I say, I don't write that way. I think Lennox, though, is more prolific than I am. I am pretty prolific but I don't write like that, that's just not my style.

Q: What is your opinion on contemporary Caribbean writing today?

MA: I'm not going to get into that. I think there is too much time spent on people talking about other contemporary writers.

Q: I am speaking generally, about the work that has come from the Caribbean in the last ten years.

MA: See, I mainly know the Caribbean writers in England and, also, mainly in theatre. I think that on the whole, not just theatre, I think that we have been producing quite a good body of work. What I would like to see is someone getting all sorts of West Indian literature together, poetry, plays, novels and really start thinking of this is a West Indian body of work; I think that that would be good.

Q: I know Errol Hill has been doing that sort of thing for some time. Why I asked that question was because I know in the '50s there was a big upsurge of Caribbean writing coming out of England and, now, that has sort of disappeared.

MA: Yeah, but they weren't playwrights.

Q: No, they were mostly novelists.

MA: Yes. I think that's the thing, that then they were novelists, now there are more playwrights, though not as many playwrights as there were novelists in those days. But, you see, the reason why I don't want to get involved in that is I always remember a story somebody, who was in that group, told me about being in a room full of that generation of West Indian writers and one of them said: "I'll tell you where West Indian literature is at this point," and he jumped up on the table and he says, "This is where West Indian literature is" – meaning that he was the guy who was the head of all the West Indian literature. Well, all that I remember now of the story is the bitterness expressed against this guy for jumping up on the table – the example of how stupid it was. You know the novelist I like – for my money, there is no West Indian novelist, regardless of the fact that people don't like what he writes – for a body of work, Naipaul, to me, is the best. And I am happy if anybody wants to quote that because I think he is the guy. The problem is I don't like his point of view, and I will say that as well; I don't like it when I see the man interviewed on television, but when I *read* his books like *A Bend In The River*, I think you're reading a real top novelist there. So, I would like to feel that when it comes to theatre, at some point people will take all my work – especially my stage plays – and put them together and see that there was a progression... where the plays in some ways could stand by themselves and be something, because some day there should hopefully be more theatre in the West Indies. There is *some* theatre in the West Indies, but I think there came a point in some places where if a play had a lot of swear words in it and it was titillating to the audience, those plays would make a lot of money, and those are the plays that they would put on. I know some people who really felt saddened by this and felt that this only cheapened West Indian theatre. They knew *more* about those plays than I did, they would tell me about plays that I had never seen. But I think it would be nice if we start having something a bit more... and there are serious plays about, but it seems to me the plays that are most popular are plays that are there to shock the audience with swear words and so. I think that was done in Jamaica, wasn't it? A lot of plays were making money but they were all topical, like plays about the gun court or whatever, but the minute you remove a gun court those plays lose their thing; they are only popular for the year they are written.

Q: What is the situation with black writers in England now? I have heard many things, especially how difficult it is; Mustapha Matura, for one, said to me once, don't even think of going there.

MA: Yeah, but you see, the point is that's what I hear from black writers here in America. I think it's not easy. You see, what I feel about it is that white audiences in America or white audiences in England are not really interested in things that are not about them, because the people who usually go to the theatre are middle-class whites and any play that is not about them is on the whole not a play that they rush to see. A play has got to be given a stamp or something, you've got to have a white person in there to lead them into that play, or a play has got to win a Pulitzer Prize.

What is worse, I think, is even when a black writer writes a play, the only critics are white critics, so they're again only talking of how they view it, through their experiences and that to me is one of the biggest problems. Because I've seen plays where West Indians have been fuming about the play, stormed out almost, or raging against the writer, and then when you read the review, the white critics doesn't know the West Indians are insulted by what is seen in the play.

Q: Do you think that the situation is any different from when you had your first premier in '73?

MA: I think it's got a little better, simply because they are seeing some plays now. But I think they always use the excuse that there aren't that many good writers anyway. I also think that, these days, one of the problems that perhaps black writers don't take into consideration is that these days plays lose money. The only plays they want to put on are either revivals or plays that they really feel are going to make money in the white theatres. What we've got to ask ourselves is: why don't we have more *black* theatres? You see, I think we are always complaining that it is so hard to get our plays in the white theatre, how hard it is to get on white television, we never want to say to ourselves: Why don't we have producers or people like that getting their own theatres together, their own television things, their own films? Because then we wouldn't need to ask ourselves that question.

Q: Well one of the reasons I have heard regarding that particular question is that – and I am speaking about in America – whereas, in the white world, they can get backers from any number of sources, to get some wealthy black backer to put up, say, $2 million or even $100,000 – is almost unheard of because people are afraid. They want to know they are going to make a profit. In other words, you are talking about people who are still new to a certain type of wealth and who are not willing to take that kind of risk. I don't know about in England.

MA: Well, in England they don't even have that many rich blacks. I'm not saying that there aren't reasons, but I am saying that there aren't that many even attempting those things. And when you do attempt them, what happens is that people then fall out among themselves or people run away – they get some grants, get some money – they run away with it, they cheat each other – instead of at least waiting until you make a profit and then try and get the money, you know. I think that those are things that we avoid, we don't want to talk about.

Q: What inspires you to create a piece of work?

MA: Stories I hear. That's got to be something to grab me, characters that grab me – or emotions, something from my past maybe. Because even though *Sweet Talk* was based a bit on this cousin of mine, it was still things that *I* felt about things that came out; in many ways it wasn't his feelings – many of those things he doesn't feel. So, it's all of it – it's different things... Like, recently, I met this black millionaire. Well, maybe some day I might write a character based a little bit on him; he told me a story about putting up some money for a ball game – football game – so it could help raise some money for black colleges and he lost something like nearly a quarter of a million dollars on that.

Q: What are some of the elements that you think shape good dramatic writing?

MA: First thing, I think, is the character, getting the characters. This is another thing that really makes the playwright. Once you can create good characters, even if you're not so good at other things, your play will be a good play. No matter how good you might be at other things, I mean, you might be able to make good climaxes and the first act might end with a wonderful scene, someone gets shot or someone threatens to shoot or something, but if those characters don't live on that stage you can forget it. *All* playwrights that have ever been noted, it's because they got those characters. You remember in *Death Of A Salesman*, the father; you remember in *Miss Julie*, the character of Miss Julie; in a play like *Eden* [Steve Carter, 1976], what I remember is the father, that wonderful father figure. It's always the character. In fact, in many cases when you see a playwright has done one play that is very good and then afterwards some of the other plays aren't really very good, it's because he never quite gets characters as wonderful as that initial character.

And then, having some sort of real gut feeling about something: anger or writing from a feeling of indignation about something. You know, one of the many things that worry me about certain kinds of white middle-class writing is that I come out feeling, "So what? What is it about these characters that grabs me?" And yet with some of the good white writers, you come out of there concerned about their characters. I mean, it's not the same with all white writing, because when you come out of a play like *Death Of A Salesman*, if you have seen a good production, you're moved, you *know* what you have been through. But sometimes you go to a play these days and you think, well, "I don't care," or you laughed while you were in there but when you come out you've forgotten it. They seem to have little to fight against; they are usually about depression or something.

Q: What do you think about David Mamet?

MA: I don't know enough about David Mamet; I know only *American Buffalo* [1975]. But I only saw an English production of that, I'd like to see Al Pacino – I'd like to see that. I want to see *Master Harold... and the Boys* [1982] because I know Athol Fugard.

Q: I would still like your reaction to the work of some of your fellow contemporary Caribbean playwrights...

MA: I tell you, I ain't gettin' involved in that one. No way! (*Amused*) I really am not going to get involved in that. I haven't got the time and the energy to do it. I like a play like – so it's Caribbean anyway – *Eden* is a play I like. I'm only interested in plays that I wished I had written and *Eden* is one of the few plays I wish I had written in recent times.

Q: What about a play like *Moon on a Rainbow Shawl*?

MA: I've read it. I wouldn't say that's a play I wish I had written.

Q: What about *Dream on Monkey Mountain*? Everybody seems to regard that play as the definitive West Indian classic. Would you agree?

MA: I think that's a play that will really last, which is the criteria. The play that I like of Derek Walcott's is *Remembrance*, I really was impressed by that.

Q: Did you ever see *Pantomime*?

MA: Yes, I saw *Pantomime*, but I think *Remembrance* is a better play.

Q: What did you like about it?

MA: I think he had a very good character in the main character, very believable, he wasn't a clichéd character. I think that a lot of black plays… I think that black playwrights are influenced by what they think would be put on by white producers and I think some white producers look for black plays to shock or at least to be so angry. It's always plays from how white people view blacks, and I think that… sometimes I am not even sure if the playwrights are aware… that's why I don't get into it… All I would say – I'll use an analogy – if a Chinese writer, say, begins writing plays about Chinese, who he knows, and shows these Chinese as human beings, and suddenly, for some reason he thinks that black plays might sell and he switches to black plays, he doesn't realize that all those black characters become symbols, while his Chinese characters were people, were human beings. So therefore it is difficult for me to talk about such plays, because as far as I am concerned, there's no warmth, there's no generosity – all those things that make black people so wonderful in those characters, because they have become symbols, just as mouthpieces of anger or whatever.

It's like when white writers write black characters. In many cases they are larger than life – they are *so* large – they're pushing dope all of them, or they're being buffoons – buffoons who might win in the end because of what they feel is a street-smart sort of thing. But, you know, it's how certain white intellectuals and liberals see blacks, as people who are larger than life, who will win out because of a certain sort of native street cunning. A typical example, in America, is *The Jeffersons* [a CBS sitcom from 1975-1985]. I can sometimes watch *The Jeffersons*, but sometimes it's *unbelievable*. There's this guy strutting his way through… but that's as conceived by whites. And sometimes you would have plays in London written by whites that are about blacks and these will be the most successful black plays, because this black is some sort of superbuffoon. This is how they have observed us.

Q: Through stereotyping.

MA: Yes – and through someone who says that he lived among blacks or he lived in area where blacks were. What he means is that some black used to give him his dope or something, so that's how he knew blacks. But they don't have any blacks really as a friend, would never know when that black cries or really unburdens his feelings; all he knows is what this black has shown him and he thinks that is the real genuine truth.

Q: As someone who has written TV episodes, do you feel, when you look at something like *The Jeffersons*, that you could have done a better job than that? Or if you had those characters to work with, do you feel you could given a much more real sense of life?

MA: Yes, I think so. But one of the best things I could say is that a friend of mine who is a university professor – he is black American – and he was talking about *The Jeffersons*, and then he was looking at some of my television work, and what he was saying was that the blacks portrayed on American television by white writers are always *frenetic*. There is no moment when they are just quiet. The black is always the one who is swaggering into the room, he's always dancing around, he's never ever quiet. And I'd never thought of it in those terms. But I'd like to think that in my plays blacks can sometimes just be still, just have some time when they're contemplative, when they're *thinking* as well as just hustling. It seems to me *The Jeffersons*' man is always shuffling into a situation, he is always the guy who comes in as a sort of bantam rooster, and he never really seems to think before he talks.

Q: The funny part about that is that he is supposed to be the black counterpart to Archie Bunker [the working class bigot played by Carroll O'Connor in *All in the Family*, 1971-79 and *Archie Bunker's Place*, 1979-83], yet the writing for Archie Bunker is far superior than for *The Jeffersons*.

MA: Because those writers know that Archie Bunker – at some point – is a man who *cares* more. He is a guy who does a turn around, he is always a guy who will defend blacks at some point, but the other guy has no real thought about things.

Q: The curious thing, too, is that Archie Bunker is based on an English show, what was that called?

MA: *Till Death Do Us Part*. He was wilder though, in England; he would talk about Jews and nignogs – he didn't talk just about blacks. That used to really get people... I had black friends who used to sit in front of their TVs and sometimes just write down all the racial things that would come out of him. But, again, he, too, was a character, he was a full character, I mean, he had other sides.

What I also find interesting is that I am now hearing that there are certain black writers who write for *The Jeffersons*, I didn't know that. But they write the same way the whites write about it.

Q: I guess if you know that you are getting a paycheck and you know that you are just writing from this formula, you do as you are told...

MA: ...And then you leave at the end of the day. I find that there is a new thing that, to me, is pretty bad as well, called *Gimme A Break!* [an NBC sitcom starring Nell Carter, 1981-87], a woman who works as a maid in this white house and she too, going into a room, she (*snapping his fingers*) swings in. The best black character on American TV is the guy who used to be in *Barney Miller* [an ABC police station sitcom, 1975-1982]; he was a good black character. I liked that series;

I'd like to write something like *Barney Miller*. I don't want to write too much more television though. If I could make more of a living from stage plays I would do that; and films – if I could break into films.

Q: What about television movies?

MA: Yeah, maybe television movies. But it's much better if you can get into films.

Q: Because there is more room, more scope, you mean?

MA: Well, I don't only mean that; there is the money... If you write one, the money you'd make could keep you going longer so you could be thinking about another one, while with television they're only going to allow you maybe one anyway. How many times have you ever seen a black film on television – a made-for-television film? The last thing I think I saw on television was by Van Peebles, *Sophisticated Gents* [a mini-series broadcast 1981, based on a novel by John A. Williams].

Q: Have you ever written any fiction?

MA: The only thing I ever wrote was a novel based on *Empire Road*. That's perhaps one time when I wrote for a lot of hours – I'd forgotten about that – because I had a deadline. They wanted to get somebody else to write the novel because I was busy, but I said no, I don't want to somebody else to put their name to it, so I sat and I wrote this novel, pushed myself. It was one of those things that they hoped would come out at around the same time as film, or the same time as a television thing.

Q: So, was it published?

MA: Oh, yes, it was published [London: Grenada, 1979]. But the series didn't come out at the same time as the book came out. What happened was that I had written the first series of *Empire Road*, then I wrote this novel, and I'd also written the second series – it was then it was to come out – but the second series didn't come out until later on in the year, so the novel didn't quite get that boost at the time to carry it on. It's like having a book of a film come out and the film doesn't come out until after.

Q: How well did it do, did it sell much?

MA: It sold, but it didn't sell as much as it should have sold if it had come out at the right time.

Q: What would be your advice to young writers wanting to write for the theatre? Would you encourage it?

MA: Yes, I would encourage it. I knew someone who writes in England, a black writer, playwright, I remember him phoning me once and asking me – and he had been around almost as long as I had – and he said he wanted to try and get a radio play on. He was asking me who should he talk to, what producers he should talk to. I found this very strange because I thought that he would have found out for himself and have learnt who it is. I suppose what I am saying is that playwrights should realize that it's not enough to just write a play, you've got to know something – I don't mean like the publicity. Before I wrote *Sweet Talk* – I said that I had written some small play before that – what I did was to find out about agents. I looked at a play from one of the playwrights I liked and I looked to see who his agent was, then I tried to get this agent to represent me or at least to read my play. But I feel that some black playwrights don't know what to do after they have written a play, they just send a play anywhere, they have no idea of what sort of places to look for, they don't think about agents. It's much better because an agent will tell you if this play isn't good enough or will know where to send plays. We've got to be serious about writing a play – professional about knowing what to do with it.

I'll tell you another story, quickly. When I was doing *Empire Road*, I was asked by one of the actors to come and talk to a young writer, and I went and I talked to this guy – he is a black writer – and he said he had written a play and what could he do with it. I gave him a set of names of people to send the play to, but he still stood there and I began to realize that what he wanted me to do was take his play and go and show it to the people, send it off to these people for him. He actually felt that I should push it for him. But I was in the middle of writing *Empire Road* and was involved in the production – I just didn't have the time. And anyway, I don't think that's what writers should expect from other writers. I mean, you should come and I should be able to help you, but if you expect that writer to do the work for you, then you are not interested. I just thought to myself, well, this guy isn't serious, because he couldn't even invest in just sending his play to the people I had told him about. I told him *who* to send it to, I gave him an address, everything, even *wrote* it down for him, and he didn't want that.

LENNOX BROWN (1934-2004)

Lennox Brown was born in Trinidad in 1934; he migrated to Canada in 1956 and earned a BA degree in journalism and an MFA in literature. He later worked as newspaper and magazine journalist, and as an editor-producer for the Canadian Broadcasting Corporation. In addition to writing plays, Brown also wrote poetry, published in Canadian and London periodicals. In the National One-Act Playwriting Contest held in Ottawa, Brown won first prize three times and the second prize once in the four-year-period from 1965-68. He also won awards for his longer plays.

An early play, *I Have to Call My Father* (or *Jour Ouvert*), was published in *Drama and Theatre* (Vol. 8, No. 2, 1969-70, State University of New York at Fredonia). In it a very sensitive young black man meets a highly neurotic white woman on New Year's Eve. In *The Meeting,* performed at the Ontario Drama Festival, 1970, in Performing Arts of Canada, a husband seeks revenge on his unfaithful wife. *Song of the Spear,* was performed by the Trinidad Theatre Workshop, and broadcast by CBC Radio in 1972, and Radio 610, in Trinidad, in 1973. In it, an African from Ghana, born with a guilt about slavery, visits North America for the first time and forms a friendship with a black Caribbean. A white woman destroys them.

Brown relocated to the United States prior to March 1972, when his play *A Ballet Behind the Bridge* was produced by the Negro Ensemble Company in New York City, directed by Douglas Turner Ward. It was set in the British colonial tropics before independence; in it a widowed mother has to sacrifice one son in order to send the other to Oxford University

That summer, another of Brown's plays, *Prodigal in Black Stone*, was presented as a staged reading at the National Playwrights Conference in Waterford, Connecticut. The prodigal is a West Indian who returns home to face an embittered mother after his father has died. In 1974, *Sisterhood of a Spring Night* was presented at the Queen's College Theatre in New York; it concerns three black women living in Canada who are unable to find satisfying male companionship. In *Home is a Long Way* (Trinidad & Tobago TV, 1974), an immigrant fights for success in a white society in Canada.

Two of his prizewinning one-acters – *The Trinity of Four* and *The Fog Drifts in the Spring* – were staged at New York's Impossible Ragtime Theatre in 1975 and at the Billie Holiday Theatre in Brooklyn by the Caribbean American Repertory Theatre (CART) in February 1976. *The Trinity of Four* (published in *Caribbean Rhythms*, ed. J.T. Livingston, NY: Pocket Books, 1974), is about how a planned slave revolt is betrayed by an infirm slave in exchange for his freedom. *Fog Drifts in the Spring* is a contemporary tragicomedy set in Paris. A black American sailor, haunted by an irrational sense of guilt resulting from a childhood incident, meets a Caribbean taxi driver. The sailor is apparently doomed to sail the seas forever and compelled to tell his story to strangers. A new meaning of black identity emerges from the meeting, albeit tragic. The play is included in Brown's only published collection: *The Twilight Dinner & Other Plays* (Vancouver: Talon Books, 1981).

Devil Mas' (1976), a ritualized interpretation of the Trinidad carnival as a powerful antidote to church dominance, was premiered at the Arena Theatre of Karamu House in Cleveland, Ohio, in 1976. It was also produced at Dartmouth College, Hanover, New Hampshire in 1987, directed by Errol Hill.

In *The Winti Train*, passengers on a train bound for Harlem are excited to participate in a Black World Festival when news spreads that two festival members plan to blow up the train. It was presented at the Billie Holiday Theatre and at the University of Hartford, Connecticut in 1977. In the 1977-78 theatre season, Brown's one-act play, *The Twilight Dinner*, about two middle-aged blacks who reminisce about their militant college days, was performed in both at the IRT Loft Theatre and by the NEC at St. Marks Playhouse. It was also broadcast on BBC World Service, Oct. 1981. *Blood Promises of a Shopping Plaza,* features a surrealist killing of a black stranger by a white teenager on a shopping plaza. The two latter plays are in *The Twilight Dinner & Other Plays*.

The Throne in an Autumn Room was performed at the Kiskadee Theatre, London, 1979; it had been broadcast on BBC Radio in 1972 and Radio 610 (Trinidad) in the same year. It deals with the reality and illusion facing a married couple and a friend, black immigrants in Toronto. Other performed or published plays include: *Summer Screen,* Frank Silvera Writers Workshop, NY; first published *Prism International* (Winter 1980, Vol. 19, No. 2, University of British Columbia, Vancouver, BC, Canada); *The Scent of Incense* (Canadian Broadcasting Corporation) and *Wine in Winter* (Trinidad Theatre Workshop).

Unperformed and unpublished plays include: *The Blues Smile, The Captive, A Clean Sweep, A Last Dance in the Sun, The Basement, Becoming Persons, A Communion in the Dark, The Conversion, The Gold Coast of Times Square, The Journey Tonight, Moon in the Mirror, The Night Class, Night Sun, The Philosophy of a Fast Half-Back, Processional from La Basse, Sunday, The Team, The Colours of a Dream Quartet, Winter is Coming.*

LENNOX BROWN

1 February 1976

Q: What prompted you to become a writer?

LENNOX BROWN: I think it's partly a matter of environment and the kind of family upbringing I had. Growing up in Trinidad, I was surrounded by unofficial black culture; it was very, very rich – with obeah, Shango, steelband – also growing up in a multiracial society where you see different kinds of people, with different kinds of lifestyles. Also, the culture that was *not* official at the time, like Carnival. Carnival is one of the basic influences on my writing. Carnival is like theatre. You know, it's like your John Canoe [in Jamaica] or Goombay in the Bahamas. The movement, the colour, the music, the dance, the spectacle of Carnival exercised a very, very great influence on my imagination. Also, I was born into a Roman Catholic family and, at one point when I was a child, was required to go to church, and I didn't like going to church because we had to get up early in the morning. But then I noticed the priests and the acolytes and so on at the mass, and the colour in that, and the music and the singing; the ritual of the whole mass made an impression on my mind as a child. In my plays today you'll notice a lot of that kind of ritual and colour. Music and language comes out of both black culture and white culture – unofficial black culture and Roman Catholic ceremony. But in addition to that, I was always a good student in school, always interested in books. And I'm the fourth of seven children, so that I had a chance to read the books that my older sisters and brothers were reading. When I was in standard one, I was reading standard seven books, because their books were around me and I'd hear them discussing their work. So that brought out a lot of ideas – from both the intellectual stimulus and the stimulus of culture – and also a very strong awareness of being black – even as a child being aware that things were not the same for black people as they were for other people. I remember distinctly when I was about thirteen years old, feeling this sense of a lack of history and feeling insulted – that the boys I went to school with, you know, whites and Chinese or East Indians would always smirk whenever they started talking about slavery; and I knew that was a reflection on all black people and on me too.

I wanted to know more about this history and started to read a lot about black people. I think I've always felt this sense of injury, not just personally, but for all black people born outside of Africa. That we should have had to be slaves – I take that as a sort of personal insult. I think that exercises a great influence on my mind – that we should have been owned by anybody else, or ruled by anybody else – that really insults me. It still gets me angry. I feel it's almost as if I were to go outside and to pick on a little boy and start beating him up because I know I am stronger than he is; I can outwit him psychologically, because I'm big and strong – it's just that kind of an insult... I can't stand. And this has a good influence on my writing.

Q: So, you could say that your writing wasn't stimulated through any sort of romantic image of the writer, seeing yourself as some great person like Shakespeare...

LB: No, no, no, it wasn't that at all. I was kind of quiet, always quieter than the average young child, and more interested in books and literature, art and so on. But also this kind of introspection led me to thinking about black people, about race, and so on. I was always reading – reading newspapers – and I would wonder why black people were always kicked around in the United States. Reading about Paul Robeson. I was a precocious reader. I would be the first, when they got the newspapers, to read all the headlines, all the stories; so I knew about Paul Robeson and other black people in the United States who suffered a lot and who sort of articulated this situation of the black man in the Western hemisphere. I was very much aware of that.

Q: So you could say that you knew then what you wanted to do?

LB: Yea. Yea, when I was about thirteen years of age, I thought I was going to start a novel about a slave, but I didn't know how I was going to do it. It's only in the past ten years that I've been writing plays; the play *Trinity of Four* [Billie Holiday Theater, NY, 1976] you know, that comes out of that kind of feeling and thinking that goes far back. How do I account for the black person? I think it's the question that a lot of black people ask themselves today; where is our history, who are we, where is our identity? I think I felt that from the time I was about thirteen and started to read... and the books in the library at that time had a lot of information on lynching in the South, and so on. I couldn't understand why it was that just black people were picked out to be lynched like this. I saw the photographs. I see this one photograph, and sometimes I still see it in my mind's eye, of a black man, a black body, the charred black body hanging from tree, just swaying in the wind with the penis chopped off; photographs of riots in Chicago, and so on – the first riots in the States. I couldn't help but feel a sense of personal indignity; I felt that these things were being done to me too.

Q: Who were some of the writers that influenced your work – your early work?

LB: Believe it or not, the people who influenced my early work would be people like – because I was born in Trinidad, when Trinidad was still a colony – those we had to study at school – Charles Dickens for example, when he wrote about the way the poor were treated in England. That made an impression on my mind. Of course the beauty of Shakespeare, Shakespeare's language, and so on. That made an impression on my mind. I mean I won't ever be that hypocritical to deny that white culture or white literature has made an impression on me… because that's the kind of education I had – a middle-class white Western European education. But I also think the really important influence came from the daily newspapers. Around the time I was growing up, the newspapers in Trinidad started to carry a Sunday supplement section in which they had a short story contest; and those short stories were written in dialect, in Trinidad English.[1] And I never thought that you could actually write down Trinidad English; when I first saw it written it opened up the whole of life for me. "But eh-eh man, wha' wrong with you'?" I thought that was only for Black people to say. But when I saw that as a printed word, I realized that we had something very, very precious in the Caribbean. And writers like George Lamming and Samuel Selvon, and some of the local newspaper columnists like Macaw [Kitty Hannays[2]]– there is a writer in Jamaica who is the equivalent of our Macaw in Trinidad – I think his name is Claude Thompson.[3] But she wrote a column in local patois, and opened up a lot of people's minds about the language we were using every day. But to say that our Caribbean writers had a stronger influence than Shakespeare and Dickens would be hypocritical; I mean I was educated in their language, their styles and so on. But the real impulse to put down words in my own tongue came from our own writers in the Caribbean – which was a lucky stroke for me.

Q: I understand that you lived in England for a while; how did that affect you?

LB: Well, my father was very adventurous. He didn't have a lot of money, but he liked to travel. He believed that before the family got too big that we should live in different parts of the world. So, whenever he had enough money, he travelled. We lived in Jamaica for a short while when I was very young. I think it was in West Kingston – although I don't remember it at all. It's just merged with Trinidad in my mind, because I was so small. Then he emigrated to England, and we lived in Notting Hill, where they had the riots years later. But again I was very young, about seven, and my memory of England was of a cold place, very, very cold. And everyday on the way to school we had to fight. We were fighting with the white kids and they started to believe that blacks couldn't feel pain. It was a kind of trick we worked on them. We decided if they attacked us we would just fight back and just pretend never to feel pain if they hit us. So we used to – six or seven of us going to school together – pick on a gang of about fourteen white kids, and just chase them, just beat them up. We spread a rumour that black people didn't feel any pain. After a while, the Jewish kids used to go to school with us because of this. This is a time I remember, because, you know, children remember these things. The white kids in England – this is the difference in black and white culture – they would never think of picking up a piece of wood, or length of steel and hitting you with it, whereas we would. When we got angry we picked up anything and fought with it. They thought that we were crazy savages, and we encouraged them to believe that, because that was our protection. That's all I remember of England. That and the cold. Not very much else, because the streets were very much like the streets of Port-of-Spain, but more narrow, the buildings the same, the driving on the left hand of the street, and so on – pretty much the same. England never impressed me as empire, to tell you the truth. I got it more in the Caribbean, than in England itself. England struck me as a very poor white country, when I was a child. No sense of empire at all. When I went back to Trinidad and saw all the Queen's photographs, the flags, the policemen and everything, *then* I got the impression that we were being ruled from overseas. But when I was in England I never got that impression.

Q: You sound like you were a prodigious and perceptive child.

LB: It's not so much prodigious or perceptive. I guess when you come from a large family, you either have an outgoing personality or you tend to listen and learn from the older ones. And if you listen and learn, you tend to absorb more. You're in a very advantageous position.

Q: How long have you been writing professionally?

LB: I started to write professionally... sold my very first professional article when I was about eighteen. I had graduated from high school – St. Mary's College – when I was about seventeen, and started to work when I was much too young. I wasn't ready for the working world, but I was bored with school, bored with learning the same Spanish, the same French, the same English, the same Shakespeare plays all over again. So I told my father I wanted to work and he took me at my word. The very next day, he got me a job in the civil service – which was a big thing in those days because you had to have an education, and so on. That put you several rungs above everybody. So I got this job, when I was about seventeen, in the magistrates' court, working in a hot court room, ninety-five degrees... but you had to wear a jacket and tie because you were the magistrates clerk. You took the notes and you conducted the court hearings, swore witnesses and so on. I used to wear this hot tweed suit with a coat and tie. The job paid about $19.00 dollars a month, and I was making more money then a lot of men three times my age with seven or eight children – just because I had a high school education. And I didn't know what to do with that money. I used to go home and give it to my mother. Then I decided that the time had come to write this novel about the black slave, that I'd wanted to write since I was thirteen. At the same time I noticed there was a lot of gang warfare in Port-of-Spain. I wrote an article on a clash between two gangs and sent it in to the newspaper unsigned. To my surprise the next day it was on the front page of the newspaper, and people wrote in saying how this writer really has a future in his pen, and so on. But I took a long time to write it, and I wrote about the causes of gang warfare in a very humorous kind of way. And that was my professional beginning, when I was about eighteen. I sold a few more pieces. Then, when I was about twenty-two or so, at university, I started to sell articles to Canadian newspapers and magazines. Then in 1965, I started to write plays. The very first play I wrote won first prize in a national competition in Canada. I won for four straight years after that. Nobody has ever broken that record. Then I started to work with a radio network as a reporter, as an editor – at the same time I was writing plays. So it's been a continuous process of always loving writing and creative expression. Even when I was a student, writing essays, I would always make sure I wrote things a little different from everybody else. I remember at the age of 9, I was asked to write something about "who was Hitler"? I was the one who had to put in that he was the good friend of Tojo and we were going to kick them out of the world, or something like this. The teacher asked: "Who wrote this?" And then he said, "Why did you put in Tojo; we didn't ask for this." So I said, "Well I just wanted to be a little different from everybody else." He said, "That's a good sign, that's a good sign". In those days you hardly ever got compliments from teachers.

Q: How was the journalistic experience for you?

LB: It was good, in that it brought me out of myself. I was much too introspective, too obsessed with reading books and thinking about life. I didn't like to go out very much, to go partying. I liked to go out, but by myself; go to the beach or go to the countryside. I wasn't mixing with people enough, and the journalist experience forced me to do that – although at times I found it painful, even as a grown man. In Montreal or New York, usually reporters, after covering a story, go to a bar, have a meal, have some booze, chase women; I would always prefer to go back to the hotel room and read. I was always observing people, but I've never been too much of an outgoing person.

Q: Do you still consider yourself somewhat of a loner?

LB: Yeah, I'm still somewhat of a loner; what I found, I think, was that I didn't have that much in common with a lot of people around me, and I just didn't know that. I didn't know the reason for not wanting to go to parties or to do the same things that other teenagers were doing. Now if I don't make contact with someone, I don't care; I'm old enough to know that. If somebody talks to me in the subway, and I don't want to talk, I just don't answer and I don't care if they think I'm crazy or what.

Q: So, you never thought of getting married?

LB: No, I always knew I was going to be a writer and thought marriage was bad for a writer. I thought that you had to work hard, that you had to make a lot of sacrifices, and you should not let somebody else suffer. And that was right, it was a good decision. I knew *that* when I was about thirteen or fourteen. Because if somebody else is not a writer, that woman will not understand what you are undergoing. But I always thought that it was good to have girlfriends, even live with a woman, share expenses and so on – but don't get married, because once you get married you step into a new role of responsibility that you cannot meet.

Q: How do you feel at this point in your career as a playwright? Do you feel satisfied?

LB: Oh yeah, very happy and very successful, believe it or not. All writers complain, but I feel very, very fulfilled. The first newspaper story I wrote was sold; the first short story competition I ever entered, I won first prize; the first play I ever wrote, won first prize. I've always had a lot of artistic success, but I've never made a lot of money from writing. And looking back now, with thirty-five plays written, about six or seven in progress, it's really quite a prodigious output for a playwright. Most playwrights write one play a year. Since 1965, I've been writing about four plays a year. Last year, 1975, I wrote the most plays I've ever written in one year– six plays – while having a full-time teaching job.

Q: You write very fast and continuously?

LB: Yes. Always. Very fast and very continuously. It's the same kind of obsession I had with reading, art and so on as a child. Everything is just cut-off and I go after writing. It's very easy for me to write. I can see my own development as a writer, the style, the deepening of perceptions. It's very fulfilling. That's my whole life really, writing.

Q: How do you go about researching for a play?

LB: I hardly ever do any research. I like to write from my imagination. For example, if I were to hear two cars outside – hear people screaming, the baby screaming, and somebody wailing "We were just going to get married", or "We were just coming back from a funeral" – most writers would want to go out and see what has happened and ask questions. I prefer to stay inside and imagine what has happened before the accident, and what would happen after. I write from a very rich imagination. I don't like reporting for that reason – it only covers the surface of things.

Q: The other part of my question is, "Do you feel there is a lot much more to be done in terms of your artistic accomplishments?"

LB: No. Actually, I think if I should die in the next five minutes, the woman in my life, who lives in Toronto, has a copy of everything I've written and has known my work now for thirteen or fifteen years. She knows the general design of my work. I feel that I have broken the back of the work I wanted to write all my life – which is to say, since I was a child. I wanted to, as I said, recreate the history, the experience of the black man in the world. Not superior or inferior, just equal. And I think I've been able to do that by writing these cycles of plays.

Q: I notice you writes in cycles a lot.

LB: Yes, broken up into cycles – the plays always related. I think it's because I sensed a lack of black history, which colonialism was trying to force on us as a child. And I have been able to overcome this by writing this way. So I think that the thirty-five plays I have written would stand as an important body of work for somebody born in a black colony, who had to question colonialism and segregation and racism, and then work all his way back to African forms of art, carvings, African music – the whole Third World. I've worked my way through the whole Third World philosophy of art, and so on. I'm very interested in East Indian, Chinese, all the races I grew up with. I don't think that I'm anti-European, but I'm very interested in other races, in other peoples' art. So I feel satisfied that I have written a body of work that has recreated the history – and not just the conventional history, but the spiritual history, the emotional history; the real artistic history – of the black race in the Caribbean. I see that in the *Trinity of Four*, for example, every time I see it.

Q: I also notice that you tend, in your cycles of plays, to repeat the same characters or use the same names. Is that symbolic?

LB: Yes. What I've done is I've created several families and they all have descendants; there is a white family called the Mahons, and they represent the whites who first came to the Caribbean either as servants or slave owners. Then I have created a black family descended from slaves, and Chinese and an East Indian families from indentured labourers, so that if I live for the next hundred years, I could just go on writing about these people as they emerge into different plains. For example, I start with slavery, then I move into colonialism, then into the independence era, then into the era of immigration to North America and Europe. I move my characters around very freely. They are not the same characters; sometimes I will start with a "Mahon" and then I would go to a "MacMahon", sometimes it's a McDonald Mahon. But it's always another generation and how they change.

Q: In your plays, do you write in a politically oriented way?

LB: Yes. I haven't thought of it consciously, but I notice that some of my plays are automatically political – have a political thrust. For example, *Devil Mas'* is a play that was written with a consciousness of the art of carnival at the back of my mind – the devil mas'. But at the same time I was writing it there was a rebellion in Trinidad, a Black Power rebellion. So it was just natural for me to make the hero of *Devil Mas'* a black man who was revolting against white authority and white foreign investment. So I tied the two together, art and politics. I think that it's very important for the black writer not just to write political tracts, or political propaganda, but to create art; even if you're going to make a political point or a racial point, make it artistically. [...] Sometimes I have quarrels with black writers about this, they say that you should write this or you should do that... and I always say, it's not "Shouldn't" or "Should" at all for the artist, it's whatever the artist feels he wants to do. Because if you're a good craftsman or good artist and you write what you honestly believe, you will write what we call the "truth", you will write it.

Q: Some people say that the artist is one step removed from the revolutionary – the revolutionary thinker.

LB: No. I think the artist is really the first rebel in society, to tell you the truth. Because the experiences you have to go through to be a writer, and the stands you have to take, the freedom you give yourself – because you have to give yourself a lot of freedom to be an artist – you're creating forms and shapes and you're taking a lot of liberties with the content of history, and so on. I think that in itself is a revolutionary step. You defy conformity by just starting to create your own view of life, your own vision of life. So I don't think an artist is so far removed from the revolutionary. I think when it comes to *action*, I think that a revolutionary, say like Lenin or George Jackson, the Soledad Brothers, I think they will act. Huey Newton or Eldridge Cleaver, Bobby Seale... they are prepared to act, whereas I would be more prepared to write about what the action should be. They would be more prepared to go out and throw a bomb or burn a building down, whereas I would prefer to shape a strategy for undermining or overthrowing the whole city.

Q: In other words, the man behind the plan.

LB: Yes. I think that's the big difference. But I don't think there's any big difference between a revolutionary and artist.

Q: So you would consider the artist as a visionary?

LB: Yes. I think that anybody who is a serious creative artist... I think if he or she takes their work seriously will eventually – in spite of oneself – write things about the future without knowing it. I've seen it in my own work and I've seen it in other people's work. But I think you have to write with a lot of integrity, lot of feeling for who you are, what you are, where you're from and what you've been through. A lot of feeling for the place you're born in and for your family and your people... And I think once you have a general feeling for these things, I think that it is very, very easy to say that we did not get true independence in the 1960s, that we are still ruled by foreign investors and by the big powers. I have written one play about this called *A Last Dance in the Sun*. It's very easy to see that, right now, Caribbean people are not paying sufficient attention to their real culture. That we are becoming too easily influenced by Anglo-American culture. I think that it's obvious that we're going to have to have a confrontation with foreign investors and Anglo-American culture before we grow up as truly independent nations in the Caribbean – or else we will always be grinning dancers for the tourist trades; we'll always be exploited; we will always be servants for Europe and America. I think we have not faced the issue squarely yet. Even though we are small, we have to do what Cuba did, say "Look, I am somebody and nobody's going to walk on me". Again, this comes back to what I've always felt, even as a child, nobody should insult anybody else's dignity. And I don't think we have done this yet in the Caribbean. I think it's about time we start telling the foreign powers, the big powers, to go to hell, get out of our country. Or if they don't like it, kill us, but we won't be slaves anymore. I think we still have a slave mentality in the Caribbean. So for a writer who's in time with his own history and his own society... it's very very easy to see what would happen in the future. In that sense, I think, a writer, an artist is a visionary.

Q: Do you see the theatre as a communicative medium?

LB: Yes. I think the theatre is really the oldest form of art. And what's intriguing to me about the theatre is its relation to the community. If you don't have a community that's connected with the theatre, you don't have a theatre. For example, in New York here, you have a tradition of white theatre. In London, you have the tradition of the British white theatre. You'll notice that with black people in the United States – although there are black theatres – there is not a tradition of black theatre as such, there is a kind of community work theatre. If in a community, the people who live there and work there also expect their entertainment there, and artists arise from that community, they communicate. This is the way the theatre should work. It's no coincidence that black people have a hard time in the theatre world in New York. It's because we're living in a white society that has not accepted them as part of the community. The day that the United States says; "All right, black citizens, you are citizens just like us, you have the same rights", then we wouldn't have to form the Caribbean-American Repertory Theatre, or the Negro Ensemble Company, or the New Federal Theatre. We would be on Broadway. We would have our own Joseph Papps [theatre director, 1921-1991, who established the Public Theater in New York] and our own David Merricks [a publicity generating American theatre producer, 1911-2000] and so on. This is the test of a good theatre. I mean if you go to any educated white person in New York, they will take it for granted that it is their right to go down to Times Square to go to the theatre, see a play that talks about their history, their psychology, their mythology, their family, and so on. It's not the same with a black person. Theatre is a very sensitive test of a community. The Greeks had their own theatre; Africans had their own theatre. A mask like that (*pointing to African mask on the wall*), or carvings like this one, they all come out of a traditional community, of people who were accepted and had rights in society, had roles to play. The only place I see as having a natural setting for black theatre as a communicative organ – two places I see – that's Harlem and Brooklyn. I think if blacks continue to live there, that a kind of community feeling will grow out and people will naturally step into theatre there.

Q: Do you think that the theatre is a powerful medium, even a powerful revolutionary force?

LB: Yes. I think that theatre is probably the most powerful force in all of human life. And I'm not saying this just because I'm a playwright, but because of the history of theatre. See, the theatre grew out of religion, and religion is really the first impulse, the first social impulse of man. In the very earliest development of man as an animal, as a human being, man didn't know anything about science; he did not know why the sun rose each morning and set each night. He did not know why the seasons changed. He did not know why the crops blossomed in the spring and summer and died in the winter. He did not know why the birds he trapped to eat for meat disappeared at a certain time of the year. To explain life, he turned to ritual. In other words, a certain person from each tribe became the priest and the scientist, even the leader of that tribe. That person was supposed to explain what were "the mysteries of life". And that's how theatre started. They believed that if they drew a picture of a lion, and they danced, chanted and cursed it… and they threw their spears at the picture, when they were satisfied that they had controlled its spirit, they could go outside and kill the real lion. They psyched themselves up. Theatre is the psyching-up. And this is what theatre grows from. In other words, there's always somebody responsible for explaining reality to man, and this is really what theatre is. This is why there is so much ritual in my plays. It becomes natural after growing up in the Caribbean. And this is why I think theatre is the most powerful force, and that all other arts spring from theatre. Theatre has poetry, great language, the visual arts, painting; it has dance, pageantry, music. A good play has all these things and can mould them into a beautiful experience. Today, when society has become very technological, very mechanical, man has lost respect for nature, has lost respect for the natural rhythms of the universe. I think man has become such a scientific rational animal that he has lost a great deal of his own human mysteries. Frankly, I would much prefer – I know it takes much more work to walk up fourteen flights of stairs to get to this apartment – but if there were no elevators, I would walk up these fourteen flights, because I enjoy feeling the muscles in my legs working – there's a sense of accomplishment for me. We have moved so far away from nature that we live a kind of artificial life, and it seems to me that at one time theatre used to stand for all of this in ancient societies, but we're losing ritual and mythology. So that man is becoming very much a kind of robot, without any real spiritual values – and I don't mean belonging to churches – I mean having values other than making money, wearing nice clothes, driving a nice car. Man really doesn't know who he is today; we have no sense of real dignity. You see a great sense of dignity in African carvings, in Oriental art, in Indian art. In all the Third World countries, there's still something left of the dignity of man in his art. But I don't find it in the dominant cultures like London or Paris, New York, Toronto. There's a kind of decadence. A loss of faith in man as one of the other animals on this planet. The other animals haven't lost it. For example – this might sound crazy to you, this is where writers get crazy – if you look at a cat or dog walking on the street, they have a natural kind of a dignity and confidence in who they are. I mean people call them dumb; I think they are very smart.

I hope the Third World doesn't lose it completely. But then as I say, the Third World really has to look at itself and work hard to retain that kind of humanity. It's not so important to have movie houses and drive-in banks and big oil refineries and so on – though those things are sometimes important – it's much more important to know how to move your body in a dance, to enjoy music, how to enjoy the sun. It's much more important to me to know how to get a plant to grow. I used to love to set eggs – when a hen sat on eggs to hatch them, and chickens were ready to come out of the shell, I used to help them – when the beak would come through the shell – just remove their shell and take them out without a drop of blood, without hurting them. In other words help bring them into life. They used to call me the "doctor" when I was a kid because of that. I think these things are very important. Things like making money or having political power don't impress me. The super powers don't impress me at all. The places that really impress me are the places in New Guinea where they still hunt with bows and arrows, where they still have laws that they could kill a man for breaking a certain tribal law I'm impressed by those cultures.

Q: Many times when I think of going back to Jamaica, I imagine myself living in the country, away from all the urban trappings that destroy you – because Kingston is becoming like New York.

LB: It's the same with Port-of-Spain. It's a big tragedy that in the Caribbean, the people, the intellectuals and the politicians don't have enough foresight to see that they have a chance to build a new kind of civilization. New values. So they force us to emigrate to London, to New York, Toronto. And we lose contact with that very important spiritual element. I remember going back to Trinidad – I used to go back every year – and I think this was about three years or four years ago, driving through the countryside with my brother-in-law and wanting to buy some mangoes. He saw a stall at the side of the street with some mangoes on it. He stopped the car and started to pick up mangoes. I said "You better shout out and say 'hello', or somebody might think you're stealing." He said "No, a woman is going to come out in a few minutes and she's going to give me a price". A very simple woman, barefooted, came out and asked him how many he had – she didn't even count them – he told her, and she told him how much it was. There was no kind of slickness or trying to steal. It was a very simple transaction, which came out with a smile. She asked him who I was, where I was from, how long I'd been away. And that was the end of it. She went back – beautiful experience. Just a straight human contact without any kind of cagey games. Like going to buy something in New York is a whole ritual of who is going to out-con who.

Q: I remember you saying once about not going back to the Caribbean until you could do theatre the way you could here.

LB: Yes. I would like to see a professional theatre established in the Caribbean. See, we have a lot talent. I grew up at a time when calypsonians used to sing for a penny, 6 cents or something like that, when people would decide after a day's work to dance and sing, play music; and they would do that for hours – and anybody could come and dance – or some friends would get together and buy a few bottles of rum – and if you were in with that group you could sit to play a musical instrument of some kind. It was a real community life. There was a lot of art and talent in that kind of community living. But times have changed. We have to learn to package that kind of art professionally, not so much to make money but to make sure it stays there, to make sure it is preserved. In other words, it's no longer feasible just to say "Oh hey! I'm putting on a play, anybody can come – I'm a writer, anybody can come." You have to organize yourself professionally, have a theatre building, make sure that the government knows that the artist has a very important place in society – that the artist is not somebody who sits around and smokes pot, that the artist is thinking very seriously about life. All of these things I think will have to change before I would go back to the Caribbean as a professional playwright. Because right now it's just a heartbreaking job. The governments are just – they are either indifferent or they oppress the artist. They are afraid of their political freedom. It's just disheartening if you're an artist in the Caribbean right now.

Q: Derek Walcott is one of the few who have remained in the Caribbean, in Trinidad, with some success it seems.

LB: With a lot of success as a matter of fact. When he first met me, it's one of the things he said that he was really impressed with, that I was able to live away from home and was still able to write convincingly about the Caribbean. Because, he said, everybody else who's left, loses that kind of creativity. Well, Derek has a lot of problems living at home. And you'll notice that now he's beginning to go on foreign tours more and more. But he has been one of the pioneers in developing art in Trinidad itself – with a lot of fights on his hands. I think he has lost… and in some ways I think he would have developed further as a writer if he didn't also have to run a workshop – which is to say function as a business manager, as a director, as a publicity agent, as a writer. He does all of these things for his company, and still writes. I think we would have had an even greater writer – and I think he is a great writer – if he had had sufficient professionalism around him to free him to write and let other people do the other jobs. He has his reasons for living in the Caribbean; in one of his articles he says American life makes him afraid – and that's why he went back home. Living in New York doesn't frighten me but I'm very much aware how it can make me dehumanized.

Q: What are your views on Caribbean and Black American playwrights?

What differences do see?

LB: There are several points you have to consider about Black American writing. First of all it was born in a cradle of protest. That's to say, writing against slavery. Then there was the abolition period when everybody wrote – everybody who was black and who could say "Oh the wicked white race and Oh, we poor black downtrodden who one day will free Daniel from the lions den", and so on. That's how Black American writing began, in that kind of protest tradition. So there's always been that element, which means that Black American writing will always be realistic. Because once you're going to protest against a social institution, you have to describe real things. And this has been one of the main things about Black American writing, that it has fallen into a trap of realism. Now I think that a writer like Amiri Baraka[4] really struck me, really impressed me because he was not only able to protest, but he had a tremendous sense of form in his writing – magnificent sense of form in his early works. Plays like *Dutchman and the Slave* [1964], *Slaveship* [1970] – tremendous, fantastic sense of form. But it seems to me that most Black American writers don't go beyond the surface. In other words, their pencils seem to function like cameras. They take a photograph of things and they just write them like that, and their writing has no resonance. I think that even though you are protesting against a social situation, what you write should go much further, should have a much more lasting value. And this is a problem with Black American writers. Again the blame is to be laid at the door of white society – oppressing our Black brothers.

Q: You were saying that Black American writers tend to write "real" plays and I was browsing through this book *Kuntu Drama* [*Plays of the African Continuum*, Ed. Paul Carter Harrison, Grove Press, 1974] and there's a quote by Bullins where he says he writes reality plays ("the theater of reality").

LB: Yes. And he does, as a matter of fact. I think that the reality that Ed Bullins captures in his plays is real reality – to use a phrase. In other words, if he's writing about the ghetto, the Black American ghetto, he doesn't pull a single punch. He just writes about it. But I think that as a playwright, a serious creative artist, you have to go several steps beyond that. There's also a big danger. If you continue to write about black people as just people who are trapped by the ghetto, then you play into the hands of white people who say "Black people should be kept in ghettoes." If you never show the potential of black people to be kings and emperors, and scientists and other things – in addition to being trapped in ghettoes – you make a mistake, you make an artistic error. I think the realistic ghetto play will not last very long because what happens when the ghetto is erased? It's very easy to get rid of the ghettoes in the United States right now. All you have to do is housing redevelopment, and then the ghetto is gone. And then where is your art? Your art has disappeared. But if you should write about the ghetto as a state of mind – and this is a kind of a negative aspect of all men's personalities – you've written something that's almost eternal. You've warned mankind "Don't make this mistake again, because you will create this condition." And I think this is where the realistic writers fall down. See, I think there is an immediate appeal, but I don't think there's a lasting value, and I think an artist should always aim for a lasting value.

Q: Have you ever thought of writing a novel?

LB: No. I find a novel takes too long to say what it wants to say. I teach the novel at school. I love to teach the form of the novel, and so on. And when I have time, I love to read novels. But I can write one scene of a play and I can make my point – give me about a dozen lines and I can make my point. A novel, it takes so many chapters, so many hundreds of pages. The form of the novel, to me, is just a bit too loose, too expansive and diffuse. I prefer the urgency and the immediacy of the play. See, I think the novel developed at a stage in literature when there was a movement towards mass education. Mass education meant lowering the standards and writing as easily as possible for the mass of people to understand. That's my quarrel with the novel; that it compromised and sacrificed, and it damaged a lot in what was a good literary tradition. The novel is not a perfect artistic device, it still has a lot of flaws as an artistic media. You asked about the theatre and its force as a communicative medium; the novel does not have that because the novel has to sacrifice, has to accommodate to meet the people who read on the subway, people who read while waiting at a bus stop. It has to be that easy to read a novel. Good art should demand some concentration and some respect. The novel is just a kind of a compromise to me.

Q: Do you ever write short stories?

LB: No, I write poetry. I write poetry and plays only.

Q: Not even as a means of making some quick money?

LB: No. In my whole life I have written only one short story. I was an undergraduate and I was completely broke. I had paid my rent and had no money for food; I noticed this competition for short stories, and the first prize was for $25 dollars. I took two weeks and I wrote a short story. To my surprise I won the first prize, and I was able to buy some hot dogs and peanuts or something like that; and that was a big meal when you're an undergraduate. And I've never wanted to write short stories after that.

I think the really difficult art forms – and I don't say this because

I write them – are poetry and playwriting – because you have to compress so much into so little... You can write a six hundred page novel; there are hardly any three-act plays on today, in New York. A play has to be two acts; and at the most you keep your audience in the theatre for two-and-a-half hours. Anything after that, they'll get tired and they'll walk right out on you. You have to be extremely sharp in writing a play; to know how to hold your audience. I think that novelists have a lot of advantages over poets and playwrights.

Q: Do you write poetry for yourself or do you write for the public?

LB: Oh no, I've published poetry. As a matter of fact, I have one that's coming out in an anthology by Simon and Schuster in April this year. The other day I wrote a poem – or I rewrote a poem called "Steelband" that I had published in 1963 for Terry Chandler [a New York-based Trinidadian scenic designer] to do a painting of a steelband for me. I used to do lot more poetry than I do now. I write a lot of poetry, but I don't read very well. When I started to write poetry, I was living with a woman who used to read all my work for me – for me to hear what it sounded like, so unfortunately I never developed the habit of reading my own work. So, now, I don't read [in public]. Again, I guess it's the introspective personality.

Q: Is that one of the reasons why you'd never act?

LB: Yes. I've never wanted to act. I've always wanted to be the person behind the scenes, who would write things and give it to somebody else to do. It's strange, because I've been teaching, I've been a journalist – jobs that call for an outgoing personality – but I myself am not outgoing.

Q: You said that you felt the theatre is more immediate, more spontaneous. Could you say more?

LB: Yes, something almost magical happens when an actor steps on the stage. And I think what I see is this long historical process in tribal society, of the witch doctor being in charge of a dance to bring back the crops next season. If the crops didn't come back, he would be killed. So, he went through this ritual and his dance, and his little mumbo-jumbo secrets. And whenever an actor steps on a stage, that is what that actor is re-enacting, believe it or not. It's almost a kind of religion for me, to see this happen on the stage.

Q: How many plays have you written?

LB: I've written thirty-five, so far. And these include full-length and one-act plays. A lot more full-length than one-act plays. Thirty-five. And I've had seventeen radio productions, four television productions, so far; sixteen stage productions. This does not include productions that are upcoming or planned. And the productions have been in different parts – in New York, in Toronto, different parts of Canada, in the Caribbean, in Trinidad, in Guyana. Even in Holland. One of the plays was done in Holland, with a translation in Dutch.

OS: How was that?

LB: The play was published in a magazine, an art magazine in Toronto that somehow turned up in Holland. The people there read it and wrote to me saying they were fascinated by the play, could they translate it. And I wrote to my agent, and my agent arranged for a five-year amateur lease. And they translated it into Dutch. It has had about three separate runs in the Netherlands, in Dutch.

Q: Was this *The Meeting*, with white actors. I was wondering about that.

LB: I started to write that in Toronto in 1965 or 1966. I was going to write a play about reality and illusion in human life as a whole – what's real and what's not real. Even as a child I always used to think about the strangest things, like: "What does a dog actually see? Or what does an ant see?" I often wondered what they see with their eyes, because we can't see for them. So, I've always thought philosophically. And I was thinking, what is really "real" in life? Then I started to think, well, let's take something like hanging. Who's responsible for capital punishment? Is it the person who commits the crime, or is it the society that has allowed the institution of capital punishment to go on? Or is it the people who turn up to see people hang? Or is it the hangman who does the actual job of executing a criminal? I started to work on this theme of reality and illusion, using capital punishment as a basis. Now, the play won second prize in a national competition. But a lot of people think that the play is about a hanging, when it is really about reality and illusion. And it has been my most successful play, commercially – and it's the one that I thought I should have done more work on, to get to the real philosophy that I was writing about. People think it's a beautiful play, so exciting and suspenseful, and so on. And it's never done in the way I really want it done – masks and a priest, the ritual and so on. It's always done as a kind of a suspense thriller. Who is the murderer? Who is the hangman? And so on. I mean, anytime I'm broke, if I want to make a quick $20 dollars, all I have to do is hustle around enough amateur groups and I'll get one of them to do *The Meeting*. It's one of these ironies about writing.

Q: What advice would you give to a young writer?

LB: I think that every writer has to find a form that suits him. I think that most writers have to go through journalism, but I advise them not to stick in journalism. After you've mastered writing for newspapers and writing for magazines, write for radio, write for television. And it only takes you – when you're young – two or three years to learn how to write a story. You should start developing a creative type of journalism and once you've started to do that, you have to make that terrible decision – and that's why you don't get married and you don't have children – to stop doing journalism and to start doing creative writing. It's a terrible decision, because usually if you write journalism you can get published and you make some money; you will be probably be taken on staff on the magazine, and you'll probably start making $20 – $30,000 dollars a year. Then you have to make a decision to stop making that and start working on your poetry or your plays or your short stories. And you'll have to decide to make (if you're lucky) a thousand a year. From making thirty thousand to making one thousand a year. I did that, and I'm very glad I did. I worked with the Canadian Broadcasting Corporation; it goes right across Canada. I started as a junior reporter and was promoted rapidly; I became an editor and then an assignment editor. My last job was making phone calls to London, Paris, all the major Canadian cities, Bonn, Moscow and asking correspondents for news stories for the radio network for that day. So it was a very, very interesting job and I was making a lot of money. I decided to save enough money and then stop working. I had started to win prizes for my plays, and that was more important than making money. Also, when you're single you don't have too many expenses, so that money isn't moving in on you so much. I think that once you've made that decision, you go through a few years of suffering to develop your creative ability. Then you start working again and you have enough technique to do a job *and* write at the same time. Then you start trying to re-establish. Pay back all the debts. One thing I think that black writers should be against is dying in poverty. Claude McKay, the great Jamaican writer, came here, wrote during the Harlem Renaissance, was one of the big voices, died in poverty.

Q: Have you ever written for cinema? Screenplays?

LB: I hardly ever go to films myself. I don't like film – although I've sold television plays. But I would write a film if anybody asked me to do one. But I really don't like film that much because of that kind of mechanical process involved in it. I like the immediacy of the stage. But the other day I thought of writing a love story between an East Indian and a Black, set in the Caribbean. I thought of it because of the growing friction between Blacks and the East Indians. And I thought I would use the film form because I wanted to use East Indian mythology and East Indian art. And there's a very good film industry in India – very aesthetic film. Very creative. And I thought I would try to use some of that in the Caribbean because I think that East Indians have a right to be in the Caribbean. We were taken there as slaves; they were brought there as semi-slaves, indentured labourers. Okay, they had a slightly better deal than we did, but the imperialists saw to that. I don't think we should allow that to divide us; I think that we are all Third World people. Also, I think we have much to learn in the Caribbean. We have all of this Asian history, Asian arts to think about; we have all of African culture to learn about. That means song, dance, language, music, secret societies, religion. We have the people living right there. The great Chinese theatre; the great East Indian films; the great East Indian play cycles – and we never get around to doing these things. When I was at CARIFESTA in 1972, the government decided to build a conference hall, and somebody came up with the brilliant idea that instead of building one of these concrete matchbox buildings, as you can get anywhere else in the world, get the Amerindians from the interior to put up what they call the *Umana Yana*. It means "a meeting place". They built this beautiful building that's just naturally ventilated. It's the most beautiful thing you've ever seen. All of this we have to learn. What we do instead, we say, "Well that Coolie got promoted over me, or that Chinese is getting a better deal, or that Black man pushed his way in front of me." We waste a lot of time, and it's because we have been taught to do that. It suits the outside world for us to be at each others throats all the time. We have so much to learn and we are not learning. We don't really use the resources of the part of the world where we were born.

Q: Do you feel protective about your ideas when you are working, or are you forthcoming about them? I ask this because in New York City, writing is very competitive and commercial.

LB: Well, we know what New York is like. It's supposed to be slick, but it's a very dishonest kind of city. It's not like the kind of traditional communities we grew up in the Caribbean, where you share art and so on. If somebody came up with a new way of beating a pan in a steelband it was copied by other people, but that first person got all the praise for it and was known for it. He may not have made any money from it, but he was the leader of the band, he was a big shot. But in New York, instead of praising a person in that way, they just steal the idea and make money from it. So I think that it would be foolish for me to have ideas and just throw them out to the public. Because one way Europeans have always related to non-white peoples has been to exploit and steal our ideas, especially in art and culture. Steal our ideas and then refuse us admission to see our own art. Jazz is a good example. The Whites stole the idea of jazz from Blacks and then formed unions that prohibited Blacks from joining the unions, The Blacks wouldn't work at the same salary as whites. I mean Blacks like Louis Armstrong would get $10 dollars a night, when a fourth-rate white musician would be getting $5,000 dollars a week, because he's a big star – but could hardly play a note like Louis Armstrong. I think we have to be protective in this environment about our ideas. But I think once the work is done and it's performed, it's out there for public consumption. And you can't stop people from stealing art anyway – stealing ideas from art. That's what art is about, it's a sharing. But at some point I think that you have to protect your work or else you'd just starve to death.

Q: Could I ask you a very delicate question… What's the most money you've ever made from your plays?

LB: I know which plays have brought me the most money. I think *The Meeting* has been commercially the most successful. *A Ballet Behind the Bridge*, which was done off-Broadway here, gave me some money. But I have never really sat down to see which play gave me most money. All the radio plays sold to the CBC – I got $1,000 dollars for each radio play. One of them called *The Throne in an Autumn Room* I think I made about $2,000 dollars off that play because they taped the play in Trinidad and I had to go with the company to work with Derek Walcott's workshop. So I got travelling expenses and so on. But I don't think that there is any one play that has made me any significant amount of money. I would think that the top price I got for a play so far would be *The Throne in the Autumn Room*. Now, in New York – and I have a lot of big plays ready to be produced in New York – those would bring in a lot of money. Plays that I haven't shown the producers yet. I'm just waiting for the right producer or the right group or the right theatre and so on. Those will make a lot of money. But I have never really approached playwriting from that mercenary point of view. Now it's a case of finishing up the plays that I want to write and then starting more on getting them produced.

Q: If your plays brought you in enough income to sustain you outside academia, would you just write all the time?

LB: Write and read, yes.

Q: My brother is an artist and he says when he's painting, the sensation from doing it is almost orgasmic. Does that make any sense to you?

LB: Yeah, as a matter of fact it's almost like being… I've never used drugs at all; I've never even taken a drag from weed. But I think I know what being high means. Because I've felt that way during the process of creating a work. Especially when it's coming well and you know it's exactly what you want to write and the formation is taking place. The physical creative process I think is… could be as intense as the spiritual creative process.

Q: Other Caribbean playwrights have spoken of the need to decolonise Caribbean theatre, build on native, popular traditions. Does that make sense to you?

LB: I remember once writing an essay… I was in St. Mary's College which was one of the two top schools on the island – St. Mary's and Q.R.C., Queens Royal College – one was Roman Catholic, one was Anglican, and we were always competing for the best scholarships. We were taught in St. Mary's College by a lot of Irish Catholic priests. I wrote an essay about living in a neighbourhood, and then going from it and coming back and finding traffic lights and shopping plazas, and all of that. I got all kinds of beautiful marks for this essay. Looking back, I was so shocked by the… "as I walk through the autumn leaves" and all of this. Where did I know of autumn leaves or shopping plazas? And the bad thing is they praised us for this. The teacher should have asked me, "Where did you ever see a shopping plaza?" I must have seen that in a magazine or something. But I picked that up as something that was good to write about.

Q: Part of the brainwashing.

LB: But it's amazing that some of us got away from this brainwashing; were able to see it and break away from it. Whereas others just got trapped by it. But I think that for my personal purposes, the best reaction is to be honest with your background and to use what's good in your background. For example, I would never throw out everything European that we got from colonialism in the Caribbean. I think we were fortunate to have been exposed to Shakespeare or Dickens; we got an idea how you could use beautiful language. We don't have to write like Shakespeare, but at least we know that language could be made beautiful that way. Our own language could. So that the people who say, "No, no Shakespeare. No Dickens", I think they are wrong; they are despising a lot that might be quite successful. What I object to is this contempt of everything Black and the putting down of Africa. I mean, if I could get a curriculum that showed Black African carving and music and dances, *and* Shakespeare plays and Chinese opera, East Indian festivals, and so on – to me that's a beautiful world. Because every race has genius – and you use the genius of every race and you get a beautiful world. I don't buy the idea of superiority.

Q: What might you say to young writers, young people aspiring to be playwrights?

LB; Well, I think the first thing I would tell them would be to make sure they have a solid intellectual foundation. Because I think if you are going to a creative artist – I don't necessarily think you have to be an intellectual – you must have some intellectual awareness of what you are doing. In other words, I know the reasons for my writing, and for the style in which I write – why I can argue with someone and say, "No, I don't want to express that in that way." I say, get an education. Then get a job. Then I would say start developing a lot of integrity and a questioning mind, about your own race, and your own personality, your own community. I think the most important thing is to know who you are, and where you came from. In our case, I think we know fully well that we came from a community where there was Anglo-American culture, and there was Obeah, Pocomania, and Shango. There were East Indian festivals, Moslem festivals. I think the basic purpose of the writer, really, is to recreate the experience of his own people. It's not a racist point of view either. I think if you're white, you have to know your white history. In other words, how did your white history come into being on this planet? I think it's the same for the Black or the East Indian or the Chinese – that you should know who you are and what your people did. And once you do that, you're free to relate to anybody at all.

I think that a writer has to develop this kind of integrity for his work, should know that he probably will not be a millionaire, that making money is not the first thing; it's the quality of art you have to establish. That you're there, in a way, to serve your people. It's going back again to the first beginnings of society; you have to explain certain mysteries. When I say "mysteries" – in quotation marks – to your people, I think you have to take your role in life very seriously – take your art very seriously, before you can venture out into this artistic career.

Q: You say that you don't think any true artist or writer should ever imagine himself becoming a millionaire in his lifetime.

LB: No. I think that if it happens accidentally, that's beautiful. I know that in American culture, in western culture as a whole, art is judged on the basis of money. But that is not the culture that we originally came from; we carry within us the seeds of Caribbean or African culture, or if you're East Indian, Caribbean-East Indian culture. You have to be faithful to that. It's almost as if that is your wife. If you try to change that you damage your art. I think that our background is one of performing art almost free for the community. Sure we charge royalties, and so on, to make sure we don't starve to death, but, I think that basically we are Third World people who are very creative, who perform art for the community and who don't expect to become millionaires from creating art. I think if you start off with the premise: "I'll be a millionaire by writing so many plays," you will start writing nonsense and not really creating from your soul.

Q: And that's a tragedy.

LB: It is a very big tragedy. It's a peculiar American tragedy in the first place. When it hits black people it's even worse, because we have so much to catch up with because of white racism. When we set out in this way, we not only damage ourselves, but we damage those who will be coming after us, those who have to learn from us.

Q: What do you think of Caribbean literature? Do you think there is such a thing?

LB: I think it's very real. Because I think that our literature was always there – except that I think we spoke it, it was part of the oral tradition. Once you start writing that down people call it "a literary tradition". Well, I think it exists before you even write it down, because you tell stories. Anancy stories – that's a short story form. You have to know *how* to tell Anancy stories. I mean, I had an uncle from Jamaica who had a whole form in telling Anancy stories. He would say: "A riddle-a riddle-a-dee and something, something, something..."

Q: "Riddle me this and riddle me that."

LB: And then he would tell you something that has an answer to it. And it used to just madden me that I couldn't get the answers. Right away, as soon as I gave an answer, he says "Perhaps not" – I'm a little child, I want to get the answer but I can't. And then he would say "Well, okay, 'water sit down, water stand up.' What's that?" Alright, then I would start thinking about it. And he would say "It's all around you." And I'm thinking about it and then I give up. Sugar Cane. And I would go "Oh." I couldn't see that. And he had hundreds of these kind of things. He knew how to get me angry – give me about a dozen of those, and he would catch me on each one. But I think that helped me to develop my imaginative qualities. I think that Caribbean literature stems from this kind of oral tradition. I think there are several other distinctive marks on Caribbean literature. One is that it's a kind of a social conscience literature – it's not a literature that's what's popularly called "art for art's sake." You'll notice that even if a Caribbean writer has a middle-class background, has a middle-class education, when he writes, he writes about the working class, the poor people, the masses. Also, we have our own Caribbean English, and we have been able to do what a lot of people have not been able to do. We have been able to take the English language and stretch it to suit our own imagination and our own experiences. And that is genius. When once you do that, you have started to form a nation, you've started to form a society, you've started to realize the genius of your race. There is a "Caribbean race", and the proof of the Caribbean race is Caribbean literature. In other words, I can sit down and I can write you an essay in completely standard formal English that could be read and understood by anyone, and I can also turn around and write it for you in Trinidad English – and if I practised enough, maybe in Grenadian English or Jamaican English. Well, we have been able to take the Englishman's English, and we have been able to stretch it to express what we want. We could not use British

English to express certain things that calypsos or reggae will express for us – certain emotions, feelings of loneliness, feelings of anger. For example, if I wanted to say "reverse the car" and I say "back-back the car" – that's because I have realized that the verb "reverse" was not enough for me. When I say "back-back the car" it means I have created my own verb from two British nouns and I've made them into a double verb. And that is a work of genius. Now, at one point, the United States did this with people like Walt Whitman and so on. Australia hasn't done it too successfully. We have a much stronger literary tradition than Australia. Canada has not done it as well as we have either. As a matter of fact, it has been said that since the great age of Shakespeare, and then after Shakespeare, Tennyson and Dickens and so on – that the only great breakthrough in the English language came with the founding of the United States, the colonies; and then with British-Caribbean literature. When you look at some of the words we use in English – take some of Louis Bennett's poems, the use of words in Samuel Selvon's novels. For example, I was listening to a calypso this morning by Sparrow – and Sparrow says that he wants to be in Carnival, and he wants to jump up and dance, and he wants to be near a woman. And then the brass goes "bram!" Now, that "bram" describes what the brass section of the band is doing. And there is nothing in British English, that has taught us that. That is our own imagination. And whenever a race of people has done this, it means that they have developed their own thinking and their own feeling, so that we have not been colonials in the true sense of the word. A colonial is somebody who doesn't have any other language except his master's language, has no other religion except his master's religion, way of dressing, cooking or eating or drinking. And we have all of these things of our own in the Caribbean. We have both; one is official, one is unofficial. For example, there's a word in Trinidad called "chinksing" – I don't know if you know the word "chink" – it means "to cheat". For example, if you're pitching marbles and if your opponent isn't looking and you want to cheat a little bit, you push your marble a little nearer to the ring to knock out the other marbles. But that's called "chinksing". And that's a word we made up completely – that's our own word. And there are words like that in Jamaica too. "Nyam", or like, "nyam something down". Or the way we express certain things – like in Trinidad we have some streets called "Turn-back Alley", and it's called "Turn-back Alley" because it's a one-way street, a cul-de-sac. When we started to write like that, British people said that "Here was a new breakthrough in the language made by people who were slaves and who we thought would never be able to speak or write. They have taken our language and have done better with it than we have." It's almost like cricket – they taught us cricket and we came back to beat them and teach them how to play cricket – and this is a sign that we definitely have a literary tradition. We have distinct marks about it. It's multiracial; it has a strong social conscience; it's very very artistic. And you see, we can switch between two languages.

Q: My mother used to say that Jamaicans are bilingual.

LB: Yeah, we are bilingual. All Caribbean people are bilingual. Now Black Americans are not bilingual. See, they can only speak Black American English generally, and once a Black American becomes middle class and learns to speak formal English, he or she does not want to go back to Black American English. Because he feels he's stepping back into the ghetto – which is wrong. You have to develop the two kinds of English. I sometimes would talk to the black students at school in their own Black English and then I would start talking to them in "White" English – and they learn more that way. I show them different ways of saying or writing things in different ways. So, I think there is no doubt that we have one of the most exciting forms of literature in the English-speaking world. I don't think since Dickens – no, I don't think since James Joyce has there been a style of novel like the best Caribbean novelists. I am talking now of Vic Reid, Samuel Selvon – not Naipaul so much – but I'm talking about the stylists: Samuel Selvon, Vic Reid, George Lamming. The things they did with language are really works of genius; there's no doubt about that. I don't think we have as many good dramatists as we have novelists. We have just a few good or good to great dramatists – but as far as novelists are concerned, we have great novelists. Wilson Harris from Guyana, I think, is the best novelist in the world today, although his name is hardly known. His name will be known in fifty or sixty years' time. People will start to look at his work. He has taken the whole Caribbean landscape and has made it into a sort of living flesh. Reading his novels is like reading one long poem. It's fantastic what our Caribbean novelists have been able to do with language. And it's because they've written the oral tradition that we've been speaking all the time. That's all they did; they just wrote it down. They developed ways of spelling it and writing it down.

Q: You know, when I was told as a child to "speak proper English" – the patois was like "bad English" – that bothered me. I couldn't figure out why it was bothering me so. Later I resolved that problem by finding that it wasn't "bad English" or "corrupt English" but it was indeed our own unique language.

LB: We created a whole new language in the Caribbean because we used an African base and we just poured English words into it. But we changed English words to suit what we wanted to say. The Barbadian who says "Back-back the car" is a man who is staring straight at Shakespeare and telling him, "No, I do not want what you are saying, I want to say what I am saying. This is the way I see it." Any country who develops a language, or changes a language, is heading for independence or heading for empire or for greatness in some way or other – at least for a while – after it might go down again. And this is what's puzzling about the Caribbean, that we have made these breakthroughs in language and art, and so on, but we don't seem to have been able to make them in economics and in politics. Some Third World states have been able to make the breakthrough in politics. Cuba is an example. Cuba has made a breakthrough in politics, and Cubans tell you they don't speak Spanish, they say they speak "creole", they speak "Cuban Spanish". At CARIFESTA, they said, "Don't confuse our Spanish with Castilian Spanish or Spanish from Spain, we speak 'creole' which is 'Cuban Spanish'."

Q: The Haitian will tell you the same thing, too.

LB: Yes, yes. Now you see, they are republics – nations with a definite identity. They may be small and poor, but nobody is just going to walk into Cuba or Haiti and take it over. See, the Spanish and the French and Dutch-speaking areas – they're the same thing with the mother tongues, they invented their own language. They stretched their master's languages to accommodate their experiences. So that you get people like Guillén and Neruda and Carpentier, the Haitian Jacques Roumain. All of these great writers are non-English writers. Aimé Césaire, Leon Demas...

Q: Fanon

LB: Yeah, Frantz Fanon. They have all broken through politically because they broke through linguistically. And it's a kind of a racial breakthrough, too. It's a breakthrough from slavery, from colonialism. So there's no doubt that we have a strong literary tradition in the Caribbean – and you could pick up a Caribbean novel and tell if the writer is just jiving. You could, because there are certain things you look for automatically, and you know if that writer is jiving. If that writer starts writing and he mentions the "yard", and he doesn't have certain thing about the "yard" in that novel, you know that he doesn't know anything about the "yard", or he's afraid of it, or he's ashamed of it, or he hasn't matured enough yet to know what the "yard" represents for us in the Caribbean – that "the yard" represents a retreat from oppressive classes, where we could be ourselves, take our shirts off and play dominoes or cards and drink rum, and beat drums, and all of that. If you don't know that, if a writer doesn't do that, you know that he's not writing in the Caribbean tradition. And this is the way

I see literature. I see literature as sort of river, and each person learning from every other person. Some getting better than others. For example, in Trinidad, C.L.R. James wrote a book called *Minty Alley*, and it was about a house. Then years passed before Naipaul wrote *A House for Mr. Biswas*, which became a landmark. I think it was in 1936 that C.L.R. James wrote his book; then Naipaul wrote his book in, I think, 1961. That's about twenty-five years before another writer could come along with the imagination to take a step further. So I think it's almost like belonging to a holy society where you learn one from the other. If you really take it seriously, you try to read everybody, and try to learn and try to develop something that will last forever, because that's what art is supposed to be. Art is really supposed to be eternal. It's eternal statements you're trying to make, you know. But to come back to what I've been saying about Caribbean literature. I think we have a lot more vigour and freshness than the American literary tradition. I think we bypassed the British tradition a long time ago. Canada does not have a sense of Canadian literature. As soon as you pick up a Caribbean novel you know. First you look at the language, you look at the way certain verbs are used, and you know it's Caribbean; or in the concepts of the society, a very strong sense of race, a strong sense of history. Remember I told you about being a child and always wondering why is it that in school the white kids smirked when we mentioned slavery. I set out to find out for myself, and got angry about it. Well, we have a strong sense of history in our novels. If you notice, the novelist always tries to fill in the background of what happened before, before they can tell today's story. So we have this strong sense of history developing in our novels that you don't find in everybody's novels. Only in the great periods of literature – like in Greek literature, Roman literature, in English literature – Elizabethan or Victorian – do you have this kind of outburst of imagination. We had that in the fifties when people like Selvon, Naipaul and Salkey went to England. I think it's one of the most important periods in Caribbean history. There was this great outburst of imagination and right afterwards Britain was forced to give us our independence. Britain had to go through the motions of saying "You're independent now", because the people had already established their own independence, in their minds. We started to beat England at Lords at cricket, then we forced them to read our own novels in *their* language, in the way *we* wanted our language written. We were no longer colonials. Canada does not have that; America had that once but lost it. I think America is just going around in circles now. A very depressing country – very sad, nothing fresh and invigorating.

Q: I've heard a white person say that "white art is dead", and black art is here to resurrect whatever can be called "American Art".

LB: If you notice, there are some white people who like to hang around black people. Once we start doing creative things, they observe us very, very closely to see what we are doing; and it's because they have no sense of form in their own art and lives. They want to see if they can copy what we're doing. And some people have succeeded at this. For example, Jean Genet the French playwright, he succeeded in ripping off a lot of Black art in this way. I think Jean-Paul Sartre has recognized this sort of ripping off process.[5] I think that Western civilization has spent itself by being too scientific and rationalistic and materialistic, and now it's looking towards the Third World countries for new art forms. And the advantage we have over them is that we – OK, so they took all of our property and our rights away, but they couldn't take our expressiveness away. So, that right now, if I wanted to write a love story between a Black and an East Indian, I have all the culture of Africa to draw on, the culture of the Caribbean, the culture of India to draw on – and I can outwrite any white writer who wants to write that story. That white writer may be able to read up on that material and write it, but I have lived it. I grew up with East Indians and Blacks and I've seen the friction, I have seen the ceremonies, I've seen the foods. He [the white author] writes from a very racist position, one that has taught him to look down on these people as despicable Indians or inferior Blacks, and so on. It's a position which goes back to a pathological period of history, a psychotic period of history where white civilization never stopped to think that the world wasn't made for everybody just to grab or to snatch.

Q: Have you ever taught playwriting? Or would like to?

LB: I don't like to – unless it's a bright creative group of students who are sort of already natural playwrights. I know I could help them by saying, "Well, I see what you are trying to do here, but you're neglecting this, or you're forgetting your character here. Or you haven't explored this situation here well enough." Normally, I don't like to teach playwriting because I don't think you can teach art. I think you're cheating students if you tell them that you can teach them to write. I think a student has to have a natural inclination first of all, and then you can act as a guide. But, I have had to teach playwriting once, and that was in Hartford. The way I taught it was as literature. I asked the students to write their idea of a play – whatever it was, doesn't matter, write a play. And all of them wrote plays – some of them fairly good plays. But I've never been able to get a group of creative students who already have something written, and I could say, well, "Okay, let me see what you have, and let me see how I can help you develop this the way you want to", by showing what they're forgetting, what they're not saying. That's the best way to approach it. I try never to teach in drama departments either, because I find that they don't (especially in the United States and Canada) teach students what drama is all about – human history from tribal society onwards, rituals, the spirit and the flesh, and so on. They don't. They teach students how to handle lights or how to put a script in a folder – things like this. They don't teach them the real literary value, the real spiritual qualities of the work they are doing. And that's why there's very little respect for art by a lot of American artists.

Q: What's the longest play you've ever written? Any three-act plays?

LB: Yeah. When I first started to write, I wrote three-act plays. There's one play I have called *The Journey Into Night* which is not really epic but it's three acts. But now I find that my plays are becoming more and more compact – they are usually two acts. I usually get quite a lot into them by using devices like symbolism, poetry, dance and movement, and using the actual physical properties of the stage – like lighting – things like that. So my plays are becoming physically shorter but increasing in depth. For example, the play I'm working on right now – I'm calling it a "dramatized" ballet because I found that the form I wanted for the content I wanted to express. It's called *The Blood Promise of a Shopping Plaza* and it's based on a murder in Toronto, where a black immigrant, a young teenager, fifteen years old, just come from Jamaica with his family, was cycling across a shopping plaza on his way to a part-time job, and a twenty-year-old white kid came up to him with a shotgun, just blasted his head right off. They said that the white kid was schizophrenic. But I have based a dramatized ballet around this whole incident. And again I've gone to my own imagination to find out the reasons for this white stranger just seeing this black stranger and blowing his head off like that. You can't explain that away in psychological terms for me – there's a lot more to it than that, I think. So, I'm writing it in the form of a kind of ritualistic ballet, where I go right back to the pilgrim fathers, on the same shopping plaza – to me, the North American shopping plaza symbolizes so much about North American civilization – then taking them up to the pioneer days and then colonial days – and I'm incorporating Blacks and Native American slaves in some very brief scenes – and I'm going to lead right up to the murder. I would show that even when the holy pilgrim fathers came from different parts of Europe to North America, that they came not for prayers, not for peace, but for wars – and that is still being fought in racism today. I think, in my imagination, that's why that white kid shot that black kid without even knowing him. Seems to me that the materialistic values of that shopping plaza dictate what you don't understand, and that white kid is just obeying his ancestral laws – which is to say whatever inner frustrations he had that could be taken out on that strange black face. I think he was obeying an ancestral code of behaviour. It's the same as the lynch mobs in the South – and they can't explain that in psychology for me either – because black people do not do that to white people, so why is it that white people do it to black people? We don't form bands and hang white people or walk up to white strangers and blow their heads off, we don't. Why did they kill off the Indians? The way I have the play developing, first there's a commercial about the shopping plaza: "Fill all your needs here on the shopping plaza… Buy everything here" and so on. And as the lights come up you see the pilgrim father praying with his wife. They say their prayer to God about clearing the forest and so on, and as the lights go up you notice there's a chain, and chained to them a Black man and an Indian woman. So, that the prayer meant nothing, really, because they had already made people slaves. Then I have the pioneer and his wife clearing the land – their farm and so on – and they're talking about the virtues of hard work, but each of them can see in their mind's eye a Black living in tune with nature and an Indian living in tune with nature – there's a tension in them; they want to be like that but they cannot be like that. Then I move it further up into an almost modern society where you get the sort of the establishment man, the bourgeois man with his briefcase, still having that same conflict within him, wanting what black people have but not being able to get it. Pretending it's inferior, and finally being so frustrated that the only way you can settle that kind of frustration in yourself is by killing. So, I'm going to write that and send it to the people in Toronto, who think that they can produce it. The murder created quite a fuss in Toronto; it was one of the first racial killings they've had for a while. Really surprising. So I've tried to show that white people brought this problem with them from the old world. The problem is all theirs; it not ours. It's all theirs.

Q: Lennox Brown, I know you're a very busy man. What kind of closing statement would you like to leave us with?

LB: That's hard to say. I would like to see a permanent monument erected to the black race. In other words, I see all races as being placed on a pedestal, but the non-white races as having been pushed off by the white race. And I would like to see the artist placing the black races back on their rightful pedestal through art. I think that's the best thing the artist can do. Without any preaching of superiority, to create that kind of monument to man.

End Notes

1. Lennox Brown refers to a period when the *Trinidad Guardian* Sunday literary supplement was edited by Sam Selvon. See *New World Adams: Conversations with West Indian Writers* Ed. Daryl Cumber Dance (Leeds: Peepal Tree Press, 1992/2008), pp. 251-252
2. Kitty Hannays wrote a satirical column under the name of Macaw in the *Trinidad Guardian* in the 1950s and 60s. Her work was gathered in *Notebook by Macaw* (Port of Spain: Trinidad Publishing Co., 1962). Later she worked as the features editor on the Express. She died in 1991. In *The Middle Passage* (1962), V.S. Naipaul described her work as "witty and inventive".
3. Claude Thompson was the author of *These My People* (Kingston: Herald Printery, 1943). But perhaps the best match for Macaw in Jamaica would have been Inez Sibley's *Quashie's Reflections: in Jamaican Creole* (Kingston: Bolivar Press, 1968) which reprinted Sibley's newspaper columns in the *Gleaner* in the 1930s.
4. Amiri Baraka (1934-), formerly LeRoi Jones, poet, dramatist, essayist, jazz critic and controversialist, has been one of African America's outstanding writers for the past fifty years. His journey has encompassed a movement from Black Nationalism to a personalised form of Third World Marxism.
5. See J. P. Sartre, "Orphée Noir": *Anthologie de la nouvelle poésie nègre et malgache*. Ed. Léopold Senghor (Paris: Presses Universitaires de France, 1948) p. xiv.

ALWIN A. BULLY (1948-)

Born in Roseau in Dominica, Bully is married with three children. At the time of the interview he was living in Dominica and later moved to Kingston where he worked as Programme Specialist for Culture at UNESCO. He is now retired from UNESCO and actively involved in many creative and cultural endevours in Dominica.

Bully attended the University of the West Indies (Cavehill) from 1967-1971, where he earned a BA degree in English and French. He began his working career as a graduate teacher at the Dominica Grammar School and Dominica Sixth Form College where he taught English, as well as art, speech and drama from 1971-1977. He was deputy principal at the school. Later he was acting manager of the Dominica Corporation, (DBS Radio); and was the chief cultural officer in the Ministry of Community Development in Dominica.

He was a founding member of the Secondary School Drama Society in Dominica, from 1964, founding dancer/choreographer of the Dominica Dance Company, and in 1966, he was chairman of the Dominica Arts Council.

Since 1970, Bully has been a prolific writer. His one-act play, *Good Morning Miss Millie,* (Heinemann, *Caribbean Plays for Playing*, 1970), republished by Macmillan in 2003, is one of his best known pieces of work. His full-length plays include *Streak* (1976); *The Ruler* (1976); the musical, *Folk Nativity* (1976); *The Nite Box* (1977); *Green Gold* (1976) and an eighty-five-episode radio serial version of *Green Gold* (1978); *Pio-Pio* (1978); a forty-five episode radio serial *Winds of Change* (1979); *Me Too*, an Educational Family Planning Film written for the Caribbean Family Planning Association; *Secrets of La Cloche*, another radio serial with thirty episodes (1980); the two-act play, *Pelée* (1981); *Fire Go Bun* (1983), a twelve-episode radio serial which was also produced for the Caribbean Family Planning Affiliation; a radio drama, *A Dance in the Dark* (1983); *J.D.; D.J*, a one-act play (1985), and *McB*, a play in four acts (1989).

He has been an active member of the Association of Caribbean Theatre Artists (ACTA), "The Caribbean Writer" literary magazine in St. Croix, advisor to the Dominica Artists Guild and many others. He has participated in scores of conferences, seminars and workshops throughout the Caribbean, West Africa, England, Germany and the United States. He has conducted theatre workshops and seminars throughout the Caribbean.

An accomplished artist and graphic artist, from 1967 to the present Bully has taught art and participated in several exhibitions. From 1964 to 1988, he worked as an actor, costume designer, stage and lighting designer, director, as well as playwright. In 1976, he taught summer school theatre programmes in Jamaica at the Edna Manley College for the Visual and

Performing Arts, and continues to conduct theatre workshops and seminars. He has composed some fifty songs, pieces of music and lyrics and a full-length cantata. Until recently, Bully was active in a Carnival band as costume designer and organizer. He has been a newspaper critic, written short stories and poems and forewords and introductions to ten books of poetry by Dominican poets.

As an amateur filmmaker and videographer, Bully has produced such work as *Super School* (45 mins., Super 8); *Carnival '78* (40 mins., Super 8); *Him* (75 mins., Super 8); *Flower Show* (1 hr., video) and *Toto and the Town Visitors.*

Among his numerous awards are the Commonwealth Fellowship Award (1986); the second-prize in the BBC Radio Drama Competition (1983); Sisserou Award of Honour, a national award given by the Dominican government, (1985); Caribbean-United States Theatre Exchange/Theatre Information Exchange Award for West Indies Theatre Achievement (1979); (1978); Best Drama for *The Nitebox*; Best Director for Derek Walcott's play, *Pantomime* (1992); Best Set Design for *Jesus 2000* (2000) and Best Director for *Oroonoko* (2001).

ALWIN BULLY

14 August 1980

Q: I've read about your concept of roots theatre or calypso theatre, and wonder if you are still working with that concept?

ALWIN BULLY: I think you're catching me at a point of transition. I saw the calypso thing as the first period in my writing, which was from 1968/69 to '78/'79. That was the period when I felt I had to try to get to the audience. Maybe I should explain that in terms of Dominica – although I think that it is something that is relevant to the entire Caribbean – we had to create an atmosphere for people's theatre, for a popular theatre in the Caribbean. Prior to my work in Dominica, theatre was a very limited in terms of audience. We had school plays, we had groups coming up, maybe forming in some kind of organized fashion to produce a play and then mash up after that. The plays they were doing were usually English plays, American plays but very seldom a Caribbean play, and this just didn't make any sense to the population. Even Caribbean plays from Trinidad or somewhere else they couldn't relate to. Why? Although the Caribbean is very closely knit – I mean all the islands have this similar vein running through them, similarities of expression, of attitude etcetera – each island has its particular nuances, definite little customs, and I think that if a people is not trained to understand simile, to understand metaphor, they can't even relate to things which are very close to their own lives. I saw it in teaching English in a secondary school, I saw students unable to grasp what very simple poems were about, because they were not talking about their lives directly. So what I attempted to do as a teacher of English – long before CXC [Caribbean Examinations Council] started to think in terms of Caribbean theatre or Caribbean literature – was to start the students off with an understanding of their own literature. In Dominica we speak patois, and I would start off teaching English each year by exposing the kids to the beauty of patois – French patois – as a language. Because that's what they knew best, and for a long time they had been put down for speaking patois – it was forbidden in many schools. If a child was heard speaking patois they would be put in detention or suspended... and they were ashamed of it, just as we were taught to be ashamed of our folk traditions – dance, drumming, folk stories – which we were told were uncivilized expressions of culture.

I think, with the whole movement of the sixties, the Black Power movement, people became aware of the beauty of those things. But in the schools, Caribbean literature is still downplayed a hell of a lot and I think it's time we start giving it prominence. We are the only people in the world, possibly, that starts off teaching literature by teaching our kids foreign literature. Never have I heard of an Englishman teaching Russian poetry first or Norwegian poetry first; they start with English poetry. And once children can understand how the imagery relates to their lives and understand how imagery works then they can relate *foreign* images to what they know and get the sense of a poem. Because the schools didn't do that for a long time, we don't have many poets *in* the Caribbean, we don't have many playwrights, we don't have many artists and I think that children are alienated from arts and culture from a very early age.

Q: Do you mean not many poets or playwrights or novelists in terms of quality or value? Or do you mean in numbers?

AB: In numbers – generally speaking. I think percentagewise we have quite a few of quality. Of course, most of these are living outside the Caribbean now, in England and the United States. And *again*, we come back to the same vicious circle: why do they have to leave? They don't have an audience, or they didn't have an audience. Things are changing gradually now, but quite apart from the loneliness of being an artist and not having people to communicate with, people were just turned off poetry. You mention the word poetry in the Caribbean, and if you had a room of twenty people, I'm sure fifteen people would walk out.

Q: And I'm sure if you put that same poetry to calypso music you'd have an audience.

AB: Of course. But then you're talking about a different approach.

Q: Because calypsonians are essentially poets.

AB: Of course. And I think it's time we recognized them as such. There are a few people making that kind of move. There's a guy in Trinidad called Christopher Laird[1] who's been really getting down to the poetry in calypso and publishing calypsos as poems etc.

Q: And there's another guy in Trinidad who does it to music as well as print… Tim Tim.

AB: Tim Tim – Paul Keans-Douglas.[2] He's calling his stuff "dialect-narrative-poetry" He's gone professional in fact. He used to work as an advertising agent and now he's gone professional… he's performing in Canada, in England, throughout the Caribbean and is really doing well. He's continuing the *oral* tradition of poetry which is intrinsic to the Caribbean. Anyway, getting back to the whole thing of education and having to educate the audience, it was essential to start from scratch. Prior to 1970 in Dominica, there was a folklorist by the name of Mabel Caudeiron – her son Daniel Caudeiron[3] is now in Canada running a black programme on TV called "Statements In Black", based on musicians, on the arts and Caribbean things in general; he publishes a magazine called *Cheer*. Anyway, Mabel Caudeiron[4] did a hell of a lot of research into the folklore of Dominica and was one of the first people to use patois *as* something worth its salt. When she did that she raised endless eyebrows, man. Like: Who the hell does she think she is to bring patois, which is the language of servants and labourers and the lower classes, into the capital or into the main theatre place, a place called St. Gerald's Hall. But she had a company called The Cairi Artistic Troupe, and that was in the '50s, and they did a number of review-type shows, variety shows, using patois songs. She used to compose her own music, write her own plays... As a matter of fact, the magazine which Christopher Laird, in Trinidad, used to publish – it's stopped now – had the same name, but he wrote it *Kairi*. Mabel Cissie Caudeiron – most people called her Cissie... Anyway, she did a hell of a lot of pioneering work. Her writing was basically skits, she would do a lot of one-act plays or even shorter than that. Or she would compose, say, three songs and build a story around them so that they could be presented. But she brought about this awareness of Dominican culture, like folk dances which she presented on stage; she did a lot of research into things like national costume, traditional costume, going back to the days of slavery, how it changed... Part of the national costume is the tying of the headkerchief, *mushwe* and, I think there is something like ten or twelve different styles of tying it, each with a different meaning...

Q: Is this African or –

AB: Yeah, basically African. And she wrote up notes on those things; I think her son Daniel has most of these notes.

Q: Is she dead now?

AB: Yeah, she died in '69 I think. I don't know what they intend doing with the notes – I think they should be published – all her research into the folk dance, folk stories, traditions, superstitions [...] So, Cissie Caudeiron did that work, but she didn't get into an organized approach to theatre, to having it accepted as an important part of the society. She would do performances that would run for one night, maybe two nights; she didn't carry it around the island. Anyway, my first interest in theatre and in culture was through her work, and I worked with her a little bit. So there wasn't any theatre to talk about; in St. Lucia, there had been the Walcott brothers in the early

50s, and it was a good time but it didn't last very long. They set up something called The Creative Arts Guild, which I think still exists in a kind of way, but since Derek left and since Roddy left nothing much has been going on. In St. Vincent, there was Tim Daisley,[5] who was the main poet who really got people thinking about arts, culture. Antigua has been very recent too, from 1970 on, mainly through the efforts of Dorbrene O'Marde[6] and he's been writing *very* political plays. In Antigua, another guy who has joined in with O'Marde, is Leon Chaku Symister[7]; in Montserrat, David Edgecombe's[8] been doing terrific work. He was in Canada for a while; he adapted this novel by Austin Clarke as a play, *Strong Currents*. These are the people who I think are doing the most work in the Eastern Caribbean. Grenada – I'm yet to find anybody who's leading any sort of writing movement. There's a guy called Chris de Riggs, who was somehow involved in culture, but I think since the revolution he's been more into education or foreign affairs so he really hasn't continued. There's a guy in Barbados, called Tony Hinkson who's been writing plays.[9] In St. Lucia, there was Robert Lee, I really can't tell you if Robert Lee[10] is into theatre now. He's been writing his poetry – he's basically a poet – he's very religious now and I don't know if he's been continuing his work. He was into Rastafari for a while – gave that up. I haven't made contact with him for about a year.

I'm sorry… in St. Vincent, I should mention Cecil Williams, Cecil Blazer Williams,[11] everybody calls him Blazer – who's been writing strong political stuff as well. And, it's strange, but quite a few of these people met at Cave Hill [UWI, Barbados], from '67 to '70. I was there, so was Robert Lee, so was Dorbrene O'Marde, so was Milton McCollin,[12] so was Blazer Williams, and, I think this is where we began to realize the potential of theatre in the Caribbean. Cave Hill was a very young campus – it still is, it's the youngest of all of them – but when we got there it had just really started moving, and we started things like an arts festival, a carnival on campus and the Cave Hill Drama Society. Walcott had been doing his plays in Trinidad and taking them to Barbados, and the Bajans were suddenly sitting up and saying, "Hey, what's happening here, man? Let's get something going." So there was the Barbados Theatre Workshop and The Barbados Writers Workshop, both of which this group I just mentioned got involved in – myself, people like Robert Lee as actors, directors and eventually as writers. My first work was written in Barbados, a one act play, a comedy. So when I got back to Dominica in '71, realizing that there was no theatre to speak of, and Robert Lee realizing the same thing in St. Lucia, O'Marde in Antigua, Blazer Williams in St. Vincent, we separately and yet collectively began to work on creating a popular theatre. We didn't want the dead theatre that existed before of doing English plays, which were understood only by a minority of people, the upper middle class or the relatively few people who've been to secondary schools – because let's face it, in a place like Dominica there's fifty percent illiteracy, maybe more, and the same could go for St. Vincent, St. Lucia, I'm sure. So an English play, an American play, a Shakespearian play, whatever, up to the '70s, these plays were understood by very few people, and these were the plays that were being done. Consequently you had art for art's sake. The plays didn't mean anything to the lives of the people; the masses of the people were not interested in them. The only kind of popular theatre which the masses attended was the calypso tent, because the calypso was talking to the people directly, in their own language, using simile, using metaphor, using the imagery that these people *lived* with everyday; speaking about their problems: the political, social, sexual...

And in the first three years of being back home working with Daniel Caudeiron, we studied the situation, trying to find out what the people wanted – at the same what we felt they needed. You have to set up yourself in sort of little dictatorial position to decide what people need. We did a play in 1972 called *Speak Brother Speak* which dealt with the Black Power situation in Dominica, and that was the breakthrough – it ran for something like ten nights to full houses. It dealt with a young man from a middle-class family, his parents reacting violently to his Black Power views, his sister going around with a white guy, he reacting to that, the society reacting to that – worked beautifully. We took it to CARIFESTA in '72 – that was the first CARIFESTA in Guyana. *Speak Brother Speak* was written by Daniel with a lot of assistance from the group; it was improvised out during the scenes, and then he wrote the script, I directed. Pretty soon after that Caudeiron left and I stayed with the group. The group, incidentally, was a group that had started in '64 under the name of Secondary Schools Drama Society; we were all at school, fourth formers, fifth formers, sixth formers.

Another important person in Dominican theatre development is somebody called Amah Harris. Her mother is Jamaican – used to act on the Jamaican stage and she brought that interest with her to Dominica. So her daughter Amah got heavily involved; we did our first play together, *The Merchant of Venice* (needless to say) in '64. When we all left school in about '67, I went to university, Amah stayed home, the name of the group was changed to The Little Theatre Group. I guess there are Little Theatre Groups all over the Caribbean. (*Laughs*)

Q: All over the *world*.

AB: Little Theatre Group, man. And it remained so... Amah left in '70 for Canada, where she still is; she's been working with The Black Theatre

Canada – I think she's left it now and is working on her own; she's been working on educational theatre along with somebody called Vera Cudjo in Toronto or Montreal. She left in '70 just when Daniel Caudeiron stepped in from England – he was living in England for a while – and he ran the group between '70 and '71, when I got back home all enthusiastic with theatre. Then Daniel left. He got into a big fracas with the government; he was on the radio as a D.J. and was doing a very controversial programme called *Teenage Tempo*, which was interviewing young Rastas and unemployed youth and definitely rubbing up the government the wrong way, so they trumped up a case against him saying that he was subversive – the usual kind of thing. Which led to a big strike – the first civil service strike, in fact, in Dominica – he was transferred from the radio station, put to work in some ministry which he obviously didn't want to do. So he left, went to Canada, went to Ryerson, I think, did mass communication, is now working in Canada in television, theatre, writing. I think he's written two plays recently, one called *More About Me*, about West Indians in Canada.

After *Speak Brother Speak* there was a period of just doing Caribbean plays. During that time we did things like *The Rose Slip* [by Douglas Archibald], *Dream on Monkey Mountain*, *The Sea At Dauphin* [both by Derek Walcott], a play by another St. Lucian playwright called McDonald Dixon,[13] called *D'able T'ent*. And Dixon is really a fantastic poet too, I don't know what's happened to him, if he's stopped writing or what, but he wrote about two or three fantastic plays and a hell of a lot of poetry; I don't know if he ever got it published. We were using those plays to study the audience. In '75, I wrote *my* first full length play, *Streak*,[14] which really got the thing going. Did 35 performances in Roseau, took it round the country and toured the various islands. And, for the first time – apart from *Speak Brother Speak* – *Streak* had reached a mass audience, *everybody*, the street vendors, the fishermen, the mechanics, the bourgeoisie, the middle class, everybody came to see this play. And from that there's been no turning back. So I think that the formula that we had hit on, of what you can call "people's theatre" or "popular theatre" was the thing we had been looking for for a while.

Q: Talk about that formula briefly.

AB: Having looked around and seen what moved the people... I've mentioned already the calypso tent and seeing how the calypsonians touch people – realizing that, we simply said, "If the calypsonian can do it, we can do the same thing through theatre." But looking around at other things like folk dance, seeing that there's a hell of a lot of audience participation in the folk dance methods – and I regard folk dance, folk stories, etc., as the indigenous theatre. So using elements of the indigenous theatre in what you can call the formal theatre, or semiformal theatre, writing *into* the play a technique whereby the audiences are allowed to participate, joining choruses as they do in calypsos, responding to the action, letting their feelings be known. You write those things in, prepare the actors to *deal* with audience participation. Now this European concept of the stage is another world – when you sit down and you applaud at the end of the scene just don't make any sense in the Caribbean. Not even in cinema. I mean, cinema in the Caribbean, people shout back at the actors and they *react* and laugh and curse the actor and whatnot, and clap and all that [...] Anyway, we're looking at other mass theatre forms like Carnival, use of costume, use of the procession – which I think is an important part of Caribbean culture, there's this love for processions. People love funerals, they love parades, they love religious processions, the Carnival is a procession in itself. Use of music, drumming, calypso itself – because the poems that I've been using in the work are very rhythmic kinds of poems... In one of the plays at the end of a poem a character asks: "Was that a poem or a calypso?" In fact I very seldom use blank verse, or what I call the more abstract kind of poetry, what I call subtle poetry, subtle imagery. I tend to go more for a rhythm in the entire poem, rhyme, a catch line repeated often, like a chorus in a calypso, which gives the audience an opportunity to join in. And then using cinema techniques because the audience had been raised on cinema – that's what they've had since the 1940s [...] Yeah. Like *West Side Story*, which I think first came out in '57, where Jerome Robbins used a lot of cinema techniques for transitions from one scene to the next... that technique I've used a hell of a lot, from 1975 onwards. Not because I knew it had been used by Robbins in the late 50s, but because the audiences had to be given cinema techniques. You couldn't have curtains closing and your audience sitting quietly waiting for the next scene to come on; they're accustomed to the scene changing rapidly in front of them. And I think these kind of things were important: the gimmicks of popular cinema like karate, a lot of action, a lot of movement on stage, a lot of colour – those things had to be given to the audience in that period from '70 to '79. What I also worked on during that period was trying to make the audience aware of the aesthetic values of theatre: symbolism, allegory, metaphor, simile, etc. I started by doing this with very simple, basic images which the people were familiar with – folk images, superstition images – like the image of the Soucouyant, for example, which is like I think...

Q: Old Hige, in Jamaica.

AB: Same stories you have in Jamaica exist in Dominica. All these various things were incorporated into the theatre as symbols. There's a character who towards the end of the play [*Streak*]tells a story which is like a folk legend, but which actually is an allegory on the entire play itself. At the end of the story the other characters ask him: what does that mean? Who is that supposed to be and what are you really talking about? And he gives a few clues which the audience immediately picks up to realize that he's talking about various characters within the play. Then in the larger sense of the work now, the *play* itself is an allegory on society, so then the audience could relate – at least I think they could relate – from the fable to the play to what is actually happening in Dominican society at the time – quite apart from the play having been based on actual incidents in Dominica during that period. There was the Desmond Trotter situation. Do you know of that? Desmond Trotter was a young Rasta guy who was accused of shooting a white man during Carnival... Last year he was released from jail. He was to hang, they were holding back on that; Patrick John eventually changed it to life imprisonment and then he was released when the interim government took over when Patrick John was overthrown.

Q: When did this happen?

AB: '75. There's a whole big movement, especially in Canada – "Free Desmond Trotter". So the play was strongly based on that incident and a number of other things surrounding the incident; a number of fires which Rastas... Dreads were suspected of having done. Some houses were burnt down, some people got killed – I think about four or five people got killed – mostly foreigners, and there was the claim that these acts were done by the Dreads as opposed to the Rastas, who were more religious, more peaceful, just living their lives separate from society, planting... forming their own community. The guys who were using the Rasta movement as a cover-up for committing these crimes were known as Dreads. So all these things were explored in the play, and I think that along with *Speak Brother Speak* – but I think *Streak* made a bigger impact in that it was better put together, better packaged in terms of story line, in terms of getting the idea across, in terms of the art work involved... it made a terrific impact. And from there on there was no turning back.

Q: Do you see Roots theatre as a viable force for change?

AB: Viable in terms of what, in terms of society, in terms of education?

Q: In terms of education.

AB: Yeah, definitely. As a matter of fact, we see ourselves as an educational force, basically.

Q: Education as opposed to propaganda? And I know sometimes being propagandist is almost unavoidable in order to get your point across.

AB: Yeah, it's hard to distinguish between the two. Two years ago we were approached by WINBAN, the Windward Islands Banana Association, to do a radio serial for them through which we would teach farmers to plant bananas. It was very elaborately set up; there was a central committee made up of agriculturalists and officials of the Banana Association who would decide what inputs were necessary; from there it went to the writers, myself as the main writer. I would structure the whole thing and I had two other guys writing along with me. I would write out the storyline and give them episodes to write and then these episodes would go back to the review committee to make sure the information was correct. It really worked well, it was the first local radio serial [*Green Gold*]. Set it up like into a soap opera: a land problem, family involvement, a romantic line running through it and all that. But into this we fed information to the farmers: what fertilizers to use, when to plant, how to take care of the crop after its harvest, what prices to expect, how to improve the crop, etc. Also, fed in other information on family planning, pre-schools, how to apply for fertilizer or how to organize village councils, how to organize cooperatives, how to got to the bank... all kinds of information was fed into it, and it had tremendous popularity. Well, it got so popular we eventually did a stage version of it.

Q: Was it done over a period of time?

AB: Um-hm, it ran for a year. [...] The play [also called *Green Gold*, 1979] was quite popular, it wasn't quite as popular as the others but it ran for about forty performances or something, which is like an average run. Following that we did another radio serial after the hurricane last year called *Winds of Change*, basically telling people how to survive the hurricane, what to do after the hurricane.

Q: Nice title.

AB: Now what happened, the title eventually caused the thing to be banned... (*Laughs*) And we chose the title quite honestly.

Q: Honestly or innocently?

AB: Innocently and honestly. We chose the title as a change for the better, having survived David, so to speak, an opportunity to improve the island. We thought that with Roseau being devastated, there would have been new buildings set up, new schools built, the roads improved... We thought all those would be happening. The serial began after two weeks, as soon as the radio got back on the air. There was no fuss about it until the election campaign started to hot up in about February or March of this year. And the slogan of the opposition party was "Time For a Change" – because the Labour government has been in Dominica for the last 20 years – so basically people were saying: "Look, man, we want a change." I received a letter one morning saying: "Your radio serial *Winds of Change* will be taken off the air because it is propaganda against the government party." Hardly any politics in the thing. I can't say no politics because we always become political. Even during *Green Gold* we were getting fairly political and a number of times the manager of the radio station called me and all that. But there's no way you can write a social theatre which is supposed to be reflecting the lives of the people and you're not political. Farmers were calling my house saying, "If Gobere is a farmer, he would be saying that it's time the government do this," you know. And then there's a whole problem with the Banana Association itself, the people who were sponsoring the programme, that they had not been spraying the bananas frequently enough and a whole epidemic of leaf spot disease attacked all the banana plantations. And the farmers were saying: "Look, man, how come the farmers in *Green Gold* are not talking about the leaf spot disease?" I discussed it with the writers and we decide to explore why. So I started calling up officials of the Banana Association and everybody was clamming up and closing doors in my face. So then we really let them have it. The whole serial backfired, so to speak, in the faces of the Banana Association. We felt that if we were going to do justice to the farmer who's suffering because of the negligence of the association, we have to come out and say it. Anyway, they didn't stop it, they supported the thing, they paid the actors, they paid the writers... right up to the end. It was 84 episodes. But the politicians...

We did *Winds of Change* on our own as a theatre group, we weren't paid for it; we eventually got support for it from the Inter-American Foundation. That was when the radio serial was into about 40 episodes before they came in and said they would support it. Actors always feel much better about doing something when they're getting something... they work hard and long hours on it. Anyway, the politicians didn't stand for any politicking that came to their skins.

Anyway, what I was saying was that these two serials were the most overtly educational or political, in terms of the work that we've been doing. The politics or talking about society, social change and so on in the other plays has not been quite so direct – they've been tied into the story lines in a more subtle way. But what has been good is that – especially when we take the plays out to the country parts, which is an essential part of our programme – after the play we would discuss with the audience what they got out of the play, meeting people on the road and getting their reactions at gut level, asking them what they would suggest as solutions to the problems that exist in their society. So we got this discussion generated and a sense that theatre was very alive and that's the most rewarding part of the work so far.

Q: What prompted you towards writing and the theatre?

AB: I don't know – I've always wanted to write. Theatre: I guess I must have been about five or six, I used to make little theatres with shoe-boxes and cut a hole in the side of the shoe-box and set up a pulley system, a screen and all that, and do little drawings as a scene and work it that way. As far back as I can remember I had an intense love for the theatre. But anyway, more seriously, I think I was heavily influenced by my mother, who was first cousin to same Cissie Caudeiron, who took part in her early plays before I was born, who also belonged to whatever kind of theatre existed in those days in the '20s and the '30s. My mother sang in things like *The Mikado* and *Pirates of Penzance* and *Gondoliers*, had an intense love for novels and passed this on to us, the three kids in my family; my sister is also artistic, she sings – she hasn't gotten into it as much, she's got bogged down being a housewife. I lived in the country, we used to live in a village in the country and my mother used to do plays with the school children there. My first stage performance was as a mango branch in one of her plays.

Q: Are you the oldest?

AB: The youngest. I have one brother and one sister.

Q: What does the brother do?

AB: He's an agriculturist. He doesn't get into performance as such, but he's a pretty good critic. He criticized my early work the best and gave it a hell of a lot of interest. So he's not a performer, not an artist in the sense I am or my sister is, but has always been strongly involved with the whole movement. I had a natural ability to write well in school, always top the class in English – terrible in math... The ironic part about it is I'm married to a mathematician now. In those early school days, early secondary school, I noticed I had a propensity for poetry. Wrote these long rhyming poems which always amazed the teachers – a good memory, better than, I guess, anybody else in the class. I remember they give us poems for homework. They'd say: "Learn one stanza for tomorrow", and I'd come back the next day and recite the entire thing. Those kind of crazy things. And a love for acting, did school plays. When I got to Barbados, I think, is when it really blossomed, because in Barbados there was an audience...

Q: How old were you then?

AB: Eighteen. I mean, a *thinking* audience who were criticizing intelligently, who were writing reviews of my work in terms of performance, in terms of writing, in terms of my directing – and also as a graphic artist. I do a lot of charcoal work, or did, now I don't paint much, I don't draw much because I find that you can do all these things on the stage. Theatre, to me, is the great meeting point of all the arts. And working at home I designed the sets, I designed the costumes, I designed the lighting, I direct the play and write it. So I'm able to do everything – and compose music for the plays. So I'm able to do all the various arts. I'd been composing before getting into theatre, writing short songs and things like that for groups of kids – and I've written two musicals so far, for which I've done most of the music.

Q: Do you play any instruments?

AB: No. And don't write music either. So, in Barbados, I think, I came to realize that this is what I wanted to do with my life. And it was a creative atmosphere because of the other people who were there, the people I mentioned, all of whom were very creative people. And then there was the tradition of literature in Barbados… you know of BIM magazine?

Q: Yes, I was going to ask you about that.

AB: I've never had anything published in BIM[15], but I've known all the people who publish it and who are the major critics. People like John Wickham and Frank Collymore, I got to know in Barbados, through my work in the theatre, doing radio work and a certain amount of television work. Then a lady called Daphne Hackett,[16] who was like the grand old lady of Barbados theatre – you've heard of her?

Q: No, I can't say I have.

AB: She's not like a prominent Bajan figure but she has produced the most theatre in Barbados.

Q: Do they have a fairly long history of theatre there? Expatriate?

AB: Expatriate. The Green Room Theatre. When I was there The Barbados Theatre Workshop came into being, as did the Writer's Workshop – it was dedicated to writing for theatre; a certain amount of poetry, too, but mostly theatre – we were concentrating on producing plays. The Green Room Theatre is the longest standing. Now there's something called Stage One. But it's not a vibrant theatre movement like you have in Jamaica, it's nothing close to Jamaica.

Q: There is a Barbados Theatre Workshop of New York run by fellow named Paul Webster, I don't know if you know him.

AB: I've heard of him.

Q: Who are some of the writers who have influenced you in your work?

AB: Derek Walcott, I think, is the biggest influence in my life. *Dream on Monkey Mountain* and *Ti-Jean* [*Ti-Jean and His Brothers*] – I think gave me the greatest insight into Caribbean-*ness* and at the same time left so many avenues open that I thought that endless writers could explore those avenues and that I should be one of them. So I say Walcott is the main influence on my life, also, to a certain extent, Slade Hopkinson. I like Slade's work a lot. Errol John for *Moon on a Rainbow Shawl*… Who else? Roddy Walcott, to a certain extent, his early plays, things like *The Harrowing of Benjy*… I think these are the greatest influences on my life, these people.

Q: Any writers outside of the Caribbean – European, American?

AB: Baldwin. I understand what he's saying very, very well. And I thought that the message he had for black people was also one that could be continued. I just want to say something about Walcott, now. In a sense he has influenced me in a negative way as well, or he has negatively influenced me in that I felt that his writing was too sophisticated for the average Caribbean man, and the things he was saying had to be brought down to their level. Now I'm saying a very dangerous thing here, because I know, for one, he feels that a writer should never drop his standards to please his audience. However, I think that if we're talking about developing the audience and if we're talking about teaching the audience, we have to start at a lower level and bring them up. See, I think in terms of Caribbean theatre today, I'd use two names as its poles: Walcott at the extreme summit of Caribbean theatre and – another dangerous statement – a guy called Freddie Kissoon[17] at the other end… I think he's been producing all his old plays over and over again… I'm not putting down Kissoon's work, because Kissoon has done a hell of a lot for Caribbean theatre, or for Trinidadian theatre, in that he has actually brought theatre to the people. But he's brought what I call "the Bacchanalian theatre" as opposed to "the Holy theatre", if you want, from Walcott. I see Walcott as "the Holy", the pure of theatre; I see Kissoon as the Bacchanalian theatre…

Q: Now when you say Bacchanalian, are you speaking in a Caribbean context?

AB: Yeah. Bacchanal, right? The backyard. And, my quarrel with Kissoon is that whereas he got the attention of the masses of the people in Trinidad, he never attempted to raise their level of appreciation, their level of consciousness, their understanding of the aesthetics of theatre, of art, of poetry or of whatever magic that theatre has in it. He kept producing the bacchanal after the bacchanal after the bacchanal… really the most clichéd image of the Caribbean man in my opinion. My quarrel with Walcott, he never attempted to come *down* a little bit to allow the masses to understand him. Now I think that both of them have the right to do that; at the same time I think that there must be some writers who are committed to filling that middle gap. In my writing, I tend to believe I'm doing that, that I'm giving some of the Kissoon type theatre and some of the Walcott type of theatre. What I'd like to do is to raise the appreciation of the audiences to such a level that they will understand Walcott or Shakespeare – and I think the two names are interchangeable – eventually.

Because, right now, doing a Walcott play at home – we did *Dream on Monkey Mountain* to a very small audience because they weren't ready for it. They didn't understand the symbolism, they didn't understand the metaphor of the play. Some people liked it because of the visual things we did, but to grasp what the man was actually talking about they just weren't ready for it. That was in '73. I'd like to do it *again* now, after the Dominican audience or the Caribbean audiences have been through plays like *Streak*, like *The Ruler in Hiroona*[18] [1976] and *Nite Box* [1977] – plays in which we've been trying to work on this appreciation of metaphor and symbolism – and *see* how they'd react to *Dream on Monkey Mountain* now. I'd like very soon to do a Shakespearian play, either adapting it in setting – not in terms of adapting the life as such – to a Caribbean situation, and see how they understand the language, see how they understand the metaphor of the play. This is the point I'm at. When we started talking tonight, Olivier, I told you I was in the middle of a transition period where I think I am moving out of the Calypso theatre per se into something approaching what Walcott is doing now. At least I'd like to attempt to do that, it's what's going to be experimented with in the play I'm working on now, something called *Pelee*. I'll continue the experiment *only* if it works with the Dominican audience; if they don't understand it I'll go back to Calypso theatre, with each play becoming more sophisticated... until I feel that audience can understand a Walcott play *fully* or understand a Shakespeare play fully.

I'd like to see a Caribbean audience being able to appreciate its own theatre – Caribbean theatre, whatever that is – and at the same time appreciate American theatre, appreciate English theatre, German, Russian – you name it. I don't believe that the theatre should be chained to one particular form, I think that it should be as free and able to operate as independently as possible. I *do* believe that it should have a commitment to Caribbean art and Caribbean issues – I'm maybe being a little stubborn in that sense – but I think that it's vitally important that Third World countries have a theatre which is relevant to their needs, relevant to the development process, their experience, heritage and culture. For instance, if you ask me how I think a Caribbean theatre company should operate, I'd say – if it was doing five plays a year, four of them should be Caribbean. At the same time I think that an artist has to be allowed his rights. And if an artist wants to seclude himself somewhere in the country and write plays which are never published and never seen by anybody else, I think that's his right, too.

Q: How do you feel about the concept of the development of a Caribbean theatre?

AB: I think it's been happening in fits and starts. Jamaica set the best example, but there must be a lot more serious work done in the rest of the Caribbean to establish a proper Caribbean theatre. If it's not, then the Walcotts and all the other great writers in the Caribbean are always going be working outside. I think, however, that there seems to be the beginnings of a professional approach to theatre throughout the Caribbean. For instance, you're seeing theatre groups beginning to pay the playwrights, pay the actors, pay the directors. We're seeing some governments setting up departments of culture, regardless of how limited their actual support is in the final analysis. We hear of people building theatres, building cultural centres; there's more attention being paid to the training of actors, training of directors. It's happening very slowly but I think it's happening and I think within this decade we'll have a serious professional theatre – though outside of Jamaica it's going to be hard for any one island to support its theatre in terms of publishing new plays, sustaining actors, sustaining directors, sustaining writers – and as such it would have to be a travelling theatre. It must travel and that is the problem.

Q: Now, Derek Walcott has said that a lot of people feel that language is the ultimate barrier to reaching a wider Caribbean audience, but that with translations it shouldn't be. How do you feel about that?

AB: But we haven't even started to approach language seriously yet. I mean, we're still talking about getting the plays through the *English*-speaking islands! We can't even get a damn play from Trinidad to Jamaica, hardly; if CARIFESTA didn't happen once every four years, you'd hardly see an exchange of theatre. Within the Eastern Caribbean there have been three groups that have been travelling among the English islands, that's my group, The People's Action Theatre, The Harambee Theatre of Antigua[19] and the Montserrat Theatre Group,[20] these are the only groups travelling. Barbados, which has, I think, three established theatre groups, never travels. I don't even think they travel *around* Barbados; they perform *only* in Bridgetown. I think Dominica has the only theatre group – and Trinidad, too, The Strolling Players,[21] Kissoon's group – that has been doing performances in villages around the island. So I think we have to first bridge *that* problem of travelling among the English islands and then, and only then, I think, we can talk about translations into Spanish, French, Dutch.

Q: So we are talking about a travelling theatre throughout the Caribbean and yet there is not even that happening *in* many of the islands.

AB: Well, in Dominica, the plays are popular not only with the adults but also with the young people at school. And the reason why is that we've taken the plays to the parents of those kids and the parents are telling them, "I enjoy the play, you will enjoy it, too, go see it." Because the kids all come to school in Roseau, in the capital, we do special school performances or matinee performances and they are sold out every time. Well, it's the same old story. If Muhammed can't come to the mountain, the mountain goes to him – must done.

There has been a certain amount – well, very, very limited – of exchange between the French islands and the English-speaking islands. There's a guy in Martinique, called José Alpha,[22] who is a writer and an actor and he's taken his work to Jamaica and Dominica…

Q: A thing called *Chose*?

AB: *Chose*, and also something called *Le Teaux*, (*The Vice*). He's been planning to do an exchange between Martinique, Guadeloupe, Dominica and St. Lucia, which are four patois-speaking countries, who can basically understand French. I think he did Jamaica because he recognized Jamaica as the be-all and end-all of Caribbean theatre, and as such he wanted the exposure there, but he's certainly making some strong efforts.

The other thing is TIE[23], Theatre Information Exchange, which was started in '74 – you know about TIE? We have all kinds of big plans for it, like exchange of groups travelling through the Caribbean, exchange of directors, exchange of actors, even going as far as suggestions such as a single play could be rehearsed in two countries at the same time, and then the cast splits. A director with half the cast goes to Jamaica and the Jamaican director with half his cast goes to Dominica… all those kind of ideas. We had our first conference in '76, in St. Lucia, and we had our second two years ago in Barbados. There's money coming from the Inter-American Foundation to run the conferences and to set up an office. What we've been doing so far is collecting new Caribbean scripts; it's also been publishing a newsletter which comes out something like once a month or once every two months. We're planning to document Caribbean theatre spaces, a playwrights directory, a directors directory. Ken Corsbie,[24] who is really the main man behind the entire movement, was to write a book on Caribbean theatre; he did one recording of Caribbean poetry, or Guyanese poetry, of the work of a guy called Marc Matthews;[25] and another Guyanese guy called Johnny Agard.[26] But the money has run out and what seems to be taking over now is a new organization which was set up last year, really orchestrated by Derek Walcott, who's been making a hell of a lot of contacts with important theatre people here in the United States, and he got the United States International Communications Agency (ICA) to set up an organization called CARIBUSTE (Caribbean United States Theatre Exchange) so it would seem that this CARIBUSTE movement is prepared to support TIE and continue the work of TIE.

The programmes that we had planned, like for instance, the documentation of the theatre spaces is going to be taken on as a project by CARIBUSTE. There will be certain number of exchanges this time between the United States and the Caribbean; they want directors, actors, designers from the United States to do workshops in the Caribbean and vice versa. Above all, we're setting up a playwrights' conference, similar to what goes on at the O'Neill, in the Caribbean, most likely in January, next year – should be in St. Thomas. So TIE, I think, has laid down the foundations for this unity of theatre activists in the region; we've recognized the fact that we've all been working in isolation, in our own separate little vacuums for too long and we've been wasting a lot of time just by not knowing what our next door neighbour is doing. There're various forms of expertise existing in each of the islands. Like, one island may have a good director, next one would have a good set-designer, next one experience in lighting – and nobody has been able to share those things. So TIE has been concentrating on trying to get these kind of exchanges happening. Which also includes Jamaica, because normally when people from the Eastern Caribbean talk about the West Indies, they're not referring to Jamaica at all. We're even talking about the Bahamas, which is even more north.

So we've laid down I think, a pretty good foundation for that work and if we can find the money to run an office, to employ somebody full-time on it – maybe employ two or three people on it – document things, photograph things, get reviews, get pictures of shows, and have them put into some form of archive, I think we'll be doing a great service to Caribbean theatre. Apart from that, I'm talking about setting up a playwrights agency for the Caribbean, because more and more of the work is getting around now – since TIE, in fact, since '76, when scripts have been available through TIE; people have been writing in to TIE asking for scripts, and the work is getting done. Talking now about royalties to playwrights; also looking into things like copyright laws. Most islands don't have updated copyright laws; I think Jamaica and Trinidad are working on theirs. So playwrights have been copyrighting their work outside the Caribbean, in places like The Library of Congress and FRS in London.

It seems to me the basic theme of Caribbean writers today is Caribbean unity, it seems that is what's bugging most Caribbean writers. Certainly doesn't seem to be troubling the politicians, which is strange; they should be the ones most worried about it. I don't think that any of these newly independent nations in the Caribbean can really survive on their own. Not one of them. Even the bigger islands like Trinidad, Jamaica. Simply in terms of making an impact as a nation, the only way that could be achieved is as a united force. We have things to safeguard, we have a hell of a lot of natural resources

– even basic things like water in the Caribbean that's going to become important to the world. There's thermal energy, all kinds of things like that. And I think we have to think seriously about uniting or it will seem that only the artists are making serious moves in that direction.

But then I'm not totally in favour of the way CARIFESTA is set up, for example. One wonders what happens after Barbados and Trinidad run CARIFESTA. Does it go back to Guyana? Because, how many of these islands can really support CARIFESTA?

Q: Or what happens *after* CARIFESTA? It's supposed to be, really, a meeting of cultures, a meeting of minds, but what happens after the meeting of minds? You make a few friends and then you go home.

AB: In some cases you don't meet *any* friends because you're so busy performing. What I would prefer to see is a series of many CARIFESTAS throughout the Caribbean.

Q: As opposed to the four year thing you mean?

AB: No, no, no, a fragmented CARIFESTA. In the sense that each island each year, or every two years or whatever it is, would host specific aspects of the festival... So that one island, say, would do the drama, one island would do the art, one island would do the dance, next island would do something else. And it's interchanged: the island that does the art exhibitions one year does the dance the next year; in that way the entire population of the Caribbean would eventually benefit from what CARIFESTA is all about. Because Dominica couldn't host CARIFESTA, St. Lucia couldn't host it. But these islands *would* be able to host one aspect. Over a ten year period or over a five year period they'd see the best of Caribbean art there.

Q: Do you ever plan to take your plays further abroad, like to the United States or Britain or Canada?

AB: No. It comes back to the same question: who am I writing for? I want the plays to be seen by Caribbean audiences. If Europeans or Americans want to see the plays, then come to the Caribbean and see them. But I think if I brought a play here, it would be like theatrical masturbation. What would I be really achieving? Would I be bringing home anything to the American audience about themselves, about their lives, about their conditions? The people I want to touch are Caribbean people; the people whose lives I want to change are Caribbean people; the people I want to educate to theatre are Caribbean people. I just don't have an interest in performing in the United States or in England. There's been an offer, in fact there were a few offers made by some people I've met here; there's a guy, Michael Whittaker, who runs something called The International Black Theatre Festival, who wanted me to bring up some work. Maybe I'll consider something for a festival... showcase-kind-of-a-thing, but certainly not to try to open a play here and run it and make money, because that would be defeating the purpose of why I write, why I want to write.

Q: In terms of an artist trying to *unite* the Caribbean, how do you go about trying to reach the varying sensibilities in terms of the differences of language even within the English-speaking countries?

AB: I write a Dominican play – make it as Dominican as possible. Because, I think, people do best what they know best. At the same time – I don't know if I've consciously done this – I try to make the story universal to the Caribbean so the situation is one that *can* exist in any island. When I did my first major play *Streak*, I was very, very sceptical about travelling with the play because I thought it was a "Dominican" play which would be understood *only* by Dominicans. But after being encouraged by a lot of people I took it to Barbados and found that it sold out every night in Barbados. Same thing happened in St. Lucia and later on with *The Ruler* in St. Vincent. I don't think it's necessary to go out and put in, say, various islanders within one play, you know, have a Puerto Rican here and a Jamaican there. I think what we're talking about is the essential spirit of the people, which exists in any island. Even if you write a purely Jamaican play it's gonna be understood by Dominicans, once they understand the basic translation of the imagery into their context. And if you're writing realistic plays – especially if you're writing realistic plays – I don't think they'd have *any* problem in understanding what's going on – and understanding that what they're seeing there is themselves. In St. Lucia, the types that were presented in *Streak*, with particular names, the audience immediately started calling them other names because they recognized the types, like, say, the chief of police or the government representative or something – they could see the person represented on stage being *totally* synonymous with characters whom they knew in their context. Same thing happened in Barbados, same thing happened in St. Vincent – in Antigua, as well. So I don't think there's any problem in this essential spirit of the Caribbean, being understood throughout the Caribbean, once it's truthfully done.

Q: Do the young writers, your contemporaries, feel the need for unification among all the islands …

AB: Yeah, it's essential that they get together. Because the last generation suffered from this isolation, and I think that's why a lot of them had to leave. Because, let's face it, although I mentioned a writer's prerogative of writing in isolation, there's very few writers who want to do that; because, well, art, I think, thrives on audience. For any kind of art whether it's painting or poetry or whatever it is, the writer is writing *for* somebody out there, for people, and wants to check their reactions. Not only that, the writer wants to communicate with another artist who he feels understands his work best of all. Because of the geographical situation of the Caribbean, and travel being expensive and difficult, the writers in the Caribbean are very lonely people. The last generation of writers went to England and the United States so that they could find people as artistic as themselves, as sensitive as themselves. Before, in many cases, they didn't even *know* there were other people writing novels, painting and writing plays in the other islands; they discovered each other in foreign territory. That's why people like Edward Kamau Brathwaite, formed CAM – Caribbean Artists Movement – in England, when he realized that there were so many *Caribbean* artists in England who had come to seek... what? Fraternity with other artists? And you have your own example here of setting up CART – [Caribbean American Repertory Theatre] – the recognition that there're a hell of a lot of you existing and working in this territory, and it might be a lot easier to run an organization like CART in America than it is to run it in the Caribbean. This is the task that TIE is facing and CARIBUSTE is facing: How do you get people together? How do you get people to communicate? It's so expensive to set up a conference. But I think the efforts are being made now, and the closer the communication is, the faster the whole theatrical movement will move forward.

Q: Do you consider yourself a disciplined writer? Let me quote something that Henry Miller said in an interview in *The Paris Review*:

> "... Every artist does discipline himself ... in one way or another. Each man has his own way. After all, most writing is done away from the typewriter, away from the desk. I'd say it occurs in the quiet, silent moments, while you're walking or shaving or playing a game or whatever, or even talking to someone you're not vitally interested in. You're working, your mind is working, on this problem in the back of your head. So, when you get to the machine it's a mere matter of transfer."

AB: That's very true – for my work, at least. My approach to it is thinking about it for months, not writing *anything* down, but working out plot, working out characters, developing characters and scenes. And when it's all ready I sit down and write down in two weeks, three weeks. That's my approach. So, I don't know if you can call this a discipline.

Q: But, it's your discipline; it's what works for you.

AB: But discipline in the other sense of the word, now, like, in terms of doing the job when it should be done, I'm not disciplined in that sense. If I were, I would have a lot more work done. I tend to postpone things a hell of a lot. I don't know if what I'm saying is really true, because it might be tied up with my situation in Dominica, where I am really involved in a hell of a lot of things. I chair at least, what? seven or eight committees, all involved in the arts, things like painters' society – getting the painters together… Rastas, going out to them, getting their work, getting materials for them – chairman of the steelband association, chairman of the musicians union, chairman of preservation of historical sights, CASOD, The Creative Arts Society Of Dominica, I'm on the tourist board, art director… major director of The People's Action Theatre, manage a dance company, etc., etc. I guess the reason why I do all these things is to keep my sanity in a place like Dominica, because were I not so fully occupied I would most likely go crazy. I create things to do, you know, like I design Christmas cards and Caribbean cards, just for the hell of *doing* something. Or illustrations for magazines and for short stories. A lot of guys doing books of poetry don't know how to illustrate the books – I find more and more and more things to do – same time knowing that what I want to do above all is to write. So, I tend to keep postponing writing plays, for the sake of these minor preoccupations.

Q: Would you like to be more prolific?

AB: Yes, I'd like to be. I guess right now I must have ideas for or plots for five or six plays in my head, carried around with me for the last four years… five years, and not being able to put them down. In fact, I'm very sceptical about the job which I hold presently, as cultural officer to the government, because I think that I'm getting into things like organizing workshops in the country, workshops of art, dance, music, etc., and drama festivals, art exhibitions, children's art exhibitions, doing all them kinda things. And I'm saying to myself, that I'm spreading myself too thin and that if I'd give up some of these things and just sit down and *write*, I'd achieve a hell of a lot more.

Q: Is that your ultimate personal goal, though? To be doing that and that alone?

AB: To write and paint, yeah. Just write and paint. Or, write, direct and paint. I love directing as well. But I'd feel guilty if I didn't get all those other things going.

Q: Have you ever thought of trying to encourage something like they have in Jamaica right now, a school of cultural arts?

AB: Yes. Actually, I've got the site. There's an old mill, about two miles outside of Roseau, and I got the government to give it to the cultural department. As a matter of fact, we had started, myself and a friend of mine, he was in England acting for a long time, and he came out with the idea of setting up a cultural training centre at this old mill. So, we started in an independent kind of way. I was still teaching; I was headmaster of the grammar school, and it lasted a few months and fell flat. When I moved from the grammar school, I told the people I wasn't intending to be a headmaster for the rest of my life – I was 29 – so, I told them I wanted to get into theatre, get into the arts. They told me come over to the ministry of education, to the cultural department. Absolutely no money put into it, not a cent; so, I raised funds on my own. They gave me the site, the old mill site, and I raised funds with people interested in the arts and we sold paintings and drawings and things like that and we opened with an art gallery and theatre and art classes twice a week. [Hurricane] David took care of that. But the site is still there. I've recently got someone in from the USA, and they're renovating the building; the architects are supposed to be working on the plans and I'm seeking funds from other agencies to develop the thing into a cultural training centre. I want it to have an art gallery, a school of art, school of drama, school of dance, something for craft.

Something which I wanted to talk about when we mentioned it earlier, was the use of television. In Dominica we only had a small, small studio that broadcast the news twice or three times a week; the rest of the time it relayed Barbados or just broadcast canned stuff from the United States, old stuff, too. And I think that television and film are two major directions in which Caribbean theatre ought to move, especially in view of our geography... It's much easier to ship round a video cassette and get the message across than to travel with even five actors. I've done a little bit of work on getting more and more into film now; recently I've got a pretty good break last year through the United Nations' Fund for Population Activities. They wanted to do this theatrical educational film on family planning, and they asked me to write a script for them. It's called *Me Too*, comedy situations encouraging men to use condoms.

Q: So is that being marketed throughout the Caribbean?

AB: Caribbean, yeah. It will be put into the educational programmes and into family planning programmes. And (they're) asking me to write two more... one on water... for Africa and another one on venereal disease. But this is educational work. I'm interested in feature films. I think if one of us makes a serious breakthrough in film, then all the rest will follow by – I'd like to believe – by us pulling strings for each other. This is the direction in which we should move. Apart from touring companies. If we could get a theatre boat, for example, a showboat, move through the Caribbean, that would be a major step in professional Caribbean theatre. But I'm still not worried about a normal travelling company using the yachts, even with the high prices, because the way I look at it, if a play can be so popular in Jamaica as to run for five months or for a year – something like the Rhone plays – means it can do six months in Trinidad, three months in Barbados, two months in Dominica, two months in Antigua, etc., etc – which means that the cast can cover their travelling costs and make good salaries. It's just that nobody really comes out and says, "OK, we are a professional travelling company." Nobody has taken that step and seriously considered doing it.

You see, I don't know what I'm gonna do when I go back home, because I'm gonna check out the new government and see how they react to my programme. If they don't, I'll most likely move out of Dominica. I've been offered a job in Jamaica – UNESCO – but it has nothing to do with theatre or culture. I think that just being in Jamaica would mean that I'd get into the theatrical scene there. And the other possibility is going to England for a while.

Q: You really want to do that? Why England?

AB: Because in England you have a platform as a Commonwealth artist – immediately – as opposed to the United States. Here, you're just another writer; in England you can present yourself as a Commonwealth or Caribbean artist. There're things like the Commonwealth Institute, who are primarily concerned with Commonwealth arts; there's the Kiskidee Centre,[27] which is very underdeveloped, but I think once the right people get in there it can really move. And there's the Royal Court Theatre, which is basically concerned with new work, experimental work and Commonwealth work… So, I think that would be a better move. But, as I told you, I'm not interested in doing my life's work outside of the Caribbean; I'd like to be in England for a period, I'd like to be in the United States for a period, like three years at the most, basically for the experience and meeting other writers, meeting other creative people, understanding what the professional theatre is *really* all about. Using that experience to go *back* into the Caribbean, set up a professional theatre. This is my plan, while continuing to write for the theatre, while continuing to direct in the theatre. I'd also like to get a lot more into music; I don't know if I'll ever learn to play an instrument but I've enjoyed composing and I'd like to get more into it.

Q: Let me ask your reaction to this quote from Derek Walcott:

> I think if the development of West Indian literature continues, my generation of writers will be known as people who had to go through a very anguished kind of identity crisis. And if we've set down West Indian roots, if we've used the language we heard around us and described the things we saw and the experiences we went through as a people, it has been to lay the foundation for whatever masterpieces would later come out of that part of the world.[28]

AB: It's true. These guys are the pioneers – maybe even we are still the pioneers. What's really going to happen with Caribbean theatre and Caribbean literature will happen in the next twenty years, maybe next hundred years – we're just at the beginning of it. And these guys have taken the brunt of it, the exiled artist, who's living in England and the United States...

Q: With the exception of Derek, to a point.

AB: I think he's still abroad, you know. I mean, how much time does Derek really spend in the Caribbean? How much work does he do in the Caribbean, now? Since he left the Theatre Workshop in Trinidad I don't know how much he has produced in the Caribbean.

Q: What do you think of the idea of daylight theatre as an alternative to night or evening theatre? It is believed by some that the Caribbean mode of living is geared towards daytime activities.

AB: Again, I can start by considering my own experience in Dominica where we've had to perform under all kinds of conditions. When we talk about going out in the country we're talking about performing under a mango tree, performing in broken-down school rooms, etc., performing sometimes – well, if it's night – by gas light. We haven't really toyed with the idea of daytime theatre, because to me, the only time daytime theatre could really work is like on a Sunday afternoon – early Sunday afternoon. The concept of theatre in-the-round – definitely. This is the only way that a real theatre is going to survive in the Caribbean, bare, in-the-round theatre, using basic essentials... making the best of a worst situation. We haven't got the money to sustain the fancy theatre with revolving stages and all the equipment and the lighting that you're gonna need. But at the same time I believe that artists like to work under the best conditions possible. So, I believe that every Caribbean island should have at least one indoor, fully-equipped theatre for those types of plays that require it and to give the artist the feel of the magic that can be conjured up with lights, with a set, etc.

I don't think that all plays should be done in that kind of theatre but I think that it should be available; because there're some plays that, to me, just work indoors rather than outdoors. Secondly, if you're talking about outdoor theatre and daytime theatre then I think the plays have to be specifically *written* for outdoor theatre and for daytime theatre, because for me, it's a different format. You're making different types of demands on your audience. You have a lot more distractions to deal with. In the average Caribbean situation, any time you perform in-the-round you can expect a hell of a lot of activity *around* the area – this is from my experience. So it would have to be the kind of theatre which *demands* the attention of the audience, that really draws in the entire audience whether they're from two miles away or whatever. We're talking about a theatre that involves music, involves drumming, involves a hell of a lot of rhythm, whether in the speech or in poetry or with song – fast-moving, loud, exuberant. These essentials would have to be there for an open-air theatre...

What is given to the actor or the playwright by the closed theatre with lighting etc. is that you have a *captive* audience; that audience is in there and you can control them; in an open-air situation you can't do it as much. This is where I see a relationship between open-air theatre and writing for radio. In writing for radio you have to keep that audience there, man, because they're not captive. There are all kinds of distractions going on in the house with people coming in, cars passing in the street etc., etc., so the movement of radio drama is much faster; it demands the attention much more, it plays on surprises a lot more, so that it counteracts the other activities which can distract the listener. So I think that the Caribbean writer, when they realize that you really have to spend a lot more time in the open-air and simple stages in-the-round, will have to write for it.

I mentioned I've been trying to incorporate indigenous forms in my plays. I didn't mention a major aspect of folk storytelling in Dominica and St. Lucia, which is a device that the narrator uses called the "me seh qwik" device. Like, what he does is throughout the story he says "me seh qwik", and the audience replies "qwak." He uses that to keep his hand on the pulse of the audience.

Q: What does that mean?

AB: It doesn't mean anything – at least, the meaning has been lost. I haven't been able to find a counterpart in African folk storytelling. Maybe I just haven't done enough research on it.

Q: That's like in Anancy stories at the end of it you say, "Jack Mandora an' me no choose none."

AB: Right. But in this case, this "mey sey qwik," thing goes on throughout the story, so what the narrator does is he's able to find out if his story is coming across, how the people like it. Because if he gets an enthusiastic "qwak" from the audience he knows he's doing fine; he might even elaborate more, put in another song and repeat another part of the story. If the "qwaks" are soft and people say it half-heartedly, he's gonna cut off certain parts of the story; so he has this ability to change the story, adapt it, depending on how the audience is reacting to him, and to me this is the ultimate in adapting to audience participation. I've been trying to use that technique, not using the "mey sey qwik" thing, but being able to find out how the play is going by checking the audience reaction and adapting to the audience reaction – an essential part of Dominican theatre which can be adapted to Caribbean theatre in general. Because all audiences react the same way. I was really surprised in Jamaica to find audiences laughing at serious... sad parts of the play; I thought Jamaica, with its wide experience of theatre, had passed that stage already. And what was happening was that the playwrights were not writing to take care of that particular aspect of Caribbean audience reaction. I've been trying, and I know some other people have been trying to deal with it, *knowing* that if you write a serious or sad, poignant kind of scene in a play that the audience is going to *laugh*. You have to *know* that and you have to accept that and prepare to deal with it. It's a direction we have to go in and our writers have to write for that particular type of theatre; right now I don't think they are writing for it.

Q: What ultimate statement in terms of your art would you like to be either recognized or remembered for?

AB: As a playwright.

Q: Do you consider yourself as a playwright solely, now?

AB: I'm considered an artist.

Q: As an artist.

AB: Yeah, in general. And I think that's basically because I just jumping round from one art to the other. I find I'm designing carnival costumes or designing carnival bands, I'm writing a poem or composing music for somebody, some singer and next thing I'm writing a play or something and I think that I'm jumping around too much. I'd like to concentrate on theatre.

Q: Well, I think that's essentially the story of the life of the artist in the Caribbean. He has been forced to be multifaceted in his talents.

AB: It would seem that most significant Caribbean artists are multi-talented and this I find not true of European artists, or very few of them. I mean, it's been said of me, it's been said of Walcott, it's been said of quite a number of Caribbean artists that we are renaissance men. And maybe it's because there *is* a renaissance happening in the Caribbean, at least an artistic renaissance, and the artists who are involved in it are prepared to deal with every aspect of this cultural reawakening. It *is* a renaissance. I mean we've been through the whole slavery bit, we've been through the whole colonialism bit, we've been moulded culturally, our minds have been bent in this direction and that. And I think, starting in the '50s and primarily in the '60s we began to discover ourselves and be reborn as Caribbean men. It's a renaissance and a renaissance will produce renaissance men continually.

Maybe this would be a good point to end on, with the play I'm writing now, *Pelée*, which is set in Martinique… the eruption of Mount Pelée, which was maybe one of the most significant aspects of Caribbean history to date – that's a pretty strong statement – but the whole story of that eruption – so political and so social in its setting, concerning the colour question, class question and the fight between blacks and whites – which caused the death of between 41,000 to 45,000 people in a few seconds – has been totally disregarded by the Caribbean as a significant point of our history. It's a story that we have a lot to learn from. Instead, our students of "O" level history are studying the destruction of Pompeii, which, to me, is not half as significant in *world* history as the destruction of Pelée mountain. This play's a departure from my former type of writing – Calypso theatre type of thing, which was full of gimmicks and of other devices which I was using to woo the audience into the theatre. Not that I'm giving up the essential style of the theatre like the audience participation I've been talking about, and the local images etc. – the things that keep it people's theatre. But the language which I'll be using will be different, will be a departure. It will be a lot more poetic, sophisticated and, in general, moving towards a more aesthetic approach to the art form, which, as I said earlier, if it works I will continue working with. It will also give me an indication as to whether my efforts to educate the Dominican audience – I can throw in Antigua, St. Lucia, St. Vincent and Barbados – have been successful, and that will spur me on to continuing my work as a playwright. So, this play I see as an important turning point in my career.

End Notes

1. Christopher Laird (1945-) was born in Trinidad. He founded and edited the literary magazine *Kairi* in the 1970s and is an anthologised poet (*Voiceprint*). He is the founder/CEO of Gayelle, an independent TV Channel, and the co-founder of Banyan Productions, Trinidad's first ever independent film production company.
2. Paul Keens-Douglas (1942-) as Tim-Tim is one of Trinidad and the Caribbean's foremost performers of narrative nation-language poetry, much loved for its humour. Since the 1970s he has self-published seven collections of poetry (and CDs and DVDs) including *Tim-Tim: The Dialect Poetry of Paul Keens Douglas* (1976); *Is Town Say So* (1981); *Twice Upon a Time* (1989); *Tanti at De Oval* (1992).
3. Daniel Caudeiron is a poet and playwright from Dominica who wrote one of PAT's (People's Action Theatre) first local plays, *Speak Brother Speak*. He published *Poems* (1973) and helped to produce the Dominican literary journals *Free Your Mind* and *Washeen*. In 1975, he moved to Canada, where he is an active writer, music promoter, and radio and television personality in Toronto. His play *More About Me* was staged by Black Theatre Canada in 1979.
4. For more on Mabel Caudeiron (1909-1968), see Lennox Honychurch,

http://www.lennoxhonychurch.com/heritage.cfm?Id=24>, and Albert Williams, "A Brief History of Theatre in Dominica".<http://da-academy.org/datheatre.html>

5. Tim Daisley was a St Vincentian playwright associated with the New Artists Movement.
6. Dorbrene O'Marde of Antigua founded the Harambee Open Air Theatre and wrote and directed *Badplay*; *Homecoming, For Real: A Caribbean Play in Three Acts* (1976); *Fly on the Wall* (1977); *The Minister's Daughter*; *We Nativity*; *Tangled Web*, and *The World Spin One Way*. See <http://wadadlipen.wordpress.com/2012/12/22/antiguan-playwrights-and-screenwriters/>.
7. Leon Chaku Symister [Chukku Wacca] is noted as having written *Voices of Protest*, 1976; *Tilting Scales*,n.d; and *Time Bomb*, 1977, performed at the Third World Theatre in Antigua.
8. David Edgecombe, (1952-), playwright from Montserrat, is currently Director at the Reichhold Centre for the Arts (USVI). He is the author of *Coming Home to Roost*, *For Better or Worse*, *Heaven*, *Kiernon's Kingdom*, *Making It*, *Strong Currents*, and *Smile, Natives, Smile*. See <playwrighthttp://stthomassource.com/content/news/local-news/2006/11/13/island-profile-david-edgecombe>
9. Anthony Hinkson is the Barbadian author of *Abortion*, 1974; *Crisis*; *The Executioner* (nd); *Forgive Us Our Debts* (nd); *Friend in Need* (nd); *Fuh Luvva Woman* (nd); *The Genesis* (nd); *Hush* (nd); *The Nemesis* (1980); *The Prowler* (1980); *Round the Bend* (1973); *Seasons* (1975); *Slave* (1980); *Teacher, Teacher* (1981).
10. John Robert Lee (1948-) has worked as an actor and director in St Lucia; he is better known as an editor and poet, author of *elemental: new and selected poems* (Leeds: Peepal Tree Press).
11. Cecil A. (Blazer) Williams (1948-) is the St Vincentian author of such plays as *Backyard*, *Bedroom not for Sleeping*, *Breaking of Chains*, *The Clearing*, *The Critics*, *Drawing Room*, *Don't Want to Bathe*, *Nine Mornings*, *War Delusions*, *The Woodworker*.
12. Milton McCollin is a Barbadian actor and director.
13. McDonald Dixon is a St Lucian poet, and author of the plays, *Diablotin* and *Tinday*. See "McDonald Dixon: Lifetime Achievement", *Saint Lucian Literature and Theatre*, Ed. John Robert Lee and Kendel Hippolyte (Castries, Cultural Development Foundation, 2006) pp. 165-167.
14. For more on *Streak*, see Judy Stone, *Theatre: Studies in West Indian Literature* (London and Basingstoke: Macmillan, 1994), pp 51-52.
15. *Bim* is the Barbadian literary journal founded by Frank Collymore which ran regularly from 1942 through until the 1970s. It was more irregular in the 1980s and 1990s when it ceased publication. It was revived in 2007.

16. Daphne Hackett (1915-1988) was a leading figure in Barbadian theatre for many years, as an actress, producer, scriptwriter. The Daphne Hackett-Joseph theatre was named after her.
17. Freddie Kissoon (1931-) is the Trinidadian author of over twenty plays including *Mamaguy* (1961); *Zingay* (1961); *Common Entrance* (1966); *Doo-Doo* (1966); *Pahyol* (1966); *Papa, Look De Priest Passing* (1967); *We Crucify Him* (1967); *God and Uriah Butler* (1967); *Fugitives from Royal Gaol* (1968); *Like Hog Love Mud* (1968); *Do Your Home Lessons, Daddy* (1968); *He Died For Us* (1971); *Boss-Man* (1973); *Crash Workers* (1973); *Lust for Power* (1973); *Girls Wanted* (1973). He wrote the radio soap opera *Calabash Alley* (1973).
18. *The Ruler in Hiroona* was based on a novel by Vincentian born G. C. H. Thomas (1911-1994) published in Trinidad by Columbus Publishers in 1972.
19. Harambee Open Air Theatre Group was founded in c1971 by Dorbrene O'Marde in Antigua. It functioned up to the mid 1980s.
20. The Montserrat Theatre Group was founded in 1973 by David Edgecombe.
21. The Strolling Players were the Trinidadian performing group founded by Freddie Kissoon in 1957, regular performers of Kissoon's own plays from 1967 onwards.
22. Jose Alpha is a Martiniquan-born playwright and director. He is the author of *Choses* (1976); *Lajan Diab* (1978); *L'Etau* (1979); *1902, La Catastrophe De Saint-Pierre* (1981).
23. TIE, Theatre Information Exchange, founded in 1979, was largely the result of activities of people such as Ken Corsbie and Alwin Bully in the Southern Caribbean. It obtained funding for at least three conferences of Caribbean dramatists in the 1980s and began a collection of Caribbean playscripts. It appears to have ceased to be an active organisation in the later 1980s. Ken Corsbie, for instance, relocated to the USA in the 1990s.
24. Ken Corsbie (1930-) is a Guyanese performer, story-teller and director and writer of radio and TV documentaries. He was chiefly noted for his role in the performing groups He-One (Corsbie alone), Dem Two and All A We and was one of the founding members and regular directors at the Theatre Guild of Guyana. He relocated to Barbados in 1978, and to the USA in 1994. He is the author of a brief survey, *Theatre in the Caribbean* (1983). See also http://www.stabroeknews.com/2010/guyana-review/10/28/ken-corsbie-is-eighty/ and http://caribbean-beat.com/issue-6/mister-theatre-ken-corsbie.
25. Marc Matthews is a Guyanese poet and performer in such theatre groups as Dem Two (with Ken Corsbie) and All A We (with Henry Muttoo, John Agard as well as Corsbie). His poetry collection *Guyana*

My Altar was published in 1987 and *Season of Sometimes* by Peepal Tree Press in 1992. He relocated to the UK in the late 1960s, where he still lives and performs.

26. John Agard (1949-) is a Guyanese poet, writer for children and noted performer. He was part of the All A We group in Guyana, published two collections of poetry there, including *Shoot me With Flowers* (1974). He settled in the UK in 1977 and was recently awarded the Queen's Gold Medal for Poetry. His most notable collections of poetry include *From the Devil's Pulpit* (1997); *Weblines* (2000); *We Brits* (2006); *Alternative Anthem: Selected Poems* (2009) and *Clever Backbone* (2009).
27. Kiskidee Centre was Britain's first arts and cultural centre for the black community. It was founded in 1971 near King's Cross by Guyanese-born Oscar Abrams and others. Its theatre featured plays by Mustapha Matura, Derek Walcott, Lennox Brown and Edgar White, amongst others. It ceased as an active centre in the 1991 when it lost funding. The building that housed the Centre burnt down in 2012.
28. See *Conversations with Derek Walcott*, Ed William Baer (Jackson: University Press of Mississippi, 1996) p. 60.

STAFFORD ASHANI [HARRISON]
(1953-2009)

Arthur Stafford Ashani (formerly Harrison) was born in Jamaica in 1953. He attended Excelsior High School and the Jamaican School of Drama; he studied film at New York University. Ashani, also a videographer and actor, is a member of the Dramatists Guild and Writer's League of America; he earned a BFA from NYU in 1985. At the time of his death he was tutor in playwriting at the Jamaican School of Drama.

As managing director at A Plus Video Production in Jamaica, Ashani was responsible for producing music videos and live concert recordings for reggae stars Buju Banton, the Wailers, Tony Rebel, Capleton, the late Garnet Silk, the Wailers and Morgan Heritage. He was the producer/director/ cameraman on four seasons of the weekly television programme "Reggae Strong," a thirteen-part television series that ran on the former JBC-TV which was also syndicated to seven Caribbean territories. He produced and directed *The Trod* TV series on Music Plus Cable channels, Jamaica.

During 1987, Ashani did a three-month stint in England performing and lecturing in the East Midlands on an exchange between Caribbean and British writers. He received an Island Voices award.

As an actor he co-starred in the movie *Klash* (1995); *Just like America*, a Hungarian-Japanese production, and was a regular on the former ABC-TV series *Going to Extremes* (1992), as well as making a cameo appearance in Steven Segal's *Marked for Death* (1989). He has also played the roles of Caliban in Shakespeare's *The Tempest* and Vincentio in *The Taming of the Shrew*.

His plays include *The Quickie* (1977), premiered at the Barn Theatre, *Masqueraders* (1977), *Anancy and the Unsung Heroes Out West* (1978) and *Foreign Mind*, produced at the Barn Theatre in 1990 and at the Paul Robeson Theater, Brooklyn, N.Y. in 1987 as *West Indian Play*, and in Canada in 2002. *Bar Jonah* was staged at the University of the West Indies Creative Arts Centre as part of the 50th anniversary celebrations of the university.

His unproduced plays include *Kill A Soun': A Dancehall Musical; Redemption Day*, a musical play dealing with Jamaica's struggle towards emancipation; *Baccanal of Black Inventions*, a musical concerning black inventors and Carnival; *Ites of Mar*, a one-act play set in a barber shop; *BooYork Runnings*, about a Jamaican street subculture in New York; and *Night Noises* about Oshun in the Jamaican dancehall.

Plays that he has co-authored include *Getta Life*, with C. Browne; *Dukunu or Blue Drawers* based on ideas from O. Williams.

Stafford Ashani's *Masqueraders* received a major production in Kingston, Jamaica, in January 2011 at the Edna Manley College. At present it is his only play in print in *3 Jamaican Plays: A Postcolonial Anthology*. Edited Honor Ford Smith (Kingston: Paul Issa Publications, 2011).

STAFFORD ASHANI HARRISON

4 January 1977

Q: How long have you been involved with the creative arts?

STAFFORD HARRISON: Well, the first thing I did, I think I was in primary school – I was something like ten plus. I used to go to rehearsals with a friend of mine, he had a part and him get direction but he couldn't really carry it out and I would just stand up on the stage and show him what to do, and I ended up getting the part. Well, the next part I did was when I was around fourteen, I was at Excelsior; they had this pantomime and the music teacher just said come along to a audition and I got the part of Sinbad – it was in *Sinbad the Sailor*, a British pantomime. I did inter-school things for the next two years. When I was sixteen, in lower sixth form at Excelsior, I started rehearsing – we opened with Barry Reckord's play, called *A Liberated Woman* [first performed in the UK in 1969 as *Don't Gas the Blacks*], up at the Creative Arts Centre. It was a big drama at the time [1971] because I was young and it was one of the first plays where a man really feel up a woman on stage and talked about sex freely. We went to New York with that to La Mama, come back home... we get good reviews. Then the last three and a half years I had a interest in writing. Year before last I actually sat down and wrote something, really based on my life and something that happened to me.

Q: Was that *The Quickie*?

SH: Yeah. And then last year it got produced and it represented Jamaica in CARIFESTA. After that I sat down and I wrote this other one.

Q: So how many plays so far have you written?

SH: Well, *The Quickie*, which was produced; *Masqueraders*, which I am rehearsing now; one on the board – a thing about the political situation in Jamaica; and there's one which I started long before *The Quickie* and really have around ten pages to finish but I haven't finished it because I don't know if the time is right for that yet.

Q: What does it deal with?

SH: It deals with a Jamaican family situation – young people. It has around seven characters, six are under twenty-two and one older brother, his mother and his sister. It deals with the youth energies in the island, the fact that some are Rastafarians, some go with the Establishment, some go abroad and come back and can't fit in anywhere...

Q: Have you had any formal training in theatre, acting or creative writing?

SH: Not really. I got invited to a couple theatre workshops and out of those sessions, when we were actually rehearsing for plays you find that you had to do a certain amount of workshop work at the same time. So that's really how I got my experience. But on the whole, most of my experience came from actually doing the work. I want to get some training but it's not a priority right now because I actually can create my own work. When it comes to creative writing, I've never been interested in writing, really – except it occurred to me that really it would be nice if I could write my own plays. The year before last when something welled up in me, I actually sat down and wrote something. But with plays, you see, I don't have a problem with them... I haven't thought about writing a novel. I wouldn't say I'm a writer; I would say I'm someone who writes plays. And I've been very good at it.

Q: Who are some of the writers that you have read?

SH: Actually I read very few writers, you know. Now, since I've been writing, certain people have been pointing out that my writing resembles this and resembles that. But most of the people I've read – I've read Derek Walcott – I like some of his stuff; I like Dennis Scott's stuff as a West Indian. There's this guy Jose Triana, who wrote a play called *The Criminals*, which I love – Cuban writer [*La Noche de los Asesinos*, translated by Adrian Mitchell]. Outside of those guys... Now after I wrote *Masqueraders*, some guy told me about *Six Characters in Search of an Author* (Pirandello). I've read some plays and others since then. I did a lot of Shakespeare when I was in school – so I've read Shakespeare. But generally I've read a few black Americans: LeRoi Jones' *The Dutchman*, *The Toilet*. I've seen things like *No Place to be Somebody* [Charles Gordone, 1969]. But most of the things I've actually seen I hardly read. It's just lately I've been reading – since people have been saying "that resembles that, so why don't you read this play here."

Q: What about novelists, black novelists?

SH: I hardly read those things. What I've read a lot though – I read scientific books. May sound strange, but I used to love reading *Scientific American*. Books about psychic power, research books about history and anthropology. If I go to a spar's house and see a book well illustrated I will go through that too. Lately I've been doing a lot of research into African art because of the sort of writing I've been doing. But all this while I've been doing plays. You see, I don't see a play as literature, I see literature as one aspect of a play. The play is really conflict – I mean, it can happen outside of literature. You can have conflict without language. So really I don't see drama in terms of literature. You can judge a play purely as literature and sometimes a play that is a great piece of literature is rotten as a piece of dramatic experience; it bores you. So really and truly a playwright, as far as I'm concerned, is not strictly a writer in the sense...

Q: What do you do outside of theatre, or is theatre your only thing?

SH: Right now, theatre is how I make a living and how I intend to make a living in the future. I've actually started writing a film script, based on *The Quickie*... I don't know what will happen because we don't have the machinery to make films out here. But I'm pretty certain it documents what happened to Jamaica over a certain period of time and with certain classes, about a middle-class youth who finds he is caught between the reactionary energies and the fashionable progressive energies in the society, with all the dishonesties on both sides. So that's what it really investigates; it investigates also reggae music and also Rastafarian religious attitudes.

Q: As a Rasta brother, do you want to repatriation to Ethiopia? And how do you see yourself: as an individual contributing to Caribbean art or as a Rasta brother contributing to your religion?

SH: All right, first thing, I don't categorize myself. Seen? When I write I write about what I know. As a Rastafarian, I know a whole heap of Rastafarian brethren, the ones in life that interest I the most, so it so happens the last two plays I've written are about Rastafarians. The one on the board is about Rastafarians. And the one that I have put down is about Rastafarians – but not because I see myself as a Rastafarian writer or I want to give the Rastafarian message. I'm just writing about what I know, and that is what I know. Now because brethren relate to back-to-Africa, lately I've been doing a lot of research about Africa to get some firmer arguments about it in my plays. Because I find a lot of brethrens at times spout off at the mouth; historically, in terms of certain details they're not really right. Generally they are right but in finer details they don't have the facts together.

In terms of Back-to-Africa, did you want to find out whether I see myself as a Rastafarian who believes in a Back-to-Africa movement, or that I should be writing about Back-to-Africa? I don't feel I have a duty to anyone in terms of these things. You see, I feel the artist's main concern is an honesty to himself and his honesty to another person. Now if what you're writing don't reflect this, you're just being pretentious. Seen? Irie. So due to how I move, maybe I might write plays for the rest of my life about Rastafarians. But at this point I'm not looking at it from the outside that I want to write Rasta plays, I'm just writing what I know.

Q: Well, the other part to that question was whether you valued the Caribbean...

SH: Well, I'm a product of the Caribbean.

Q: But do you see yourself as rejecting the land you were taken to in bondage?

SH: It's not why I reject Jamaica, why I will leave here; it's not that I reject I parents, why I will leave here now, but I feel my reaching Africa is continuing something that started thousands of years ago which someone like me is an end product of. Seen? Black people were disenfranchised and put into a separate part of the world against their will. Seen? I see myself as a Black man collectively and I see that black people collectively should have the right to go back to the homeland if they desire. No doubt if I settle in Africa, that many a times I would come to Jamaica and rest for a while – and America and even Britain, if I decide to do a work. I not goin' chain myself in a part of the world because of somebody's religious ideas. Seen? But to me, part of the continuing story of the Black man in the West is that he must have the freedom to go back home. And the only way him goin' have this freedom is if some brethren actually go back home and pave the way.

Q: I'm going to ask a very sensitive question ...

SH: Free, man.

Q: When I've mentioned your name to certain people, I've gotten various reactions about you as an individual and I've heard people say you're not a "true Rasta", that you're just an "opportunist", and that you are just there to get what you can. Your reaction?

SH: People will say this about anybody that gets X amount of attention above the normal man in the street. They will find things to cry him down, and on the opposite side, will try to build him up to be greater the he really is. So, I don't care about these things; all I try to do is to make sure if a man has something against me, him don't get a chance to split me head... and don't get fooled by people... who may feel that I'm greater than I am and start to get vex with them – I don't worry about that. That's a lot of bullshit. By the way, though, I man has been a Rastaman long before I dreadlocks; long before a lot of ones who are now Rastafarians. In fact, since I been wearing the trappings of Rastafari – dreadlocks – and been accepted as a Rasta, I've started to see things that people could say is anti-Rasta – because really and truly I realize that there are negative things in the movement as well – and I'm not going to sit down and stomach it because I have a Rasta image to keep up. The main problem with that sort of thing is that people have stereotypes of what a Rastafarian should be. Seen? And I really don't fit into this. I don't believe that I should kill my personality to fit into a stereotype of what the Rasta is, because that is not true. The stereotype of the Rasta, really, is a lot of ghetto sentiment is involved with the Rastafarian religion because that's where it evolved. Seen? The earlier stages. Now, me, as a middle-class youth will not accept some of these things: feeling that every white man wicked or every man with a car is a capitalist… I don't believe in that sort of bullshit. Mark you, a whole heapa brethren don't believe in this either; in fact, very few brethren do. But the society seem to think that that's what Rasta brethren believe in. Seen? I'm a vegetarian, and I will sit round a table with people eating pork and I don't say a word! And them same people who eating will say: "Then how come the man no want piece?…" Feeling embarrassed, hoping that I will take up the other portion so that they can call me a fool. Now when I don't do that, they feel like a fool, so they find some other reason to keep the reality the way they want to keep it. So they say: "Well, you not a true Rasta because you sit down while I was eating this pork." I can't bother with those sort of people. Seen?

You see, there's whole lot of things about Rastafarianism that has nothing to do with God. And that's why I'm a Rastafarian, because them is the first set of people who show I a fullness, that God is in every man. Seen? Now there's a lot of things to do with Rastafarianism which have *nothing* to do with God. And I will not take up these things just because somebody says I'm a Rasta. In fact, I will even tell some people that I'm not a Rasta if I feel what they're trying to fill you into is something that I don't believe in. In fact, sometime a man ask me if I'm a Rasta, I'll say, "What do you mean by that?" Seen? Now if him ask me if I believe that God is in Man? That Emperor Haile Selassie is The Christ? That every man must be equal on the earth? Seen? And every man must work for whatever he gets, a fair share for him work, and that if a man believe him right – like, truly – and believe in Jah, and get the Grace of God that we can inherit life? Yes, I believe in this – which is the important thing of Rastafari. But if a man say you blood a man who eat pork and you make your woman wear a long dress, smoke herb all day, chat a lot of rhetoric – right? Well, if that's what a one look at in Rastafari, I'm not a Rasta. Because I don't partake in that sort of thing. To me it's a waste of everybody's time. In fact, you have a lot of brethren – you reason with a brethren about a project, for instance, moving this table from here to there, and, instead of talking about the problems of moving the table from here to here, them is tellin' you about doctrine. Now I'm not into that. Seen? In fact, part of this came out through… a interview; Neville Willoughby[1] started this thing: "Now that you're under locks…" and I said: "Hold on, man. I don't *locks* my hair you know; it's not that I do something to my hair, it's that I *stop* doin' something to my hair; I just let it grow freely. So this is not no *locks*, this is just my hair." Now a lot of people, Rastas and others, took that as a statement to say that I wasn't a Rasta, which wasn't the case, it's just that they wanted to hear that – the middle-class people – because they can't afford to have it that a Rasta has written a play that has been successful, so they'd rather not see me as a Rasta. And there are Rastafarians who would rather not see me as a Rasta because I deal with the Babylonian people. So they have interpreted this situation for their own ends. You see, the thing that I'm trying to get out of is: I don't want to fit in the strappings of what a man is supposed to be, I'm just me. I'm dealing with Jah. Not with Rastafarianism or Christianity or Buddhism – them things is just religion. And religion and God is two different thing.

Q: I've heard it said in arguments that Haile Selassie was in fact a dictator, and he – I read this – backed down when he saw the throngs of brethren out there at the airport, refused to come out of the plane, refused to accept that he was Jah; on the other side that there are historical facts that prove he was a descendant of the Queen of Sheba and that there are certain parts of the Bible that indicate that this may be so.

SH: First thing is this: Emperor Haile Selassie in my understanding is Christ. Seen? Christ, meaning the realization of God in man to the fullness that man commands this power of God. Seen? Which in effect makes that man God. Irie. Now whether the Christ see Himself as the Christ or not is beside the point, it is the effect that this Christ has on His fellow man. Seen? In fact, most of the Christs that have come on earth – or most of the great men that have realized God – have come on earth regardless of what religion, have never claimed themselves to be God. They have left it for other men to do. Because to realize God, you have to have an ultimate humility. You see yourself as God, your ego would swell to an extent where you'll never realize God. That is one thing. Number two, it don't even matter to me if him did see himself as God because the important thing is that, *because* of where I'm coming from as a human being, he has helped me to realize God in me; you understand?

The thing about Rastafarianism, too, they not looking on the externals of Emperor Haile Selassie the man and say that man is God, they are looking on the realization of that man. And the energy that man has tuned into, which is the external energy of God; you understand? So for all intents and purposes that man *is* God. But it's not the external man you dealin' with, because the man go bathroom an' him have sex. Seen? So, really, is a man you dealin' with for all intents and purposes. Now in His own personal life – I don't know the full political situation – I have heard that he has shot down thousands of people. I don't know either way and that don't matter to me. Seen? Because really and truly people have their reasons for reporting what they report in the press. And I wasn't there. But apart from all of that, that really don't matter to me, because the important thing is that Emperor Haile Selassie, in terms of *my* experience in Jamaica, right? has influenced the Rastafarians who is the only set of people who seriously saying that God is *you*, which is the key.

Q: I have heard people say of Bob Marley when he speaks of returning to Africa, they say: "Well, he has millions of dollars and he can return anytime he wants, so why doesn't he go?"

SH: But him can't return and leave him brethren over here. It's boring. Listen: Man is a child of the earth. In all the countries on the earth a man is free to go. If I have the bread I would got to Japan, and I'd go to Europe and see what those human beings are doing over there. The point about Africa is that Africa must be united as a continent before all the black men on the face of the earth can feel any real pride and unity as men. Part of this Africa uniting will mean that the disenfranchised black people who were brought to the West against their will, will get the right to go back home if they so desire. But if I want to have a vacation in – *anywhere* – I'm free.

Q: I was talking to a friend of mine and he said that they really needed some kind of alternative theatre to the type of theatre that exists in Jamaica right now. He mentioned something about the creation of a "roots" theatre. I'd like to hear your comment on that.

SH: Roots theatre is what I'm interested in, but when *you* say you want a roots theatre I don't know what you mean – whether you want a theatre for the grassroots people to get a chance to see and take part in, or you want a theatre *about* the grassroots. What has been happening right now… most of the more progressive writers like Dennis Scott – well, I would want to see myself as one too – are investigating the grassroots situation and using our folklore to put it on stage. But right now we're still putting folk things in a middle-class situation. Now that has to do with certain realities of living. If you're a playwright and you only write one, maybe two plays at most every year, you have to think in terms of making all your money from this.

The only people who are going to give you a decent living are the middle-class people who can afford to pay $3 dollars a ticket to go and see your play. The only way to go around this is if the government decides to start subsidizing theatre which, right now, I'm sure they can, even if not to the level of other countries. But they haven't seen the real importance of doing so yet, so a writer like me is caught in between what he has to do and what he'd like to do. There are ways of going around this though, which I may try. For instance, you run your play to your middle-class audience, make your money and then try get a place like the Ward Theatre or a place in western Kingston, advertise a big show, charge a minimal fee for an audience to come in just to cover your expense – is one way of getting around it. But the only way to really get a Roots theatre that appeals to the masses is if the government subsidizes it, or private enterprise, say, buy a house one night and donate it to people in a certain area. Then again – and I'm going to come down hard on them now – this so-called masses that we feel can't afford to pay $3 dollars to go see a play, the reality is them pay a $1.50 *each* for them and them girl to go see a movie every week. I hate the word "masses", but I'm giving the masses the benefit of the doubt there.

Q: I remember speaking to a cast member of *Summer Dread* [by Slade Hopkinson] of the tragedy of a play about "the people", but the people are not going to see the play because it is in the established theatre.

SH: We took that play *Summer Dread* in Trench Town once and the reaction that we got down there was a *world* of difference than we got up at Jamaica House [Garden Theatre]. Towards the end of *Summer Dread* when the Chief was goin' get dead an' everyt'ing, the audience down West was goin' so (*whipping his fingers*) Seen? And up Garden Theatre everybody just… (*folds arms and leans back*) and appreciate it purely intellectually. They didn't get involved because they didn't see realities of where it coming from – something they read about. There's one other sort of Roots theatre I guess you could have, is when somebody, a *roots* person, starts writing about their experience and don't have the money… and they're forced to put it into their backyard. That hasn't evolved yet in Jamaica to my knowledge, because I don't know anybody from the grassroots who's actually doing any writing, or if they do any writing, have actually gone about trying to get it produced even in their own small area. Because what happens here, even when a man not dealin' with society he still thinks in terms of the society. He will write a play and knows the society won't put it on, so rather than put it on himself, he doesn't put it on at all. To me a man who is anti a society is just as much a part of the society as the man who is at the top of it.

I don't know what else you could define as roots theatre… We need more theatre from the grassroots and we need more progressive writers who, even if they are middle class, are writing about a grassroots situation. Another thing too, the so-called roots people have to talk to themselves. I am roots, not economically or as a result of my class or education, I am roots because of how I see myself, as a very basic human being; and I will talk to everybody from all sections of society. But I don't necessarily see myself as a "roots man". I'd be bending my headspace to say I am. To me the only real Roots theatre will have to be coming from the roots people – whoever the roots people are. I hate them words though, like "roots" and "masses"; them don't mean anything to me, you know, because I'd really like to see the individual rather than see them lumped up in a big *mass*. So even though I answered that question, I still can't relate to it. Well, the truth is, right now, most of the things that's going on stage here, is just TV in life form. A light comedy about middle-class situations and middle-class contradictions, really.

Q: How do you feel about the stuff that you get on television? What would you like to see them do?

SH: I could tell you what I'd like to see on TV but I'd have to consider it in terms of what is real. Let's face it, JBC has a business to run, and they can buy canned films from the States for a fraction of what it would cost to put on a local production. They're not getting the sort of money they need to run a decent TV station. The other thing is this: Jamaican writers are not taking the responsibility to go to JBC with enough material to convince them that they must start doing something.

Q: Why do you think that is?

SH: Well, incentive is one; JBC is not asking for it. As well, when the Jamaican writer now – 'cause he has to make a living – decides he's going to do something, he'd rather put his energy into it and make it a full length production that can go on the stage. Lately I've been thinking in terms of TV, but right now there's no incentive. I have a lovely TV plot and me not goin' get no money to do it, so it's better me put me energy in writin' something else because I have to make a living – there's no two ways about that. [...] The problem is with live plays that don't respect the TV audience and their hang-ups, and they get into certain scenes that people don't like to see on television. They did a segment from my play where I would just be chatting-up me woman, and I had a half a page in the *Daily News* about it – that it was too suggestive to be on in prime time. I didn't kiss the girl or anything, you know! It was just arguments, and they said it was too suggestive. The one so-called liberal critic too – Verena Reckord – she felt that it was too suggestive to be put on in prime time. So you have all those things to deal with. And for a writer to cut up his work – it kills it. You understand what I mean?

I personally would like to see more Jamaican things on TV but I don't know how *real* it is right now to expect it. We don't have any private film companies that can even take on a project like this and try sell the film. Now how it could work now, if somebody like Vista – you have some film companies in Jamaica but they don't make movies or films, they only make ads – quick money – if someone could convince some of these to take on projects with local writers, make half-hour into hour films that they can not only sell to Jamaican television but to other Caribbean islands, or even Britain and the States. Maybe something could start from there. But a lot of these advertising companies are only in it for the money.

Q: You said that the writers don't have enough incentive. Couldn't they form some kind of union that could deal with this?

SH: I don't know if they have any writers' leagues in the island, maybe they do, because sometimes a lot of established writers have their own little things on the quiet, and you will see something in the newspaper, but it's not a real force. But I wouldn't be surprised if you hear that they do have one in some corner. You have schools of writers who could get together, like you have the older set – Dennis Scott, Mervyn Morris – in fact, they *are* together, for all intents and purposes. And then you have younger man like me, Oliver Samuels [an actor, later a popular Jamaican comedian with a TV show, *Oliver at Large*] and Michael Everett (who wants to write) and you have in-between man who has been established, like Trevor Rhone and Carmen Tipling.

But for all of us now, to come together and have something – the time isn't right yet. Because a lot of us have different opinions, not only about life but about our writing and what we want to do. Like the actors have been trying to get a union together. But the way the culture is right now it's as if we're not really ready for this step yet. I, personally, in my life am ready for it, but on the whole I don't know if the culture is ready. It's necessary though. It's been necessary for years.

Q: Possibly that will happen when the drama school starts to produce more actors and writers, where people get a more professional attitude.

SH: What I say is when we have more writers, and a writer isn't an exclusive thing, a luxury. Right now, in our society, when a man is a writer, you know, it's a certain luxury the society can afford... We don't look at a writer as just another human being who's helping the society to function. It's a luxury. Theatre is a luxury, it's not even looked on as a necessity – which to me it is. And the writers *look* at themselves as luxurious beings who must spout intellectual... It's disgusting! Right now it's necessary, but I don't know if the writers themselves see the necessity for it. Because, art is a part-time thing in a place like Jamaica for a lot of people.

Interview 2: 17 October, 1980

Q: What do you think about Derek Walcott and his work?

SH: I don't even know the man to think much about him – outside of his work. I met him in Jamaica once, where he asked my opinion about *O Babylon*. Generally, I rate him as a playwright, as a great poet of the theatre – maybe more than a playwright in the strictest sense. The fault I find with him – if you can call it a fault – is that him is too much of a intellectual for him purposes and his audiences. As a result he stands up in the way of his work; you see him and you see the work he's writing; you see the poet and you see the result. To me, it should be you see the result; you should see the artist creating and not him apart from it. And to see him apart from it you have to deal with him and his obsessions, his love of words, the thickness for symbolism and so forth. And a lot of times it gets in the way of the drama. So that is as a playwright, but him as a playwright don't stop there, because as you know he used to direct his own pieces when he just came out. And I think that's another thing that stands in the way – not that a playwright can't direct his own work, but because of the things that he's caught up in. Most of his plays run on for over three hours; the dynamics of *drama* don't rule, but the dynamics of literature rule his performances. And I think it's a pity – maybe that's a reason why he hasn't had a big hit, because he has the ability to have it. It sounds weird from an artist, especially a Rastafarian artist, to say this, but an artist who is not a success monetarily, I have to ask myself questions about why.

Q: Is it because of certain compromises an artist won't make?

SH: I don't know if it's compromises either. The audiences aren't fools; you know what I mean? There're certain compromises that a man – a lot of people sell out to make hits but at the same time I feel people accept good work. Good work is not just because the writer thinks it's good or some bunch of critics feel it's good, it must touch people, it must reach them.

Q: How do you see yourself now compared to four years ago? At that time you were acting and writing.

SH: At that time it was pure intuition. As a person and as an artist. I've learnt much more since then; I've even gotten cynical of the thing that I am doing – which I think is a healthy sign. You can't be too absorbed in something like theatre, you get too self-important, and feel like only you know what is happening and your audiences don't matter; that's what was happening to me at a certain point. And I feel this cynicism help free the artist from the absorption in his work to the point where we cannot see and relate to other people. In fact, I find most successful theatre people have this, what I call cynicism.

Q: What about the kind of cynicism that people find in Naipaul's work?

SH: Well, I don't know much about that … Most artists have this cynicism and it comes from looking at life in a certain way. You're forced to come to this cynicism because you realize everything that happens to you is not on the level. But the cynicism I was talking about is to your work; I don't have any illusions about theatre; I don't feel that I can put on a play and change the society. I had those feelings earlier on when I just started to write. I still feel you can change a society in a lot of ways through the arts, through theatre, *but* I'm seeing theatre on a different level now. I'm not looking to change the world from the next play I do.

Q: But a few people if you can?

SH: I don't even know about that any more. I just want to write a good play along the theme that I have in mind. And if it's a good play I will accomplish a lot of what I want to say out of it. And, I may even change people, but that's not the function of theatre, essentially.

Q: What *would* you say is the function of theatre?

SH: I can tell you what I think and what I know. Well, performance is important in every society for a number of reasons: sociologists talk about "liminality" and talk about "communitas" and the fact that the society needs to exorcise certain spirits at certain points in order to renew themselves and continue. So on that level theatre is essential, or performance is essential to every society and in Western society, and Caribbean society to a certain extent, theatre is a major aspect of performance. So theatre should do what performance does in all cultures: rejuvenate, exorcise, bear a reflection, so the society can get a reflexive view of where it's at, so they can continue.

But the truth is, Western society could function if there was no theatre around. While in certain societies, like for instance, the Yaqui Indians in Tucson, if they don't perform their annual Easter ritual, the society can't work, it breaks down; it is essential to society. In the Western society, theatre – British theatre I'm talking about – isn't needed on that level; theatre is purely entertainment. So you have to succeed in the areas of entertainment; you have to keep the people glued to their seats and you have to please them – whatever that means.

Q: So do you believe your function as a writer in the theatre is to entertain?

SH: Yes, it's to entertain. But the word entertain now, I don't see it as purely a negative thing. You see, once upon a time, maybe I would have regarded that as purely negative.

Q: Do you see it as something that can heal?

SH: Well, that's the part of the whole thing – entertainment in this society heals too.

Q: Well, there are some writers who feel that their function is to impart something that can heal a world that needs healing.

SH: All of that is well and good, but that's kind of bullshit. I mean, you can *want* to heal people and if them never come into the doctor's office, them never get a cure. Him could set up all him equipment and nobody comes to the office, and even when they come, if they walk out, him don't heal nobody. In other words, if somebody comes to see your play you got to keep their ass seated for the one, two or three hour that you have them in that place. So that is entertainment; the science of keeping them in there – is *entertaining*. It *has* to entertain or the people won't get cured. Now I don't think that the theatre should stop at the dynamics of entertaining. When I said satisfy I meant more than just titillate them – satisfy is to be titillated in a wholesome way. It's a difference between just fucking a girl on the street and fucking your woman; one please you purely on a physical level and one please you on another level. Sometimes you don't even have to fuck your woman; you just have to be with her. But satisfying them doesn't just mean making them laugh, it means appealing to the intellect and giving them a message to leave with, giving them a *reason* to come and be entertained.

Even with the Yaqui people with their Easter ritual, though they don't have to worry about entertainment, in fact, they go looking for the entertainment values, they have a lot of sideshows going on each time. Even the most serious thing is still regarded as having an entertainment value. In our society now, the message and the dynamics of entertainment are kind of more separated and we have to work to fuse them together. But I don't think I'm a shaman, though those are some of the reasons why I write, personally.

Q: What are the driving forces that compel you to write or make you want to say something?

SH: Well, I love drama – the whole idea of a paradox, that two people can be wrong and feel them right... this whole idea of paradox, of conflicts interests me, and being a playwright, I *control* it. Writing was a progression from my acting, really. Because I feel I have more control as a writer and I get to dramatize the type of conflicts that I want to deal with, rather than just be a robot for some guy; even though the actor still a creative process, he's still working for the writer's vision.

Q: You like being the one who pulls all the strings.

SH: Exactly, exactly. But it's not *such* a powerful position when you know the business. You can write your play and a producer does it and *nothing* of your message comes across. But the act of creating as writer is more fulfilling to me then the act of creating as actor.

Q: Do you ever see yourself writing novels or any other forms of fiction?

SH: Funny, I never ever did. *Recently* I've gotten an interest in research projects, the sociology or anthropology of performances. I could see myself writing couple papers on certain aspects of entertainment that interest me. I have thought that at least one aspect of my life would be interesting if I tried to write it as a story, meaning novel. But I don't have the interest, really, because I don't read much. I read a lot of plays, mainly because I feel I have to, and it's part of the business, but really, I don't like reading – the whole idea of lying on your back and looking at words, especially in a society that's so active, with all this stuff going on. Reading is important – but in decades gone by; it was a way of getting what you can get through a lot of other mediums in this society at this time. At the end of the last century, you had to read to find out about certain things; reading in this society is more about leisure, relaxation and I can get that relaxation through other areas. And though I love words, it bores me to death to sit down and read, unless it's a journal or something with specific information I had to get. I'll browse through a magazine or a paper because I want to see what this writer is saying. But, generally, to keep up with all the novels – you know how some people have read all the new novels? – that don't interest me.

Because I don't read much I don't know if I would want to sit down and write something for somebody to read. But because I love performance – I love the excitement of the presence of being – I feel I can write the same thing I'd want to write in a novel more easily in a drama. Because it comes alive; and I think the performance is much more exciting than reading. It's a personal taste.

Q: I remember when we spoke in Jamaica you said that one day you'd like to get some formal training. Do you still feel that?

SH: Well – going to school – I found out that half of the thing with me is the fact that I still haven't shaken off my middle-class aspirations or inheritance, or whatever it is. It's both an inheritance and an aspiration because I'm not truly middle class in the truest sense of the word. College is unfinished business with me; I felt I had to go through it at least to get the idea of what it's about, that is one. Secondly, I always thought it would be great to just sit on my ass for four years and concentrate on what I really love and I *must* get something out of it – which is the case here. I *am* learning a lot at school, but I also realize that I know a lot too. In other words, what I should be doing at this point in my life is working with a theatre company. I'm wasting my time in school. But as far as me as a person in society is concerned, I wanted to be a bit whatever, whatever, whatever. I need college, I need to be a much more educated person; I need to know more of what I would write about – and all these things that are there that I'm gonna be compared with, whether I know them or not, so I might as well know them, so that I'm sitting on *top* of the situation. And

I'm feeling more like I *am* sitting on top of the situation – which is from going to college. The problem with the school thing is that it can paralyse you too. You can realize just how great all these other people are and you can come to the conclusion that you'd be a nobody. In fact, this is how education changed me over the years, from doing a lot of plays in Jamaica. Since the last interview I've produced three of my plays [*Anancy and Unsung Heroes Out West*, 1978, *Masqueraders*, 1978], plus a Broadway show. I get to see how the business is *really* set up – and it's a little politics involved. When I'm in Jamaica and I read a play by Tennessee Williams, for instance, [*A*] *Streetcar Named Desire*, I'm paralysed by the greatness of this man – how every jacket fit perfect. And it could never be *that* perfect. But after I come here and I work on a Broadway show and do three more plays and so forth, I realize, "But wait, when this guy wrote the play first time *nobody* was satisfied with it." So he had to do another draft, then a director took it and changed it around and *he* hated it, and then his publisher convinced him that the director was right and he sat with the director and then after that they took the stage manager's copy and transcribed that and asked the playwright to work on that, and that was finally published. In other words, the end result, what I see as a product, really goes through a process and I never see the process. And it's the experience in theatre that has taught me that process, and I think the process is very important especially for a lot of Third World people to realize, especially when you're dealing with a superculture. And when I say superculture, we're all colonies… We still live by a system that we inherited: the English, European, American. And as far as theatre goes, I have to deal with that because that's the area I'm working in. When you come from a colonial situation you only see product and not process. And when you see product you're so overwhelmed by product that it paralyses you from doing any fucking thing, and that is the danger of education for a lot of people. Now I was fortunate in that I *worked* in the thing, got to a point of feeling and knowing in my gut – and then expose myself to the education, so I'm not overwhelmed by it. I understand it organically.

Q: Tell me about the Broadway experience; did you actually write or did you just consult and advise?

SH: No, I wrote. What it was is this: I'm in Jamaica, 1977, Michael Butler and a writer [Kendrew Lascelles] comes down there and they have a basic story and they're asking around, they hear about me, they come and I talk to them. They have this basic story that this girl comes to the island to learn reggae music and they want to make a musical about it. I showed them about certain structures in the society and where the drama could go. I told them about the rude boy phenomenon, the paradox between the righteous and the revolutionary. And that's where the whole character of Rockets – who, incidentally, is one of the more exciting characters in the piece – came from. In other words, I put the Rockets character in. I didn't write the first draft of *Reggae* [Musical, Biltmore Theatre, 1980] though. Two years later I'm invited to New York and I see a draft written by the writer I spoke with in Jamaica and by Melvin Van Peebles. And I was given this draft to work on and I redraft that with the director looking over my shoulders. In other words, I would rewrite a scene and before it would go in the script I'd have to go and explain to him what I'm driving at and a good amount of what I wrote was accepted; I ended up rewriting all the scenes that Melvin Van Peebles wrote. He put in the character of Natty, which was very successful in the show – it got good reviews. And I rationalized the character in my rewriting; it was a bit too ridiculous to fit into the Jamaican frame of things – that of the young Rastafarian searching for Jah – I had to make it credible. So in the end what I did was make the language as authentic as could be so that this audience could understand it, and also I changed the structure of the story insofar as making it true for the Jamaican situation. But if I was given that thing to write I would not have written that particular story, because the symbol, the poetic image of that story isn't very Rastafarian – same old Babylon trip. So the story never really interest me but the whole experience interest me and I felt I did something for the play.

Q: So what did you get from the experience?

SH: Boy, it was frustrating in a lot of ways but it was more enlightening than anything else. I realize that Broadway is like anywhere else, only say them have more money. It's the same damn incompetence and the same greatness too; but them have the facility and the structure to consistently really do great work. Also, I realize it's biased and prejudiced and full of stupid hype like everything else. Most of the Broadway shows I saw were shit – well done shit and some of them badly done shit too and they still got good reviews and ran for a while, even ran longer than the piece that we did. So in other words, I'm not awed by the whole experience. I don't hate Broadway; in fact, I'd love to work on Broadway again. I love the idea a man spend a million dollars on my show; it feels good, it feel like you join something important. (*Amused*) But it's not the be-all and end-all of where I'm coming from, because I realize it's just another American hype.

Q: Where do you see yourself going after you're finished with school? Do you see yourself going back to Jamaica or do you see yourself staying here for a while?

SH: On two levels I'll always work in Jamaica. Well, the type of projects I'm doing now – because I'm very interested in writing folk-type or Jamaican things with a certain international eye, I'd like to put some of the Jamaican myths and Jamaican characters on the stage in such a way that the world appreciates the quality in these people and the beauty of their art and so forth. So I'm very much involved in Jamaica and I always will have Jamaican subjects on my mind and consequently I'd like all my plays to open there or at least to be done there. So I'm always concerned with Jamaica. On another level, just in terms of shrewd craftsmanship, it's a great place to try out your plays. If I write a play here that I know is gonna cost $100,000 dollars just to showcase here – because I love these big cast things – I mean, I can go to Jamaica and do it with $25,000 dollars and see how it work – so there's another reason why I will always want to work in Jamaica, though I don't know if I'll always be able to afford to.

There's another thing happening there too. I'm not just interested in Jamaica alone, because I see a man like Trevor Rhone, the greatest Jamaican playwright undoubtedly, and he has never had a hit anywhere else. Him too narrow, too myopic, the whole Jamaican concern. And what would work in Jamaica a lot of the time is just the fact that the people them never see this thing on stage before. You could be in Jamaica as a "great" playwright and really you can't write plays at all. In other words, I need the international scene as a touchstone for where I going. I'm not just content to make a lot of money and put it in a Jamaican bank and be a great guy in Jamaica – and I'm still not affecting anybody. Because Jamaica is one island in the whole of the Caribbean which is one region in the whole of the West, which is one half of the world and there's a whole lot of stuff going on.

Q: Would you ever want to go to Africa?

SH: I intend to.

Q: I mean living there for a while and dealing with whichever country in Africa you'd go to in terms of theatre.

SH: I don't know why, for a long time I've always liked Nigeria, although I've never been there. I know nothing about the place. I know them have a big city named Lagos and them have a part named Ife where a heap of great sculpture come from and supposedly you have the Yorubas who populate Jamaica came from that part of West Africa. I would like to do my masters at the university in Ife. I want to study some of the masquerade dances they have there because I'm interested in the whole idea of African cultural retentions in Caribbean lifestyles. So I'd like to go to a place like Nigeria to see the root of it and how it changed and understand it in that context.

Q: What about Ethiopia?

SH: Ethiopia, I'm only interested in it from an image, poetic point of view. As a Rastafarian is I and I Zion. And it is an image of the whole of Africa as a majesty; so it's more a poetic image and concern I have for Ethiopia and I regard the whole continent of Africa as Ethiopia. But I have no particular concern or anxiety about this place that some Marxist control. But I've no anxiety about going to Africa; in other words, if I never get to Africa soon, it don't matter because I know as long as I'm around I will get there, because it's part of a logical thing. But I would like go London first.

Q: The last time when we were in Jamaica, we were talking about repatriation and the involvement of Rastafari...

SH: Well, the key to repatriation is this, and I've always maintained it: the *whole world* must regard black people as Africans. We're not niggers or negroes or black man and all this type of stuff. You must *look* at a black man and know him come from Africa. Now it may seem a pretty banal thing to say for a lot of educated people, but the truth is, when I was growing up, I never knew why my skin look so! I never made a connection that I come from a part of the world or my forefathers came from a part of the world where African people are. Man write it in songs, man write it in book – it's come to be a cliché now – the fact that in Jamaica the Chinaman man is a Chinese, the Coolieman is Indian, the white man is European and who is we? We's negro. I never had that concept of being an African; I think it's very important for the *world* to recognize this. It will lift black man from out of the level of being a beast in the eyes of a lot of people, even himself, to be a human being – just that recognition. That him black because him come from Africa is a *key* for black man psyche, that's the first thing.

Secondly, as a result of that, the black man will get more respect around the world and in the continent. If we know, for instance, the OAU (Organization of African Unity) have a concern for black people, that there's a body in Africa that if the white man them in America decide that them going to fucking burn twenty blocks of Harlem because the blacks rioting, and kill all the blacks up there, we know that in Nigeria and North Africa the black man them will *lock* down the fucking oil if that happen. So *that* is another reason why I feel we *need* to see weself as Africans; and that is where repatriation come in. Unless a bunch of black man get mad and say: "Rass claat, man, me's an African, man, an' I'll lick down de *fuckin'* door till I'm accepted!" Until that is done nobody is gonna pay us any mind. Because the Africans don't want us, them feel one step ahead of us just because them still in the continent.

Q: They call us distant cousins.

SH: Disgusting bullshit! Is because they stay in the land and allow the shit to happen to *them* that they had to drag *us* three thousand miles to do it to us. And we have things surviving in our Western culture that they in Africa have forgotten. Notably, some of the Surinamese culture. So, they're no better off than us, and they must fucking well realize that, or *we* is the one to make them know that. So whether repatriation make sense, or whether we'll ever get there, or whether nobody want us, or whether we goin' go there and cause problems, or whether we not goin' help the society, or whether we runnin' away from our problem here – all that don't mean nothin'. Because somewhere on the continent some black man must get up and say: "Me's a fuckin' African, man, and I need to be respected like that!"

Q: How do you feel about the whole Rasta movement, both here in America, in New York City, and in Jamaica? Do you see it as a force that is developing?

SH: No, we going through a thing right now. See, Rastafari caught on two levels: it caught between the grace of Christianity and the realization of God, and the idea of Karma that Eastern religions have. Now, you have a lot of brethren who been looking at the King and following very much like how people follow Jesus Christ. You have another set of brethren who – the King is there and him very important, but that's the last thing them worryin' about – them want be like the King in them own light. You have these two things going on with Rastafari. Now in the last couple of years you have had a battle between these two things, especially with the news from Ethiopia that the King is dead. The religious ones – ones who want to believe in the following type of mentality – they maintain that the King escape and him off somewhere and him gonna appear on the top of the Euphrates at the right time and all of this. And some other man say it don't even matter because whether him is there or not, them still have them own fight with them own spirit.

And I feel we going through a point now where *what* we're doing and *where* our energy should be focused – I think we're at a point now where we're *feeling* that out. Consequently, a lot of slackness going on. Whole heap of Rastaman have no direction so them a turn criminal; some a them inna New York, just a fuck white woman every weekend and nah deal with nothin', or dem sell herb… Them just don't know where them a go right now because that certain direction get cut off. Some of them love the imagery and them feel comfortable as a human being within the whole Rasta lifestyle, but them doubt certain aspects of it because of what has happened in the last couple years. So I feel we going through a point where we sorting weself out to see which is the best move to make. Because what we have proven to ourselves is that we have validity and we're very powerful, and the turns in Jamaican society in the last couple years have helped us to feel that. The fact we're getting respect internationally as well; the fact that we music touching a lot of people internationally; the fact that we philosophy, we look, we attitudes spreading all over the Caribbean. We realize that there're certain strengths and rightness to what we're doing. So we're keeping that tradition, but it's not as focused as it should be right now because people trying to feel out which is the best thing and how them fit in to the whole scheme of things.

Personally, I feel Rastafari have to start define them own reality. Them can't make the Bible do it for them, or journalists outside or a religious leader – we have to define we own reality and I feel the *artist* have to be the vanguard in this area, which is really what me want get to. And they *have* been the vanguard...

Q: How do you feel about Bob Marley's work?

SH: That's what me a go say, Bob Marley, whether me like him personally or not, is a great example of this. Single-handedly him do more for Rastafari than any amount of book and preaching and Bible. Just him presence as a creative person and a dynamic force, and him define a whole heapa things for not just Rastafari but the whole Jamaican culture. And I feel the artist have to define these things, especially in this type of cultural revolution. It's not a intellectual revolution.

Q: So do you still see yourself as playwright in that light?

SH: Yeah. Of course. [...] Rastafari to I is not a religion, you know; it's a *cultural manifestation*, it's a *cultural expression*. So religion *is* culture, in a lot of cases, but in this Western world our minds have a schism between where we're coming from in Africa and what we have learnt here. So from a thing have religious connotations it tends to close off the spirit; it's when I realized the *cultural* aspect of Rastafari that it free I. Anytime I see it purely as a religion it becomes bullshit, and I just want to either cut off me locks or just give up me life altogether and become some kind of religious walkabout, which is not like me at all. But when I see it as a dynamic force I feel *alive*, I feel I have a sense of purpose, I see the world clearer.

Now it would be great if a lot of man out there who have locks and shoot people would cut off them locks and stop confuse the issue. It would be great – but the world is not like that. The world is a complex fucking thing and I want it to remain that way. I mean, I'd love it to improve, but at the same time it don't seem that's the nature of creation – that everything would be handed to us on a platter. Part of the struggle is to be alive.

Q: How would you like to see yourself after you pass on?

SH: Is some serious question you ask me there, you know. Is a very wicked bloodclaat question, too!

Q: Your legacy as who you are and what you've done, what you've tried to do.

SH: I want to have a ball! (*Amused*) You see, I have a million answers I could give you, but when I get this type of questions I more want to say, just don't even ask that question in the first place, rather than answer it. But, right now, I'm caught up in dramatizing certain folk myths and folk situations and I really want to show Jamaican people, or any other people in a similar position, look, man, you have a wealth of material more important than anything that you're yearning for. I want to show me and my people them how important we are, so consequently, I want to dramatize a lot of we myths, a lot of things that people in Jamaica even want to *hide* and be afraid of. I'm also interested in subculture things, just as a human being. So, I'd like to be known as one of the first people to do that, because that's where I'm working. But, I guess the thing I'd like to leave with people is the idea that living is just about being alive. I mean, it's just something you endure and enjoy at the same time. I think in the end if a man ask me what I'd like to leave with people: just be alive, man, everything irie, don't worry about anything. Everything have its own order – even the chaos, there's something to be understood there. And there's another thing: my plays tend to urge people to be reasonable, but not good because I don't believe in good, but I like a certain reasonable... If a man fuck with you and you feel like shot him, him don't really deserve to dead – him have pickney and all that; forget that – rather than thinking shotting is necessarily wrong; it's not that we dealing with. So in other words, I have an interest in imparting a certain amount of good, but it's not from a value judgement of goodness; I want people to be reasonable; you know what I mean?

Q: That's all one can really ask in the end.

SH: A lot of people not reasonable, though, you know.

Q: I know that.

SH: Fuck!

Q: In fact, there're a lot of people who delight in being unreasonable.

S.H. (Laughs)

End Notes

1. Neville Willoughby (1937-2006) was a journalist and broadcaster in Jamaica. He published a novel, *Jamaica Boy* (1981).

ERROL GASTON HILL
(1921-2003)

Errol Gaston Hill is widely recognized as the father of the English-speaking Caribbean theatre. It was Hill who told the young writers of the 1940s and 1950s to stop imitating European drama and start writing in their own vernacular, and use the experiences of their immediate surroundings.

Hill was born 5 August, 1921, in Trinidad, to Thomas David and Lydia (Gibson) Hill. He was awarded a British Council Scholarship to study drama in the UK, where he graduated from the Royal Academy of Dramatic Arts in London, where he also won recognition as an actor and announcer for the BBC. In 1956, Hill married Grace Hope of Barbados. In 1958 he travelled to the United States to study at Yale University and the Yale School of Drama where he earned a B.A., an MFA in playwriting and Doctor of Fine Arts in Theater History in a record four years.

As extramural staff tutor in drama at the University of the West Indies between 1953-1958 and 1962-1965, Hill travelled throughout the English-speaking Caribbean, lecturing, conducting workshops, adjudicating at festivals and directing performances. He also held teaching appointments at the University of Ibadan, Nigeria, for two years was a Rockefeller Foundation teaching fellow, and spent an academic year teaching at City University of New York. In 1968, he took up a post in the Drama Department of Dartmouth College, officially retiring in 1989 as the John D. Willard Professor of Drama and Oratory, Emeritus.

During his tenure, Hill taught thirteen different courses on acting, directing, playwriting and theatre history, and directed thirty-three full-length productions. As the first tenured African American faculty member at Dartmouth, Hill also served as the university's first official Affirmative Action Officer.

He died of cancer in 2003 at the age of 82 at his home in Hanover, New Hampshire.

As early as 1946 Hill had founded a Trinidadian acting company – the Whitehall Players, along with the future international dramatic actor and playwright, Errol John. To break from the European dramas that comprised almost all theatre performances, Hill began writing in the vernacular and his plays focused on important aspects of Trinidadian culture. *Ping Pong* (1958) featured steel band players, *Wey Wey* (1958) referenced the Trinidadian Chinese numbers game and *Dance Bongo* (1965), written in free verse, moved towards a ritual dance for the dead. His best known play, *Man Better Man* (1964), performed at the Commonwealth Festival in Britain in 1965, used rhymed calypso verse and original music.

Over the course of his life, Hill produced and directed over 120 plays, classic and modern, and pageants in the Caribbean, England, the United States and Nigeria, which encompassed amateur, semi-professional and professional companies. His work ranged over European, American, Caribbean, African American and other African diaspora theatre.

In all, Hill wrote twelve plays: *Oily Portraits* (prem Trin. 1947); *Square Peg* (prem. 1949); *Priscilla's Wedding* (workshop, 1953); *Dilemma* (prem. 1953); *The Ping Pong* (prem. 1953); *Broken Melody* (prem. 1954); *Wey Wey* (prem. 1957); *Man Better Man* (prem. 1957; revised with music, 1960); *Strictly Matrimony* (prem. 1960); *Dimanche Gras 1963, a carnival scenario* (1963); *Whistling Charlie and the monster* (1964); *Dance Bongo*, a fantasy in one act (prem. 1965).

He authored or edited fifteen major books and wrote many articles on drama and theatre history, including researching and writing 33 entries for *The Cambridge Guide to World Theatre* in 1988 and 83 entries for *The Cambridge Guide to American Theatre* in 1993. His study of the African American and Caribbean theatre earned him a worldwide reputation as the foremost historical scholar in these fields. His historical research produced such works as: *The Trinidad Carnival: Mandate for a National Theatre* (1972); *The Theater of Black Americans* (1980); *Shakespeare in Sable: A History of Black Shakespearean Actors* (1984); *The Jamaican Stage 1655-1900: Profile of a Colonial Theatre* (1992); *Cambridge Guide to African and Caribbean Theatre* (1994); and the recently published *A History of African American Theatre* (2003) co-authored with James V. Hatch.

Awarded the 1996 Robert Lewis Medal for Lifetime Achievement in Theater Research, Don Wilmeth, Professor of Theater at Brown University, said, "Errol Hill has done more to further the serious study of African American theatre and drama, as well as the theatre of the Caribbean, than any one scholar in the world."

Hill served on the Executive Committees of the American Society for Theater Research and the American Theater and Drama Society and was a member of the College of Fellows of the American Theater. He was an Evaluator for the National Association of Schools of Theater, a Visitor to the Loeb Drama Center at Harvard University, and a former president of the Dartmouth Chapter of Phi Beta Kappa. He served as visiting professor at universities in England, Canada, and the United States.

In 1983, Errol Hill was named the Chancellor's Distinguished Professor at the University of California, Berkeley and, in 1994, the Mellon Visiting Professor at Tulane University. In 1999, he received an honorary Doctor of Letters from the University of the West Indies.

Among his many awards were British Council and Fulbright Scholarships, and fellowships from the Rockefeller and Guggenheim Foundations, the National Endowment for the Humanities and the Theater Guild of America. He won the Bernard Hewitt Prize for theatre history, the

Bertram Joseph Award for Shakespeare Studies, and a Gold Medal in Drama from the Government of Trinidad and Tobago. In 1991, Hill was awarded the Presidential Medal from Dartmouth for outstanding leadership and achievement.

Asked about his careers as actor, teacher, historian, director, and playwright, Hill said: "At different stages of my life certain things were more important to me. I enjoyed directing a lot because I could choose plays that I wanted to do, from every conceivable period of theatre, and I had the freedom to do them with the best available students, talented students. That was wonderful. Acting and directing – I loved that, [but] nobody was getting the history right; nobody was interested in what went before. So I started it, it had to be done. Whenever I felt there was a need, I took it on."

A "Jamaican style" adaptation of *Man Better Man,* was put on by the Jamaica Youth Theatre at the Philip Sherlock Centre in September 2007. The play was performed in Jamaican patois with musical references to dancehall DJs Beenie Man, Bounty Killer and others.

ERROL HILL

8 November, 1981

Q: Your name is synonymous with Caribbean theatre, and you are considered to be one the major pioneers of what we understand as Caribbean theatre today. What are your feelings on that?

ERROL HILL: I have had some remarkable opportunities to be a part of the developing Caribbean theatre and I imagine that is one reason why my name has been associated with the beginnings of Caribbean theatre. Of course, I have been researching, recently, the true beginnings of Caribbean theatre. I hope before the year is out I will have finished the first draft to my book on the 19th Century Jamaica theatre [*The Jamaican Stage 1655-1900: Profile of a Colonial Theatre* (1992)]. But we know that theatre in the Caribbean of one sort or another has existed all the way back to – well, the earliest mention of a theatre in the Caribbean is in 17th Century Jamaica. But we are talking, I suppose, about the more recent development of Caribbean theatre. Before my time, no less a person than Marcus Garvey made his contribution, with theatre at Edelweiss Park in the late 1920s and the '30s.[1] People like Archie Lindo,[2] in Jamaica have written plays that are Jamaican based, a lot of them based on the novels of De Lisser.[3] So that there were people there *before* me.

I think the reason that my little contribution is remembered is that after I received a British Council Scholarship to study at the Royal Academy [in the UK] – this was in 1949 – I came back to the Caribbean in 1952, to Jamaica, and I was appointed by Philip Sherlock, as a drama tutor at the University of the West Indies, in the Extra Mural department, as it was at the time. And, Philip gave me carte blanche to develop drama; the way he put it was "special oversight in drama in the West Indies." With that sort of mandate I took it upon myself to spread the gospel of a West Indian or a Caribbean theatre throughout the length and breadth of the West Indies. And I travelled, literally, between 1952 and 1958, when I went up to Yale, to almost every British West Indian territory, teaching, directing, acting a little bit, producing, sponsoring summer school, so that at one time it used to be said that if you addressed a letter "Errol Hill, the

West Indies," it'll find me. (*Laughter*) And that's the kind of opportunity that I speak of, and the reason why I think my name has been associated with the true beginnings.

In '58 we had Federation and I was associated with the drama component of the whole Federal Arts Festival; indeed, it was under Noel Vaz[4] and myself – Noel joined later – that we got the Federal Arts Festival done in Trinidad, and got Derek Walcott commissioned to write his *Drums and Colours*, and to put it on – it was directed by Noel Vaz, with myself directing the Jamaican part of that whole epic drama. It's the only time that I know of when a West Indian playwright was commissioned to do something for the whole West Indies, to mark the inauguration of the Federation. The play was later published in *Caribbean Quarterly* [CQ, vol 7 nos. 1 & 2, 1961; a revised version was published as part of *The Haitian Trilogy*, 2002].

So I made very strong contacts and had many very loyal supporters throughout the West Indies, from British Honduras (now Belize), all the way down to Guyana; I worked, I lectured, I ran training schools, I worked on productions, I wrote critiques, I did whatever was necessary. Sort of one-man bandwagon promoting the gospel of West Indian theatre. I said several things, some of them I'm not proud of now. I urged people to stop doing Shakespeare and start doing West Indian plays. Several people wanted my head for that. It isn't that I didn't like Shakespeare or didn't think that Shakespeare's the greatest writer in English; I did feel that West Indian *writers* writing under the shadow, as it were, of Shakespeare, would never get rid of their inferiority complex. Shakespeare's a *symbol* of English culture – and people would always find a reason for doing a non-West Indian play because they could find a better English or American play. And I said, "Forget that, let's start with our own, let's develop our plays." And I promised people that anyone who wrote a play in the West Indies, in the six years or so when I worked at the Extra Mural Department – I went back after '62 and worked for three more years in Trinidad – I was actually in the field for about eleven years and four of those years I spent up at Yale, when I went back for my advanced degrees. But I promised that any play that could be done, that anybody who would write what I felt was worth putting on, I would see to it that it was done – if I had to put it on myself. That was a means of *encouraging* people to write plays. I started a collection of West Indian plays [*A Time and A Season: Eight Caribbean Plays*, 1976]. I still have, I think, the most complete collection of West Indian scripts up to – oh, I don't know – about the last eight or ten years.

Q: Was that the series that is put out by the Extra Mural department?

EH: I started that. I got some money from Foyle's in London, to do the first systematic publication of West Indian plays. That same series called *Caribbean Plays*, was started by me in '58 or '56, I think. *Sleepy Valley* [*A Jamaican Morality* (Knox Summer School, 1955)] and Derek [Walcott's] first play *Sea at Dauphin*, that was published and others. Indeed, I said that I would print plays that I thought were exceptionally good, and those that were good but I felt didn't quite make it up into the top class – because money was limited to publish plays – I had mimeographed at the office. And it was after I left Trinidad that Esmond Ramesar took all those plays that were in mimeograph form and began printing them, because he was able to get a lot more money. These were plays that I had worked with the playwrights on and then got them up to a scratch to where I think they were worthwhile presenting.[5] And I put out two or three volumes of plays since I left there. I did one for CARIFESTA. The latest one has three one act plays that was published in England with Carmen Tipling in it. [During *Lunchtime They Had the Revolution*, in Three Caribbean Plays (London: Longman, 1979)] I promised to do one for Barbados, and settling on the smaller islands; I'm still working on that but I just don't think the plays written by people like Bully and Edgecombe[6] and O'Marde[7] and the current writers in the smaller islands – I just don't think the plays are good enough for anthologizing.

Q: Why is that?

EH: Well, for very many reasons. I mean, the most popular play of the lot is *The Nite Box*, by Bully [1977], and *Nite Box* is a detective tale. It really has very little to do with the Caribbean. There are two stories there and the most important story is a detective thriller having to do with a murder by a young a boy. But the idea of the strike and the nurses' problems with the hospital, the general social malaise is something laid over the strong tale of a psychotic young man. They don't have anything very *profound* to say. I did see Edgecombe's play about a politician, and that's one of the better ones I thought. But even that seemed to lack a strong grounding in dramaturgy, how to make a play work.

Q: Well, one of Derek Walcott's criticisms of young contemporary Caribbean playwrights – writers in general – is that he feels there's this tendency towards laziness and indiscipline.

EH: That's true. I mean, their plays look like warmed over television serials. I am very disappointed in the work that they've done. But then I can't blame them; where are the models? Who is doing the job that I did for eleven years in the Caribbean of sitting down with a playwright with his work and giving him criticism and urging that he do the rewrites, and so on? Who's doing this?

Q: Well, Derek Walcott has done that, and Dennis Scott.

EH: Dennis now, through the school, yes. Dennis. Well, I found a great lack in the teaching of Caribbean playwrights so I must say that I'm very pleased with what I suspect has been going on in Jamaica. I was there this past summer, and they do have at the school – this is the cultural training school – a special experimental programme devoted to the development of a Caribbean theatre. They're not assuming the models that come out of the western world of North America are necessarily the models that they have to follow. They are breaking away, they're trying to look at some of the indigenous models growing out of the folk theatre; and from that, *Shepherd*, is one of the plays that was done by a young Trinidad writer [Rawle Gibbons, 1981] who has been working with Dennis, that was quite good. And then there is Dennis's own play *Dog* [1978 and reprinted in *Champions of the Gayelle*, MacMillan 2005], which has tremendous possibilities I think. But there are people who don't have an opportunity to work with a Dennis Scott or a Derek Walcott, those writers primarily from the smaller territories who attend conferences such as the one at CARIBUSTE in the Virgin Islands, last year. I understand that there was a director there who is a young Englishman, just been out for a couple of years, and he was directing these plays by West Indian writers and helping, as any premier production of a play would do, to *guide* the writers as to what would make their plays more effective. But I think that's highly dangerous, because the models he will use would be models that may be quite irrelevant to the West Indian writer developing West Indian plays. I feel that he would be unlikely to be acquainted with some of the folk-forms of the Anancy storyteller, of the John Canoe dancer, of the Shango rites, of the mourning ground, all the things that we're looking at to give inspiration and to become a model for the kind of form out of which West Indian theatre should develop; all these would be totally unknown to this expatriate. And it seems to me a subtle form of neocolonialism where people like these are in positions of authority to *guide* the destiny of a West Indian theatre or West Indian writers. I think it's totally wrong at this time in our history.

Q: So how was it that he was allowed to participate?

EH: Oh, he went as representing the Cayman Islands. He had gone to Jamaica first, I believe, for a short time and then went over to the Cayman Islands. I was in CARIFESTA, as I said, and there were still a number of people who went there who didn't seem to have the *grounding* in West Indian cultural history to become mentors for others. Even now, I do believe, apart from Dennis Scott in Jamaica, I don't believe that at any of the various universities centres throughout the West Indies, anything is being taught of this nature. Which is a great pity.

Q: Not even at the Cultural Centre?

EH: Apart from the Cultural Centre. I mean, there are the three or four major centres of the university, in Trinidad, Barbados, Jamaica and in Guyana and then there are university centres in so many of the other territories. But who is helping to guide, to open up the ideas of young people as to their cultural heritage? Who's helping specifically in the whole matter of the writing of their plays?

Q: Well, I know that some of the younger people like Alwin Bully regard people like yourself, Derek Walcott, Errol John and other writers of that period as being pioneers, but that he also considers *himself* a pioneer because he thinks that the work is still as yet not done.

EH: I'm sure that many of these younger theatre people in the Caribbean are doing useful work; *my* particular interest is not that there should be the production of West Indian plays or the formation of West Indian theatre companies doing plays, my *real* interest at this time, is the development of a *recognizable* indigenous theatre. And that is something far different from the writing and production of plays about the West Indies. Far different.

Q: Before I had met Alwin, I had read about him and his work and how he was attempting what he called "Calypso Theatre" in Dominica, which is the same indigenous type of theatre coming out of –

EH: But his best known play *The Nite Box*, is anything *but* Calypso Theatre!

Q: Well, he said he had moved away from that kind of indigenous theatre at the time when I met him, which was last year, but he said that he was planning to get back to that concept.

EH: Why had he deviated?

Q: He was trying other things. In Jamaica there is talk of "reggae theatre", as well as "roots theatre", meaning grassroots theatre; so there have been attempts at different levels to deal with what you were saying.

EH: Yes; my concern is that there are *individuals* – that Harrison chap [Stafford Ashani], in Jamaica, for instance, is one. What is needed is a very systematic approach; this is a scientific business. This is something that needs the gathering of forces. I mean, if CARIBUSTE, which seems able to get money from the United States – and the man who has been running that is an old friend of mine from Yale, George White, who runs the O'Neill Theatre Center at Waterford – if that money, which seems to be able to bring people from all over the Caribbean to a convention and to get some of their new work presented in experimental productions – now if the *focus* of work like that could be on *what is an indigenous Caribbean theatre*, then it would be doing something useful. Something revolutionary.

Q: How do you define who are Caribbean people?

EH: It's a very simple analysis here. The truly indigenous, aboriginal peoples of the Caribbean were the Amerindians, and they no longer exist; if they do it's in small pockets. They have very little impact on the cultural development of the place. There is some, but little. With the passing of the Amerindians, two waves of people came into those Caribbean islands: one were Europeans and the other were Africans and later on Asians (East Indians). There is a vast difference in the psychology of these two streams. The Europeans came as colonisers who looked on the Caribbean islands as a place where they made money and returned to Europe, returned to their culture. They were not interested in transplanting a culture to the Caribbean because they never looked on the Caribbean as their home. I'm speaking generally. The African slaves had no option of returning to a home anywhere. So, when they came to the Caribbean *that* was their new home. It had to be. To all intents and purposes, *they* became the indigenous peoples of the Caribbean with the passing of the aboriginals. To a lesser extent, coming several generations later and only to two or three of the territories – Trinidad, Guyana and to a small extent, in Jamaica – the Asiatic Indians first came to Trinidad in 1845, I think it was, *they* came as *indentured* labourers, they *could* return but most of them elected to *remain* in these islands which became their home. Now, the Europeans, eventually, some of them became creolized and elected to remain here. But at *no time* did they look on the Caribbean as their *cultural* home even if it became their physical home, because their cultural home *remained* Europe. And that's the difference.

So when we talk about the indigenization of Caribbean culture, we're talking about the culture that was *created* by people who had no other home but the Caribbean. You have to start from there.

Q: But the whites, the Chinese, the East Indians are just as much a part of the Caribbean as the African or black population.

EH: The whites in Jamaica represent one or two per cent, now, of the population; similarly in Trinidad. So if you compare the actual percentage of the population as evaluated with the importance and impact of the culture that they represent you have done something that is very disproportionate and should not be allowed to continue. And it continues because the creole class – which is a mixture of black and white – or the black intellectual class – by history has grown up believing that they could justify their learning, their position as the successors to the ruling white class, by adopting upper class culture. So they have tended to perpetuate ruling class culture – the white culture – although they themselves are black; but slowly, sometimes with great revolutionary fervour – the whole Rastafarian movement among the middle-class blacks is an indication of the violent rejection of past generations of middle-class blacks who didn't see anything *good* in the indigenous culture – and saw everything laudable in white culture. And that is being rejected by young people as part of the nationalist movement.

Q: And which is also affecting theatre and people such as Stafford Harrison – which is what I was talking about in terms of roots theatre.

EH: But I think that there is a discipline of theatre which requires very careful thought – including *serious* experimental work – so that in *tossing* out the bathwater of English culture you don't also toss out the baby of dramaturgy. And I'm not saying there is only one form of dramaturgy, but there is a discipline to be followed depending on what kind of material you're working with. The discipline of making sure that the material that you use develops a form that is adequate to that material. One of the problems with *Shepherd*, which I think was aiming in the direction that I'm talking about, is that it has become too private, too eclectic in many ways and you lose the audience. The author and director – Dennis Scott directed – they become so steeped in the kind of material they want to use that they put forward symbols and so on, which the bulk of the audience don't share. There is no excuse for that.

Q: Would you consider that to be part of the lack of discipline that Walcott talks about?

EH: It's *partly* that; it's partly a lack of the discipline of the theatre. I think Derek is thinking much more, when he speaks of discipline in the theatre, of the use of language, which he is very strong on, making the language *work* for you, and that's a very hard thing to do. But it is also the question of making the *form* work for you; making your symbols and *images* work for you; not *privately* but publicly. Theatre is a public art and it's an instantaneous art. People have to get it as soon as it is presented on stage. Derek himself has problems with this.

Q: In what way?

EH: Derek suffers from the same problem, I think, of not being able to communicate with *clarity* to his audience, *partly* because he is a poet. And much of his poetry of late, I believe – though less so than earlier – has a density which makes it difficult to be understood when it's spoken on the stage. One *reads* poetry, one goes *back* to poetry; people don't go back to plays with any regularity. You've seen a play, you've seen it. If it really seizes you, you may go back once, but people don't go – as you pick up a poem six times – back to see a play six times, of the same production. People may go to a film much more often, but people don't really go back to see a play more than once or twice. The most popular theatre in the Caribbean today, and always has been – and I am talking about formal theatre, I'm not talking about Carnival – is the Jamaican pantomime. And that appeals to all classes and all ages – and I don't think that people, as a rule, go more than three times to see a Jamaican Pantomime in any given year. Now, you are a Jamaican, how many times have you been to see any pantomime?

Q: I mean, it's a full house every night.

EH: I know. It's a full house because it appeals to all the people. That pantomime experience, in my view, suggests the kind of crowd the true West Indian theatre should be able to draw on. It's really the national theatre, and it tells us something about what the theatre in the West Indies could be: the incorporation of dance and music and singing – all West Indian material. My one complaint about the Pantomime is that they have not used it for more than light entertainment, because they should be able to do much more with it than they have done.

Q: Derek (Walcott) feels that way, too, that this should be where the theatre in the Caribbean should be going.

EH: Absolutely. You see, it started with the English pantomime but it has changed completely from that. Maybe there will be many forms; I don't think there is only one form that will develop as our indigenous theatre, but I think that this is what people should be working on. When I wrote *Man Better Man* [1964], which is one of my two claims to fame as a playwright – the other one being *Dance Bongo* [1965] – I did it using calypso verse, carnival music, dancing, costuming, choral singing; it was purely an exercise in some of the basic ingredients that should be part and parcel of any truly West Indian play; and has been *tremendously* successful wherever it has been done, professionally or by amateurs.

Q: I know Stafford Harrison has been making attempts in that direction. I know he believes in the whole idea of creating one's own mythology.

EH: Well, the problem of creating one's own mythology is that other people do not share it, and a mythology that is so private and not shared by your community, well, that is not a mythology.

Q: What I think he means is using the folkloric images around him. In fact, he regards *Dream on Monkey Mountain* as a perfect example of where you can go with that sort of thing.

EH: I think it is a very fine play. Some parts of it that are a little dense but I do think it is a very fine play. Though I can't understand Derek's fascination with the image of the white woman; there is a strange kind of

Q: What problems do you have with that?

EH: Well, I don't know what she stands for. I don't know why this Makak, this old man of the mountain, should have deep within his psyche an image of a white woman. Why is she there when he goes back to Africa? She is there – as an ethereal creature.

Q: Well, do you think it could be the fact that the white woman has always been a strong sexual symbol from slavery on up?

EH: That is stereotypical, I don't accept that for a moment.

Q: I am offering that as one possibility. What do you think it is?

EH: I don't know; ask Derek what it is. I have never discussed his plays with him.

Q: As a principle?

EH: Oh, no, we have not had an opportunity to sit down and talk about his plays. I hope sometime to write a book on Walcott the playwright, and if I do then I will try again to understand this.

Q: Errol John talks about the early days when it seemed that all the West Indian writers converged on England. What were those times like in London, in the early days?

EH: Edgar Mittelholzer went at first and was several years older than I, but people of my generation included Sam Selvon, George Lamming – were two of the main ones that I was very friendly with...

Q: What was the mood like in terms of West Indian writers in England? I understand that there was the *Caribbean Voice* programme on the BBC...

EH: Henry Swanzy was an Englishman who ran *The Caribbean Voices* programme – he also ran one on *West African Voices* – and that was good because this was the one avenue through which West Indian short story writers and poets could get their work read and publicized and for which they would be paid – what we thought then quite handsomely – a pound a minute by the BBC. So it was always a great cause for jubilation on a Sunday evening at seven o'clock when everybody switched to the BBC in the West Indies and heard what stories and poems were being read on the BBC. The only other organ was *Bim* magazine, which [Frank] Collymore was putting out, and that was another place where one could be published; in Guyana, *Kyk-over-al* began to be put out every quarter and then in Jamaica, it was *Focus*, which came out in three or four issues over many, many, years. It was not a regular publication at all.

I got up to England in '49 and Errol John followed me the year after. Louise Bennett[7] had been there a year or two before me – she had spent a year at the Royal Academy. I went in for the full course at the Royal Academy; Noel Vaz followed me, I think, a year later – he went to the Old Vic Training School. I was at the Royal Academy and Errol came up as a visitor of the British Council and decided to stay on. Times were hard. The BBC, through people like Swanzy, would use West Indian material. They had two programmes, as I recall, one on Saturday evening that read the news and I was offered that job, and used to read West Indian news regularly. And then when

I left in '52, I handed it over to Errol John, and he did this. But I was also with Errol on the BBC radio drama series, and when we were called in to perform that meant you got a nice piece of change for acting in plays on the radio and you met some very important people. I do remember a production of *The Golden Asp*, with Dylan Thomas in it and I was in that cast. For the whole day or two days that we rehearsed and presented that play I was buddy-buddy with Dylan Thomas, which is a nice thing to reflect on. It was after I left that Errol won the *Observer* Competition with *Moon on a Rainbow Shawl*. I directed the BBC's Derek Walcott's *Henri Christophe*, and then I did it on stage with Errol John playing the lead in 1951. Then I directed *Antigone*, with Errol John playing the lead and put the whole thing in a West African setting. This was done in London at the Hands Crescent Theatre. These, I think – even before I went back to Jamaica – were milestones because it was the first opportunity for a West Indian company to come together and perform a West Indian play. In *Henri Christophe*, for instance, there were people from Jamaica, Grenada, Trinidad, Barbados, St. Lucia, Guyana – just a whole host of West Indians. And, indeed, I would like to think that it is the experience of Walcott's Henri Christophe, that kind of convinced me that we have the potential for a West Indian professional theatre, working on our own material. It never materialized.

(At this point the conversation was interrupted by Prof. Hill, who asked me into his library to show me his scrapbook of photographs from the *Henri Christophe* production. The conversation resumed with Prof. Hill talking about the condition of the arts in Trinidad.)

EH: Trinidad has the money but there isn't a decent theatre in Trinidad. Eric Williams did a lot of good for Trinidad, he also did a considerable harm by neglect. If he felt that he couldn't control something then he would refuse to endorse it. And I guess he felt that artists were uncontrollable. Certainly there were many, many proposals for starting various kinds of institutes and cultural centres and so on. I mean, his treatment of Beryl McBurnie[8] was just scandalous, look at all that talent she had there – she is the dancer/choreographer who was the real, true pioneer of West Indian dance – and she has never been able to fulfil her potential in getting a company of professional dancers (Trinidad or West Indian dancers) established, which, like the Mexican Ballet Folklorico could be sustained and travel the *world* over with their dancers. It was all there. No sponsorship from the government, no help.

Q: Do you think that will be rectified in any kind of way?

EH: I hope so. This week there are national elections in Trinidad and Tobago, and we don't know whether the PNM will be returned to power or whether another government will take over, I think it is time for a change after 25 years, but, one doesn't know. [In fact the PNM was returned to power with an even bigger majority.] All the structures are there; I mean, there is a national cultural foundation with a hundred million dollars assigned to it and there is a national cultural council with a budget of its own, and so forth. But that's just the formal structures; they don't meet or they seldom meet, they have no programme, they don't know who to report to and all that kind of thing.

Q: You know, when we had the company in New York, a lot of the people who were involved were Trinidadians and I thought, well, there must be a lot of things going on in Trinidad because I met some extremely talented people.

EH: Talent is just prodigal in Trinidad.

Q: And the funny thing was that they said while there are some things that *are* happening in Trinidad but they said Jamaica is the place.

EH: Jamaica is the place because Jamaica in its poverty has done *more* for the arts than Trinidad with all its prodigality. And now, there is the fact that at the university you have – although nothing much is done with it – the Cultural Arts Centre. There is no such space in Trinidad. Then there is the Cultural Training Centre, which puts all the performing arts together using dance, drama, even painting – no such thing in Trinidad. It's scandalous! It really is. I have put in, myself, at least six proposals to the government. Months before he died, I wrote my third letter within two years to Eric Williams, begging him, "*Please* do something, Eric, don't let this desert continue to exist in the culture of Trinidad." One reason is that we have the carnival, and that is a year-round activity. People really put everything into the carnival. So you know if you have your Carnival coming up every year and you are busy with that then there is not too much else. But there is a lot happening, now. I was there this summer for ten days, and Lennox Raphael[9] and two or three or four different people, Jimmy Lee Wah,[10] down in San Fernando, had started a theatre festival. Margie Padmore died – she was in charge of the National Cultural Council and she had put on a festival, and died as a result of all the efforts, and so on. So people have been working without a great deal of support and, what is most distressing, without the correct facilities for doing the work.

Q: Errol John has spoken of his dream to see a Caribbean Theatre, as a pan-Caribbean ideal…

EH: I think it must have been in 1954 when the idea came of forming the first Caribbean-wide professional theatre group. The idea was that we would perform, produce only West Indian plays and that we would travel throughout the Caribbean, up and down, with a base in Trinidad and a base in Jamaica where we would stay and do the plays and then we'd travel up and down and we would run courses; essentially it would be a performing company and we would have our playwrights associated. The two leading actors at the time were Slade Hopkinson and Errol John, who was in England, and we would bring him back (and I spoke to Errol about it.) Derek was to be our leading playwright. Indeed, when I founded the Federal Theatre Company, in Jamaica, in 1957, we opened with Derek's play *Ione* [1957, UWI Extra Mural series]. Jean Brown, used to be one of our leading actresses, at that time, Cicely Waite-Smith, [Anglo-Jamaican author of *African Sling Shot* (1957), *The Creatures*, *Uncle Robert*, *Return to Paradise*, *The Impossible Situation*, all 1966] who was the only non-West Indian, though she had written several West Indian plays, a professional actress, was to be a member of the company – the only white person I could think of that had totally identified herself with the native movement. She wrote *Uncle Robert*, it was inspired by Roger Mais... though it wasn't on his life story at all. People were so enthused by this whole idea, because at the time Federation was in the air; we thought that this would solve all our problems. Of course, you know what happened to Federation.

Q: Do you think that the Caribbean would have been better off had we committed to Federation?

EH: For the artists, certainly. Because it was bringing the artists together. The Federal Festival was the first, really, CARIFESTA. Before that there was *one* festival in Puerto Rico, but the Federal Festival in 1958 was the first *real* CARIFESTA, when several things were going on all over Port of Spain at the same time – the artists that came down brought their dances and theatre, and so on. It was of a very high order, the quality was very good. I think we would have been much farther along now... What happened after the break up of the Federation the islands became very parochial once more. Only efforts like Walcott and The University Players, who, occasionally would travel with their troupes, maintained that contact. But as far as the politicians were concerned they didn't want to have anything to do with the other islands. Great pity.

Q: Lennox Brown once said that he would never go back to the Caribbean to practice theatre unless there was some sign of professionalism or professional attitudes towards theatre. He said he felt that possibly the only country where he felt a strong sense of nationhood was Guyana – in terms of a place that he could settle in.

EH: Well, I don't know what you mean by nationhood. There was a time when, under Burnham, Guyana seemed to be the leading West Indian nationalist country. Jamaica has always been very politically oriented, there is no doubt about that – unfortunately, they have tended to look north rather than south, and that was part of the problem with the Federation, that Jamaica never really accepted that her identity belonged with the other Caribbean islands; she is too close to America and Cuba, and too big compared with the rest of the others. But where has this nationalist thing led to in Guyana? – I doubt Lennox would say the same if he went to Guyana today.

Q: I think he was referring to the time when he was there for CARIFESTA.

EH: Well, I was there for CARIFESTA [1972], myself, and I understand what he meant by that. Trinidad has always been laissez faire when it comes to culture; under Williams for the last 25 years any support of culture was done for political purposes: Better Village campaign and better this and that, all getting the people in the country to support PNM because PNM would go out there and pick groups from the country and send them abroad, and so on, and ignore the really sophisticated talent that was in the town, which couldn't be directed in any one channel or another. Williams had this unfortunate penchant for picking politically oriented people and putting them in charge of the artists. So that George Wong Sang became the sort of cultural commissar of Trinidad, or this other person, loyal to him, regardless. This didn't happen in Jamaica. In Jamaica, the integrity of the artist was respected and support given because of the quality of the work they were doing. This is not to say that some people who were on one side or another didn't get shafted when the different parties were in power, but at least you could deal with the artists in Jamaica, not so in Trinidad, you had to deal with politicians.

Q: Coming back to yourself; when and how did you first become involved with theatre?

EH: I must have been about 14 years old when I took the leading part in a play put on at the Sunday school – this must be sometime in the '30s. And then I belonged to a scout troupe in Port of Spain, which was known for its theatrical propensities; and we took the Princess building and put on plays – by people like Osborne Ashby[11] … And from there I was one of the founding members with Errol John of the Whitehall Players, which was started in '46. Whitehall because we met at Whitehall, which was the British Council headquarters – they gave us a room there in which we could rehearse our plays. The British Council sponsored us for several years, getting expatriates who would come into the island to come and coach us in speech and movement and things of that kind, getting plays for us because we had none. It was because we started putting on these foreign plays that the critics – Alfie Mendes, Albert Gomes and people like that[12] – in Trinidad, began on one hand praising the group for their efforts and on the other criticizing the group for working on foreign material. Then we got together and said: "Look, we must write our own plays, there are no West Indian plays that we have, so we must write." I wrote one and Errol one, and those were the first two Trinidadian plays put on by the Whitehall Players; mine was *Square Peg* and Errol's was *How Then Tomorrow*, and then we wrote some more plays and put them on [including plays by Douglas Archibald[13] and Derek Walcott] and then we began to try and do West Indian plays along with plays from other cultures.

There had been some attempts being made to put on plays before that time. De Wilton Rogers,[14] was my old schoolmaster, and he had written and put on some plays. Errol Sherry had done some musical operettas that he had written. So, from time to time there were the odd play being put on by a Trinidadian, but these were not companies that existed; someone would write a play and get together a group and put on the play and at the end of the play their group would disperse. There was a schoolmaster called Roberts who every year would put on a very fine comedy, a satire, plays about the social situation, about scandal at the hospital... and he would do these with his schoolboys at Nelson Street, and thousands of people would pack in to see those plays. But they weren't trained and they would be done with scant respect for rules of theatrical production: just get these young boys to stand and speak. They were really extended charades. But when we began, in '46, '47, with our plays, we began by getting training for the actors and that's why I think the Whitehall Players would always be remembered – and it still exists. It changed from the Whitehall Players to the Company of Players and then it changed to another name, and so on, but the company is still there.

Q: Who is running it now?

EH: I know my sister, Jean Herbert, was one of the people running the company, I don't know who is in charge of it now. Ronald Amoroso,[15] I believe, who is a playwright, and who teaches at QRC, is also one of the strong members of the Company of Players. But out of that came people like Horace James,[16] Freddie Kissoon,[17] Leo Bennett, who went away and became a professional actor, Errol John, myself, and a whole lot of people. Very talented. Barbara Assoon[18]... so many people came out of that company that have made theatre their livelihood.

Q: As a writer, who have been some of your influences?

EH: I have not consciously patterned myself on anyone. I remember when my play *Ping Pong* [1955] was done, people said "Ah, this has a flavour of J.M. Synge, the Irish writer." I wasn't aware that I was following Synge at all. I have read widely. My tastes are very catholic; if you look at the plays I have produced, everything from the Greeks all the way down to Tennessee Williams, so I never know who was influencing me more. It's different with me because I have not written anything like as many plays as a regular writer, but I could look at most of Derek's plays and say: *Dream on Monkey Mountain* [1967], that is straight after Strindberg's *Dream Play*; or *The Sea At Dauphin* [1954], that is straight after J.M. Synge's play *Riders to the Sea*; *The Charlatan [1974],* that is straight out of Brecht, and I know that Derek works this way. Derek models himself on some of the great writers, playwrights of the past, and he has always done it. I have not done that; there is never any conscious patterning of my work on anyone; maybe that is a fault with me but I write as I feel.

Q: Why do you think that is a fault?

EH: Well, because I think one can learn a great deal. I mean, Picasso became the greatest painter of modern times by sitting in the art galleries of Spain and just copying from the classics and getting his form, his pen working and examining. I don't think one should slavishly copy but one should consciously adapt and I don't think that Derek slavishly copies either. But the *ideas* – at one level art is universal and I think that one can gain a great deal by imbibing, as it were, the essential ingredients from the great writers from the past. I also feel that when Derek lets his imagination *loose* he comes up with something like *Ti-Jean And His Brothers* [1958], which is straight folk material and it is beautiful; and I can't find any playwright that it is modelled on. There are several correspondences that exist in so many of his plays, established plays that have become recognized as classics.

Q: Would you regard *A Dream on Monkey Mountain* as a West Indian classic?

EH: I think it takes longer than a decade or two before a play can be called a classic. I certainly think that there are some of Derek's plays that belong in any repertoire of West Indian drama and I would imagine that *Dream on Monkey Mountain* is probably one of those. I think that *Ti Jean* is certainly one. If I did *Dream*, and if Derek were around, I would see whether it would be possible to clarify some of the things for the audience a little more. Some *powerful* scenes in it. As I say, I am worried by this recurring figure of whiteness in Derek's plays; it's something he has to get out of his system.

Q: How long were you in England?

EH: Three years. I applied and received a British Council Scholarship as a result of the work that I was doing with the Whitehall Players; and so I went up to The Royal Academy in 1949 until '52, then I received an invitation to return to Jamaica from The British Council to help run a summer school in Jamaica, which was one of the first big drama summer schools that was done at the campus at Mona. So I did that, gathering around me all those Jamaicans of theatrical experience at that time: Greta Bourke Fowler and Henry Fowler[19] and Elsie Benjamin-Barsoe[20] and Harry Milner,[21] you name it and they were all part and parcel of it, Orford St. John,[22] and so on, it was a great gathering of theatrical clan. And then I went up to Knox College where I helped develop the first playmaking effort up there; and then by the end of that year Philip Sherlock[23] had been working strenuously to get the university to appoint me to his staff and that was confirmed, so that beginning in '53, I was with the university in Jamaica. And I stayed there with the Extra Mural Department for two years and I was sent to Trinidad and stayed there for two years and I went back to Jamaica in '57. In '58 I was sent up to Yale by the Rockefeller Foundation on a fellowship, because it was clear that, having got my professional qualifications in London, I needed academic qualifications, and I stayed at Yale for four years finishing up with a doctorate. By this time, Noel Vaz was in charge of drama in Jamaica. I went back to Trinidad and worked for three years there; continuing to work in the southern Caribbean – Barbados, Guyana and Trinidad and Tobago. In '65 I was sent to Nigeria, again by The Rockefeller Foundation – because Philip Sherlock had said I would be coming back to lead the Creative Arts Centre that was being built in Jamaica. Well, I hardly got to Nigeria before I got word that Jamaica did not want me to come back as director of the Creative Arts Centre.

Q: Oh, really?

EH: Oh, yes. That was part of the whole breakup of the Federation. Why should the Creative Arts Centre be run by a Trinidadian? Philip wrote to me and said that he was hoping to put me in the English department, and I said I didn't want to be in the English department. I had finished a doctorate in drama and I wanted to stay in drama. It was a messy business. It finally transpired that I told him that he had appointed me as heir designate and I was returning to do that job. He wrote and said: "OK, you can come back; I have just appointed John Hearne as your deputy," I knew that Hearne had been angling for the job all along. Hearne is a novelist. I wrote and said, "Philip, if I am directing the Creative Arts Centre, you don't appoint a deputy without at least conferring with me; you are making it impossible for me to work... If we are going to have only a little money to run the Centre, the last person I want to appoint is a novelist. I want a scene painter, I want a lighting expert. Good God, what am I going to do with John Hearne?" So I resigned after 14 years with the university.

And that is how I managed to be in the USA. I did not just come here, I wrote to all the [UWI] campuses and said that I wanted to work in the West Indies, in the theatre, what could they offer me, and nobody could offer me anything.

Q: Did you feel very bitter about that?

EH: Very bitter.

Q: I asked you earlier about what the mood was like in the '50s when all those writers were converging on England. Was there any bitterness among those expatriate writers?

EH: No. There was a great feeling of optimism among those writers, there was no bitterness. There were really no publishing houses in the entire West Indies; *The Gleaner* [as Pioneer Press] was the only one that I know of that began putting out in a little paperbacks some of [W.G.] Ogilvie's novels,[24] and so on; but that was for local consumption. And these novelists could go to London – particularly the novelists – and get published by Jonathan Cape, by Methuen, and they would literally have a worldwide public. This was exciting. Moreover, a number of them felt that whilst writing in the Caribbean was a very lonely thing, they began, now, to become part of a literary community in London. Very exciting. But they were prepared to serve an apprenticeship period with the hope that they would eventually make it. And, in fact, many of them did... I mean, Selvon, Lamming, Salkey and Naipaul, who came a little later. Oh, there was tremendous enthusiasm every time a new book came out – great celebrations. I think that the mood changed. I can remember seeing Sam Selvon, several years later – he is now in Canada – and he said "I can't live any more in London." They did not want to publish his work any more; he used to get his work regularly on the BBC and they didn't want his stuff any more. It became very, very hard. Lamming now lives half the year in England and half in the Caribbean or in America, or where he finds work, visiting appointments at universities and then he goes back to London to write or he goes down to Bathsheba, in Barbados, to write. But it's not the same at all. This was in the postwar era when lots of West Indians were in Britain and the British people were becoming very much aware of West Indian culture.

Q: How often do you go back to Trinidad, now?

EH: Oh, I never think of myself, now, as a Trinidadian; I think of the whole West Indies. But whenever I can, at least once in every two years, sometimes more often. This summer, for instance, I was five weeks in Jamaica at the university; I gave lectures, I researched my book on Jamaican theatre, I went down to CARIFESTA in Barbados and I went to Trinidad; those are the three places that I touch all the time. If I could afford it I would go to some of the smaller islands.

Q: Would you go back there to live or to work?

EH: Yes, I would indeed. Trinidad – where I had hoped that I would eventually go back to work – I was really so disappointed with this last visit, because on the one hand there is all that affluence and on the other hand nothing seems to work at all. None of the infrastructure or the telephones work; you don't have water, the streets are in a terrible condition, the traffic you can't get through. Those kind of basic things that can so hobble a creative artist. I came away saying "Look, this is the last place I am going to settle down to work in." On the other hand, I had no sooner come back [to the USA] than I spent three weeks editing Atilla's manuscript of the Calypso [Raymond Quevado, aka Attila the Hun, *Atilla's Kaiso: A Short History of Trinidad Calypso* (1983)] which I have sent down there to be printed, and writing up yet another proposal which I sent to Dame Hilda Bynoe to be handed into the government on a cultural arts centre for Trinidad. I think what would be nice would be to live in a place like Barbados and go to Trinidad for specific projects that would be worked on with freedom. I would hate to be subjected to having to report to any politician; I can't do that any more, not after working with complete freedom and integrity. In any of the proposals that I have made to go back I said: "You want the cultural centre built? OK, you appoint me to do so and so and so, in so many years; there is the money – I'll go and I'll do it for you." That is the condition under which I would go.

Q: What has been your output of plays since you've been teaching drama?

EH: Oh, it is very difficult to write plays; and it is not only because I have been teaching but because I think that there are many, many playwrights – many better than me – throughout the Caribbean, who are living in the environment and therefore can be stimulated by it more than I can. I am so far away. But I have also felt that no one, except one person who I have been working with in Jamaica, Wycliffe Bennett,[25] who went to Yale, has been doing anything about the *history* of theatre and culture in the Caribbean and I think it is important to know our heritage. Ever since I came to Dartmouth – and I have been here 15 years – my free time has been spent in writing about Black theatre – which embraces Africa, the Caribbean and Black America – and I have been able to put out several books on the subject in addition to anthologizing plays and so on. I think that contribution will be greater than if I started writing plays; I would like to write one or two more plays but I have got so much on my plate to complete.

I used to edit a little bulletin for The American Theatre Association called *The Black Theatre Bulletin*, and I did this for a few years, and one of the things that I tried to do is to present news from those three areas of black culture. I put out – I was hoping to complete this but then they suspended publication of it, financial cutbacks – listings, a bibliography of Caribbean plays. I did one for Jamaica, one for Guyana, I did not quite complete one for Trinidad, based upon both of my collections and my records of all the plays that were written by Caribbeans or set in the Caribbean.

Q: Spanish, French as well as English?

EH: No, I did have some in French but I could not do the Spanish plays – that was something else I wanted to get on to, but this was primarily West Indian. I listed, for instance, 160 or 170 Jamaican plays; 200 odd Guyanese plays. I would say that there must be something like 1500 plays written by West Indian writers as of today. That is a lot of plays. I mean, you ought to able to get 30 or 40 scripts that form part of any professional West Indian repertory. I edited Michael Gilkes' fine play *Couvade*, set in Guyana.[26] The publisher – this was the English publisher – wrote and said they had this play and would I be able to do it and I said yes. So it is *Couvade*, edited with notes, the three Caribbean plays for schools, the anthology – these were the three ones that I have done since I am here.

Q: How do you feel about the present state of Caribbean theatre as you see it? Generally.

EH: Well, what is Caribbean theatre? I do not think theatre, formal theatre, can exist without its writers. Those in England – Matura, Abbensetts, Errol John – Derek Walcott; I don't know what Slade [Hopkinson] is doing – he had promise but I have never been very impressed with Slade's playwriting. I've only known two of his plays, early plays, I have not seen his more recent work and I would like very much to see them. Dennis Scott, some of Barry Reckord's work,[27] not all. But they are all away. Dennis Scott is the only one who is there and a couple of the younger writers – Freddie Kissoon, Neville Labastide,[28] a chap in Barbados, Anthony Hinkson,[29] who has written dozens of plays. But you search in vain for something that you really feel will last; I think I found one of his plays, *Teacher Teacher* [1976], that I think I would consider for that anthology. Of the others, I just don't see it there. I'd like to see Ken Corsbie's[30] plays; I would very much like to feel that out of CARIBUSTE or some other organization like this, we could get the writers together to work on their material, to seriously criticize the plays. What I am really saying is that the process of training is an ongoing process and has to be done with each generation; we cannot assume that someone in playwriting is going to come, like a novelist, and just suddenly begin to write beautiful plays. One of the interesting and promising things is that people like Earl Lovelace,[31] with his *Dragon Can't Dance*, which was dramatized by Errol Jones[32] and done at CARIFESTA, became very excited with the possibilities of theatre; and when I left him he was going to write a full length play based on *The Dragon Can't Dance*. And there is a whole new area of all these wonderful West Indian novels that have rich material for dramatization, but nobody has really worked on that at all. You asked me what I think of West Indian theatre: there is *so much work to be done*, training at all levels, experimentation at all levels and the manpower and the facilities for doing this kind of work and experimentation does not exist – except through that one centre which is only partly – and for understandable reasons – devoted to developing West Indian theatre, a segment in the Dennis Scott Jamaican cultural enterprise. I don't see it anywhere else. Everybody else is working on their own with their own ideas but I don't think that is part of a movement, because they are all going off in all different areas.

Q: Well, isn't that the reason why people should be there trying to contribute?

EH: You're saying I should be back there. Well, I did do the groundwork and I was ready to do work at a more advanced level and was rejected.

Q: Derek [Walcott] also stuck it out for a long time.

EH: Derek is a professional writer; as a professional writer you really don't need an institution. I am professionally a teacher; I need an institution. I trained as a teacher of drama. I have not been acting, myself, but I decided long ago that I was not interested in becoming a professional actor outside of the West Indies. I am a teacher and short of going back to the West Indies and setting up a school of drama – which would have taken someone with far more faith than I have... or one can start a popular school – having a lot of people there and so on. I am not interested in that. I was interested in training through the university where people have already been admitted and have a certain sophistication and intelligence so that one could get the best minds devoted to this – not to go and open a big public school where you are just taking everybody for their money. I could have gone back like an Aubrey Adams[33] and got a job with the government, but my temperament would not permit me, as I said, to work with politicians – I must be free to comment and criticize, and you can't do that in the West Indies.

As you know, I was invited to do two of the big Carnival shows in Trinidad in 1962 and 1963. In 1963 I produced a play called *Whistling Charlie and the Monster*, which is a satire on Trinidad politics – I was almost run out of the country for it – but it was a great success; but then you certainly burn your bridges when it comes to working with the government. That was the year Williams had his "red scare" and bought judges and started saying that he was tracking down communists and all kinds of things. It was just *made* for theatrical burlesque which is what I did with the Carnival show. And then he had C.L.R. James under house arrest and I would go to C.L.R. James, who I admired, and talked with him and so on, and I am sure they put me down as one of the people to watch; that kind of thing is too petty... You see, you can't really retain any independence of spirit unless, as I say, you are doing a kind of job where you don't need anyone. Derek wrote a lot of criticism and so on, for *The Guardian*, but essentially he is a professional writer and poet; started his theatre group in order to get his plays done. One of the interesting things about Derek's theatre group is that it really was begun as a means whereby he could develop his playwriting craft and put on his plays himself. He did very few plays by anyone else. Eric Roach's, I think, was the only other Caribbean playwright whose play was done.[34] I don't want to seem to be carping at Derek, but it happened that Roach was also a critic at *The Guardian* and was criticizing Derek's plays, so it was good politics to do Roach's play; and then he did a production – a radio production – of one or maybe two of Lennox [Brown]'s plays in Canada at the CBC, but other than that Derek has done no other – as far as I know – not even his brother's plays, Roderick Walcott, who is a fine playwright.

Q: I guess it would be safe to say that you are not terribly satisfied with the work that is being turned out by contemporary Caribbean playwrights.

EH: Well, as I say, I went to the festival in Barbados, this past summer, and what did I see? I saw *The Nite Box*. I had read it before I saw it, and seeing it only confirmed my view that it is a television thriller and little more than that. I saw a very poor play from the Cayman Islands, I saw two plays in Jamaica, *Dog* [by Dennis Scott] and *Shepherd* [by Rawle Gibbons], both with tremendous possibilities, which I would like to see developed. I think they are working on the right lines with regard to pantomime, song, to some of the ritual elements that they incorporated in them. I did not get to see the dramatization of Lamming's play [1981] but I got to read it (Lamming dramatizes, you know, his novel *In The Castle of My Skin*) and I understand that that went for all of three to four hours long and that it was tedious in spots, and I could imagine that. I was very pleased to see the dramatization of *The Dragon Can't Dance*, and I feel that has great possibilities. And I saw a political play from Montserrat by [David] Edgecombe, which I felt lacked form in playwriting [*Strong Currents*, based on two Austin C. Clarke novels]; he adopted a novelistic technique that I didn't think he needed and because the episodes were so short and going so rapidly you could not feel the sustained drive of the play, and that, I think, shows that the writer has not quite mastered the form of playwriting.

I did see a play in Barbados, a play that was developed in a sort of creative playmaking process from Anguilla, a very exciting play; there was some lovely mime and so on. I went and asked the person in charge of the company whether he had a script and he said just an outline and he would send it to me. Well, of course, I am sure I would never get it from him. But, the play, again, was one of tremendous potential: telling the story of Anguilla, a historical story, in a very sensitive way with many episodes dealing with the life of the people there [probably by The Mayoumba Folkloric Theatre]. I liked it very much indeed. Very nicely disciplined company. I remember one particular scene of people who were cast away on a boat and the way in which those men pantomimed water on stage with one piece of rope, the idea of sailors on a ship and the women coming down to the shore looking for them and not finding them – it was very sensitively done.

I was saying that in the same way as we talked about experimenting with the *form* of drama, we also ought to begin to experiment with the *place* in which the theatre is done. Actually, a very fine thesis was written by a Trinidadian, [Rawle Gibbons, "Traditional Enactments of Trinidad – Towards a Third Theatre", M.Phil. 1979] and I was asked to read it for the university and to evaluate it. It talks about the form of Trinidad theatre and about the *place* where Trinidad theatre should be done. He is really giving some deep thought to the development of an indigenous theatre based on folk-forms. We ought to consider that the proscenium stage or the arena stage, which we inherited, without thinking, from other cultures, may or may not be suitable for us. Certainly, a lot of our folk theatre is processional, it is peripatetic and we should consider how we can have the kind of stage or platform or ramp that permits the actor to do a great deal more movement around the audience or through the audience than is normally possible in the physical theatre of today. It is the *pageant* kind of theatre that is more suitable for the Caribbean than the straight play that is done indoors. The pageant requires space, dimensions, a great deal more participation and movement and song and so on. It is this way that we should be going.

Q: You said that after the Federation failed that the situation became rather parochial again, do you feel that way about the writing now? What should the focus of our playwrights be: nation or region?

EH: No, no, I don't think so; I think that efforts have been made and are being made within the region to establish a kind of federal spirit on a much sounder basis than was originally done, as imposed by the British. The original Federation was imposed, people were not ready for it. I think, now, through the Caribbean Economic Community and other means of this sort, that people are beginning to realize the need to work much closer together. There have been, much more than in the past, theatre companies, on their own initiative, and with some help from industries, travelling from one country to another.

Clearly there will be writers who feel more comfortable with writing about the Caribbean experience per se, or even a certain segment of Caribbean society. J.M. Synge wrote about the people on Irish [Aran] islands primarily, and wrote some great plays about them. Other writers take a more catholic, universal view and they may be able to see that experience in terms of other peoples and other cultures. I don't think it matters whether one writes about what one knows – and that is a very limited view – or whether one writes about one's people in relation to other peoples, what will matter is how *well* one does it and with what *integrity*. Not many people have had the opportunity that Derek Walcott has had to rove all over the Western world and to see so much. One would expect that he would be able to bring a much larger vision to his work. But that is not to say that a person who is writing from one of the smaller islands and writing with deep conviction, who has got mastery over his craft, would not put out something equally valid.

Q: What are some of your favourite Caribbean plays?

EH: I have to admit that being away from the Caribbean, now, for seventeen years – which is a long time, nearly a generation– and I have not directed a Caribbean play in the Caribbean since that time – it's hard to judge a play purely by reading. I have *seen* quite a few plays since that time, I saw Abbensetts in London – and I have seen Matura both in Trinidad and in Chicago, I have seen Derek Walcott's [*Dream on Monkey Mountain*] at The Negro Ensemble; I have seen Lennox Brown's *A Ballet Behind the Bridge* [1972] also at the Negro Ensemble, but these are odd instances. I have directed a couple myself, here, but in the Caribbean I have not done any, and none by the current crop of playwrights, so it is so hard to judge. You can see from the ones that I anthologised and published myself the ones that I think that are best. They include Derek's *Sea at Dauphin* and *Malcauchon*; Roddy Walcott's *Banjo Man*, which I think is a great play; *Couvade*; I think only one of Freddie Kissoon's has great possibilities and might very well last, and that's his *God and Uriah Butler* [1967]. He's written dozens of other short and longer plays and very popular, very stageworthy plays, but lacking in depth. Of the Jamaican writers I still think Barry Reckord's *Adella* [1954] was one of his best, not the later version *Flesh To a Tiger* [1958] that was done in London, but the original *Adella*, which I thought was very good; *Echo In the Bone* [1974], by Dennis Scott, I have read, I have not seen it done; I think it's very possible. I love a number of Lennox Brown's plays; he gets a kind of magical quality in his plays, a kind of large metaphor and theatricality; it's a pity that I haven't had an opportunity to direct any of them, but I do care very much for some of his work.

Q: I am going to ask you for your reaction on some other writers and you can probably go a little more in depth. Errol John.

EH: John wrote a magnificent play with *Moon an a Rainbow Shawl*, and then he published three screenplays [*Force Majeure*, *The Dispossessed* and *Hasta Luego: Three Screenplays* (1967)], some of them he has rewritten. I have had an opportunity to see three or four plays that he has been working on recently including one spectacular television play that he wrote for the BBC – which they bought and had never used [*The Insider* (1969)]. John has a great poetic gift – prose poetry not formal written poetry – and a large conception; his plays, however, now seem to sort of explode on the page and he doesn't seem to care very much about writing for a theatre that has a limited physical space and he's writing for a theatre that is almost filmic in production. This is not to say it can't be done – I mean, people do Shakespeare this way – but he is going to have difficulty getting it done. I think he is writing with a triple purpose: his plays can be done on film, on television and on the stage, and because of that his plays seem to meander and flow as if you have a camera working in it rather than the actors on the stage – that is part of his difficulty right now. But his plays are very fine works, very moving; and he works and works and works them over, down to every word practically; that discipline that Derek was talking about, in terms of language, he has.

Q: Lennox Brown.

EH: Perhaps he writes too quickly, but I like his vision and I like his magic and the feel he has for music and movement on the stage which, I think, is even more authentic, when you come down to it, than Derek's. Derek has a feeling for the poetic language, but Lennox is a poet of the theatre; at his best his images are *theatrical* images of movement and spectacle and so on, which I think is wonderful. I am thinking mostly of his Trinidad plays and not his Canadian plays and not of the one that we saw at the Negro Ensemble, which I think was an old potboiler – *A Processional from LaBasse* [1973] and *A Ballet Behind the Bridge* [1972][35] and all these sort of things with counterpointing voices is wonderful theatre. I would love to see them well done, I really would.

Q: Trevor Rhone.

EH: I must confess I have grave problems with Trevor Rhone's plays. I have seen rave notices and reviews of his play *Smile Orange* [1971]. Everyone has said it is his greatest play and it is so good that it ran for *years* in Jamaica. I haven't seen it on stage… It is superficial. *Old*

Story Time [1979] reads like a 19th-century play but updated to 30 years ago. Although there are couple of sentimental scenes in it with regard to the old man and old woman and the boy who goes away to study and comes back and doesn't get to marry the girl that he wanted, and so on and so forth, there is nothing really, I think, profound or new or of any intrinsic merit in the play. The writing is the most pedestrian one can think of: "Black Sambo pose off with you in wedding picture. Lawd, against my better judgement I keep the peace, but after your performance here today, raise yuh hand to kill yuh Ma, there is no power on God's earth could convince me say is not obeah that woman obeah you." [Old *Story Time,* p. 60] (He reads again from another section of the play.)

LEN: Toto. Toto Tomlinson. Who else? Me.
GEORGE: Oh shit!
LEN: That's all right.
GEORGE: I didn't realise.
LEN: How could you? It's been years.
GEORGE: How's your mother now?
LEN: Not too good, George, seeing how you owe her three thousand dollars on the house deal.
GEORGE: Boy, I hadn't realised. [p. 46]

It's banal, you know. But the people love it, they eat it up. And Trevor Rhone is considered to be one of the finest West Indian playwrights; he has a reputation that he doesn't deserve.

Q: Maybe not the finest, but the only West Indian playwright who has been really successful financially with his work.

EH: He has been successful. *Smile Orange* – I saw that in Guyana, when it was done for CARIFESTA there – I hated it! – and I know there are other people who share my view. It is supposed to be a satire on the whole tourist industry but it turns out to be a satire on Jamaicans themselves – which I didn't care for. *School's Out*, the same sort of thing. I really sat down and read these plays *carefully* to see what the hell is in them. Trevor Rhone has popularized theatre, that's true, but in the process I think he has – I don't want to say degraded the theatre – but he has not uplifted his audiences. Derek Walcott has said: "Come up to me"; Trevor has descended; he has even gone down, in my view, *below*, to the lowest common denominator of the audience he is speaking to; I don't think that a serious playwright should descend to that level.

Q: There are some who feel he has depth.

EH: Well, I wish they would show it to me. I have read a number of the reviews of *Old Story Time.* In particular, Mervyn Morris is very, very strong and has written long reviews about it.[36]

Q: Dennis Scott.

EH: I would like to see some more of Dennis's work. I have read *Echo In the Bone*, I have seen *Dog* and read *Dog*; I think Dennis could produce some very fine work, I'm not sure he's done so yet. I respect his mind, I respect his integrity and I respect the direction in which he is moving. I can't say the same for Trevor, I think Trevor is all commerce – there is nothing *wrong* in writing to be popular and to get your plays done, and it's good that he's brought a number of Jamaicans into the theatre who would never go there, but at the cost of a feeling of the live theatre, which it's something more than what he is offering.

Q: Alwin Bully.

EH: I have seen nothing yet from Alwin Bully to lead me to believe that he will be a strong West Indian playwright. I have read *Good Morning Miss Millie* [1970] and I have seen and read *The Nite Box* – and I think there is one other play he sent me – but no, I've seen nothing yet.

Q: Carmen Tipling.

EH: I love two of her short plays that I have seen [possibly *Straight Man*, 1974 and *The Skeleton Inside*, 1976]; I haven't seen much of her work, but I liked it enough to want to publish it. I think there is real feel for the community of which she is writing – a real feel for it. Compare Carmen with Trevor Rhone and you see the difference in their language. Not that she is writing elegantly or anything, but the *reality* of what she is writing is there; there is a naturalness, an easy flow about it which is there; Trevor doesn't have it.

Q: Slade Hopkinson.

EH: As I told you before, I saw a couple of Slade's early plays [probably *The Blood of the Family* (1957) and *The Fall of the Chief* (1965)] which were very pretentious. He tried to write poetic plays and I don't think that it was working at all. I have always looked on Slade as something of a poet, a *brilliant* actor – really brilliant. I think probably with Errol John, the finest actor that I have seen anywhere – and a very good critic. But I have not seen any of his plays that led me to believe that he's made any serious contribution to West Indian theatre as a dramatist.

Q: Derek Walcott.

EH: Well, he is the finest West Indian dramatist, undoubtedly. He is the most professional among them; he has written all kinds of plays. I am on record for saying that I wish he would trust his inspiration more and have less belief in what he says about genius as an anthology, ["One's own voice is an *anthology* of all the sounds one has heard" (*Conversations with Derek Walcott*, 148)] so he goes back to the greats all the time not for any inspiration but as models for his work. It may be that Derek may have gone even further if he had a good director working on his plays, but directing his plays himself, he can't realize the fullest potential in the work because he thinks he has put in it what isn't there, and that is always very difficult for someone to see. However, he has been at this a long time and should by now have sufficient objectivity to see what is in the work and what isn't there. And, he has had professional directing, now, abroad – though he hasn't had it in the Caribbean since he has done most of the work himself. But, certainly, a magisterial West Indian playwright and maybe even one of the top playwrights writing today. I wish that it were possible for Derek not to be as dense at times in what he is saying, because I believe that some of his images begin to be too private, so that you will only understand certain things, which is a great pity. Poetry is a private thing unless it is epic, playwriting is not private or shouldn't be and that is a problem with Derek. The minute he becomes too poetic in his plays then he becomes personal, private, and that's hard to communicate.

Q: One of the playwrights that I interviewed, Stafford Harrison, said he felt that Derek Walcott has this "thickness for symbolism" and that he is "too intellectual", that his intellectualism interferes with the work, that if he could remove himself from the play and let it speak for itself that it would be to his advantage.

EH: Well, I think this is part and parcel of not having a director. I mean, if I am directing one of Derek's plays and something is there that doesn't come across I can go and say, "Derek, look, I am afraid this is a flaw, this is not communicating, there is something there that needs to be done about it," but if he is directing it himself he *knows* what he has written and he thinks that the audience is also going to understand it because he understands it. I think a poetic playwright, even more than a prose playwright, *needs* a director, sensitive director, someone in tune with what he is doing, someone who believes in what he is doing, but he needs one. To direct it yourself then all the images are in your mind.

Q: His brother, Roderick.

EH: A very fine playwright.

Q: You don't hear as much about him.

EH: No; but I read a lot of his work. The last play that he sent me, however, I have been bogged down with because he is trying to write something that is so very different: a play about Frank Worrell, the cricketer, with cricket onstage and all kinds of things in it and it is very, very difficult. But obviously, Roddy is trying his best to explore new forms and I am all for that, but to do it in isolation is hard; he has to do it where there is a group that can read and give him feedback and attempt to stage bits of his plays and so on.

Q: How do you compare him to his brother? Do you see a similarity?

EH: Not really, no. Derek has a poetic vision and Roddy has a theatrical vision and the two are quite different. I think Roddy is farther along the way of developing folk-forms than Derek, for instance. Derek always will take the folk and try to merge it with the so-called universal, which means plays that have worked and have become classics and he has a marvellous ability to take those classical plays to find parallel situations in the West Indian experience and then to adapt and adjust those plays to that experience. That is the technique he uses – omnivorous reader, always has been from a child. But I think that Roddy is more – gives me the feeling of being much more in touch with the reality of the folk-forms; that when he writes about them he is writing straight from the heart and he is writing without the encumbrance of trying to find a poetic metaphor for what he is saying. So, on the one hand, Roddy becomes far more easily accessible than Derek, but on the other, Derek's plays, when he succeeds, will have more depth and more meaning because he is writing at different levels. Roddy is a good actor, good organizer. I think he is as much, if not more, responsible for the success of the Arts Guild in St. Lucia, than Derek; Derek provided the plays, Roddy was the one who saw that they were done, kept the group together, directed and all that kind of thing.

Q: Coming back to Caribbean theatre in general. Do you think that the development of Black Theatre in America has had any marked effects on theatre in the Caribbean – particularly the protest theatre of the '60s?

EH: I think, indeed, that Baraka – I think of all people, Genet, and his play *The Blacks* – I know that was done very early on in Jamaica and in Trinidad; Derek did *The Blacks* and a few other plays of his and some of Baraka's work was done in the Caribbean; and the occasional other play like *Eden* [Steve Carter, 1976]. But I don't think the effect was very pervasive; I think it was the black movement as a whole – Malcolm X *and* the whole Rasta movement – the black cultural revolution was what affected the theatre rather than that the Black American theatre affected the Caribbean theatre. I think the black social revolution influenced some of the fringe theatre but I don't think the serious theatre in the West Indies was affected very much by it. What happened in Jamaica was very unusual. The cinema has always had a stronger appeal in the West Indies than the live theatre, right? But in Jamaica, the cinemas, certainly in the cities, began to be very rundown, began to be unsafe for people to go to, and so people were looking for some other form of entertainment (I am talking about the middle and lower middle-class audiences – respectable members of the community, not the street people) and at the same time as that was happening, little theatre groups like the Barn Theatre and so on, began to spring up with Trevor Rhone putting on plays which were very accessible to the people. And there is where the people started going to theatre; I mean, you go to Jamaica now, there are eight or nine plays running simultaneously four or five nights a week in Kingston. And the so-called theatres are tiny little rooms and tiny stages seating 100 to 120 people, but running constantly and the people are getting a lot of practice in staging. Unfortunately, this tends not to make for a great deal of flexibility in the theatre because you are forced into these narrow confines and you just do things that work there. Occasionally, as in the Sistren group, there are people doing some exciting things.

Q: I have never seen them, but I know Honor Ford-Smith.[37]

EH: I have seen two of their productions; very interesting. They have only done about three productions but they have been good, very different [*Down Pression Get a Blow* (1977) and *Bellywoman Bangarang* (1978)].

Q: I understand that the way they work is through improvisations and that is how they script.

EH: Yes, they do a lot of improvisations. Of course, that is a technique that is very limited, because I do believe that once they get a script from the improvisations, that is where the playwright then should come in and begin to put that script in a more elegant form, that they shouldn't leave it at the level of improvised dialogue all the time because I think then it tends to be rather vernacular language and you don't get the *density* of the language – too conversational, too everyday.

Q: How do you see the potential for more West Indian plays being presented here in the United States? We tried to do it with our theatre group (CART) and it was fairly successful.

EH: Well, there are two ways of looking at it. One is whether the plays will sell themselves as Derek's plays sell themselves, to be done by American actors, or whether the plays should be done by a West Indian community for that community, and for the wider market. It would be nice if indeed there could be a strong West Indian theatre in America, as there used to be a Yiddish theatre in America and so on, because I think that the plays would then receive a much more authentic kind of interpretation. I do think that many of the plays will fail to be picked up by American directors who feel that they can't handle them, they don't know enough about the West Indies to do them and I think that is unfortunate.

Q: What kind of prospects can you foresee for the future development of Caribbean theatre? Do you see it as positive or negative?

EH: Well, hope springs eternal. I think I know what has to be done and I don't think we will have any really serious exploratory scientific development in the theatre unless it is done. We will continue to have lots of theatre but I think we will miss a glorious opportunity to develop, to become a *force* in contemporary theatre if we do not, pretty soon, get together and build our professional company with our best talents and go into a period, well supported by governments that can afford to, like Trinidad, to develop our theatre and then expose it to the world for world criticism; that is what has to be done.

End Notes

1. On his return to Jamaica in 1927, Marcus Garvey organised cultural events at Edelweiss Park St Andrew Jamaica, which the UNIA had purchased, mainly involving European classical music. See Wycliffe and Hazel Bennett, *The Jamaican Theatre* (Jamaica: UWI Press, 2012), p. 195.
2. Archie Lindo (1908-1990) was a Jamaican playwright – *The Maroon*; *Forbidden Fruit* (1941); *Under the Skin* (1943) and the adaptation of De Lisser's *The White Witch of Rosehall* (1945) – poet, and short story writer – *Bronze* (1944) and *My Heart Was Singing* (1946) – photographer, radio broadcaster and producer, a journalist and reviewer who played an important part in the Jamaican connection to the BBC Caribbean Voices programme.
3. H.G. De Lisser (1878-1944) was a Jamaican novelist, journalist and newspaper editor. His early novels *Jane's Career* (1914) and *Susan Proudleigh* (1915) were the first genuinely competent works of modern Caribbean fiction that dealt mostly respectfully with the lives of the black working class. De Lisser was himself a member of the white creole middle class, and his later novels display the cultural and ethnic prejudices of that class in the 1930s and 40s. At least two of his novels were dramatised by Archie Lindo and Ernest Cupidon.
4. Noel Vaz (1920-2009) was a Jamaican playwright (*The General: Alpha and Omega*) but best known for his work as a director and leading light of the Little Theatre Movement and founder in the 1960s of the New Theatre Company. From 1955 to 1986 he was staff tutor in drama at the Creative Arts Centre at UWI. He was involved in the scripting and direction of many of the LTM's annual pantomimes. He also worked in the theatre in the UK. In addition to Caribbean plays, he brought 20th century international theatre to Jamaica (Ionescu, Weiss's *The Marat/Sade* and Soyinka).

5. The Extra Mural Drama series published by the University of the West Indies in the 1950s and 1960s and intermittently through the 1970s is the single most important repository of Caribbean Theatre, edited initially by Errol Hill and latterly by Esmond Ramesar.
6. David Edgecombe: see interview with Alwin Bully, note 8.
7. In addition to her international reputation as a poet and performer and champion of Jamaican Creole, (*Jamaica Labrish*, 1967) Louise Bennett-Coverley (1919-2006) made a major contribution to the development of Jamaican theatre, particularly the Jamaican pantomime. She wrote, sometimes with others, *Bluebeard and Brer Anancy* (1949); *Anancy and Pandora* (1955); *Anancy and Beeny Bud* (1956); *Busha Bluebeard* (1957); *Queenie's Daughter* (1963); *Bredda Buck* (1964).
8. Beryl McBurnie (1915-2000) was the pioneer of Trinidadian dance, drawing on the country's folk traditions. She studied in the USA under Martha Graham and Katherine Durham. She founded the Little Carib Dance Company and the Little Carib Theatre in 1948. See Molly Ahye, *Cradle of Caribbean Dance: Beryl McBurnie and the Little Carib Theatre*, Heritage Cultures, 1983. And see: http://caribbean-beat.com/issue-20/beryl-mcburnie-first-lady-dance.
9. Lennox Raphael (1939-) is a Trinidadian born playwright based in the USA, whose play, *Che!* (1969) was closed down by the public morals police for explicit nudity and profanity. His other plays include *Dracula the Dreamer* (1980); *The Politicians* (1981); *Blue Soap* and *Ziggerboo.*
10. Jimmy Lee Wah (1931-) is a Trinidadian director and theatre promoter based in San Fernando in South Trinidad. From 1956-76 he led the San Fernando Drama Guild. He taught at Naparima College until his retirement in 1998, bringing a Shakespeare festival to the college. He founded the San Fernando Drama Workshop in 1976. See <http://u.tt/index.php?articles=1&article_key=1584&for_internet_announcements=1>
11. Osborne Ashby was a Trinidadian playwright involved with the Whitehall Players. His plays included *The Doctor in Spite of Himself* (1953) and *Sailors Ashore* (1966).
12. A.H. Mendes (1897-1991) and Albert Gomes (1911-1978) were leading figures behind the publication of the Trinidadian literary magazine, *The Beacon* (1931-1933). Mendes was the author of two important novels, *Pitch Lake* (1935) and *Black Fauns* (1936). Gomes was better known as a pre-independence politician; much later he published an autobiography, *Through a Maze of Colour* (1974) and a novel, *All Papa's Children* (1978).
13. Douglas Archibald (1919-1993) was a Trinidadian playwright (and historian) whose work was an important staple of the post 1950s Caribbean theatre. His published plays included *Junction Village* (1958); *The Rose*

Slip (1962); *Old Maid's Tale* (1966); *Ann-Marie* (1967); *The Bamboo Clump* (1967); *Island Tide* (1972); *Defeat with Honour* (1977) – all published by the UWI Extra Mural Department, Trinidad. Other plays include *Back of Beyond*; *Drink and the Devil*; *My Good Friend Justice*.

14. De Wilton Rogers was a Trinidadian novelist and playwright. He was a teacher and a founding member of the People's National Movement, though he later fell out with Eric Williams. His plays included *Columbus – Man in Chains* and *The Silk Cotton Grove*, both circa 1940s, and *Blue Blood and Black* and *Trickidad*. His novel, *Lalaja,* was published in 1944. See http://www.newsday.co.tt/commentary/0,147393.html.
15. Ronald Amoroso (1935-) is a Trinidadian playwright, actor and writer of folk musicals. His plays include *The Blood Clot* (1970) *Blood and Steel*; *The Brother, Five*; *Pan Rising* (all undated) and *Master of Carnival* (1973/1986).
16. Horace James (1927-) an actor and producer was involved with the Carnegie Players of San Fernando and the San Fernando Theatre Guild. He was the producer of Trinidad's first local drama series. He worked in TV and established "Play of the Month". See <www.ttpba.org.tt/index.php?option=com-content&view=article&id=79:horace-james--2010-winner&catid=39:hall-of-fame&Itemid=12>.
17. Freddy Kissoon: see interview with Alwin Bully, Note 17.
18. Barbara Assoon (1929-) is a Trinidadian actress and dancer who performed in Trinidad, the UK (for almost twenty years in the 1950s and '60s, including a role in *Coronation Street*) and the USA. She was lead dancer at the Little Carib Theatre and had a senior post at Radio Trinidad before she retired.
19. Greta Bourke Fowler (d. 1978) and Henry Fowler (1915-2007) were stalwarts of the Little Theatre Movement in Jamaica and the Ward Theatre. The Fowlers established the Jamaica Theatre School which became the Jamaican School of Speech and Drama, which was handed over to the government and is now the Edna Manley College for the Performing Arts. Henry Fowler was a white Jamaican from an old planter family, but was an early activist in the People's National Party and editor of the anti-colonial weekly, *Public Opinion*. The Fowlers were writers of such pantomimes as the much revived *Queenie's Daughter* (1963) and *Morgan's Dream* (1965). See http://www.guardian.co.uk/news/2007/may/25/guardianobituaries.obituaries and http://www.ltmpantomime.com/pages/History/thefowlers.html and Bennett, *The Jamaican Theatre* (pp. 271-275).
20. Elsie Benjamin-Barsoe was a Jamaican actress (she played a part in the film *A High Wind in Jamaica*) and theatre director of W.G. Ogilvie's

[see below] *One Soja Man* (1945) at the People's Theatre. The cover of the programme proclaimed that the play was "under the kind patronage of the Jamaican people". See http://www.jamaicaobserver.com/columns/Self-discovery-essential-for-national-development_13259068#ixzz2KgoUjwOn.

21. Harry Milner was for forty years the leading newspaper critic of Jamaican theatre, and respected for his judgements. He was an Englishman granted Jamaican citizenship in 1962. See Bennett, *The Jamaican Theatre*, passim.
22. Orford St. John was an English-born theatre director and reviewer working in Jamaica from the 1940s to the 1960s. He founded the Repertory Players in 1957, committed to promoting an interracial theatre group and doing much to bring a wider and more modern range of plays to the Jamaican theatre.
23. Sir Philip Sherlock (1902-2000) was recognised as one of the great West Indians of the 20th century, principally for his work as the first Vice-Chancellor of the University of the West Indies. His importance for the theatre and literary arts was in his vision in placing culture at the centre of the campus, in the Creative Arts Centre, now the Philip Sherlock Centre for Creative Arts. He was an important historian and a fine poet and founder and first editor of *Caribbean Quarterly*. He also wrote many books for children on Jamaican folklore such as *Anancy the Spiderman* (1956) and *Tales from the West Indies* (1966), both still in print.
24. W.G. Ogilvie (1923-1992) was a Jamaican novelist, writer for children and dramatist. His plays include: *One Sojer Man* (1945) *Double Trouble*; *Hi, Miss Cleo*; *Jezebel* (1966); *The Legacy*; *Me Tief*; *One Dollar for Dog* (1964); *The People*; *The Sudden Guest* (1962). His two novels, *The Ghost Bank* and *Cactus Village* were both published by the Pioneer Press in 1953.
25. Wycliffe Bennett (1922-2009) was a producer and director of theatre, radio, film and television, organiser of Jamaican national arts festivals, general manager of the Jamaican Broadcasting Company and Chairman of the Ward Theatre. His book, with Hazel Bennett, *The Jamaican Theatre: Highlights of the Performing Arts in the Twentieth Century* (UWI Press, 2011) is an invaluable survey.
26. Michael Gilkes (1935) is a Guyanese dramatist, director, poet and critic. His plays include *Couvade* (1974), *A Pleasant Career* (1992) and *The Last of the Redmen* (2002). The first two are forthcoming (2013) in the Peepal Tree Caribbean Classics series. His collection of poems, *Joanstown and other poems* (Peepal Tree, 2002) won the Guyana Prize.
27. Barry Reckord (1926-2011) was a Jamaican who came to the UK in 1950 and made a major contribution to British and Black British theatre with such plays as: *Della* (1953); *Adella* (1954); *Flesh to a Tiger* (1958);

You in Your Small Corner (1960); *Skyvers* (1963, 1971); *A Liberated Woman* (1970); *Give the Gaffers Time To Love You* (1973); *X* (1974); *The White Witch of Rose Hall* (1975); *The White Witch* (1985); *Sugar D* (1988); and television plays *In the Beautiful Caribbean* (1972) and *Club Havana* (1975). Three of his plays were published in *For the Reckord* (a collection of three plays by Barry Reckord: *Flesh to a Tiger*; *Skyvers*; *The White Witch*), Ed. Yvonne Brewster (London: Oberon Books, 2010).

28. Neville Labastide is a Trinidadian playwright whose plays include *Lost on My Hands* (1961); *Cousin Adriana Coming* (1963); *One for the Road* (1965); *Sans Everything* (1965); *Something Old, Something New* (1961); *Voice of the People* (1978); all but the first and last of these were published in the UWI Extra-Mural Series.
29. Anthony Hinkson: see interview with Alwin Bully, note 9.
30. Ken Corsbie: see interview with Alwin Bully, note 24.
31. In addition to his fiction, Earl Lovelace (1935-) has written the following plays: *The New Boss* (1962); *My Name Is Village* (1976), *Pierrot Ginnard* (musical drama, 1977); *Jestina's Calypso* (1978); *The Wine of Astonishment* (adapted from his novel, 1987); *The New Hardware Store* (1980); *The Dragon Can't Dance* (adapted from his novel, 1986, published in *Black Plays: 2*, ed. Yvonne Brewster (London: Methuen, 1989); *The Reign of Anancy* (1989); *Joebell and America* (1999). His play collection *Jestina's Calypso and Other Plays* was published in the Heinemann Caribbean Writers Series, 1984.
32. Errol Jones (1923-2011) was a Trinidadian actor who was a founding member of the Trinidad Theatre Workshop, working with Derek Walcott and performing as a notable Makak in Dream on Monkey Mountain. See http://www.trinidadexpress.com/news/Errol_Jones_dies-114766104.html and http://caribbean-beat.com/issue-106/errol-jones-gentleman-and-player.
34. Aubrey Adams (1919-2007), was involved with the Trinidad Little Carib Theatre. He wrote the play *Bamboula* (1966). He earned Hill's ire by becoming cultural advisor to an increasingly autocratic Eric Williams.
35. Eric Roach (1915-1974) was a Tobagonian poet, journalist, teacher and dramatist. His poetry, amongst the most important before the work of Walcott and Brathwaite, remained uncollected until Peepal Tree's *The Flowering Rock: Collected Poems 1938-1974*. Roach was the author of three plays: *Belle Fanto* (1967), *Letter from Leonora* (1968) and *A Calabash of Blood* (1971) which were published in the UWI Extramural Series and widely performed. *New Dancers in the Dooryard* (1971) and *A Home Flight of Pigeons* (1974) were unpublished.
36. Lennox Brown's two Negro Ensemble plays were *A Ballet Behind the Bridge* and *Twilight Dinner*. It's not clear where *A Processional from*

La Basse was performed – or which play Hill regarded as a "potboiler".

37. But see Mervyn Morris's critical introduction to the Longman edition of 1987, which is very far from negative about Rhone's play..

38. Honor Ford Smith (1951-) is a Jamaican poet, dramatist and theatre director who since 1991 has been resident in Canada, teaching at York University, Toronto. She was a co-founder and artistic director of Sistren, a theatre collective of working-class Jamaican women established in 1977, and the editor of *Lionheart Gal: Life Stories of Jamaican Women* (1986). She was also involved in theatre work in Jamaica as a member of the Groundwork Theatre Company, created in 1980 as the repertory arm of the Jamaica School of Drama, where she taught. She published a collection of poems, *My Mother's Last Dance* (Toronto: Sister Vision Press, 1997). Sistren's plays included *Down Pression Get a Blow* (1977); *Bellywoman Bangarang* (1978); *The Case of Iris Armstrong* (1984); *Domestick* (1982); *Ida Revolt Inna Jonkunnu Stylee*; *Muffet Inna All A We* (1985); *Nana Yah* (1980); *Sistren Song*, musical (1985); *Tribute* (Jam. 1983).

ABDUR RAHMAN SLADE HOPKINSON
(1934-1993)

Born into a middle class family in New Amsterdam, Guyana, Hopkinson's father was a barrister-at-law, his mother a nurse. A few years after the death of his father, his mother took him and his sister to live in Barbados where he attended Harrison College. In 1952, he went to the University College of the West Indies on a scholarship, coinciding with Derek Walcott and Mervyn Morris as students. While at UCWI, Hopkinson became active in university theatre, performing and directing in Sophocles' *Oedipus Rex*, and in *King Lear.* He obtained his BA in 1953 and a Dip. Ed. in 1956.

In 1962, Hopkinson and his family went to live in Trinidad where he joined Derek Walcott's Trinidad Theatre Workshop. In the company's first public presentation in 1962, he appeared as Krapp in Samuel Beckett's *Krapp's Last Tape.* He played in scores of other productions, including Jean Genet's *The Blacks*, Derek Walcott's *Dream on Monkey Mountain* in the role of Lestrade and in *Ti-Jean and His Brothers,* as Devil. In 1964, Hopkinson appeared under Errol Hill's direction in the Trinidad Dramatic Club/ Phoenix Players quarter-centenary production of *King Lear*, in what was described as a "towering performance of Lear that would have been acclaimed on any stage in the world." He studied at the Yale Drama School on a Rockefeller scholarship between 1965-66, taught at the University of Guyana, 1966-68, then returned to the TTW. However, by 1970 there was a falling out with Walcott and he founded the Caribbean Theatre Guild in 1970.

The first CTG production in 1971, directed by Hopkinson, and taken to Guyana for the 1972 CARIFESTA, was Douglas Archibald's *Rose Slip*. Subsequent CTG stage productions included plays by Wole Soyinka, Errol John and Hopkinson's own *Sala.* His *Scent of Jasmines* was also presented on television. In 1985 Hopkinson was selected to be honoured by the Trinidad National Drama Festival.

He became a Muslim in 1964 and was now known as Abdur Rahman Slade Hopkinson. By 1970 he was suffering from kidney failure and by 1973 was on regular dialysis, which brought his acting career to an end.

While living in Jamaica during the 1970s, he worked at the Jamaica Tourist Board, and as a teacher and newspaper editor, before moving to Canada as Vice-Consul for Guyana. He later worked as a classroom assistant and teacher before taking long-term disability leave.

Hopkinson's writing career began in 1954 with the publication of *The Four and Other Poems*; the plays, *The Blood of a Family* (1957), *Fall of a Chief* (1965), *The Onliest Fisherman* (1967), *Spawning of Eel* (1968), rewritten as *Sala* and *The Long Vacation* (or *Summer Dread*, 1975).

In 1976, the Government of Guyana published two companion collections of poetry, The *Madwoman of Papine,* which contained mainly his secular poems ranging over his Caribbean experiences, and *The Friend*, which contained his religious and philosophical poems, written in the process of discovering the teachings of the Sufi Muslims.

In addition, Hopkinson wrote a couple of short stories, and his poetry was widely published in journals such as *Bim*, *Savacou*, *New World* and in anthologies such as *Anansesem, The Penguin Book of Caribbean Verse and Voiceprint. Snowscape With Signature*, a selection of the poems written between 1952-1992, was published by Peepal Tree Press in 1993, with an introductory memoir by Mervyn Morris.

His daughter, Nalo Hopkinson, has been making a name for herself as a fabulist writer with such books as *Brown Girl in the Ring* and *Midnight Robber*, and his son Keita Hopkinson is an accomplished painter.

He wrote that for him, "the stern craftsmanship, the deftness, of verse is the basis of the high art and pleasure of poetry: only finely cut stone should be used to build a temple." As a poet, actor and dramatist, Abdur Rahman Slade Hopkinson made a major contribution to the Caribbean arts, which would almost certainly have been greater had not serious illness intervened.

ABDUR RAHMAN SLADE HOPKINSON

28 September, 1981

Q: What prompted you to become a writer?

SLADE HOPKINSON: That would go a very long way back, but I'll try. Memory takes one back to the early teens. I remember a set of books that my mother had acquired somewhere. Both my mother and father were reasonably bookish, my father especially, and books were part of one's domestic life. And I remember very vaguely – I'm talking about the age of twelve, thirteen – a set of books that we had acquired, and my diving into these books – they were second-hand – and my hauling out a collection of – it was Keats, and reading this thing straight through. And it was as if my eyes had been opened. I suddenly saw the world differently; and the quality of the imagination behind this work became something that was very admirable to me.

And, of course, from here, as a starting point – I think Keats was the first writer that I read seriously, if you ignore the boyhood classics like *Tom Sawyer*, which, of course, I had read earlier – but from there, I moved through the Romantics and through whatever each writer led me on to, to a different area. Keats led me to Shelley and Shelley led me to Wordsworth and so on all around. And Shelley also led me to Shaw from reading critiques of Shelley that mentioned Shaw's interest in Shelley and so on, back and forth across the spectrum of English literature. And it started to appear to me to be a very admirable thing to want to do – to want to express that kind of feeling about the world and about life. And I started very early, in the middle teens, to try to write verse. Plays came later. So I don't know if that is a satisfactory answer. How did I start?

Q: You were opened up to a whole new world as a West Indian youth.

SH: By the accidental perusal of a volume of Keats which I used to read through and through and mark and remark and make notes about – in the margins and on the back leaf. It really haunted me for three or four years, that volume. And I remember, too, that this was – Keats of course is a certain *type* of poet, he has his limitations, he has his subject – the extravagant loveliness of nature – but at that time I had just gone to Barbados at the age of twelve, and the beauty of that island, coming from the coastlands of Guyana where I lived before, where I was born, struck me with a similar impact, and to me, the two things went together. I can remember walking during full moon on the Worthing beach in Barbados, as a boy of thirteen, with a volume of Keats in my back pocket; sometimes sitting on a boat and reading it – the moon was so bright there, what with the reflections off the white-painted buildings and the white sand itself – you're sitting in a kind of ocean of light – and it was quite possible to read. And I don't know if you could call that a poetic affectation but, I mean, I think for a boy of thirteen or fourteen probably not. I mean, affectation comes a little later. But I can remember doing this, and to me, Keats with his intoxication with the English landscape was – the landscape that I had in front of me in Barbados was not excessively different, it was certainly beautiful, too.

Q: So at that time when you started writing verse, at twelve, thirteen?

SH: Probably a bit later. Say fourteen. By fifteen I was certainly writing.

Q: What was the reaction around you –

SH: I didn't show many people… I showed… I remember I had a dear friend – my mother ran a guesthouse, you see, in Barbados, and this gentleman I talk about, he was a Mr. Didley, he was a solicitor – he's now dead – a friend of my father. But I have always, throughout my life, been able to have friends who were separated from me by many, many years, either upwards or downwards, you know. I've had dear friends who were children, dear friends who were very old people, and at this time when I was fourteen, this man, who at the time must have been perhaps in his early seventies, was a very good friend of mine. I used to show my stuff to him. I mention him because he used to come and stay at my mother once a year for his holiday; he was a Guyanese solicitor, a colleague and friend of my father's, and he became a literary friend of mine. He was an intellectually very curious person coming out of colonial Guyana. I don't remember too much what his reaction was except encouragement. He was a Marxist in those early days and so maybe probably not too turned on by a Keatsian romantic. But other older people I used to show the stuff to – teachers – and usually got a lot of encouragement.

Q: What about later, as you got older?

SH: Well, I mean, one's tastes changed, one got involved with school and in real life, and one went to university and one's tone of voice changed and one also got very interested in the theatre. I remember my early stuff; I don't have any of it and maybe it would be a deep embarrassment to look at it now; but it certainly was very Keatsian. But that changed rapidly as one got exposed to real life in the colonies.

Q: So what was your reaction then, as a young writer, going to university and coming in contact, I would assume, with a lot of fairly prominent West Indian writers, the likes of, say, Derek Walcott, to name one –

SH: Yes, well, Walcott's life and mine ran – parallel is the wrong word – intertwined with each other for quite a distance. And of course, when I went to UWI, one of my great curiosities… and purposes was to meet this great man; and, yes, we met and we became friends and we worked together a lot. Of course, he was then becoming interested in the theatre and so was I. I used to show him my verse and he used to work at pruning its extravagance and its off-the-cuff quality and tried to get me to be more premeditative rather than spontaneous, and I think that my intellectual influence was at that time entirely his. He introduced me to writers who would help to enforce a discipline upon a too rampant imagination. At that time (and I'm talking about '52, '53) he was very keen on the critical qualities of Ezra Pound, and he used to set me to reading Pound's critical essays and this put a certain amount of restraint upon that romantic impulse – to the good, of course, I think. The critical restraint probably resulted in my clamming up from then on. When I say clamming up, I'm not blaming Walcott for clamming *me* up, but I mean something happened inside me which said that this extravagance had to be watched – and it's something that I've never lost. What I'm saying is that teenage romantic hothead quickly cooled, or hotheart, if you want, quickly cooled.

Q: What did you think of Derek at that time as a poet? I mean, you did mention the fact that he was regarded as a great man at that time.

SH: Well, I thought so then and I still do. His poetry at that time was very difficult; his poetry has become clearer and clearer as he has got older. That is not atypical. As I was intoxicated with the Romantics, so, I think he was with Dylan Thomas at the time. And if you can remember – if the *world* can remember – a poem like "The Yellow Cemetery": "All grains are the ash to ashes drowsing in the morning…" [*Caribbean Quarterly* 5.3, 1958]. A very early Walcott poem, I mean, if you read it you can hear his voice – looking backwards you can hear his voice. But there is certainly the voice of Thomas there. And I can remember hearing a joke from him, I can remember him telling us, a group of us some place, maybe at the student union at UWI, that he had heard that Thomas had asked in Britain about this West Indian poet that he had heard about who was trying to write like him. (*Laughs*) Thomas had heard about him, of course, because in those days the BBC was very interested in the West Indian poets and Walcott's stuff used to be transmitted on the BBC, and, indeed, so was mine. Henry Swanzy, was it? *Caribbean Voices*, if I remember correctly. That was the early radio magazine that was an important launching pad for a lot of the earlier writers.

Q: Well, the next question I was going to ask you: Are you still actively pursuing your career as a writer and if so, to what extent?

SH: I tell myself so. The last stuff that I've had published was by the Barbadian poet Bruce St. John.[1] He writes some cunning little dialect poems and reads them – he gives performances – very subtle and very good. He edited a volume to coincide with this year's CARIFESTA; he came up here to meet some poets and to collect stuff, and I submitted three poems to him, of which I think he chose two [It is not clear this anthology was ever published]. Incidentally, in this book, the poems will be under my new writing name, which is Abdur Rahman. I have – not so recently – become a Muslim. But those poems are the most recent stuff that I have published. I've also been trying a little fiction, but it becomes painfully difficult to do because of what I told you. You see, the brain isn't good everyday. Today, for instance, I'm reasonably lucid. Tomorrow I'm going to have a dialysis and depending on how strenuous that is, the next day I may be not so lucid. So I really have now about maybe a fifth of the time, and maybe less than that of the energy that I once had. The rest of the time is devoted to dialysis and recovering from it, and there is considerable loss of mental vigour and clarity. Considerable. But I still write. I have a poetic short story now that I'm putting the final touches to and then I'll try to get it published somewhere.

Q: Coming back to speaking about poetry, what do you feel about Derek Walcott's view of contemporary West Indian poets as lacking in discipline and basically lazy?

SE: Well, if this is a view of those immediately contemporary, that is, over the past, say, eight years, then I don't think I'm qualified to say. As a generalization it probably holds true. After all, isn't that true of the whole West Indian character, whether it is operating in the field of poetry or industry? Or agriculture or whatever. Our spontaneity and spark are beautiful but they are not enough. They're not enough. We learn this very quickly when we participate in the international world. Maybe this is what is wrong with the West Indian poets that he is talking about, that with the new nationalism they will probably consider it culturally wrong to think of themselves as participating in the international world, and so they would lose that. But if you take, say, our cricketers, they learn that discipline of living in the international world as a sportsmen – I'm not talking about personal discipline only, I'm talking about the discipline of cricket. They learn how to resist the temptation to hit a six and take a great chance doing it and get out promptly – they have learnt that. And our writers who see themselves as competing with the best in the language – as Walcott does – *he* has learnt it. Naipaul has learnt it;

Naipaul is a magnificent writer. I don't always agrees with what he says, but he's a magnificent writer. But you see, to learn that, you cannot call yourself a West Indian writer; you're a writer who happens to be a West Indian. I mean, Hemingway made this point already, that when you take up your pen to write – he didn't make it in these terms but this is essentially what he was saying – you've got to see yourself as taking on the lions of the past. You are with them, you're not doing some little parochial thing – unless you see yourself in those terms, unless that is what you are trying to do. Then why are you trying? Don't bother. It's not worth it. And those, you know, those like Walcott, like Naipaul, who see themselves in those terms, have certainly learnt the discipline, so it doesn't apply to Walcott and it doesn't apply to Naipaul and possibly to a few others.

Q: Outside of the two poems you mentioned, have you worked on any books or anything outside of that?

SH: I am struggling at the moment – maybe it is bad luck to say this – but I'm struggling at the moment with an idea for a novel that is tempting me. I haven't started working except to write notes – got a lot of notes, maybe a book full of notes, but I haven't started. Or rather, I made a start – which I'm going to discard – and I'm going to start again. Hopefully, eh? And one doesn't want to act.

Q: What about plays, have you written anything since *Long Vacation*?

SE: No. I considered rewriting *Long Vacation* the other day partly because I thought that I could get somebody in Canada interested in maybe doing it. But I rethought even that. I think I've become just more hesitant; I decided that I would let the fellow read it as is and see if he likes it. If he wants to do it then we could rewrite it then, you know, a working rewriting. *Sala* [1975] – do you know *Sala*?

Q: I never saw that but I've hear a lot about it.

SH: *Sala* is alternatively called *A Spawning of Eels* [1968] – horrible title. *Sala* is better. But that has just been done in Trinidad, I believe, and has been done in Jamaica, it's been done in Guyana – it's been done in Trinidad now twice. I'm just amazed at its popularity.

Q: Did you ever earn much from writing it?

SH: Now when it was it was done in Jamaica, it was directed by Dennis Scott, done at The Barn, yes. Because that whole enclave of artists in Jamaica – you know, Scott, Trevor Rhone and so forth – they are professionally minded and they believe people should be paid for their work, so, oh, yes, certainly I got paid for that. I haven't heard anything from this Trinidadian production, never heard anything of it. It was done by a group which I founded somewhere around 1970 or so when I broke away from Walcott's Trinidad Theatre Workshop – a group called the Caribbean Theatre Guild which, happily, to me, still functions in some sort of way. It may well be that they consider me a member and so maybe no royalties – well I haven't heard anything about royalties.

Q: Why I mentioned this was – well, there's always been a question about professionalism. I remember speaking to Lennox Brown, and he said – this was around '76 – that he'd never go back to the Caribbean until they had a better sense of professionalism about theatre.

SH: Well, that may be a rationalization of his own position – he didn't intend to go back to the Caribbean, anyhow. I think he was living wherever he was living, was quite comfortable there – maybe. I'm guessing. But to me, I think that would be wrong. What you do is – if you can – join the scene and help to create that sense of professionalism. And, you know, we're really asking for something, which evolved in Europe and America, to suddenly appear in the Caribbean full-grown. It has to be nurtured along. First the artist has to take himself professionally seriously – that is, he has to produce a quality of work which is deserving of that kind of respect, and he has to do this for free at first. And then by his own seriousness he gets an answering seriousness out of the public, and by the very quality of his work the public will be delighted to pay to see it. I mean, he can't just say, "I'm an artist and I want you to pay." He's working at home in a new, raw situation.

Q: Lennox said that the only country in the Caribbean that he thought had a proper sense of nationhood, that he thought he could live in and work as a playwright, was Guyana.

SH: He might find difficulties practising as a professional playwright in Guyana. I thought he was going to say Jamaica, because you know in Jamaica – and Trinidad also – I'll deal with them separately – in Jamaica people like Trevor Rhone have worked *very* hard in the way that I suggested as the right way, *very* hard at being professionals and Rhone has made it, I think. Rhone has convinced the Jamaican public that he is worth paying money to see.

Q: From what I've been made to understand, he is probably the only West Indian playwright –

SH: Living off playwriting. And you would have now, for instance, people like Dennis Scott, who are at least *partly* living – or maybe *only* living – isn't he principal of the Jamaica School? – so he's living off drama. Somebody's paying him to practice the skills of his craft and to exercise his talent. But the work has to be done; you don't just arrive and say that I'm worthy of it. You can do it in a developed country but this is a raw colonial situation where you have to grow with the growth of everything else, and you have to contribute to the growth. I mean, all of this spade work that was done by people like Walcott and Errol Hill and so forth, in the early days, it has got to be done. You don't make claims upon the people without having done your work there with them. Now I think that workers like Walcott – talking about Walcott now not as a playwright but as a teacher of drama, as a director, as a teacher of acting, as the head of the Trinidad Theatre Workshop – has worked *very hard* to instill into his actors the self-respect that I'm talking about, the self-respect which will eventually cause others to respect you in terms of coming to the theatre and paying to see what you have done. *Very hard*! But you don't insist from the word go that you be paid. You make that claim a little later when you think it is about time people see your point. I think that claim can be made now. But not from the word go. Not in our situation in the Caribbean.

Q: Is there any kind of active West Indian theatre here in Toronto?

SH: There are West Indian artists of the theatre around the place; they form no coherent movement. There're people in Toronto like Ralph Campbell,[2] the Trinidadian actor; Daniel Caudeiron,[3] who's a Dominican, he's a writer, he's a public relations man, vast sort of energy and very broadly based interests.

Q: He has a TV programme, too, doesn't he?

SH: Yes, he does *Black World On Culture* – multilingual television. And a few other people like that. Roddy Walcott may well be here. But they don't cohere together. And, indeed, one doesn't know – if you're talking about a transplanted West Indian theatre – one doesn't know whether such a transplant can live here, whether the temperate zone will grow this tropical plant. It will change, you know, if these people are serious about living here, living in Canada. They may begin in the early stages by putting on West Indian plays – I mean, the plays that we're talking about from back home, and they may try to keep that going. But in twenty years they will be putting on Canadian plays written by West Indians about Canada. Indeed, that is already starting. There's the Guyanese who just had a play on – Hector Bunyan – his play was put on at the Theatre Passe Muraille earlier this year – what was the name of the play again? [It was *Prodigals in a Promised Land* (Canada Press, 1981)] Oh, dear... You see, this is an example of lapses in memory – it's a play about Guyanese trying to live here. Now that kind of play is going to be written. I mean, I don't see any point in striving very hard to put on an authentic version of plays from back home and making that your guiding light for evermore; you know, it will change. We begin that way.

Q: Have you tried to follow the theatre scene in the Caribbean or in Jamaica or Guyana?

SH: You mean recently?

Q: Yeah.

SH: No. Something has happened to me. While I think I want to continue writing and, indeed – though more slowly – I'm still writing, I think I'm less and less interested in the theatre as a performer. Now that may be a self-protective device because the truth of the matter is that I can't perform in the theatre any longer and I've been unable because of my illness to do so since – oh, I think 1971 or '72 was the last time I appeared on the stage. I no longer have the stamina, myself, to act or to direct. And it may well be that I tell myself I've lost interest in the theatre because I can't bear to contemplate the active theatre and know that I can't participate in it. It may well be, you know. That's for somebody wiser than me to say. But I still go to the theatre when I can. I try to go to Stratford every year and I try to see things around Toronto. But as a member of the audience, you know, I have temptations; there've been times when I said, well, is there something inside here you can do? And I was very tempted earlier when I saw Bunyan's play. In fact, the director of that play and myself, we got in touch with each other and we have talked. I showed him one of my plays, I showed him *Sala* and I want to show him another. I don't know – you get the temptation, nostalgia; but you know that if you're going to get back into that it would probably be as a writer, certainly not as a performer or as a director – it's physical work which I can no longer do. Although I did make a film in Jamaica in '76 when I was ill; of that film, the less said the better. It was a totally horrible film. Horrible, horrible. (*Laughs*) I acted in the film called *The Marijuana Affair* [Directed William Greaves, 1975, but never released]. Yeah. I did a short part in it. It was a pretty grim film.

Q: At the time you left Jamaica, what did you think of the situation there with theatre?

SH: There're some extremely gifted people. There's one person who used to really – well, it's not only one, but I'll mention her – who used to take care of me to the extent of trying to make sure that I saw things, and that was Carroll Dawes.[5] She and her friends, Rawle Gibbons[6] and David Carty,[7] were absolutely beautiful to me when I first reached Jamaica in '73 with my illness, and they were trying to pull me out of it. And Carroll used to come and pick me up with these good friends of hers, these disciples of hers, really, and take me to see all kinds of things and it was beautiful. Because I was weak and unclear in my head and needed a lot of propping up and toting around. But to try and answer your question, there was David Carty, who, to my mind, is a brilliant actor. And when I say that I don't mean a brilliant West Indian actor, he's a brilliant actor. I wonder what happened to him? He came from Anguilla. Anguilla is a very tiny island with a tiny population, and I believe he wanted to go back to Anguilla and develop theatre there. Strange, because, I mean, I don't think the theatre in Anguilla – if such a thing isn't regarded as a contradiction in terms or an absurdity – theatre in Anguilla must necessarily be small – I don't know if he could be thinking of the kind of theatre that we call theatre – I'm talking about not the quality of people but just the *numbers* of the people. It's a small island with a population of a few thousand at the most. As far as I know, David wanted to go back to Anguilla. But he was a *brilliant* actor. *Brilliant.* I saw *The Zoo Story* [Edward Albee, 1958] that he did there in Jamaica. Terrific performance. There was Rawle Gibbons, who I believe is still functioning. I saw his name somewhere recently. Very intelligent about the theatre and young and clearly serious. There were the older persons – Dennis Scott, who is a very valuable artist. But there was a lot of young blood coming up, awful lot.

Q: What do you think of Stafford Harrison, who was in your play?

SH: Yes! Strong instinctive actor. What has happened to him?

Q: He's in New York studying theatre at New York University Drama School. He worked with a Broadway production, musical called *Reggae*, which was not successful.

SH: Yes, he's a strong actor. There was Oliver Samuels,[8] very gifted, and he has a sort of a comic stand, but there're greater dimensions, fuller dimensions to him, oh, yes.

Q: What do you think about Carl Bradshaw?[9]

SH: He was starting to get limited and mannered. Possibly because of becoming a great success at one thing. That central role in the Rhone film, *Smile Orange*, he has been becoming very good at that kind of thing. And he worked a lot with Rhone, so he got a lot of chance to do that kind of thing; but I think he was a gifted actor who needed testing.

You see, we're going through this nationalistic phase in the West Indies, and of course, it is necessary that our writers should write about us. A writer should always write about what he knows, he can't write about what he doesn't know. At the same time, if this is an act of exclusivity, if it means that you cut yourself off from what other people are doing, then it's harmful. And while the actor must be good with his national, local material, I would say he should play other things as well – even if the idiots will call the stuff "foreign". They have to strain themselves to test their limits. He should play Shakespeare, yes; he should play Ibsen; he should play the Greeks. Strain himself. It'll make him better at his own stuff. All knowledge comes from God; it all comes from the same source. You can't value this and not that; it's all human. I think we will outgrow that phase soon. In politics as well as in art. We'll have to; it's a form of adolescence. We all have to go through adolescence, nations too.

Q: Yeah, that's what's happening.

SH: Yeah, I mean, America had it too, at the time. But, I mean, in North America, now, you look at Canada – you can come to Canada and see Shakespeare, you could see a play like *The Visit* by Dürrenmatt, you can see it here. Canada, of course, is a little earlier in that history, I mean, Canada is getting very nationalistic, too. They have to do that before they get bigger; but they have to get bigger *after* the nationalism. You have to grow out of it, it's a form of adolescence.

Q: I see that with Black Theatre in the United States also, that whole wave of theatre that took place in the '60s, which was a reaction to the civil rights movement and the Black Power movement.

SH: Which is a necessary thing. Which you have to get beyond. Well, the blacks in the United States are in a state of war against their oppressors, that is true. But that fact doesn't strangulate *all* of the writers and it doesn't limit the *literary* ambitions of *all* of their writers. What about Baldwin – who is as black as you can get, and who is as pro-black as you can get? Not every black will agree, but he's a serious writer, and an international writer.[10]

Q: There's been this idea or concept that has been going around for some time, now, and it's the concept of Caribbean Theatre. Let me put it another way, how do you view the idea of a Caribbean Theatre?

SH: What do you mean?

Q: Well, a theatre coming out of the indigenous people of the Caribbean not the sort of expatriate theatre –

SH: Who are the indigenous people of the Caribbean? You mean the Arawaks? (*Laughs*) Who are the indigenous people? The Arawaks and the Caribs? We're all imports. And the white people, if that's what you mean by expatriates, in the Caribbean – those who have lived there and are as Caribbean as any of us. They may be able to see themselves as Caribbean and European in the same way that we have only recently learnt to see ourselves as Caribbean and African or Caribbean and Indian, but they're Caribbean, too.

Q: There's been this talk – in Jamaica – of roots theatre, and more recently *reggae* theatre, and in the Eastern Caribbean, Alwin Bully from Dominica has been talking about the concept of *calypso* theatre, which, again, is the roots thing, dealing with the grassroots –

SE: Of course, the theatre, if it is going to be true to the life of the Caribbean, is going to make use of those forms; they're part of the life. It is the same adolescence that we talked about, you know. It's like a boy who has just discovered that he has genitals, so he's genitally obsessed until he gets used to the idea. We're just discovering. We're still at that stage. We're just discovering that we are black, we didn't know that all along. We discovered it recently and we're very excited about it. And some of us are narrowing that down now and we're discovering reggae if we're Jamaican or calypso if we're Trinidadian. And you grow out of that. Yes, we're Trinidadian; we're human, too. Of *course*, one must make use of these beautiful musical elements, they are further richness for you to make use of, but make use of them and press on. But why limit? Why limit? Why back into a corner all the time? Why cut off? Why exclude? What are we running from? Because when all is said and done, when a man two hundred years hence – if the world lasts that long – picks up the text of a West Indian play and reads it, that man will want to be touched by the fact that it's not only West Indian but it's human, too. The man may be a Chinese, he might be a Norwegian, he may be even a West Indian two hundred years down the line when we have all changed. The thing that remains is the humanity. The local colour is just local colour, that's all it is. A play should be able to move across national frontiers and be understood across national frontiers; its proper character, if not its poetry, should be capable of translation. Otherwise, what? Are West Indians a different race of animal, a different species? Like as different from the rest of humanity as a lion is from a lizard? No, I don't think so. I don't think so. At the same time one understands what is happening. The boy who was unaware of his sexuality when he was eight, has suddenly become pubescent and he has gonads and he's very aware of them and very proud of them and so on. We've discovered that we're black and proud or Indian and proud or whatever it is, mulatto and proud or whatever. We're proud and that is healthy and good; we have to move away from that now, move *beyond* it. We have to encompass that, digest it and grow. There's no point in this backing into corners, hiding, defending yourself.

Q: I'd like your honest, candid feelings about certain playwrights, some of whom I know you know, and what you think about their work.

SH: I may try (*Laughs*).

Q: I'll mention the name and you can tell me what you feel. Errol John.

SH: *Moon on a Rainbow Shawl* and *Tout* are the two plays of his that I know. *The Tout* I really don't remember very well. *Moon on a Rainbow Shawl* is a very actable, very producible, very theatre-worthy sentimental play; it is a nice play, it's a charming play; it is very competently written, written by a man who knows the theatre very well. It's got a beautiful lyric quality about it like the early Tennessee Williams, I find. It's a sweet play. I like it.

Q: Lennox Brown.

SH: I'm not familiar enough with his work to say.

Q: Trevor Rhone.

SH: Trevor Rhone is a very important person. He has made that contribution of taking himself seriously as a professional and getting the Jamaican public to take him seriously as a professional. His work is a lot richer than you may think from the fact that he has a mass following, and I know this because I've seen a lot of it in the course of being prepared at The Barn. I used to knock around there a lot in '73, '74. Dennis Scott is a man who appreciates this, that his work has comic depths to it. You know, for instance, there's this play of his called *School's Out* [premiered Jamaica 1975]. Now, it's set entirely, as I remember it, in a staffroom where the teachers are – only one schoolboy appears, but you get a total portrait of the school from these teachers sitting there in the staffroom. At least, I came away with the feeling that if the teachers were like that, then why blame the children. It is a deep play. But like many good playwrights and many playwrights greater than Trevor Rhone, he is all things to all levels of understanding. He can meet you at the simple dialect level – kya-kya-kya – and if you bring more to it than that, he can meet you there too. This is what I like about Rhone, he has depths.

Q: Dennis Scott.

SH: Dennis Scott is a more intellectual, symbolic playwright. Clever, a poetry of the head, but I think as Dennis gets older – this is a guess – the genuine poetry, the right-side-of-the-brain poetry, which is certainly there in Dennis, is going to come out more and more. And the very great structural cleverness will play less of a part. I think there's a real poet inside there and we know that from his poetry, still very cerebral, very intellectual, very controlled. I think he will develop into a very important playwright.

Q: Carmen Tipling.

SH: Again, I only saw one play of hers and I remember it only vaguely. I wouldn't care to offer comment.

Q: Have you ever seen anything by Alwin Bully?

SH: No. Alwin Bully is somebody I knew, have met in Trinidad and so forth, when we were all at this thing together. A nice boy. I've not seen any of his work at all.

Q: Stafford Harrison.

SH: I've not seen any of his written work.

Q: Errol Hill.

SH: Errol Hill told us all at the time, when we ought to have been told, that we should be looking at the West Indies and you should get your material from there. He was the High Priest of West Indian drama in those days, and he taught all of us, he taught a whole generation of us to look at the West Indian scene, to write in dialect, to use the dialect. He taught us this. He taught us that it is nothing to be ashamed of. His own plays, I find, are well made in the 19th century sense; I find them almost artificially well made, you know, things like *The Ping Pong* [premiered 1953] and, the great one, *Man Better Man* [premiered 1957]. They're well made and they have a slight feeling to them, but that maybe hindsight speaking. In these days when we first met *The Ping Pong* and plays like that, they struck us as not artificial but how true; because he was talking about something that was real and alive all around us. I find looking back at *Man Better Man*, which was somewhat prettified for Yale, he took it to Yale and they liked it up there, and rewrote it in verse, the original version was in prose. The original version I think was better than the versified version. But when I read *Man Better Man* today, the view of Caribbean life that he gives is picture-postcard; it's flat, it's like a cartoon, it's not got any depth. But certainly, he taught a lot of us the rudiments of theatre and he has immense importance as the man who did that. All of us learnt under him. All of us have quarrelled with him or disagreed with him – when I say all of us, I mean people from Derek and myself down. So he has that importance as somebody who taught us in the beginning and with whom we have grown to disagree and who has moved away, too. He lives in New Hampshire now, I believe, and he's making a living, nobody can fault him for this. His plays have a nice sort of sparkle, but they lack the depth that has since come out of the works of richer imaginations. But certainly, Errol Hill was the man who told us many years ago, at the beginning of the 1950s, that this is the direction we should be looking.

Q: Derek Walcott.

SH: Walcott's plays – and here again I do not know plays like *O Babylon!* [premiered 1976] – I don't know anything that he has written since – since I got ill, about the past six years. But he took the West Indian thing a stage further, he tried to marry the stage and verse, the stage and poetry in the way that the early Irish theatre writers did – John Synge. And he is our Shakespeare in the sense that if you want to be tested in all your technical apparatus as a speaker of verse, as a man articulating complex and subtle emotions, then he's the playwright... he's the one who tests you most, he's the one that has tried the most, tried the deepest things, the hardest things, not always with success. He is the most artistically ambitious of the playwrights and the work of his that I've worked with, that I've worked with as an actor, is to me very enriching. Very enriching. We had our differences and we did indeed part company in the early 1970s – that due more to administrative than artistic reasons. And of course, I must say that at the time when this happened, I myself was getting sick and did not know that I was very ill. I don't know how much that contributed to our parting, but it was over the way in which the heroic job he was doing in running the Workshop – to my view at the time – couldn't handle it properly, but he was doing it, and I was irritable with my own illness and I just couldn't take it anymore and I left.

But that doesn't in any way alter my respect for what he tries to do, what he's been doing. He has always insisted on self-respect, on the artist's respect for himself and respect for his craft and giving of his best, and he's always hated shoddy work and God knows many of us need to be told that. He's a very fine – apart from being our Shakespeare, as I said – by which I mean the man who will test the actor and the audience the most. He's also a very gifted teacher of actors – I distinguish that from director. Because he's a writer he can give you nuances of emotion and of gesture that he is seeing in his mind as he composes the verse. He's a good teacher of actors – providing he has good actors who can give him back something, who can discipline, who can give him something to run against.

But his plays – I think, for instance, *Dream on Monkey Mountain* is a magnificent attempt that worries me in some respects. To me it is a great flawed work, and in spite of its flaws it may still be the greatest play we have in the English-speaking Caribbean. Some of the things that bothered me – because I played Lestrade for a run inside there, and I also played Lestrade in the film version – sometimes I'm in doubt as to who is the hero, Makak or Lestrade, and I want to think it's Lestrade, you know. A lot of the things that bothered Lestrade bothered Walcott personally – that's not really a complaint. One of the things that has never been clear to me is that at the end of the play Makak goes back up into the mountain, but one is not sure his dilemma has not been solved, one is not sure that he's now going to get another brainstorm. Nothing has happened in the course of his dream to change what it was that went wrong in the first place, that caused him to go mad. Nothing has changed. He has decided to accept his home up in the hill. But he was there before and he may get another storm. I think the symbol of the white witch to the moon – the white goddess – is a little blurred; it is the white goddess who tells Makak to go back to Africa. I'm not sure what that means. I'm not sure I understand. At the end the white witch is the one who must be beheaded in order that Makak may claim his own blackness. I'm not sure that they're the same woman – that the one who told him to go back to Africa is the one who must be beheaded. I'm not sure I understand it – the symbol. But it's a strong play, it's a beautiful part for Makak, for Mustique, for the Corporal, some wonderful acting parts. Then, too, you know, it has so many comments about the colonial situation. You get a little character like – what is his name? – Pamphilion, that ass. I remember him played by Claude Reid, in his bush jacket, the perfect colonial ass, the inspector with his accent and his postures and so forth, just a slave of the expatriate administration. You know, that is something that Walcott uses very well.

I retain a profound affection for some of his shorter plays, particularly *Malcauchon* [premiered 1959] and *The Sea at Dauphin* [premiered 1954]– they're nice little plays. *Malcauchon*, which of course – Derek is so eclectic, you know, he's widely read, he reads everything, because as I said, he sees himself as a human being, not as a limited Caribbean man – has memories of the Japanese film *Rashomon* [Dir. Akira Kurosawa, 1950] where a truth is seen from several angles. It's a very complex thing. It's a director's delight. I tried it once as a director. Just didn't know enough then – I'd like to try it again if I could, but of course, I can't. *Malcauchon* I like very much. I like it nearly as much as *Dream*.

Q: How do you see him compared to his other half, Roddy?

SH: Roddy wrote some very playable short plays in the early days, we were all very excited by them. *A Flight of Sparrows* [premiered 1958], *Benjy* [*The Harrowing of Benjy*, premiered 1956], very playable. Roddy is different. Of course he has done a lot of work which I do not know. Roddy wanted to work very close to the St. Lucian mythology, and it's very rich for such a small place, the figures of myth and folklore. Some of this is in Derek also, but I think Roddy wanted to narrow it down a bit more. He doesn't have his brother's language, his own language gets a bit dense and a bit unnecessarily complex; sometimes, for instance, in *Malfinis* [premiered 1960] it gets a little unnecessarily unclear.

Q: People are always curious about how writers conceive and produce a piece of work. What is your approach on conceiving an idea and your actual execution of the work – whether a play or a poem?

SH: Well, they're conceived differently. And then, with the poem it might well depend on its length. As a writer, I don't know too much about long poems, having written but one long poem, and that's so long ago I can't remember. But a short poem comes as an emotion associated with a phrase. The phrase maybe – Robert Graves said this once, I think – the first line and a half of the poem comes just like that; sometimes it's like that, sometimes it may be a phrase in the middle of the poem. But to me it's always an emotion associated with a form of words. How it does *not* come is an argument that I want to deliver to somebody or a point that I wish to make. It *never* comes like that. And poems that read like that are nonpoems and there're a whole heap of them. You know, poems that wish to prove something about blackness or whiteness or colonialism or Marxism or something like that. Poems that come as ideas are nonpoems from the word go and can never go anywhere. To me, a poem comes from a strong feeling associated with words, a rhythm, a turn of phrase, a sentence, a line, an image – they must go together. If you have the emotion but not the words – no go. If you have the words without the emotion – no go.

A play, now, comes as the resolution of a fragment of a story, a problem, so that you might say: I wonder what would happen if so and so and so and so got into conflict, how'd they work it out? You see from above the conflict down to the end, and then you have to build up the beginning so as to bring them to that point. I haven't written a play for a long time, but that is how a play comes, I think, as a dilemma that can be enunciated as a plot, a problem, moving towards a clash and a conclusion. So and so versus so and so.

Q: In other words, you figure how you would resolve the conflict.

SH: Um-hm. In other words, you see people, not ideas and not phrases. You see people. People in conflict.

Q: Earlier you mentioned something about Naipaul. I remember Derek Walcott saying that it's unfortunate that Naipaul, being such a great writer, is so cynical and his own cynicism is destroying his art, but he has written within the context of his own cynicism and that is what has made him a great writer. What is your feeling?

SH: I have to take him – I can't go on a Naipaul binge and read three or four books one after the other because the point of view is too depressing; he has too many truthful bad things to say about colonial man and I will get depressed. So I can't read three Naipaul books one after the other. I can read one of them and enjoy his criticisms of us. He's such a beautiful writer that it is a pity, but there's a hollow yearning inside there for something that he can believe in and that he could attach himself to; he is a lost man; he is a citizen of no country; he is a human being, but he is lost, depressed and depressing. And great within this, great because of his honesty, because he makes us admit the truth of these things. But to me, his vision of what is negative and bad about colonial man is so obsessive that I think he's going to shut up long before he should.

There is very little about colonial man that he can see as redeeming, and maybe he should try a little bit more to find *something* without being untrue to the facts, because I believe that there is some light. A lot of what he says is true but he's obsessed with the whole negative part, and I think that way madness lies. What I admire about him is being able to perceive without any illusions whatsoever.

I fear, however, that the persona that appears all the time, the "I" figure, always *feels* like the same person: The "I" who tells the story in *A Bend In The River* [1979], is the same "I" in all the other books. He has one character: himself. He has this one character which he develops very deeply and very beautifully, but you don't get that Shakespearean richness of many characters, equally strong. He's got that one obsessive "I", the person at the centre of all of his books, this lost colonial, lost and bitterly truthful colonial. That is both his richness and his limitation. I cannot remember any of his other characters since he stopped writing short stories.

I think his writing life breaks into two – somewhere after *Biswas* [*A House for Mr Biswas*, 1961]. The books before *Biswas* are not to be underrated; there are some beautiful stories where what I'm saying now does not apply. There's a story like "B. Wordsworth" [in *Miguel Street* (1959)], which I think is one of the most beautiful stories ever written. Wordsworth, there, is a character. But somewhere after *Biswas* something happened. I think it's like he fell down a precipice; he was always on a ledge, but he went down – *Mimic Men* [1967]. I think somewhere around there he went down. You know, I saw him on TV the other night talking to –

Q: On Dick Cavett.

SH: Dick Cavett. And he's funny and he's bright and he's light; I don't get that when I read the books – there's this deep, angry sorrow, an angry despair. Well, I heard him say – Dick Cavett was asking him "what will have made it possible for these societies not to have turned out that way?" And he said: "The development of intellectual life, perhaps." I would like him to follow that premise, I would like him to imagine. You see, maybe he sticks too close to reality, to truth. I would like him to imagine a corner of Caribbean society or colonial society in which that development of intellectual life happens, because there *are* corners where it has happened – they may be small ones – but I would like to see him write *that* novel. A novel in which there are some colonials as bright as he but not as negative; colonials who find the intellectual wherewithal to pursue all of the roads that make man civilized. I would like to see him write that novel. Even as a fantasy. Even as a fantasy.

Q: Well, they claim him to be one of the best writers in the English language.

SH: He is. He can stay negative for the most part, but just a little ray; just a little ray. You see, to me, in a story like "B. Wordsworth", the beauty behind the ridiculousness of Wordsworth, *lifts* the story above the level of being just a put-down of a poor, ignorant son-of-a-bitch with pretensions; he's got a little glow about him that makes him a poetic figure. I would like to see him do that again in a big book, a longer book, something that has that poetic glue. He didn't have that despair in the earlier days – you could see that he was always laughing at us. *Biswas* is not a depressing book; *Biswas* has two characters who make a heroic struggle; they fail, but you admire the struggle. But colonial man, Third World man, as he appears in the second half of Naipaul's life, doesn't have the equipment to make an heroic struggle; he's just too crass and stupid, and this is depressing. Now, the humour is gone, the poetry is gone. At the same time, to me, Naipaul is a great writer. He tells me things about myself that I praise his honesty for. As a colonial, he tells me things about myself. I'm happy that somebody tells me.

End Notes

1. Bruce St John (1923-1995) was a poet and playwright who, in the 1970s and early '80s, pioneered the serious treatment of the Barbadian nation-language voice in ep recordings such as *Foetus Pains*, and publications such as *Joyce, Eros and Varia* (1976) and *Bumbatuk 1: Poems in Barbadian Dialect* (1982).
2. Ralph Campbell was a Trinidadian actor and playwright, a founding member of Derek Walcott's Trinidad Theatre Workshop. He studied acting at New York University and later formed a company to do West Indian theatre in New York. He is the author of *The Death of a Crow* (1971) and *Caribana Jab Jab* (1986)
3. Daniel Caudeiron: See Alwin Bully interview note 3.
4. Hector Bunyan a Guyanese playwright, no details found.
5. Carroll Dawes (1932-) was a Jamaican theatre director and actress, working from the late 1950s, directing both classic drama and the revived Jamaican pantomime with Louise Bennett. She was head of the Jamaican School of Drama. In the 1970s she taught in Nigeria. She was the first wife of the novelist and poet Neville Dawes.
6. Rawle Gibbons (1950-) is a Trinidadian dramatist, director and theorist of Caribbean theatre. His plays include *Shepherd* (1981), *I Lawah* (1986), *Sing de Chorus* (1990), *Ah Wanna Fall* (1992) and *Ten To One* (1999). The last three are published as *A Calypso Trilogy* (Tunapuna, Canboulay Productions, 1999). He is currently Director of the Creative Arts Centre, UWI St Augustine.
7. David Carty: Anguillan writer and local historian. See http://

mtmkobbe.blogspot.co.uk/2009/12/david-carty-jack-of-many-trades.html#!/2009/12/david-carty-jack-of-many-trades.html

8. Oliver Samuels (1948-) is a Jamaican comedian and actor who began performing at the Barn Theatre in the 1970s and is associated with the plays of Trevor Rhone. Samuels starred in the film of *Smile Orange* (1974) and the very popular JBC series *Oliver at Large*.
9. Carl Bradshaw is a popular Jamaican theatre, film and television actor (and former Olympic athlete) most famous for performances in *The Harder They Come*, *Smile Orange*, *Countryman*, *The Lunatic* and *Klash*.
10. Hopkinson alludes to the fact that James Baldwin had come in for criticism for not being sufficiently Black Power oriented, though a good deal of the criticism was deeply homophobic – see Eldridge Cleaver *Soul on Ice* (1968)

ERROL JOHN
(1924-1988)

Errol John was born in in Port-of-Spain, Trinidad and attended the Tranquillity Government School. After leaving school, he initially pursued a career as an artist and journalist, and also followed his desire to act, founding the Whitehall Players acting troupe along with Errol Hill and Errol Jones. Then, at the age of twenty-five, like so many writers of his generation, he went to England.

He began making small appearances in television and film, including *The Heart of the Matter* (1953), *The Emperor Jones* (BBC, 1953) and *Simba* (1955). He then landed the starring role in the *BBC*'s *A Man from the Sun* (1956), which was followed by larger roles in *No Hiding Place* (BBC, 1961) and *Rainbow City* (BBC, 1967), a five-part series written for him by John Elliot. But despite such efforts, John was able to find only small acting roles in such films as *Assault on a Queen* (US, 1966), with Frank Sinatra and Harry Belafonte and Sidney Poitier's *Buck and the Preacher* (US, 1971), which also starred Belafonte.

His first play, *The Gateway* was performed in 1947, followed by *The Tout* (1949). His most famous play, *Moon on a Rainbow Shawl,* about a young man's struggle to leave a Port-of-Spain slum, won the *Observer* Play of the Year in 1957. The play was widely performed in Britain and elsewhere throughout the world, most recently being revived in London at the Cottesloe in 2012. It has probably never been out of print and is widely studied in Caribbean schools. Other scripts for plays include *Easter and I'll Come for You* and *How the Tomorrow*, a fantasy in one act.

He wrote a series of film scripts *Force Majeure*, *The Dispossessed and Hasta Luego: Three Screenplays* (London: Faber, 1967), which were never produced, but in 1969 his *The Exiles* was part of the *BBC*'s *Wednesday Play* series.

He died in Camden, North London in 1988. He was posthumously awarded the Trinidad & Tobago Chaconia Medal Silver for Drama in the year he died.

ERROL JOHN

September, 1977, Chelsea Hotel, New York

Q: So, we're talking about theatre in Trinidad.

ERROL JOHN: We better because I'm gonna have to confine myself to that particular area. And the thing is there is also an enormous gap because I have not really lived in Trinidad for almost six years, you see. As a matter of fact, I'm now engaged in doing an article for a magazine in Trinidad, called "On Looking Back" that's looking back over my – call it – career – how things developed… abroad. Because '51, when I went away, it was not my ambition to be an actor or a writer, although I can function in *drama* – I call it that, the amateur drama in Trinidad – as an actor though, eventually, we were told by what one would call progressive, liberal, British, well-meaning people, that what we were doing was not good enough – and this was the premier group in Trinidad amateur drama, called the Whitehall Players… (*Laughs*). The Whitehall Players, that was the name we chose, and it's significant not because of the word white – but because this is where we had a place – where the Prime Minister's official building is now – it's significant in that way. And this is where the group was formed and it came about because of the activity of the expatriate British dramatic companies that performed in the country itself.

And so when we thought that we wanted to form this company we naturally had some admiration for the work these people were doing and we sought their assistance. It was harmonious – that's right – harmonious for this sort of condition. And we began by studying the plays that were available and the plays in those days they came from London, mainly. Of course there was Shakespeare…

Q: What period is this that you're talking about?

EJ: This is the '40s, late '40s. And there was Shakespeare, which, naturally, most of us had studied in school, all that, and being part of the British Commonwealth or whatever it was called in those days… This then became our function as students studying… And finally we decided that after a period of exercises – voice, music and so on – that it was necessary to do – that we would do public presentations.

Q: Did you have workshop situations?

EJ: No – those words didn't come into being… (*Laughs*) at that time…

Q: That's why I said *situations*.

EJ: (*Still amused*) Yeah you know, those words, I mean, didn't come into being till recent – later American relationships and so on, and even drifted over to England, but certainly it didn't exist in those days. We presented a play by A.A. Milne called – you must forgive me, there are things I'm not going to remember at all – *Bird in Hand* was the name of this play [the author of the play was John Drinkwater, written in 1927], at this first show of ours, and it was directed by this Joan Kirby, who had been an actress in England and the daughter of a very famous actress in the British theatre... and she directed this show – the kudos was *quite* fantastic... it was a happy event. But as I think about it now, this woman – wonderful, wonderful woman – died right after, so we were immediately left adrift. And so there was another woman who had been brought in by Mrs. Kirby, a woman called Mrs. Wilson, who was quite an ancient lady, but she had also come out of the British theatre, had been a Shakespearean actress, she was very grand, and again, here we are part of the British Empire, and so naturally the emphasis was on language – which is as it should be in any kind of theatre – and the kind of thing that happened here earlier – I mean in America, here – among the early American theatre schools, the way people were taught to speak. So much so that eventually when Hollywood went into sound, a lot of actors couldn't function because they could not speak; it was only the actors from the stage who had these trained voices and these voices were nearly always close to being English.

But we have a confusion here because we're talking about a little island, at that time with less than a million people, and we're talking about local dramatic societies. We mentioned Hollywood, we mentioned dramatic speech and all this, but that is an absolutely *professional* area. Ours was amateur – call it entertainment – and maybe a few of us did fancy ourselves. I don't know. But certainly the play, the presentation was a huge success. We were left with Mrs. Wilson and Shakespearean classes and after that, I think, there was another young lady at the time in Trinidad, June Grimble, and she was an academic of some kind, I don't recall, but her father was a very British commissioner of something in the Philippines and the whole Hawaiian islands. He wrote some very important books on the people of those Pacific islands and all that. [Arthur Grimble, *A Pattern of Islands*, 1952] And she, I think, was teaching at one of the convents in Trinidad, and she took over the classes we used to attend once or twice a week. And it was during this period, I think, that this group, which included Errol Hill, who's at Dartmouth now, chairman of the drama department, one or two other people and myself – I mean, I only mention names that might really mean something. Well, Errol *is* one of the important people involved... There's another person, also, I should mention: Mr. Cecil Gray,[1] who is now the university in Jamaica, he teaches English literature or something like that.

And it was with June Grimble that we began rehearsing another play... not rehearsals really, but just – I don't want to use the word "workshop" because it hadn't come into being. But we attended these afternoon classes and we used to perform scenes from a play called – again, it was another West-end hit – *Distinguished Gathering* [James Parish, 1936] and, as plays go, it was a beautiful, dramatic sort of piece. I could even remember one speech, the character that I was mainly involved with who eventually dies... does the big thing by taking off in an airplane and killing himself. He had done something earlier on in his life that had hurt his sister, so all along he had been having "walking ghosts", as he said, because he had more or less killed his sister. This kind of part was very useful for dramatic purposes and so on. And of course there were characters like Sir So and So and Lady This and Lady That – that kind of society. So really it was if one looks back at it – penguins or monkeys in dress... (*Laughs*). Although we didn't think about it in that way, because one of the marvellous things that comes out of the Caribbean – *long* before we knew other pressures – and I'm talking about Trinidad now – it's from a time when one was quite small or in one's teens, one went to the cinema, and the people *looked* at the characters on the screen and they identified with the condition. We're not necessarily talking about the great dramas... but the films, in the period of John Garfield, like *Dust Be My Destiny*, and maybe John Steinbeck's *Grapes of Wrath*. They could identify with the *whole* world, whether they be Japanese, Chinese or otherwise – with the myth of the Western – the cowboy walking down the main street. As a *male*, one identified with these characters and I think there was also a tremendous – a *curious* – I shouldn't say curious, because that makes it sound pretentious in a way – but there was a way of *appreciating* performances on the screen. But down there in the pit you had guys, man, who would, when certain things happened on the screen, throw their hats in the air. When an actor did something they'd throw their hats because they appreciated what was done. So it would seem to me that always there was this appreciation, this *undercurrent* that developed to a certain extent and it *should* have gone much, much further in the period that I'm talking about – when we were performing – in terms of the appreciation that one remembers from people in the cinema, *reacting* to performances by some of the great performers of the screen in those days.

But after the period of Kirby and June Grimble and the distinguished gathering, we had a meeting to decide when we were going to stage a play – I mean, after all these classes, otherwise what's the point? You need an audience, so you present your work to the local audience – what? Three hundred people, two hundred people or five hundred people. These are the people you'd be presenting your work to. At this meeting there was a split in the decision about presenting this particular play – I can't remember the reasons why – but eventually the whole thing was thrown out, the idea of presenting it was thrown out. I remember one time it may have been *before* we arrived at this decision, that I was talking to June Grimble after one of the afternoon sessions, and she said, "You know, you all are not really doing anything presenting these London successes; I think that you should make some attempt to present your own plays." Now June Grimble was not the only person, I think, that would have made this remark; other people had probably said this as well, but anyhow, because of the decision made against a presentation by our "distinguished gathering", it was decided that we would write some plays, and Errol Hill wrote a play – I hope I have the sequence right – called *Square Peg* [First performed 1949] and I wrote a play called *How Then Tomorrow* [A Fantasy in One Act, 1947]. Omar Khayam was rather popular in those days, and out of this Omar Khayam sort of quatrain I titled this play of mine. And we presented these two plays and *bridged* them with the love scene from *Romeo and Juliet*, in which I played Romeo and a young lady called Barbara Assoon[2] played Juliet. This was our first performance – public performance, I mean, performed in schools. And the plays went down very well. I don't know whether I mentioned the title of the programme, it was called "Beyond the Veil". That too was a quote from something.

Anyhow, we presented these three plays and the reaction was so good that we began to think in terms of presenting local drama. And we followed that up with a presentation of three other short plays, one of them was *The Tout*, [Errol John, first performed 1949] which you mentioned earlier; soon after that Errol [Hill] left to go to England on a British Council scholarship to study at The Royal Academy of Dramatic Art. By that time I had begun to have some personal feeling about what theatre required – I mean, as a learning process. And I felt that in this learning process one had to find plays that had some form of identity; it didn't matter where the play came from. I'd been doing a lot of reading, as we do when we're in these backwoods, and the sort of thing that surprises people who come from abroad, and you can talk *as if* you have *been* abroad. I think there was a period when I *was* abroad when I knew *less* of the theatre, practical things about the theatre, and what was going on in the theatre, than I knew in the years before, when all one did was go to the library and pick a book and sit down. And I found this curious identity with American drama – it was a political period – the play called *Waiting for Lefty* [Clifford Odets, 1935] was really almost the beginning of a sort of total dramatic identification with the working classes in this country that included Kazan's *On the Waterfront. [1954]*

I had been reading Eugene O'Neill for a *long* time, I mean, even before I was in any way connected with actually performing in the theatre – other than just looking at shows, going to shows and so on. I used to read a lot drama and Eugene O'Neill's one of my favourite playwrights. I felt that some these dramas were so masterful. I've read reviews, recently, knocking him, *Anna Christie* [1921] and so on, but there were things that I loved about *Anna Christie*, because though I hadn't *been* in this part of the world there were certain things that seemed to *touch* me so closely. And then he had a series of one act plays published called *Homeward Bound* [renamed as *The Long Voyage Home*, 1917] this is when he was a sailor, it was from the early period when he went off to find himself; he went on tramps around the world and then he wrote this series of plays that had to do with seamen. And the story that was played here on Broadway, I think it was called *The Hairy Ape* [1922] – a story about a man who worked in the engine room, he was a stoker. And these dramas really got to me. There were the stories by Clifford Odets, Elmer Rice and these people. One read these things and one felt not a personal identity but a dramatic identity, because there were people around me who were like these people.

And then in reading these dramas one found these effective pieces of – it was a kind of poetic theatre. There's a line like: "A bleeding underneath my shoe." This was language – and one came to Tennessee Williams and that was language, again, out of this world – I mean, something else.

But we were also still putting on British plays. We had a big success again, with a Priestley play – a kind of play about socialism called *An Inspector Calls* [J.B. Priestley, 1945]. That was the character that I was telling you about where I felt there was some curious kind of spiritual something in that performance and there were most extraordinary things said about it – I mean, my performance. I'm being objective, because I didn't think of myself as an actor, you see. We were performing, we happened make a decision we would do *An Inspector Calls*. At that time we felt that this was a play that pointed out that people needed to love each other, needed to help each other, that if they didn't, the world would be just chaotic. And so this play was quite an important play – and Errol [Hill] was also in it, just before he went away; and we had some success with it.

It was then I began to feel that the workings of American drama – I had also been reading a great deal of academic works published on the American theatre, the *growth* of the American theatre – came closer to the island [i.e. Trinidad] than Britain with its theatre that goes way back, I mean, beyond Shakespeare to the priests performing the Bible plays [The Mystery Plays] because people couldn't read. American theatre was much closer to me. And a lot of what I was reading about was just community theatre and not really professional theatre, community and university theatre. I began to feel this strong pull towards the development – the *hope* for the development of a *Caribbean* theatre, not necessarily a Trinidad theatre, but a theatre in the *Caribbean* itself, the English-speaking Caribbean, the possibility of bridging the thousand miles between Trinidad and Jamaica – this is what I began to think about.

Because in this kind of research that I was doing, one found that the first true identification with America and the American theatre didn't come until the late 19th century, and I think in a production of one act plays. In one of our productions – I can't tell you which programme of one act plays we did – there were *two* local plays plus this one American play, which was directed by Cecil Gray. And this short play was, in terms of the dramatic theatre I'm talking about, one of the earliest plays that really established the American drama – this was before *Lefty*. So then I moved away from The Whitehall Players and formed a company of my own called – with my five closest friends – The Company of Five, and our first production was *The Glass Menagerie* [1944] by Tennessee Williams. After one has lived abroad and one has come across all this racism – and there is racism wherever one happens to be – when you *look* at the world in a certain kind of way, you don't see the division as relating to just the kinds of people that Williams is writing about – I mean, for him they were special: they were Southern people, or dispossessed people. You saw these people as being dispossessed, too – a son who left the family because he couldn't take what was going on. That's how you saw it and so you did the play for that reason – not only for that emotional reason but for its *technical* excellence. And you felt by staging these kinds of plays – having also written a couple – I mean, you were doing yourself a kind of favour and developing within the limits that you had, your knowledge of the theatre, and your techniques – seeing, for instance, the working of the lights. I mean it's not like the lighting of Melzine or whatever his name was, Joel Melzine – he lit most of Tennessee Williams' plays, he was a great lighting man here, recently dead. Now, you didn't get this, but you got – you began to get the feeling of the sense of light in the presentation of a play. And therefore, also, in thinking in terms of writing, you began to think in terms of *areas* of lighting as you *wrote* your play. And if you had to take over a production as a director, *these* things help to give you the knowledge. Because [in Trinidad] you didn't have available to you a professional theatre like here, where you could leave the Bronx, or wherever you happen to be, and travel in from some back-route area and come to New York and sit down and really *see* some really high quality theatre – so this is how one began to develop.

As things grew and people reacted, and thought all sorts of marvellous things should happen, and even then, in those days – I'm talking about over a quarter of a century ago – people were talking about the *need* for a theatre. I suppose I had begun to move mentally in another direction and I remember writing an article saying, "We don't need a theatre, all you need, really, is four boards and a passion." And that is really true about the theatre; you can perform right outside of that street there. You can go on a corner and perform and present the most *marvellous* production. You don't *need* all the technicalities of the commercial theatre. I mean, this is part of the beauty of the theatre – the fact that one wants to create and create *out* of the community.

It was interesting, a couple of years ago when I came back to New York from Mexico, I read Joe Papp [American theatre producer (1921-1991) who premiered several important African American plays] writing that theatre should not be a social affair. And I'm sure what he meant by that is, in those days and even the days we're talking about in Trinidad, for dramatic presentations, you *had* to be dressed up, you put on your Sunday best even to go to see an amateur performance that may run two or three nights. Now that is theatre at a level in which you are leaving out too much of your population, which is where, in another sense, the *power* of the theatre is, you see. So, again, as I say, for me the plays of O'Neill, very many of them, were very personal plays; the plays of Williams dealt with the *kind* of people, as in *A Streetcar Named Desire* [1947], amongst whom one could recognize a lot one knew. So *despite* one's British background, there was this – again, for me – curious sort of *equation* with American drama. I don't think that it could have come from films – or *that much* from films – but you can never really peg these things down. I remember talking to my brother the other day, and it was the first time it occurred to me that my father must have been a theatre buff. He'd been to England – he was an international cricketer [George John, (1883-1944), whom C.L.R. James writes about in *Beyond a Boundary*] – and I remember there was a framed photograph on the wall of Tallulah Bankhead in the green hat. Not so long ago I was reading something about Tallulah Bankhead, about her life story, and how she stormed England with the green hat – one of her performances was as this character in the green hat – and there she was on our wall. I also remember the times when he'd come back and talk about that he'd seen. I remember there was a picture called *The Prime Minister* [1941], with John Gielgud as the young Disraeli, and my old man was in raptures about the speech and the manner of the man in the film.

My first Shakespearean experience, one that I could remember vividly (of course in our school primers there were scenes from Shakespeare – and these were things that one had sometimes to learn by heart) my first experience of professional theatre – was in the days when they used to have travelling companies come down through the Caribbean. I don't know whether they went to Kingston, but they certainly came all the way down to Port of Spain and performed at the Prince's Theatre, and the first was *As You Like It*, with this professional English travelling company. They still do it, but I think now they only got to the Bahamas. They don't go to the islands anymore.

I can't say whether this was a spark that had anything to do with my interest in the theatre, except that there was a period, before The Whitehall Players, which is very, very important in the development of what happened. These were all schoolboy things. There was a schoolmaster down there called Roberts who wrote several satiric and other kinds of dramatic pieces for his Nelson Street School Boys, and these performances used to be done sometimes not only in schools but later on in large theatres, seating nearly 1500 people or more, and I can tell you, you couldn't get in. School boys performing these shows and you couldn't get in. The laughter was fantastic. And it was out of this group that Cecil Gray came – he was one their leading actors, and as a youth, he, if I remember correctly, played a number of female roles because he was slim and, I suppose, the quality of his voice and so on. This would have been, I suppose, just before the war. And there were other people like C.L.R. James, who a long time before had been writing plays for dramatic presentation [*Toussaint L'Ouverture*, performed London, 1936]. But most of the titles escape me at the moment [It appears James planned a second play about Harriet Tubman but abandoned it]. And there was – he probably belonged to the same period as C.L.R. James – Alfie Mendes.[3] It was all mainly – I would think the poetry was all mainly in the British tradition, but not the theatre, not the plays, *certainly* not the things that C.L.R. James wrote. He also wrote a novel that's come down through time, one of the earliest Caribbean novels called *Minty Alley* [1936].

All along that period there were people who tried to establish some kind of dramatic presence. The need to perform is there because I think the acting potential [in Trinidad] *is* extraordinary – I think so. I *believe* that some of these people would have done well in a professional theatre if such a theatre had begun to function…

There's something in people everywhere, I think, even in small communities where they don't have a physical theatre – well, theatre is a repetition of dance, a presentation of a festival of some kind – it doesn't necessarily have to be written drama in the sense that we're talking about. And I have a feeling, having been away from the country for all this time, that the country should have established a deeper kind of theatre, because there's an *extraordinary* amount of drama. I mean, turn left, right, anywhere, on any street corner there's an *extraordinary* amount of drama. Some people think that you need to write political dramas to have a theatre; this is not absolutely necessary, this is not the only kind of theatre that one would want one to have. And in these troubled times, if you did attempt to write that kind of drama, it is likely that your action would be suppressed because of fear of revolution in our country. It is very possible that it might offend someone and you would not get support…

I feel that an enormous contribution has been made by the dramatic societies that do exist – a lot has taken place. And while I have certain personal objectives, so far as theatre is concerned I feel almost like a mental cripple – except I remember one time being asked by one of the fellowship foundations here – who were apparently prepared to give me some kind of money – what was I prepared to do so far as Trinidad theatre is concerned? I said: "From where I stand, whatever contribution that I make and however I make it… it's an attachment that comes out of there [Trinidad] and it goes back there." Well, I believe my contribution had already been made – I mean, locally, if you know what I mean – although when I went away first, my intention was only to stay away for two or three years and study as much as possible of the theatre.

This means community theatre as they called it in England at that time. And then to go back and try to function in that way. Because I remember the first day when I stepped off the boat in Southampton, I had been invited by the British Council to England for a period during the Festival of Britain for some three months to see some of the theatre there, but the invitation was extended *if* I could pay my way. I'm glad of these things because it means that if you pay your way, you make your way as an individual. I remember getting off the boat there, and for some reason – these things are arranged – some reporter came and started talking to me and asking me questions about this and that. And one of the questions that came up was about playing Othello and I said: "You know, that was never in my mind." I had no thought of that kind, of doing that kind of thing at all. There were two reasons for that. What one read and what one felt and what one knew in one's ignorance at that time was that everyone imagined Othello to be physically a *huge* black man – which may not have been Shakespeare's image. Certainly an actor of any kind, I mean particularly a black actor could fulfil the role of Othello if you have the talent, if the talent is developed enough to perform it. Indeed, one has seen small men with great talent on a stage look as huge, and huger than the tallest man on the stage because of that presence and his capabilities. Why I'm telling you this is because it was never in my mind in the beginning to make that kind of professional theatre. But two things happened; one was that I decided that I would stay in England with the hope that, apart from the tour of community theatres, my attachment to a small theatre company, studying backstage and helping around, with no salary – that was the only way they would engage me – pushing handcarts with all the scenery through the streets and all that kind of thing, I mean, doing the real dirty work so far as the theatre was concerned – would come to something. This was in order to fulfil my knowledge and work with directors who were really outstanding. Peter Cokes ran that theatre, he had a great standing with the British theatre at that particular time. So, one was really into something effective.

Then, while I was there I had this extraordinary opportunity when the telephone rang inviting me to do a BBC Saturday programme, called "Calling the West Indies" or something…

Q: Was it "Caribbean Voices"?

EJ: I can't remember. It was either "Calling the West Indies" or "Caribbean Voices" [Launched in 1939 as *Calling the West Indies*, it became *Caribbean Voices* in 1943]. But that was a Saturday programme or maybe it went out on a Sunday night, I don't remember. I used to do this programme – this is coming to me… it's like memory really playing tricks… and just coming back as we talk. Why I'm telling you about it is because it had to do with my first appearance on television. Working these Saturdays, while at the Kensington theatre we did Walcott's [*Henri Christophe*] – this is 1951 [actually 1952 at Hans Crescent]. I didn't know Derek at that time, I don't even think I knew anything about his poetry or anything. But Errol Hill, I think, knew him; and we did *Henri Christophe* [*A Chronicle in Seven Scenes*] which Errol directed. It was Lloyd Reckord from Jamaica, who went off while he was playing Vastey or whatever the character's name – Lloyd then went off to the Bristol Old Vic Theatre school so he had to give up his part while we were rehearsing. Errol took over Vastey and also directed the production. I played Christophe.

As I said, I did not go with the intention of wanting to be an actor, but mentally and physically there was something *driving* this inner thing. And this is something Errol Hill will support. And that's why I was keen on reading all the historical things that one could read about all the great actors like Kean and Barrymore and Wolfit – Laurence Olivier was not the great actor then – I'm talking about Henry Irving and all these characters.

I played Christophe and this is a part where the performance brought me to the attention of the professional people who had come to see the play, mainly from the BBC, who had come through Errol's invitation. And one of the good things that came out of that was that I got a booking to perform on BBC, again with Errol Hill. This was radio, "World Theatre" radio, directed by R.D. Smith, [Eugene O'Neill's] *The Emperor Jones*. Now, I didn't play Emperor Jones; Gordon Heath, [1918-1991] the African American actor [and folk singer] who'd gone over to France in '51 or something like that [as a gay man to escape homophobia in the USA], went over and remained there the rest of his life; I think probably he had two short visits here to this country [the UK], played in Paris and played guitar – played guitar and sang. He was brought over from Paris to play Emperor Jones. And it was because of R.D. Smith having seen me in *Christophe* and he'd known Errol before, that I was given a *gift* of a part. My line in the play was: "Hey, man, what you hittin' me for?" And that was it. (*Slightly amused.*) "Hey, man, what you hittin' me for?" But you know what happened? That meant that from then on whenever I was booked as a professional actor and whenever the BBC wanted me on their Caribbean programme for the readings, I got two guineas more than the basic three guineas that everybody else got. (*Chuckles*) And it went beyond that.

This, again, came from a connection with the Caribbean service which at that time – believe me – was a very small service. A group of people who, when you got in, you were in – it was a very small, tight society. To get in you really had to fight. I was lucky because of this theatrical connection, okay, and I got to read short stories and stuff. Again, I had the advantage of being booked through drama and got more than the other people, depending on the length of the stories. What came out of this was that there were from time to time attempts to develop a theatrical community of black actors in London – but, again, you had no audience and the plays were few, if there were any at all, and the few parts went to a few people in film. But one day I was called to the telephone at the lodgings where I stayed, and somebody said to me: "You are wanted at the television station for an interview for a television serial that they're doing on Sunday afternoons; it's going to last three months," or something like this.

Now, the only thing I knew about television then was there's a place called Crystal Palace where they had the television station, and I was preparing to get on the tube and go to this interview, when for some reason I got on the telephone and called up to check where I should go for the interview – it was at Shepherd's Bush, in the opposite direction (*laughs*), not too far away from where I lived at Rose Court. So, I got to Shepherd's Bush, and there was Lloyd Reckord, there was Errol Hill and the few young people who had some connection with the theatre, and students and so on, all going in for interviews.

So, Lloyd went in, he had his interview and he came out, and then Errol went in and he had his interview, he came out – they had been to these things before, I never had – and both reported the same thing – that they'd said: "We'll let you know." And I go in and I talked with the man (Michael McClemmo was his name) and he asked me what my plans were. I told him what I'd been doing at the Knightsbridge theatre and that I was planning to go on to study theatre at one of the academies. We got to the end of the interview and he said, "All right, I will let you know." And I got up and I walked away. As I got to the door, he said, "One moment, where do you come from?" And I said, "Trinidad." "All right, come on, sit down. Let's settle this right away." He gave me the part. Now what coming from Trinidad had to do with acting as an African prince who had for some reason found himself in England working with a circus as just one of the hands, I don't know. But it gave me *three* months of television – which was my actual professional beginning as an actor in the theatre. I always say how extraordinary the theatre is – how chance plays its part; where sometimes the people who come out of the academies with the strongest recommendations are not the people who make it when eventually they go before the public. But here was this odd chance that gave me an opportunity to begin my theatrical career as an actor, as a professional actor. And it seemed that it never stopped, for quite a while, both on the stage as well as the odd part on television.

Q: This was when?

EJ: This was 1951. I got married in 1952. And this went on for – up until, I would say, 1956. Films, you know, the odd part in a film. In 1955 I went out to Kenya, played again – a "beautiful" part [The film was *Odongo* (1956)]. I was an African, and although he was written to be a fool, it was a challenge to an actor, if you were an actor. It was a challenge for an actor to play it the way the director wanted it played. As they say, film is the director's medium, but I really enjoyed playing it, really, really enjoyed it – as well as being in Kenya, having the opportunity to see Africa for the first time. It was a comic role but I didn't make it comic in the sense that I somehow managed to keep the guy in place. But it was also a very *dramatic* time to be in Kenya, because it was during the Mau Mau emergency. If you were a black, I tell you, and you walked across a street in Nairobi, somebody would run you over. And you saw all those guys walking around the place with two guns on their hips – revolvers on their hips – like some old cowboys in town and you really knew that they would put a bullet right through the middle of your forehead and have no problem at all. The hotel where I stayed, because I stayed there with the film company – it was in Nairobi – no African, no black African, no matter what his level, chief or chief's son, could have stayed at that hotel. He could have not gone into the dining room *at all* – unless he was invited as a guest by one of the Europeans. I don't *know* that I felt any identification. What I do know was that I sensed the need to be careful, because in any country that you go, whether the people be black, or whether the people be white, if they belong to that country they will take sides. Therefore one had to be very careful not to think that somebody, because he was black and you are black, was your brother and say what you really felt one way or the other. It was during that time when I went off to Kenya that I decided that I would not perform as an actor any more in any of the kind of roles that I had played. I felt that I had performed my apprenticeship as an actor and I needed to know a little more about the particular roles that my agents decided, or somebody decided, they wanted me for, before I accepted. I said to my wife – I was married about four years then – "This is going to make things a little rough, but for a time I am not going to accept acting roles at all." I had written *The Tout* and a couple of other things...

Q: When did you write *Moon*?

EJ: This was about the time that I wrote *Moon*. This is why I just jumped back a bit –

Q: This is during the mid fifties?

EJ: In the '50s, yeah. This is why I jumped back again in what I'm telling you. Sometime before that there was some kind of award being given – from the British Arts Council – to young writers if they presented their work, and they'd be given money for maybe a year to pursue their writing. I presented *The Tout,* something else and the reports of my work in the theatre, and I learned that I was on the short list for a grant, but then, eventually, I did not get the grant. This was maybe three years before the decision to hold back from acting roles. So I thought, well, you know something, I've been with a travelling American theatre company, for a year, first as general understudy, which means understudying *all* males roles and then finally playing, I think, three of the parts when the actors left. I moved up from playing the policeman, the sailor and then the brother. Lloyd Reckord replaced me when I left the company. As I said, going back to the business of writing, I'd decided that I had performed my apprenticeship in acting and that there was no function for me in the British theatre, even though I was a very *British-English*-spoken actor. To find that there was no room in the British theatre for somebody who *talked* like me... you understand? And the roles, again, were flat; whenever you had to play them it was just one single idea –

Q: One dimensional.

EJ: One dimensional, okay. So I thought, if I got on the short list among these writers who applied for this Arts Council Award, you know what I'm going to do? I'm going to stop this business of fooling around and I will now sit down and write a play. And this is how *Moon* came into being.

Q: What year was that?

EJ: That was 1955, it must have been – for the original draft of *Moon*, which I left with my agent when I went to Kenya. And why I'm telling you this around the African connection was that a cable arrived from my agents while we were on location way out in this place which I understand now is a thriving town – then it was just *grassland*. There was no other kind of life around there at all but us actors and the film company. Then the cable came saying the script had been read and they [The Royal Court] thought they could do something with it. Suddenly I began to get the attention of the commissioner of the area, who came asking me questions and so on. Where was I from? I said from the southern hemisphere. He said, "Yes, but where, exactly?" And then eventually, when I felt why press the situation, I said, "Trinidad." He asked me what I thought of Kenya. Well, what I did was describe the clouds and the mountains and the grass. (*Slight chuckle*) You know, I had no political views, but I believe it was there, seeing the treatment, and seeing the attitudes in that African country, that I began to turn over *inside* as a theatrical person. And finally, when *Moon* was performed, it comes out at the top of *The Observer* award. And this was twenty years ago – 1957. It doesn't seem as long ago as that because it was done here in New York with tremendous success in 1962. One of the interesting things about the *Observer* competition for new playwrights or new plays, was that the plays had to be entered under pseudonyms. The final judges were, I think, Peter Ustinov [an actor and dramatist], Peter Hall [one of the UK's most distinguished theatre directors], Alec Guinness [stage and screen actor] and two other people I can't remember – but these were all top people in the theatre then. They had several panels of readers to decide which plays should go forward to the final twenty-five, and then from the final twenty-five plays they picked the final five, of which a play marked *Moon On A Rainbow Shawl* came out on top. What, again, was a pain to me – I don't know if this is necessarily what it was – not necessarily a matter of colour, but *you* may be capable of doing something, but somebody will look at you and decide *you're* not the man for the job and go and get somebody else, and you'd probably be able to do a better job than the other guy, but the other guy gets it anyhow because of the way he looks. The *belief* was, I was told afterwards, that the play *fascinated* all the readers who had touched it until it came through. Diana Wynyard [1906-1964] – I'm talking about people who were long past, a beautiful actress, classical actress – and lots of people who'd read this play were so moved by it, but the belief was that the play had been written by an Englishman who had lived out in the Caribbean for a very long time and had a tremendous command of his own language and the descriptive passages and an ear for the speech. It was only after the decisions had been made and the envelope opened that the name of the author was found. (The pseudonym was Robert Lawson, my son's first and second name.) And here was this play coming out on top of this extraordinary collection of plays, and as a Caribbean person and as a black person, you found people, who certainly knew what the rules of the competition were, making the comment that naturally it had to be won by a black writer – they had to present it with their political bias as a setup – despite the quality of the judges and everything mentioned.

It was after this that I went to another African country, and this was the Congo – just before it blew. Here I was in Kenya and then I was in the Congo [For Zinneman's film, *The Nun's Story* (1959)], and here again is the image of people like myself in these European-conceived pictures, based on novels written by Europeans about black people, and we're going into these countries and playing the parts of Africans when there were Africans there who I'm sure were quite capable of representing themselves. It was an opportunity, okay, a career opportunity because it was one of the great directors, Fred Zinneman [1907-1997, maker of *High Noon* (1952)]. And there is the difference also, when you're making a professional picture, you're looking for professional actors. It was Zinneman and his producer Henry Blanke who were, apparently, so moved by my contribution to the picture [Errol John played the part of Illunga] that they recommended me for a big lead, feature lead in Hollywood right after *The Nun's Story*. *The Nun's Story*, of course, had been with Peter Finch and Audrey Hepburn and this other one was, again, with Peter Finch and also Angie Dickenson, famous later in *The Policewoman*, a beautiful young actress at the time. [The film was *The Sins of Rachel Cade* (1961), also set in the Congo, in which John played the part of Kulu.] But all the time what was happening was this: the actor in me felt somehow that there was a need to reach out to something bigger, something more substantial, yet here you were, here was a person in the eye of the public regarded as being a star, and being this and being that, but you yourself felt completely unfulfilled. But, again, this is not a thing limited to the black actor, it's limited to people in the artistic profession – in a *lot* of the professions. Sometimes no matter how much they appeal to people, they themselves feel unfulfilled. Like you look at some people, women and men, and you think them the most *astonishing* people you've ever seen – and they themselves don't know this. Probably keep looking in the mirror all the time and wondering who the beautiful thing is that people talk about, and they cannot see it. One arrives at this when you are in this kind of profession – what I'm talking about is a loss of identity. I'm no longer a Trinidadian, I'm no longer a Caribbean – I'm talking about what I'm presenting, what is coming out of myself, how one has, as a matter of fact, established some other kind of – it's not image – some kind of – well, you're like an invisible man really.

Because – if we come down now to talk about it – this is why I think the development of the Caribbean theatre is so important. Maybe as an individual one has got so much to do, but there're certain projects that I have in my mind. But hell, if the area can turn up people like Walcott and so on, there must be other young people coming along now that these countries are independent. And because, technically, people are learning so much faster now, the opportunities that are presented are so much greater than in our time, when what we did was imitate rather than create. So this is why I come down to the point that I feel there is a tremendous opportunity, a tremendous, tremendous opportunity in developing the Caribbean theatre. I'm talking now about the English-speaking Caribbean. What must happen, though, is that the people must learn to take a *professional* pride, no matter *what* their position is if they're interested in the development of the theatre. So that when a call is for seven-thirty in the evening, you're there at six, man. Sometimes, no matter how *good* somebody is and that person can't arrive on time, you have to say: "Out. We don't want you." There's always somebody to replace them, because we all die at some point. *Out* you go. What I'm saying is that the total *sense* of theatre must be within these people. And in a community like ours there are some people who are performing, who really should be in the audience. There are some people who should really think more about what their capabilities are, that maybe they can't ever be any more than a small part player. There're other disciplines for people in the theatre... particularly for somebody who has got that particular genius to be a director. All these things are special – as I said before to you – special *sciences*. I mean, Kazan [Elia Kazan (1909-2003) one time leftist, social realist theatre and film director] was an actor, he was a good actor but he eventually turned out to be an *extraordinary* director. So was George Roy Hill, [film director 1921-2002, credits include *Butch Cassidy and the Sundance Kid*] so were a lot of people in the theatre – in the professional theatre here.

And I feel that with the inner identification that we have now – and I say "we", though "we" is more or less in inverted commas because I'm also thinking of "them" – the inner thinking and picking up of dramatic possibilities in terms of the society, in terms of what occurs in the newspapers, that maybe a whole new form of theatre could be formed. This is not to think that anybody can sit down and write a play, because it is not true, but it can happen because of the nature of the people down there. I think Trinidad happens to be the most cosmopolitan of the islands – of the English-speaking islands. I don't know how to identify the blackness of the island, because most of those people, if they came to this country [the USA], they're all black. But down there you have a specific kind of black, and then you have another set, a *whole* regiment of colour and I don't know how that's going to get together, but what I'm saying is – here you've got a whole different set of people who all live there and you're *sure* to find among these people the new roots to push this theatre forward. I think apart from all this there're young people in schools now who are thinking quite differently from the sort of middle income – I don't want to call it class – middle income and upper income groups of people there. These young people are seeing the world quite, quite differently. I think the kind of theatre we're thinking about will come from them.

But in the meantime so much has happened. I mean the Jamaican theatre flies down to Trinidad for a performance there. The Trinidadian theatrical companies – you can almost call them semi-professional now – flying up to Jamaica, going to Antigua, going to Barbados, and all that. You have this exchange, you have this movement and that is *bound* to create a connection. Now we also have things like television, we've got film and such – though I feel that the making of films needs to be done in a different kind of way, because we can't afford to make them, and if we're going to make films, forget the glamour and the nonsense. I've been in Hollywood, I've been in Pinewood, I've been in Rome, you know what a hard world it is. And how difficult it is for the few, the handful who make it, because ninety-five per cent of the people in the profession don't make it. What we want to get together is film made on tape; you can get stories, you don't have to make a 90 minute film – we don't have to do that down there. We can make forty-five minute films. The Cuban film companies do that. You make a 45 minute film and most of their directors and the technical people who are trained – the Cuban film makers go way back – have been trained in Italy, so they come back full-fledged people.

And to speak of theatre, I'm not talking about being away for training for just a year, you don't learn about the theatre in a year, you take a *lifetime* to learn about the goddamned theatre and among theatrical people you take a lifetime to grow – ten, fifteen, twenty years. But we can do it. We can make films on tape and exchange films between the islands, and all the time the technicians are growing, your lighting is growing, your actors are growing. To mention one actor I will never forget – old man, from out of the Caribbean – you'll probably know his name – I can't remember – this guy was an Olympic prospect and he was in *Smile Orange*.

Q: Oh, Carl Bradshaw [Also lead parts in *The Harder They Come* (1972), *Countryman* (1982), *Third World Cop* (1999) and many others].

EJ: Yeah. Now, I'm telling you that guy is one *hell* of an actor. You hear me. Believe me, I can see that guy playing any part in the theatre, *any* part! – in the world theatre I'm talking about. And talking now about the development of the Caribbean theatre, we don't have to sit down and wait for $300,000 dollars to make a movie...

End Notes

1. Cecil Gray (1923-) is an important Trinidadian educationist, one of those responsible for getting Caribbean literature onto the curriculum of Anglophone Caribbean schools, for which he edited several important anthologies of Caribbean writing. He currently lives in Canada. His collection of poems, *The Woolgatherer* was published by Peepal Tree in 1994. He wrote one unperformed play, *Family Name* (nd).
2. Barbara Assoon. See Errol Hill interview, Note 17.
3. A.H. Mendes: See Errol Hill interview Note 12.

MUSTAPHA MATURA
(1939-)

Matura was born in Belmont, Trinidad, attending Belmont Intermediate School, where he recalls being a below-average student who was "undermotivated" and wanted get out of school.

After his father died, he was forced to become the breadwinner and found jobs as an office boy in an attorney's office, did a stint at the Hotel Normandie, then became a casual labourer on the docks of Port of Spain. Like many of his generation who felt the limits of living on an island, he found escape in movies. He wanted to become an actor like James Dean and was making plans to go to America. Instead, after going to England in 1961, Matura and his fellow countryman, the future film-maker, Horace Ove, found their way to Rome where they got hired for a film about building a railway. It was in Rome where Matura got his first taste of the theatre, working at Teatro Goldoni, the only English-speaking theatre there at the time. It also allowed him his first experience of black theatre, a production of Langston Hughes' *Shakespeare in Harlem*, which he attended.

After returning to England, he married and began writing, holding down an "undemanding factory job" while he wrote his first play, *Black Pieces*. The play, produced in Amsterdam, was the turning point for Matura's career as a playwright which prompted him to decide to gave up his factory job to write full-time. He returned to Trinidad in 1973, where he gathered material for *Play Mas'* (1974), a play that examines the effects of independence seen through the lives of an Indian tailor and his mother. Plays such as *Rum an' Coca Cola (1976) Independence (1979)*, and *The Coup* (1991) also explored different levels of Trinidadian life. Even his adaptations, *Playboy of the West Indies* (1984) – based on J.M. Synge's *Playboy of the Western World*, and *Trinidad Sisters* (1988) – a Trinidadian reworking of Anton Chekhov's *Three Sisters* – are all set in Trinidad.

As he told Simon Lee ("The Man in the Corner House", *Sunday Guardian*, Dec. 19, 1999), even after being in the UK for nearly forty years: "I'm a Trinidadian, my plays are about Trinidad" and "Living in the UK and writing about Trinidad, that's the perfect distance and the safest way." Only his first plays, such as *Black Pieces* (1970), *As Time Goes By* (1971), *Bakerloo Line* (1972) *Nice* (1973) and *Welcome Home, Jacko* (1979) dealt with the Caribbean experience in England, and were seen as groundbreaking at the time in British theatre because of their grassroots approach.

Matura's other stage plays include: *Another Tuesday* (1978); *More More* (1978); *A Dying Business* (1980); *One Rule* (1981); *Meetings* (1982). Matura also directed this production.

Matura's television credits include the highly successful series *No Problem!* a joint project between Black Theatre Co-Operative – which he founded in 1978 with Charlie Hanson – and London Weekend Television/ Channel Four.

He also wrote for the 1983 LWT/C4's *Party at the Place*, a live show and the British entry for Montreux in 1984. He scripted Kid Creole's Christmas Spectacular, *There's Something Wrong in Paradise* (Granada TV, 1984), and devised and wrote, in collaboration with Rudy Narayan, the BBC series *Black Silk* (1985).

In 1971, Matura won the George Devine and John Whiting awards for his first full-length stage play, *As Time Goes By*. In 1974, he won the *Evening Standard*'s Most Promising Playwright Award for *Play Mas'*. *Playboy of the West Indies* was toured in the UK and the USA, and its Chicago production was nominated for four Jefferson Awards. Matura also wrote the television adaptation of the play broadcast by BBC2 in 1985.

In 1991, Matura received the Trinidad and Tobago Government Scarlet Ibis Award for achievement. His other awards include The Helen Hayes Award (1994).

Benedict Nightingale asked in an article in *The Times* of London: "What makes Mustapha Matura our finest dramatist of West Indian origin? A wry humour, warmth of feeling, a knack of observing human oddity and for embodying it in quirky, unpredictable dialogue, and the fundamental seriousness with which he writes of people who, like himself, have in some sense become severed from their roots. He ranges from the usefully mischievous to the wickedly funny."

MUSTAPHA MATURA

New York, Tuesday, 17 May, 1983

Q: When did you first begin to write?

MUSTAPHA MATURA: About 1968.

Q: And how did that process start? What prompted you?

MM: I felt an urge to write. I had no literary influences or formal education; I didn't go to university, and so I didn't have that kind of discipline or exposure to writing as a discipline, but I had the urge; it may have been a fantasy, but I had the urge. I sat down to write a play because I didn't have the academic training, and I thought theatre and dialogue would be more direct in getting to the point of something – the content. This was the late '60s when the Black consciousness and anti-colonial consciousness was taking place in England and we were becoming aware of our place as a people of colour or ex-colonials in white British society. Of course it was influenced by what was happening in America with the Black Panthers and Huey Newton and all these people; we were picking up those signals and translating it into our own experience and coming up with amazing answers and asking more questions. It was a very exciting and creative time because we were becoming *free* of a lot of hang-ups and a lot of concepts and attitudes that we'd been carrying around with us for a long time; we were just throwing them off, man, in a matter of *seconds* and days and replacing them with pride and imagination and strength. So it was a very creative time, and I sat down and started writing. I was writing about what was going on at the time, about how *this* consciousness was being active and the forms it was taking. So what came together was (a) the *fact* that I was writing, and, (b) what I was writing about, and they were feeding each other, you see. Which was wonderful, because the energy was coming out in the plays, and the energy was taking place outside as well, and because I was reporting on that, they were complementing each other. The actual fact of writing – me, a young Trinidadian – well, not so young, I was in my late twenties or early thirties – the very fact that somebody who had no formal education and no formal training – I used to go to the cinema more – suddenly sat down to write a play was quite an act in itself, you know. From not doing it to suddenly doing it and doing it as a means of expression was quite something – and that was symptomatic of the times. It's like opening a door and finding a room full of beautiful objects – you know what I mean? And, I always write in dialect, which was another *act* of revolution. I was *asserting* our language, and that was a part of the times as well.

Q: Were you influenced by people like Baraka[1] and Bullins[2]?

MM: Yes, yes. They were our models. Not Bullins, so much, because I think I only saw one Bullins play. I may not have been influenced by their work but I was influenced by their *presence*, to know they were there and doing work, and Baraka was being respected for his work and the ideas of his work – of the very fact that a Black writer was saying these things. I saw Baraka's play, *Dutchman* [1964]; that was powerful stuff. I may not have been influenced by the actual *writing* because the American connection was very hard, especially the *Black* American connection, to make in London at that time... Now I'm aware of a lot of things we have in common, but at that time I wasn't aware of it.

Q: What about other Caribbean writers?

MM: Other Caribbean writers, no. I'd read Naipaul – that was an influence, because he was respected and it must have influenced me in some way that, here was a man from my background – we shared half of the same race – being given respect and approval for writing about this sleepy little colony that you never thought the world knew existed; that must have encouraged me in some way.

Q: What about some of the other writers who were in self-imposed exile there, like Selvon and –

MM: Oh, no influence at all. I thought they were all has-beens. By the time the '60s had arrived those guys were old-hat; they were classed as everything we were fighting against at that time. We used to call them the "BBC writers", because a lot of them had come with their artistic and literary ambitions, couldn't make a living with their writing and so went to work for the BBC Caribbean Service – and to stay within that cultural situation. I came to London with a lot of ambitions, but with no basis for these ambitions. I was working in a factory, and in a hospital as a porter. So I arrived there and operated on a working-class level; they arrived in London and operated at a academic, cultural level by working at the BBC. They were exposed to that intellectual situation whereas I wasn't. So, at that time, those guys – they used to wear suits and ties, and they were kind of academic and intellectual – I mean, this is how we saw them – I'm not using this as a criticism of them, you know, I'm just saying how they were perceived by a lot of other people who were emerging – they were the old reactionaries; these were the people we had to knock out of the way to get our things heard. We used to put them down and give them a hard time. But then, after a while we got to know them as human beings – because before that they were seen as "writers" – but once we started rapping and socializing, you begin to realize that these are human guys and we had a lot of things in common. Also, they were moving closer towards us; we were attacking them, but those guys were – I don't want to spend too much time talking about them, but I'm trying to paint the picture of the period – probably isolated. More isolated than *we* were. We were part of a movement – everybody was experiencing this thing. But those guys, when they arrived in London, they were probably so isolated, that probably helped to form a lot their attitudes at the time. But I'm sure we gave them a lot of strength and they felt stronger by having this larger group of creative people coming through and stating that they could be less afraid of speaking out. And so there was an interaction going on between the two groups.

Q: What year did you arrive in England?

MM: 1961.

Q: Do you see yourself going back to live and work in the Caribbean or in Trinidad?

MM: As a hope, as an ideal, yes. As a practicality, I doubt it. I mean, it's my home, I'd love to live there, I'd love to be there, eat the food, feel the sun, listen to the language, listen to the old talk. But practically, I doubt it. It's not a psychological obstacle, it's an economic obstacle. Pure economics.

Q: With all that money in Trinidad?

MM: Yes – but they're not giving it to creative or cultural activities. If by some kind of fluke the arts was seen as something to put government money into, like cricket or steelband or calypso or football, and they put forward a scheme to get people to come back and lay the foundations for some kind of theatrical institutions in Trinidad, I'd love to. That's my ideal.

Q: How many plays have you written to date?

MM: Oh-my-God... I really don't know offhand... I would think about twelve to fifteen, all-in-all – full-length and one-acts.

Q: How would you evaluate the development and success of your work to date?

MM: It's been climbing. Let's put it this way, if you're looking at a chart, from the time it started to where it is now, it's been forever climbing, but it has wavered up and down at some points. I mean, because of circumstances, I have written some plays that were not as intellectually or critically well realized as some others; I've written some that came out of an urge... Some plays I've written have sprung from an idea, a natural idea inside that I didn't plant; some of them have sprung from deliberate concepts, or I wanted to write something dealing with something; and some of them have been better than the others. Obviously, the natural ones that spring out – but this is for other people to judge – of their own momentum, that force you to write them, they've usually turned out to be better than the more deliberate, self-conscious ones.

Q: You've been getting a lot of plays across the Atlantic in the last several years,[3] are you now able to survive solely from your work?

MM: Yes, now. But that's because, quite recently, I've started writing a television comedy series which pays very well.

Q: You have received grants, in England, though, given by the British Council towards creative writing?

MM: Oh, yes, I've had grants. Only for, say, six months of the year. It's not that substantial.

Q: About how much would be the average?

MM: About four thousand pounds – that's the highest – two grand [£2000] is the average – that could spread you to about six months of the year, but that's about all. I think playwrights in America are better funded – I don't know, I'm just guessing, but I think they are. Until only recently I've been catching my backside...

Q: How did you survive in between?

MM: I was married and my wife had a regular job, so it was that way.

Q: What is the state of Black Caribbean theatre in England today? There seems to be quite a bit going on from what little I've been hearing.

MM: It's growing, it's growing. The Brixton riots and the Scarman Report[4] didn't start it, but they brought a lot of things into focus – the racial discrimination that has been going on in England for many years focused on the Blacks – and because of that a few doors have been opened. They haven't stopped – but they've kind of slowed down their pace in terms of denying opportunities to Blacks. But also now, in 1983, we are getting the fruits of the '60s. The generation that's coming through now are the fruits of the politics and awareness of the '60s – and so they're more assertive, they don't have the hang-ups that we had. They didn't have that experience, which I think is a disadvantage, but you can't turn back the clock. But they are coming forward and finding a situation that was created by the politics of the '60s. They don't know at what cost they have benefited from it, but they are finding a world where they have more confidence, they have more assertiveness and strength about them, and they're coming forward. They're finding things wrong and they're saying, "Why the fuck didn't you change this? We're gonna change it, we're not standing for this," and they're moving forward. Which is good. I mean, they don't have the sense of limits that we had, and so they're getting into all kinds of things – they want to be dancers, so they're going ahead and dancing; they want to be singers, they're going ahead and singing; they want to be actors, they're going ahead – it's healthy. And, so we're reaping the benefits now of the '60s.

Q: Are there a lot of Caribbean groups now forming in England?

MM: Yes, yes. We formed a company called the Black Theatre Co-operative in 1978, and we're the leading Black theatre company in England. We've got a good reputation; we've also created a Black audience for theatre. This is something that's come together because of this younger generation coming forward, who're interested in the arts, and we're doing plays that address the problems of young Blacks. We have found an audience and young people have found *us*. It's good, it's healthy – we play to good houses.

Q: What about playwrights – are there any new Black English playwrights?

MM: Yes. There's one called Caz [Caryl] Phillips,[5] who is getting a lot of respect and attention.

Q: When were you last in Trinidad?

MM: I was in Trinidad three months ago.

Q: How do you view the condition of theatre, in particular, and the arts in general, in Trinidad? I know you mentioned a bit about it earlier but I'd like you to go into a little more depth.

MM: The arts in Trinidad are struggling. There are a lot of people with the will and the ambition to do things; what they don't have are the institutions to go in and do them, and so they have to create that. They will probably spend their lifetime laying the foundations for the next generation to come in and do it. But it's spasmodic, it's disorganized, there's no centre – I'm sure Jamaica is much healthier in that respect. The only people who did theatre in Trinidad were the English colonists who came down there and did plays – their amateur productions.

Q: The expatriates.

MM: Yes. But they didn't leave a structure after independence for us to build on; we had to form it ourselves. It's a struggle. Everybody's trying to do everything; people who are not trained specifically in any one discipline of theatre have to do everything; they have to act and try and direct and try and design and try and produce, and, so you get the results of that kind of situation, which is hit and miss.

Q: It seems tragic, because people like Errol Hill, Errol John and Derek Walcott have spoken about that same sort of situation that existed there over twenty-five years ago, and also of coming up from the late '40s.

MM: Yes. It's because we don't have a pioneer with vision, a sacrificing pioneering spirit, down there to stand and draw people towards a centre. We're all busy leaving the island, trying to make a living, trying to get our work done in the outside world.

Q: Derek Walcott tried it with the Trinidad Theatre Workshop, and I think it's still there, isn't it?

MM: Yes, the people are still there, but they're all doing office jobs; there are no full-time writers; there isn't that much theatre to support a full-time actor.

Q: It's funny, because when we founded CART, the majority of the people who were involved were from Trinidad. And I thought to myself that there must be a whole lot of things going on in Trinidad.

MM: That's why we're here! That's why we're here! We export our talent. It's a drain on our natural resources, but our island is too small to accommodate our talents; we have to leave. The creative environment is not there to utilize our talent, so we have to go abroad; it's tragic, but that's the way it goes.

Q: One of the good things that came out of the Manley government was the creation of the Cultural Training Centre in Kingston in '76.

MM: But even before that Jamaica had a tradition. Norman Manley's wife was a sculptress – when you get that kind of model, someone in that position pursuing artistic activities, it must filter down through the rest of the island. Our heroes in Trinidad were cricketers; calypso was the only kind of creative activity in the island – and steelband – that could have influenced artistic activity in the island. But all the other creative people like Boscoe Holder,[6] Geoffrey Holder,[7] Naipaul, Samuel Selvon, they had all gone abroad, so we would read about these Trinidadians being successful on a creative level – but thousands of miles away. We couldn't feel their influence, so we didn't have that kind of direct creative encouragement to draw on.

Q: Are you in any way embittered about that?

MM: Oh, no. I'm not. I accept it for what it is. Trinidad is too complex and organic a society to try and impose an ideal on. A lot of people have tried and failed and were last seen running to the nearest mental hospital. I don't know where the foundations of that ideal come from – if it's a European concept we want to impose on Trinidad – it just is not the society to absorb that kind of thinking because of it's historical influences. I smile at its lack of intellectual – it's not a thinking society – but I wouldn't get frustrated or bitter about it – it's one of its virtues.

Q: While we're still on Trinidad, a review of your play, *Meetings* [first performed 1974], in the now defunct *SoHo Weekly News*, Carlos Clarens says: "Depending on which character is holding the stage, the kitchen is either a threatened outpost of reason and progress in an island doomed to superstition and underdevelopment, or an alien imposition on the Caribbean order of things. And when *Meetings* is really working, the views blend into each other." He asks the question: "Is the kitchen the best metaphor for Trinidad, a country in danger of losing its natural flavour to either socialism or capitalist democracy?" Your answer?

MM: Yes. I think the kitchen is a good metaphor for it. This probably came out of the play unconsciously; it was one that – as I was talking about earlier – grew out of itself; it had to be written. And, like Trinidad, the kitchen in the play was *complete*, completely occupied by manufactured objects all manufactured abroad, and it was a shell, an empty shell that was filled with things but it is still empty. And in a hundred percent of ways it represents Trinidad, because Trinidad is a shell that – intellectually, culturally, industrially – has been manufactured by things from abroad that have been put into it. This has been our greatest faults.

Another metaphor for Trinidad is as a huge sponge that has been absorbing things, and things have been poured on it, and the only people who squeeze that sponge are the writers and the creative people. We have been squeezing that sponge to see what comes out of it and trying to make sense of it, but the sponge is too big, it's too strong, it's too resilient – and it just continues absorbing American influences – now, because it's independent – and Canadian influences. And it has a very pseudo-sophisticated veneer, but right under that – it's very thin, that veneer – is all the conflict and contradictions of an ex-colony. That's what makes it fascinating for me. It's a very thin veneer. In its history, the African influence and the Indian influence – the two major racial groups in Trinidad – are very strong. It all resides under this thin veneer of modern sophistication brought in by television, the movies, people travelling abroad, so, yes, that's Trinidad. On one level, very sophisticated and brash and confident and worldly; the latest craze – you'll find it in Trinidad. They'll try anything – whatever is the latest, that's what they're interested in. That's on the surface. But beneath that, it's a primitive, brutal, sadistic society.

Q: I'd like you to go into that a little more: the brutal, sadistic side.

MM: The death penalty is still in existence in Trinidad; there is no liberal conscience in Trinidad; there are no liberal institutions to defend human rights in Trinidad; the power comes from the ruling party; there is no institution, no blocking civil rights or liberal left wing, no liberal conscience or left-wing bourgeois liberal. We don't have a middle-class bourgeoisie with liberal leanings to act as a blocking mechanism to create an atmosphere of justice and civil rights and fair play and *civilized* – whatever that may mean, or what we have come to accept as civilized behaviour – we don't have that power group to intervene in matters of injustice. So, in that respect, the society is brutal. It's a good and evil society; you're either good, clean and pure or you're evil. There is no group to put forward a sociological argument for evil – what they see as evil, like crime, I mean. There's nobody to say, "This man is a thief because he has been poor all his life, and hungry all his life; and he has been hungry and poor because of the political and economic structure of the society." There is no room for that kind of argument to find a resonance, so, in that respect it is brutal and cruel. You are bad and so you will be punished; it is that kind of a society.[8]

Q: You are saying that there is no room or freedom for dissent in Trinidad?

MM: You pay the price for it. And the price is social, economic condemnation; you are an outcast. It's a very conformist society, because it is a small society.

Q: It sounds almost totalitarian.

MM: It is. We don't have a dictator but we have a dictatorship mentality. I mean, it would be better if we had a dictator – we might get rid of him. But it's a very conformist society; and it's a very repressed society. But on the other hand, it's a very spontaneous society because of that repression; the kettle boils, you get the steam coming out.

Q: If the kettle is boiling, will it explode?

MM: Oh, yes. Oh, yes. Because Trinidad has just experienced a financial euphoria – an economic euphoria – because of the petrodollars, and they've overspent. They've thrown money away like water – and the corruption… Trinidad is a money country; that is the only thing people are interested in: how to make money, how to make more money and how to spend it. That is the national pastime. *Meetings* was not fiction, *Meetings* was *fact*. Trinidadians go to Miami to shop, they come to New York to have affairs because they don't want people to know their business – their extramarital affairs – so they come to New York and stay in a big hotel to fuck! (*Chuckles*) They can afford to do it. They go to Barbados to have dinner. *Meetings* is true.

But what's happened now, because of the recession and the cutbacks of the oil crisis, oil is no longer so sought after. The superpowers are not stupid, they have engineered it, they have cut back on their oil consumption because they were giving too much power to these little colonies and these little dictatorships – as they see them – and Trinidad is suffering because of that now. Trinidadians cannot put on the brakes, they cannot change into another gear – they are too extreme a people – they can only rush forward. And so the effects of the drop in oil prices is going to be catastrophic, because we're not a responsible, disciplined people; people have been handed money and they're still going to spend – and they're going to spend more, they can't readjust. So the effects of the recession are going to be – as well as socially – psychologically disastrous.

Q: But a lot of what you're saying, in terms of the behaviour and even the brutalism and the decadent behaviour on the part of those that have money, is also true of Jamaica – and Jamaica doesn't have the economic wherewithal that Trinidad has. So, therefore, is this a form of behaviour left by our colonisers, and have we taken the baton and gone on to greater heights?

MM: Yes. What I find fascinating about Trinidad, is that it has gone full circle and returned to the point where it started off, and has stayed there. Trinidad was a British colony, and had all the problems and all the contradictions and all the effects of British colonialism, right? The '60s came and we had a revolution –

Q: Of sorts.

MM: Of sorts. It was cultural as well as physical. We came very close – we went to the brink – but we didn't move on from there.[9] All the rhetoric, all the awareness, all the sense of destiny and pride that was generated at that period has not influenced or has not made an impression on the fabric of the society – it's as though it *never* happened. It has returned to being a country where the colour or the shade of brown you are and the friends you know – to get you a job or do you a favour – is what matters. Not your ability, not your humanity, not your intellect or character, it's who you know. It has returned right back to how it was as a British colony. The only difference is people smoke more dope, sniff more cocaine, there is more homosexuality because of the liberal times, people spend more money, but in terms of social behaviour, social conscience – no way. It has gone *right back* to being a British colony, but there are no British running it any more; they have reimposed colonialism on themselves.

Q: Neocolonialism.

MM: *Neocolonialism*. They *volunteered* to be a British colony again. Because, the alternative for them is communism – that's how they see it – and they don't want to do that. So they have chosen to be a middle-of-the-road British colony – amazing.

Q: You don't paint a very pretty picture.

MM: That's what it is.

Q: Someone told me about the moral breakdown in Trinidad, that's rampant even in the school system: teachers having babies with students, and about the large amounts of money that students walk around with to spend.

MM: Sure, sure. You go into a cafe at lunchtime, and schoolchildren are in front of you. I used to go home for lunch when I went to school; what they do now is they go in a restaurant and eat lunch – buying things at the cafe with hundred-dollar notes. But with all the money they have, kids have to go to school in *shifts* –

Q: In shifts?

MM: In shifts. Now we're talking about the brutal side of the society. I mean, if you think I paint a bad picture, I'll just give you some facts… They've got so much money but there aren't enough schools for the kids, so one lot of kids goes to school for a morning session and another goes to school for an afternoon session; they haven't built enough schools for the kids! You go to the hospital, you have to take your own blankets, sheets; there're two people sharing beds in the hospital; newborn babies are wrapped in brown paper –

Q: You're not putting me on, now.

MM: Look – I mean, people see this beautiful island… party… Carnival… happy-go-lucky people… *This* is the underbelly of the society. They're building a new hospital now; it's going to be the best equipped hospital in the Western hemisphere. It's going to last – this is my opinion – say, five years. When something runs out or breaks down it's not going to be replaced or repaired, it's going to be thrown away or just left standing there. I mean, this is the society – this is the society. Look, if you want to check my story, you just get a weeks' newspapers from Trinidad and you'll see what goes on there – just read the reports in the newspapers.

Q: So where's the money going?

MM: The money is going into people's pockets; it's going on yachts and ranches in America, and it's going up people's noses.

Q: But that's seeds for revolution, man.

MM: But nobody wants a revolution! Nobody wants to change; everybody wants a piece of the action, so, they're not going to revolt against it – they want a piece of the cake! They're all chasing dollars, man, so nobody wants to upset that situation. There's no social conscience in Trinidad. It's your bad luck if you can't afford a private nursing home; it's your bad luck, it's not my problem, it's poor you! "You're a fool, why don't you get off your backside and get money so that you can afford a private nursing home?" That's the society.

Q: So, a play like *Meetings* was directly talking about some of that behaviour. Do you find yourself drawn more in that direction of telling that story?

MM: No… no.

Q: Is it that you don't feel motivated to do that?

MM: No, no.

Q: That's why I asked you before if you felt in any way bitter about the circumstances there.

MM: Oh bitter! – I've passed the stage of bitterness. Of course, I find it tragic; but I'm not a crusading writer in that respect. Maybe if I was a journalist, but I have an artistic urge to satisfy, you know.

Q: Do you regard that as a luxury, for yourself?

MM: No.

Q: Or a privilege?

MM: A privilege more than a luxury. It fluctuates – but in many cases it's for my development and benefit as a human being, as well as an opportunity to focus on aspects of humanity. This might sound pompous, but it's not meant to.

Q: Still on Trinidad, for a second. What do you think are some of the things that could improve the cultural sphere there?

MM: Well, what we need is a love of our self, of our history, of our roots and to take pride in that reality and to value it. And until we do that, until we stop looking at the West, Europe, as a reservoir, as the only source of civilization and culture and things of value, we'll never value our own history. It's too painful, it's a party society. They don't know how to experience any kind of painful recognition of things; they want to have a good time! So, that has to change, too. It's a society that refuses to grow up and stand on its own two feet. We are like little children, we want sweets, we want to have a good time, we want our mother to say, "You're a good boy." I can't see change happening unless it undergoes some kind of social upheaval… a catharsis, to make people stop and think and say, "Hey, where are we going?" or "Where have we been going?" or "What are we doing?" But nobody does that in Trinidad, they want to have a good time and party. You know, party, party.

Q: Moving along. Over the past several years there has been much heard about people in the various islands attempting new approaches to theatre, searching for a true indigenous folk form: "roots", "reggae", "dub" and "calypso" theatre. What do you think about that?

MM: I think it's healthy. I personally think reggae has been overemphasized as an art form. I'm sure a lot of people will attack me for it, but, I don't know if it's because there has been nothing else to focus on and so people have focused on reggae. I know reggae was an evolving form – it was ska, it was blue beat; because of its commercial success it seems to have petrified as reggae. But I think the searching for an indigenous Caribbean form of storytelling is healthy. We may not see the fruits of that searching immediately, but it will eventually emerge, and that's good. Because, we have – Trinidad, I'm talking about, I don't know about the other islands – the influences and the racial historical forces operating there – the two largest groups, the Africans and the Indians – we have got thousands of years of tradition and resources of storytelling in those two groups of people. When that comes out it's going to be fantastic.

Q: I know Roderick Walcott, for one, has stuck closely to creating a

Caribbean, or a St. Lucian mythology, drawing a lot from the folklore and folktales, etc.

MM: That's good. In my case I've gone for the language.

Q: You said earlier that when you first started to write you wrote solely in dialect –

MM: Yes, and I've never stopped. It was the key for me, it was the key to open the door – the language.

Q: Some of the older generation will tell you that Errol Hill was the one who really pointed their eyes in that direction. He said, "Start writing in your own tongue." Lennox Brown told me something similar, that when he first saw his language on the written page it opened up a new realm for him, and he took that and ran with it.

MM: It's like finding you've got money in the bank. Suddenly somebody puts money on the counter and says, "This is yours." You say, "What!?"

Q: But really, it's an inheritance. Like some money your grandfather left you that you didn't know was there.

MM: Sure, sure. And you've been carrying it around with you all the time and you didn't know it. It's quite something.

Q: Some have gone to considerable lengths in discussing the need for a definitive concept of a Caribbean theatre. What is your view?

MM: Oh, God – I don't know. We come back to the problem that there has to be an institution to draw these things together to make things happen. But because of our political history we're very divided and scattered islands. I mean, I didn't know about other islands when I was growing up because it was not our colonial masters' interest for us to know, so we didn't know. Years to come we'll get closer together, artistically and otherwise. We are still influenced by the superpowers. If you look at the American attitude to Grenada – and Trinidad is very anti-Grenada because Grenada is going into a Marxist-left wing situation, Trinidad is going toward an American-capitalist situation, and so there is an antagonism between the two islands. And that's going to exist for as long as it suits the superpowers to have that situation.

Q: It's like what has happened now with Jamaica and Cuba.

MM: Right, right. Artistic activity should transcend the political but we're not that sophisticated or civilized for it to happen – it may happen in the future. But we have to get the lead from the top or somewhere in the middle, the institution has to be there to create that exchange.

Q: Do you regard yourself as a socialist?

MM: Yes, I think so. A socialist-humanist.

Q: Why I asked that was because Derek Walcott says that there's no writer coming from the Caribbean who could not be anything else but socialist, coming from those kind of conditions.

MM: Sure, sure. I think so. I agree. I don't know if I would call Derek a socialist, but I think his statement is right.

Q: He also believes that a writer whose beliefs or integrity were threatened under a dictatorial or totalitarian system would rather be shot than to kowtow or renege his beliefs. How do you feel about that?

MM: I think that's a romantic vision. I don't believe it; I'm much more realistic than that. It's a nice European-based romantic Bohemian concept that comes from Lord Byron...

Q: Have you had many plays produced in the Caribbean?

MM: No, no. Two – just two.

Q: Were any done at CARIFESTA?

MM: No, no. Trinidad took *Sizwe Banzi* to CARIFESTA – which tells you something – to Barbados – the last one. There was a big stink about it.

Q: So which ones were produced and on what island?

MM: *Rum an' Coca-Cola* [premiered 1973] was produced in Trinidad, and I went down a few years afterwards and directed *Independence* [premiered 1974].

Q: How were they received?

MM: They were well received. They didn't create the kind of intellectual stimulation that I would have liked; but Trinidad is very blasé, conceited society and thinks that everything is all right. We'll do it and see it, but it's not going to make us think; we're too clever already – that's the society. Trinidad is a society where the only satisfaction a writer could get from it is to shock them. But they're too smart for that, you can't shock Trinidadians, and if even you do they'll pretend. They don't want to be seen to be shocked because that would mean they've a small-island mentality and they see themselves as sophisticated so they wouldn't give you the benefit...

Q: I know you've talked a little about how a play comes to you, but I'd like to get a little more into that. How does the idea first come to you and how do you develop the play from its genesis?

MM: It usually comes from an idea... I look for certain signals – and this has developed through experience – and I look for certain other signals to go with that, other thoughts and ideas to go with the signal and I let the idea germinate and grow until – again, this is because of experience – I get the feeling that the baby is about to be born. And then I sit down and give birth to it.

Q: What are the themes that you like to pursue?

MM: Well, my early area of interest was the effects of colonialism, the contradictions; I was writing in many ways about my experience as well, my learning, growing awareness, and trying to apply that growth to other people in different situations and at different stages of learning and awareness. Showing people in situations and showing how they grow out of them – that was my earlier interest. Perhaps, maybe, it still is.

Q: I was just about to ask you about now?

MM: Now? I don't know about now. This is not a fact, this is a feeling, but I feel at this stage that I want to go into other areas... What's funny is that I started off writing in a certain way – not in a *certain* way – an ironic vein using comedy, not jokes, but with an inkling of humour. And then I started writing consciously more seriously. I left the comedy or the humour – the ironical humour – behind, though recently I wrote this television comedy [*No Problem* (1983-85)], and I enjoyed it.

Q: Has that been going well?

MM: Yes, yes, it's been more successful than anybody imagined; the feedback has been fantastic. The Black community loves it and wants more; it's the only Black comedy series on British television. I'd forgotten the pleasure I got from writing humour and I feel as though I'm going to go back. It's funny, I was sitting here yesterday thinking that American plays are more humour orientated than English plays. And I was thinking that maybe it's presumptuous, maybe it's shortsighted to think you can't write serious plays with humour in them.

Q: If it comes from a natural place.

MM: Yes. And I enjoy writing humour and using that *eye* to look with, if you know what I mean. I feel a pull in that direction.

Q: Another playwright told me that he thinks it is healthy to write from a place of cynicism. Do you agree with that notion?

MM: I don't know, I wouldn't like to make any rules. I wouldn't go as far as to pick any one standpoint and say it's healthy or unhealthy. I mean, if it's healthy and productive for the writer – that individual writer – it's good. But, in my case, I'm restless, and I like to explore and be in other places. Maybe I will settle down eventually. I have been going in varied directions, which probably accounts for the up and down nature of my work. Some of my plays have been brilliant and some of them have been not so good – I wouldn't say rubbish – because I have a set of standards that I try to maintain. And I think it's because I've been exploring different areas. I felt at one time that I was the only Black writer in England – and at one time it was like that – doing work and getting my work done. And I felt I had to – because I was the only one carrying the can, as it were – covering so many areas. If there were, say, ten of us, and we were writing about different areas, that's cool, we could pursue our own narrow things. But as I felt I was the only one carrying the flag, I had to wave it all over the place, if you see what I mean. Now it's changing, there are more writers coming through; maybe, now I've got older, I can pursue a narrower, more singular direction.

Q: Lennox Brown uses a formula whereby he writes in three different cycles, using several racial families whose descendants keep popping up in the various plays, and uses this to represent the journey of the Black man from African to the Caribbean and the Western World. He has plays that are set in Canada, America, the Caribbean, England, etc. He says, with this formula and the characters that he has set up, he can write plays in this manner for as long as he lives.

MM: Ssshhhhh! I mean, one of the things that keeps me writing is the unknown, the difference, the variety – that's what I get out of it. I couldn't work Brown's way, there'd be no enjoyment or mystery or newness or excitement about it for me. I need the difference.

Q: Do you write quickly or slowly?

MM: Quickly.

Q: How many drafts do you go through before the final one?

MM: One. I mean, I do a bit of trimming and rewriting here and there, but pshew! (*Claps hands in a suggestion of forward motion.*) It's got to be one and that's it; and it's very intense...

Q: Longhand or typewriter?

MM: Oh, longhand, yes; it's got to be longhand.

Q: How do you, to date, compare the Black writers in England, Afro-American writers, and Caribbean writers?

MM: I don't know. I mean, what I think about them is I think that what is lacking in their work is any political perception.

Q: Here, in America?

MM: In America, in the Caribbean, all the areas you mentioned. I'm sure they'd all throw bottles at me, but I think that is what is lacking in their work. I'm not talking about the kind of militant-right-on-kill-whitey politics – and that's in some work – I always suspect it's like a dog barking and it's not going to bite. I always suspect overcompensation and overbarking; it's a condition common among black writers that they have to justify their existence as black men and have to be seen as militant blacks in order to get credibility in their work. I don't have a precise or clear view on this situation, but this is how it appears to me. And I always find the more militant the writer is, the less militant his work is; the more the militancy appears like an appendage to the work and not as a part of the whole thing. I feel that a lot of black writers write of over-romanticized political situations, and they're pure fantasies; they don't reflect the dilemmas that I see existing in my own self – and the conflicts – that I know must exist in other black people as well.

It could be because I live in a country that has a majority of white people, and so that conflict is alive all the time; maybe if I lived in an all-black country – if I lived in the Caribbean, which is not all black, but has more black people in the majority or as one of the majority groups – I wouldn't be aware of that conflict. But, I live in a white society so I'm aware of these conflicts and they're there, but I don't see them reflected. And maybe it doesn't have to be a white group that create these conflicts; it could be any other racial or cultural group. But I don't see these dilemmas reflected in their work; it's as though they're not there but it *is* there and these people write about it as if it doesn't exist; and this is what I find lacking in their work. All homemade bombs and bullets should be delivered to my address. (*Laughs*) This is not a putdown, it's just something I don't *see*, if you know what I mean.

Q: Derek Walcott, Errol Hill and some other Caribbean writers have been fairly critical of the younger generation of writers for lacking discipline and for being lazy with regard to craft.

MM: That's too European. As soon as I hear people talking about black people in terms of laziness, I think in terms of the plantation man saying that "the slave isn't working hard enough because he's lazy." Maybe they're right, but they don't *put* it right for me to give it any consideration. I think it's too simple.

Q: For example, Walcott says, "It is very easy to say I'm black and beautiful and I don't need craft..."

MM: Yes, but these are people who have moved on from that situation who are criticizing people who are going through that situation – it's too simple. I think it's a generation problem more than literary one. I think they're old men. But they're academically trained and place more value on discipline because some teacher used to cut their ass for being undisciplined and they just want to pass that on. Maybe the young ones don't have that concept of discipline or value it so much. It might be a deliberate rejection – they've got to allow for that – of that value of discipline and love of craft; I don't see why they have to accept those values.

Q: I'd like to ask you what may be a rather sensitive question, because I'm sure you've dealt with it. You call yourself black but physically you do not look African. I know that you are racially mixed. I'm also assuming that during the '60s that you probably had a lot of these conflicts. How did you resolve this for yourself as a writer and as a human being, in the milieu that you were in at the time and still are?

MM: (*Laughs*) God... I don't know... I don't know... It was finding an identity, it was finding a shared identity and it's because of my roots; I grew up in Trinidad with Black people. That's my life and I can't see another – if you know what I mean – I grew up as a black person in Trinidad. Whatever I look like, whatever scientific reasons for me not being black, I am. Do you know what I mean? It's an *instinct*, it's a natural –

Q: I understand that. What I'm saying is that I'm sure you've been asked this quite often by the press.

MM: Oh, yes. Oh, yes. It's like asking you that question.

Q: Well, I'm racially mixed, too.

MM: This is what I mean – it's not scientific; you could measure the blood –

Q: You know that, I know that. I'm saying the realm that we live in does *not* understand that, and they only see you at face value. They don't deal –

MM: How I dealt with it was by overcompensating and overemphasizing certain things. I went through certain phases. I used to wear a dashiki and robes and this kind of thing; I don't need to do that anymore now. But that's not how I dealt with it, that's how it dealt with me! (*Amused*) I overstated certain things and got very aggressive and very belligerent and was very antisocial and unsociable – that's how it came out. But how I dealt with it – again, it was like going to the bank and finding you had money – I loved it. I had dilemmas because I was very idealistic and thought every black man was pure and a walking God until I realized that it was human beings we were dealing with and their faults. I am wise enough to see the effects of colonialism and oppression in people and see how their faults are manifested, and know the cause of the faults, and so I can put it in a perspective. Does that make sense?

Q: Yes, it's clear to me. But, to change the subject, I'd like to ask you your honest, candid and critical opinion on the work of your fellow contemporary West Indian playwrights.

MM: Okay.

Q: Lennox Brown.

MM: Yes. I think he writes good domestic West Indian dramas, but I feel there're levels of conflicts in those dramas that he maybe is not aware of, or he doesn't write about. Again, it's what's missing, it's what's not there. But I don't find them – I can look at his plays and admire them – engaging or moving or gripping.

Q: Interesting. Michael Abbensetts.

MM: Again, I find something missing in Michael's work. I think in many cases in Michael's work I see a lack of courage in his writing, that there may be things too painful for the writer. This is a writer talking; I'm not a theatre critic, I am a writer, and I know the processes and the pains and the intellectual courage, the moral courage that one has to go through to arrive at a certain situation. I know the upheaval in your psyche when you have to examine certain things. I don't think Michael uses his own experiences and puts it into his work. Boy, I'm going to get slaughtered.

Q: Everybody's getting slaughtered. (*Laughs*) You've been slaughtered already.

MM: Oh, well, okay, that's all right. I know what people think about me – well, I don't know what people think – I know what they say about me, I don't know what they think about me... No, I think Michael – I'd like to answer this question much better – what I find about Michael's work is that it's limiting. He's not adventurous, he's not brave, he's not prepared to be wrong, he's a safe writer and he limits himself. I'd like to be really objective about people's work and not get into personalities, you know.

Q: Well, sure. Edgar White.

MM: I think Edgar is a young, young writer. I think he's got a long way to go before I would consider Edgar a real playwright. I think he's still finding his way, and feeling his way and searching for inspiration – but that's healthy. I think it may happen. I just saw a play of his in England, and it was not very original; it was like seeing a Black play ten years ago. And for a new writer coming through there was not much credit to it.

Q: Errol John.

MM: I don't know Errol John's work at all.

Q: Trevor Rhone.

MM: Trevor Rhone I find a trivial writer – which surprises me for the kind of recognition and reputation he has got. I find it very surprising that a writer could come out of Jamaica, with such harsh social conditions, and write the trivia he has written. I've seen his *School's Out* and *Smile Orange*, and I find it *unbelievable* that a Black writer coming out of Jamaica with so much social upheaval – and this is what he writes about. It's unbelievable! I don't know anything about him, about his social background or his history or what his parents were or what his childhood was like – I don't know. But it's *unbelievable* that this is a Jamaican writer writing about Jamaican society in the 1980s. I can't understand it. I feel as though he's living in a tunnel – it's strange.

Q: Financially, he's one of the most successful playwrights living in the Caribbean.

MM: Yes, I know. I hear he's a great hustler; he takes care of business like nobody else. Good luck to him, good luck to him. But there's a vacuum in Jamaica for a good, strong Jamaican playwright to come through, because nobody is writing about Jamaican society that I know about or what's going on there.

Q: Dennis Scott.

MM: I don't know him, and I don't know his work at all.

Q: Alwin Bully.

MM: I don't know him.

Q: Roderick Walcott.

MM: I don't know him or his work.

Q: Derek Walcott.

MM: Derek is a poet. Derek is a good poet. I have never found any connecting lines with Derek's plays. I don't know if it's a generation thing – this may be unjust – but my impression of Derek's work is like 'Nancy stories – the mythology thing – it always seems second-hand to me; that it's how he thinks it is and not how it really is – that's my impression of Derek's work. That it's very much a writer or an artist imposing a picture as opposed to reflecting a picture. Maybe he tries too hard, I think, to paint a picture or to impose a picture. I get the feeling he's a bit heavy-handed with his plays. I find his poetry very, very full of images, moving and magical, but his plays I find always heavy-handed, clumsy.

Q: A writer told me that he felt that Walcott was our "Shakespeare of the Caribbean."

MM: (*Chuckles*) Well, I wouldn't agree, but I would just say he's welcome to that opinion.

Q: I mentioned that to Trevor Rhone and he said that Shakespeare wrote for the man down the street and that he, Rhone, writes for the man down the street.

MM: It's always amusing, it's always interesting to hear how other writers see themselves. I'm sure I suffer from that blindness as well. I err on the side of modesty because I know how deep that precipice is on the other side and I don't want to fall down there. I wouldn't rate Derek as the Shakespeare – we can all say we're the Shakespeare of the Caribbean. Maybe we all are. Derek writes *Julius Caesar*, and I write *Othello* and Trevor Rhone writes *Hamlet*; maybe we all write one Shakespearean play each! (*Laughs*)

Q: Errol Hill.

MM: I don't know Errol Hill's work.

Q: Slade Hopkinson.

MM: I don't know – I mean, what's going to come out of this is my ignorance of Caribbean playwrights.

Q: That's all right, there are a lot of these people who aren't familiar with each other's work... There're some writers who feel a heavy obligation to the vast literary inheritance every time they sit down to work. What do you feel?

MM: I don't feel a damn thing. That's my luck, that's my blessing, I never went to a university; I never had this heavy academic history of great novels, of great works of art – I never had that. So I don't feel it all, I don't have that influence, don't feel that weight on me. I was never in awe, I was never told: "This is a great work of art, it will never be surpassed in two million years." I never had that drummed into me. So, I don't put any writer on a pedestal or anything.

Q: Did you ever feel a desire to go to a university once you got into writing?

MM: No, no. In many ways I educated myself. I left school at thirteen – Belmont Boy's Intermediate – this was a secondary school. I didn't even go to a high school or college.

Q: I saw that you dedicated your recent book of plays: *Play Mas, Independence & Meetings* [1982] to Frantz Fanon. Were you influenced by Fanon in any way?

MM: Yes, yes. Fanon changed my head in many ways; he confirmed a lot of things that were scattered thoughts in my brain, and reading Fanon joined them up; he was like a glue. You know when mercury is all in little pieces and suddenly it's joined together and it becomes a whole thing? It was like that with Fanon.

Q: What sort of advice would you give to a young person wishing to pursue playwriting?

MM: Somebody asked me this recently, and I'll try and say exactly what I said to that person. You've got to have a tough skin, you've got to write things the way you see it and don't be afraid about what anybody says about what you write – just write it. If you want one sentence: go to your roots.

Q: What would you consider to be the ingredients for a well-made or well-written play?

MM: It should engage the audience – which is quite an achievement because an audience in Trinidad is a group of Trinidadians who share a lot of things in common, but an audience in, say, New York – you're getting people from different backgrounds sitting in one room watching a play; to involve them all at the same time is quite an achievement. What would I say are the ingredients for a well written play? Jesus, I don't know.

Q: Do you think theatre should make you think or purely entertain?

MM: It should engage you. Entertain, make you think, whatever – don't think there're any rules, but it should change you. But, I mean, human beings can't take too much, there's only so much you can change a human being – but it should change you.

Q: Another playwright said that he doesn't write to entertain but rather he writes to heal, because the world needs healing.

MM: Well, when I started off writing I had a lot of different kinds of ideals about the power of the play, and so on. But this was the '60s when change was happening quickly, but I don't think it's as easy as that now. Because I've been writing for a long time and a lot of other people have been writing for a long time – and people are still killing one another, beating the shit out of one another, and there're still fucking fascists in the streets in England terrorizing poor fucking Pakistani people, and there're still police in England brutalizing young black kids. And all the fucking plays you do about racism and so on, it's still fucking going on.

Q: Do you think theatre is a powerful medium?

MM: No. Not compared to television – television is much more powerful. I don't want to over-romanticize theatre, I think too many people do that and I think that's for their own benefit and to justify themselves. I think television is ten times more powerful – on a superficial level – than theatre. I think theatre is highly overrated, actually (*laughs*). It's not a necessity – not to me, and, I don't think it is to a lot of people. I don't go to the theatre unless out of love, if I know an actor is in a play or I know the writer who wrote the play or if it's a Caribbean play. I'll go to see what this person is saying about the Caribbean, how he's representing it or what areas of the Caribbean he sees. If I'm going out to have a good time, or if I'm going out with my woman, I'm going to see a film! It's not to say I'm not a theatre-goer; for love I go to the cinema and I would much rather see a bad film or an average film than see a bad play. So my natural thing is to the cinema – I love cinema.

Q: Have you ever worked in any of the other forms, poetry or fiction?

MM: No, no. I used to write poetry, but I wrote the definitive poem and I stopped.

Q: Well, you've now gone into television; I take it you feel good with that.

MM: Yes. But it's crazy, you bust your ass writing plays for the theatre for so many years and you don't get any money, and suddenly you write this real nonsense, really, not any great work of art and you're getting better paid. What you get paid for a half-hour comedy series you get paid as if you'd written three plays that you bust your ass to write, and put all this great hope and expectations into it. The black community love this TV program, as I was telling you. Suddenly, people come up to me – and I've been writing plays about the black community that I thought would uplift them and educate them and change their heads and now I'm writing this silly comedy series – and they say: "Man, you write that? Fantastic!" They've only now discovered I'm a writer, and for what? A comedy series, which is totally absurd, but that is the power of television. This is why I'm telling you television is powerful – I respect its power not its content.

Q: What about screenwriting?

MM: Yes, yes. That's another ball-game altogether; that's dealing with corporations and money, and there're too many villains in that business, you know.

Q: Some of the criticism that I heard about *Rum An' Coca Cola* when it was done here in New York [1976], was that it was incomplete, that it should have been more developed; others felt cheated, that the second act was anticlimactic. What's your response?

MM: What can I say to that? That's the play I wrote. Some academic who has been to university and has studied great literature and read two hundred thousand plays – which are supposed to be great plays – could easily sit down and look at all my work and come to that conclusion. But that's what I wrote, that's my vision, that's my story, that's what I did.

Q: Do you believe in the notion of writing from inspiration, or, as you said earlier, take an idea and develop it?

MM: I think both. I don't like to make rules and don't think any rules apply, especially with a creative thing. Sometimes, as I said, I sit down and the idea comes and it's written, and sometimes I deliberately sit down and write something, so it goes both ways. I just finished adapting *Playboy of the Western World* [premiered UK, 1984] – the Irish play – to Trinidad. That was really enjoyable – to find parallel things, and I want to do some more of that. And, as I said earlier, I feel as though I'm going into another phase now which is interesting – I don't know where it's going to lead.

Q: What about the adaptation of novels?

MM: No.

Q: How would you like to be remembered as an artist?

MM: Wow! (*Laughs*) Oh, shit! We have so many bad examples in front of us, Van Gogh and other artists who, after they've died, then they become immortal – which is a terrible example to lay before people because you get this kind of sufferation complex like: "Is only when I dead they go be sorry!" (*Laughs*) You know what I mean? How would I like to be remembered? I would like to blow people's minds when they read my work. I would like to be sitting on a cloud in heaven and looking down at people – I'd probably be frustrated and angry and say, "Why the fuck didn't you do it before!?" But I would like people to examine my work closely with open eyes, and see the trails I have mapped out in my work. It's like a code – I'd like people to break my code – I don't feel anybody has done that – and see what has gone into my work. All artists feel this way, I presume, that they're not appreciated for their real value and I'm no different in that respect. I feel as though I've left maps – but you have to follow the trails – and that's what I would like people to do. I'd like to be remembered as a person who left things of value behind and to be remembered for the steps that I have made.

My father was a motorcar salesman who died when I was thirteen. We were poor. My mother sold in a department store – behind a counter. Neither had any kind of education in the academic sense; and I grew up in a little back street in St. Francis Valley Road in Belmont, with no intellectual or artistic disciplines or anything. And to have made that step from those beginnings to being a playwright – I'm not Harold Pinter – but to have made that step, to have my work done and considered valuable is quite something, I think. I mean, my work is a result of my childhood, it's Trinidad, it's my roots and it's all there.

End Notes

1. Amiri Baraka: See Lennox Brown interview, note 4.
2. Ed Bullins (1935-) is an African American playwright amongst whose almost forty plays, *The Electronic Nigger and Others* (1968) won early attention and his *The Taking of Miss Janie* (1971) won an Obie award.
3. Matura's plays in the USA include: *Rum an' Coca Cola* (Brooklyn Academy, New York, 1976); *Nice* (Arena Stage, Washington, 1980); *Play Mas* (Vinnett Carrolle's The Urban Arts Corp Theatre, 1977, New York City; The Goodman Theatre, Chicago, 1981); *Welcome Home Jacko* (New York, 1983) and *Meetings* (Phoenix, New York, 1981).
4. The Brixton uprising in South London exploded in April 1981 following a period of heightened tension stemming from a number of incidents of police brutality in a climate of regular harassment of young black people arrested "on suspicion", the infamous "Sus", and following the New Cross massacres where the black community believed a racist act of arson was not being properly investigated. In the aftermath of the riots Lord Scarman was asked to report on their circumstances and the conduct of the police. Scarman found that stop and search powers were being used disproportionately against black people and the report pointed to the deprived socio-economic situation of the black community.
5. Caryl Phillips (1958-) was born in St Kitts but came with his family to Leeds, Yorkshire as a baby. By the date of this interview he had not yet published any of the earlier novels – *The Final Passage* (1985); *A State of Independence* (1986); *Higher Ground* (1989) and *Cambridge*

(1991) – on which his reputation as one of the UK's best younger novelists was founded. He had, though, written the plays *Strange Fruit* (1981); *Where There Is Darkness* (1982); and *The Shelter* (1984).

6. Boscoe Holder (1921-2007) was a Trinidadian artist, designer, dancer choreographer and musician. In the 1950s and '60s he was based mainly in the UK with his troupe, Boscoe Holder and his Caribbean Dancers. In the late 1960s he returned to Trinidad to concentrate on his art. See Raymond Ramcharitar, "Boscoe, holder of one more award", <http://launch.groups.yahoo.com/group/limers/message/136>.
7. Geoffrey Holder (1930-) is a Trinidadian actor, dancer, painter, musician and writer who appeared in a number of British and American films (including the James Bond film *Live and Let Die* [1973]), and Broadway musicals including *The Wiz* (1975) and with Tom Harshman wrote *Black Gods, Green Islands (*New York: Doubleday, 1959).
8. It is worth noting that Matura is speaking at the point when the Trinidadian Left and the project of building a creative, participatory and egalitarian civil society that Lloyd Best and the Tapia movement and other radical groups had been trying to construct from the mid 1960s onwards was at probably its lowest ebb, but it would not be true to say that there weren't those trying to make Trinidad a more humane society.
9. Matura refers to the 1970 "Black Power Uprising" which brought together urban workers, students, sections of the army and the young urban poor in opposition to the "Afro-Saxon" government of Eric Williams.

TREVOR RHONE
(1940-2009)

He was born in Kingston and raised in Bellas Gate, a rural community in St Catherine. He was the youngest child of 23 children. Although it was a childhood of poverty, Rhone regarded Bellas Gate affectionately and it became the subject of his last play, *Bellas Gate Boy*. He felt that his upbringing gave him the will to succeed. Rhone donated his family home in Bellas Gate for the construction of a basic school, community/skills training centre and visitor's lodge.

He attended Beckford and Smith's secondary school in Spanish Town where he became involved in the Secondary Schools Drama Festival, and the annual pantomime of the Little Theatre Movement. He wrote radio plays for the Jamaica Broadcasting Corporation (JBC) and, in 1960, went to London on a scholarship to attend the Rose Bruford Training College of Speech and Drama for three years. Back in Jamaica he worked as a teacher for a time then returned to England to look for work as an actor. There were few opportunities for black actors and in 1965 he returned to Jamaica where he formed a dramatic arts group, Theatre 77, with Yvonne Jones-Brewster and other colleagues, and later opened the 150-seater Barn Theatre.

Shortly afterwards Rhone began writing and producing the series of plays that gave him the merited reputation of being probably the only dramatist in the English-speaking Caribbean who was able to live solely and successfully from the efforts of his writing and productions. These have been highly popular in Jamaica, the wider Caribbean and many other parts of the world, including Port of Spain, Barbados, Nassau, Paris, Toronto, Montreal, New York, New Haven, CT; Chicago, Washington, Lexington Kentucky, North Carolina, Nairobi, Kenya London, Bristol and Martinique.

He wrote, acted, directed, produced and invested in his productions throughout his career.

In 1967, with Daryl Crosskill and Jackson Martin, Rhone co-authored *It's Not My Fault Baby*. His own plays include: *The Gadget* (1968); *Cinderella,* a musical (1969); *Smile Orange* (1971); *Sleeper* (1972); *Comic Strip* (1973); *School's Out* (1974); *Old Story Time* (1979); *Everyman* (1980); *Two Can Play* (1982); *Music Boy* (1989); "Family Planning Musical" (1989); *The Game* (1989); *The Power,* commissioned by BBC Radio (1992); *One Stop Driver* (1992); *Dear Counselor* (1997); *Bellas Gate Boy* (2002).

His published work includes: *Old Story Time and Smile Orange* (London: Longman, 1987); *Bellas Gate Boy* (London: MacMillan, 2004); *Two Can Play and Other Plays* [*School's Out* and *The Power*] (London: MacMillan, 2008).

He wrote and directed the screen adaptation of *Smile Orange* (1974); and co-wrote the screenplay for *The Harder They Come* (1969); *Milk and Honey* (1988); and *One Love* (2003).

Rhone played a supporting role in the 1992-93 Miramax ABC-TV series *Going to Extremes*, as well as a supporting role in the Miramax feature film, *Revelation* (2001).

In 1987, he guest lectured at both the Drew Medical Centre, UCLA, Los Angeles, and at Haverford College in Philadelphia. He was a guest lecturer at the University of the West Indies, Mona, assisting students of the Executive Masters in Business programme, as well as assisting students of the Masters in Arts programme to maximize their communication skills. In 2003, Rhone was a guest lecturer at Harvard University, Cambridge, MA and at Deerfield Academy, MA.

His awards include: in 1988 the Ward Theatre Season of Excellence Award given for significant contribution to Jamaican theatre for over twenty-five years; in 1988 the Musgrave Gold Medal Award; in 1989, the Cross Cultural Communication through the Theatre Arts Award; in 1996 Living Legend Award Awarded by the National Black Theatre, USA, and the Norman Washington Manley Award. He was awarded the Commander of the Order of Distinction by the Government of Jamaica.

According to the actress Leonie Forbes who regularly performed in Rhone's plays, he was a playwright who had his fingers on the pulse of Jamaican culture and society.

TREVOR RHONE

Way Out Theatre, Pegasus Hotel, Kingston Jamaica
10 February, 1982

Q: What were some of the ingredients which contributed to your becoming a writer?

TREVOR RHONE: No ingredients, really, I guess it was just the fact that the sort of play that I wished to see or the sorts of dilemmas and problems that I wished to see dealt with on the stage were not being dealt with at that time. I hadn't intended at all to become a writer. I was an actor, took acting school in England for three years and my primary concerns, really, were with the stage as a interpretive artist or an actor. Took up writing quite by accident, or discovered I had a talent for it quite by accident. Again, that is not totally true, because long before I had been to drama school I had attempted the writing of radio material, the odd play. So, in fact, I would say the germs, the thoughts, the ideas were possibly in me long before what I call the "renewal" happened, which is about '68, twelve years ago, in fact, since when I have been writing seriously. My first thing was with a pantomime at school, simply because I could not find the right sort of material that would satisfy the needs of the children, so I rewrote the Cinderella story for the Christmas pantomime for the children, setting it in an environment that they could readily appreciate and understand, using the original story, the original characters, and setting it in Kingston. I did these pantomimes for about two or three years, and that is about where it all started.

Q: Who were some of your early influences, writers that influenced you?

TR: Nobody, really. Molière fascinates me, and there is this other playwright who fascinates me for another reason – Ibsen – for form and structure – Molière for a different reason altogether; Shaw as well, although there has been no sort of overt influences. *Methods* rather than material or intent, or content. But by and large I try and do my own thing; I try and discover a form that works best for me and my own style. Because one is working in a new environment that has not really been tapped all that much, I am still in the process of finding out what works best for me rather than modelling myself on any previous writer.

Q: You are acknowledged as the most financially successful playwright in the Caribbean. How do you feel about that?

TR: That's not true. Derek Walcott, in Trinidad, has got a grant for about half a million dollars – US dollars. But I have never had a grant in my entire existence. I don't know about financially – secure you said?

Q: Successful.

TR: Successful. Pledged to make a living, I guess, from the art, the craft; I live solely by the box office; if nothing comes in then I starve. The other day I lost – must have been about $30,000 dollars on a show in a week. It happened. Just plump! As one examines the finances of the theatre and how it works – for example, any given month now that I put a play on, I need to make, depending on whether it's a play that's just newly been put on… for any given week one needs to make about twelve, fourteen thousand dollars before one begins to see a penny for oneself. It's really a high risk business and I just *barely* manage to get by – in truth, better than most people who are writing plays because most playwrights don't manage to make anything at all. I make a fair living. But, again, it's an expensive business; you need to make a lot of money. I would say ten years ago I was possibly better off, because one charged $1.50 then, but one's expenses were minimal; now one's expenses are at the maximum and, in fact, the fare that one charges – like $7 dollars now – only just covers – it's a tight business. [In 1982 the exchange rate was $1.72 J to $1 US] But as you say. I am possibly the most successful at the box office of all the other playwrights in the Caribbean.

Q: What has the experience been like for you working in the theatre in Jamaica?

TR: Satisfying. And I can tell you why I think it's satisfying: Because one has watched something grow. I can remember looking back, say, ten, twelve, fourteen years ago when we would put on a play and we would expect a two week run, three shows a week, maybe nine shows in all for the run of the play – one found that one spent more time rehearsing the play than one actually spent performing the play. This has changed drastically over the years. A play, now, is expected to run for three months, four months, five months, six months, longer – a year, two years. *Old Story Time* has been on since 1979, which is approximately in its fourth year; we've taken breaks but it's a continuing process. Just this logistics is satisfying – from two weeks to three years, the same play attracting people, attracting audiences: that's one level of satisfaction. Another satisfaction is the fact that one gives people a lot of pleasure, one helps to establish a sense of self, helps to restore the spirit of black people. One tries to dig in oneself and to dig within the society to try and create pathways that will help us as a people grow and develop, and help us establish our own selves, our own sense of self, our own identity, so to speak. The other layer of satisfaction is simply the fact that people come up to you and express gratitude for what you have done for them, giving them good entertainment, pleasure. So there are all those levels. It also helps if you examine the thing about the creative process, that one of the dilemmas for black people is that for years they have been told, "You can't do nothin'. You really ain't equipped to do nothin', you're second class, second rate." And all the people have believed that for a long time and they feel that unless the stamp of approval comes from outside the society, from Europe or from North America or someplace, then it's invalid. What I'm *trying* to say to them is that we are very valid. That we are totally valid. We have all the necessary equipment; it's simply a matter for us to get it together. When a man can create something of himself and for himself, it's really a major leap in his development and his survival – both spiritually and economically. So, I find that whatever little contribution I can make towards those major goals gives me pleasure and that gives me the energy and the drive to continue working.

Q: You seem to have a fairly firm grasp of typical Jamaican characters.

TR: It's not so much a grasp, you know, it's more a probing. Each play for me is a problem, I mean, it is not an easy proposition. It can take me two years, three years of working on it almost every day, over a great portion of the day, and when you look back to, say, the finished two hours of material, you say: What the hell have I been doing for three years of my life trying to produce this two hours? I need to feel when I have finished something that I myself am satisfied with it, that it gives *me* a certain amount of pleasure as well, from doing it out of what is there. Also, I suspect that I have a knack and a talent in saying things a little bit *differently* than the next person. Basically, people say that my thing is comedy – maybe. It's the method I find that for me – in the Caribbean – helps to tell my message best, whatever it is that I want to say – message is a curious word – whatever thoughts I wish to transmit, I find I usually transmit best through the medium of comedy, and through *knowing* my society fairly well. But that, again, is a conscious thing, because when I went to England in the '60s, literally most things that related to oneself were sort of beaten out of one's mind. We were told that where you come from ain't valid and the way you talk isn't valid, your thoughts are not valid. So it's been a very conscious return, almost to oneself, to where one spent one's early life, literally going back and digging it up all again and examining very closely the levels of pleasure that I had left from my own childhood. Nobody could ever say that I wasn't valid or the people who lived within *my* community weren't valid, you know, but it was simply *reaffirming* that validity in oneself. Have I answered your question? I think so. In a vague sort of way.

Q: Errol Hill, in seeking to anthologize a new volume of West Indian plays, says that he is very dissatisfied with a lot of the things that he has been seeing lately. As an exception to the wide acclaim that your work has received, he seems very critical of your work; he regards it as being "superficial". The dialogue in *Old Story Time* as being somewhat "banal". He also feels whereas someone like Derek Walcott has tried to uplift the audience, he feels that you have descended to the "lowest common denominator". He says: "I don't think a serious playwright should descend to that level, I don't think it is necessary for him (Trevor Rhone) to descend to that level." How do you feel about that?

TR: Hill is rather fortunate, in fact, that he is an academic. Closets himself in an academic background, an academic setting. Okay, the man might be a scholar, but he doesn't have the courage, obviously, to face a live audience. Could he survive the way I survive as a playwright? I could survive in an academic world as well as he could. I think the man *is* just possibly jealous. He has, I gather, expressed similar negative views – always been in an attacking position. But you must understand, as well, that it's the dilemma of black people – some black people – who are not willing to give, pay homage and honour when it is due. I can understand Mr. Hill's position. As I said, he closets himself in a scholastic area where he is obviously paid for his work. Well, I guess the people that I'm trying to reach… they were all sorts. For four years – I mean, that, in fact, speaks for itself and nobody can question that – the plays have played all over the globe and have stood up, have moved people to tears and to laughter and people have looked within themselves out of what I am saying, what I have said, and I think that stands up and speaks for itself.

Q: He said of *Smile Orange* that it was supposed to be a satire on the tourist industry but he felt that it turned out to be a satire on Jamaicans themselves.

TR: I don't take Mr. Hill too seriously. As I said, anybody who doesn't have to go in the marketplace – because Mr. Hill doesn't have to be a playwright, Mr. Hill can stay on his university campus and hide away from the reality of the world and live quite happily. Now I can't do that – so until he can come out into the marketplace, the theatre, put on a play, ask his audience to pay seven dollars – and they are the real judge – if the play is no good they're not going to come, if the play is meaningful to them they will readily pay their seven dollars – until Mr. Hill can do that, give up his academic position and have faith in himself with his audience... until he says to me: "OK, I will give up my academic work, I will go out into the world like Mr. Rhone does, I will write plays for a living, I will put them on, let my audience be the judge" – let him survive on the same terms, the same level that I survive, until he can do that, I think what he is saying I would disregard, really.

Q: What do you think of the more recent crop of Jamaican playwrights?

TR: One must never be too harsh. I think the most wonderful thing that has happened is that people *are* writing. Sometimes the quality of the work isn't so good but one must realize that there's levels of inexperience, and when one looks in the long term, a guy might write two plays, his first two plays, they may not be totally satisfying, but what we are talking about is the guy gaining experience, learning from this early work and then hopefully developing; and where this will lead us in the long term could be *very* fulfilling.

Q: How do you see the wider Caribbean in terms of contemporary theatre writing?

TR: There are a fair amount of people in the other islands. There is David Edgecombe[1] in Montserrat, there is (Alwin) Bully in Dominica, there is Derek (Walcott), couple other guys from Trinidad. I think we are all trying to fashion a form that is going to take a long while before it really begins to crystallize, because I think we're all of us of this generation, this era, all coming out of similar backgrounds, where we were always told that Shakespeare was best and that was the standard. That was it. One looked toward that sort of hallmark. So I think all of us really are in a situation of probing. I spoke with David (Edgecombe) in Montserrat and Bully, and people like that – and it's probing, it's probing. I don't think one is really going to see the fruits of all this for another maybe fifty, hundred years from now.

Q: Bully would like to regard himself as being one of the pioneers of what is happening now in the theatre, just as much as the generation that preceded him, such as Walcott and Errol Hill, of twenty-five years ago. He feels that they were the pioneers of a theatre emerging out of the expatriate theatre that existed prior to the beginning of the indigenous theatre, but he feels that he is still a part of that pioneering process.

TR: Yes, he is possibly right as well. He's possibly right. Yeah.

Q: You said you take about two to three years, sometimes, to work on a piece. I therefore assume that you write fairly slowly.

TR: Yes. I try and think things out fairly well. I write in a language that the audience will understand. I think the whole process is about communication – this thing about lifting people up I think is a whole lot of nonsense. People lift themselves up. And in terms of language, you don't use language to lift people up, you talk to people in a language that they will understand, through which you can communicate thought to them. For me, it is useless going to a play, as I have been to plays – some plays – here, and you leave absolutely bewildered, wondering what the hell was that all about. I mean, I am not an ass. Sometimes you go to a play and the whole thing befuddles you. That's not communication for me. The language that our people use I think its very valid; it's the one they think in; it's the one they express their own ideas in, the one they express their hopes, their frustrations and their joys in. The language that Mr. Hill might want them to speak in or to listen to is alien and foreign to their thoughts and to the way they think. That reminds me again of the sort of Eurocentric thinking that says unless you sound like a European or write in that sort of style, then it isn't valid.

Q: Well, I don't think that is true in the case of Errol Hill because he was one of the first people who said, write in our own language and get away from Shakespeare. He was the one who encouraged people like Derek Walcott and Dennis Scott, etc.

TR: On the question of language, you talk to the man in a language – I have a very special ear where I hear what very few people else hear, and I am able to use that as my medium, my wave, my level of communication.

Q: When you say you hear things that very few people hear, James Baldwin once said that in order for a writer to be in touch with his environment he must always listen not to what people say but to what they don't say.

TR: That, too, makes a lot of sense to me.

Q: What do you think about the present state of Jamaican theatre?

TR: Healthy. When you check where it's coming from, I am always, I'm afraid, willing to forgive shortcomings at this time, because when I check back to what it was like when I just left college, what it was then to what it is now, boy, it's like north pole-south pole. I am not saying that we are always achieving a sense of excellence – far from it. I think a lot of it is very exploratory. Some of the stuff that goes up has, well, shortcomings, and sometimes if you analyse the motives for writing plays you find that the financial concerns are uppermost in their minds, rather than concern for unity. But these people quickly fall by the wayside, because if that's your concern, your major concern, then you're not going to survive very long.

Q: Do you think there is a more professional attitude towards the theatre here now, since, for instance, the Cultural Training Centre has been turning out people.

TR: Not necessarily. People that I primarily work with are people of my own generation who – and you must not always knock this – like when we went to England and they told you that your past ain't too valid – people like Charlie Hyatt,[2] Leonie Forbes,[3] Yvonne Brewster[4] had this incredible sense of discipline, a real absolute discipline. Charlie Hyatt, for a performance, gets here two hours before showtime; he really gets involved in it. I don't know that the school has had that much, profound an effect on the theatre. I wouldn't see it as being marked, at this time.

Q: How do you see the development of Caribbean theatre as a whole? You have travelled around and you've seen what's going on elsewhere; how do you feel about what you have seen?

TR: By and large I'm a professional in terms of what I try and do. I know I have a possible audience of about 50,000 people in Jamaica; in Antigua, that's almost the size of the whole country; Montserrat is level, Dominica is much less, St. Lucia is tiny. It's harder in those islands. The sort of development that one hopes to see – what is seen here – in Antigua, say, it's almost impossible because the audience will soon have exhausted itself. For an actor to really develop, he needs to be able to perform regularly and for long periods – to organize his craft, sort out his craft, that sort of thing. Those are some of the physical problems for theatre that I see. It doesn't hamper the writer too much, except that, one, he can't make a living from his work in a town with such a small audience. Doesn't necessarily hamper the quality of his work... there are outside markets that one can tap. I've been around the islands – and there's not much happening in Trinidad, not too much that really relates to the person in Trinidad.

Q: Surprising you should say that, considering there are so many talented playwrights and actors coming out of Trinidad.

TR: Yes, but it is true what I say. Derek's there, but the theatre in Trinidad has just never generated any enthusiasm among the populace, the people, the man-in-the-street. I have made the man-in-the-street come to the theatre; he doesn't see it as something for the elitist class. I have tried to work in Trinidad – not too successfully, although there is good talent there. I don't know... I don't know if it's getting any better now; I couldn't make a living in Trinidad, from the theatre.

Q: No?

TR: No, because I was there for long enough, you know, willing to go through the sacrifices that one made here initially, because the first ten years of my life here was a sacrifice for development, and I don't think anybody has made such a sacrifice in Trinidad. I know Derek Walcott started up with the Workshop [Trinidad Theatre Workshop, founded 1959, and still in existence] and worked for a long while in it, yet I think when it collapsed, everything else did as well, and I don't know why. If I die tomorrow or if (Rex) Nettleford dies then dance will continue. There has been a root that has gone very deep here; it was planted long ago; people like the Fowlers,[5] who were major contributors, Ranny Williams,[6] Louise Bennett,[7] Noel Vaz,[8] Orford St. John[9] all sacrificed, and they all worked in the region. They weren't like Mr. Hill – if you will pardon my sarcasm – living in North America, enjoying North American fruits and making pronouncements on the region. The people that I am speaking of, who made contributions, *lived* and *worked* here. I know Noel Vaz, I have a lot of regard for the man; Orford St. John spent *years* of his life without reward, literally, encouraging, developing, working – the list is endless of people who actually *sacrificed* here.

Q: Well, as I understand it, Errol Hill was also a part of that movement at the time.

TR: Before my time, maybe.

Q: With the Fowlers, etc.

TR: I started here in the '60s. But it is the ongoing sacrifice that I speak of, you know. People like Yvonne Brewster, who gave up ten years of her life to building and creating The Barn and watching it grow and develop. I'm not knocking Mr. Hill's development, I don't know very much about it. But I made my choice not to live in North America or live in England. I've lived and worked in the region, that is what I know and where my spirit lies... and there have been people like that – lots of people – who have done this; and it's like a cumulative thing where there have been layers and layers at all different areas of the society. There is [Ed] Bim Lewis,[10] [Ernest M.] Cupidon,[11] Louise [Bennett], Ran [Ranny Williams], the Fowlers, Noel Vaz, Mr. Hill, himself, maybe, Derek, who was here (another good friend of mine), Dennis Scott; the Festival office – the government's input – so there has been multiple layers that helped the thing grow here, while in the other islands I don't think they have the same input or the same level of ongoing sacrifice.

Q: As someone who co-authored what has now become a classic in the movies, *The Harder They Come* [1972], what was that experience like, that is, from its inception, to the wide critical acclaim it has received in many parts of the world?

TR: It was a curious experience, because what it taught me was that I had an incredible amount of courage in making the conscious choice that one could do something that related to black people, to the black spirit and the black dilemma in a language and a style that black people understood and could relate directly to. It is so easy to follow a North American model for the work that you do, but the movie was very pure – it had to be heavily subtitled. I think it was one of the major Black cultural breakthroughs in the entire world. The fact that it has survived for – how long? – its eleventh year, stands up and speaks for itself.

Q: It has been regarded as one of the best Black movies made.

TR: By far.

Q: Was it your idea originally?

TR: No. The original thought came from another partner of mine, a guy called Perry Henzell[12] who, in fact, approached me on the writing of that film. But it's eleven years and still playing all over; in fact, it made a lot of money here [the USA] two months ago. It is one of those things that will last forever. In fact, it's like most of my work, I think it will simply last forever. I did *Smile Orange*, and again, ten years later, the issues that it dealt with are as alive as they were ten years ago – even more so, now, funnily enough. Yeah.

Q: I understand that the translation to stage of *The Harder They Come* wasn't as successful.

TR: It wasn't as successful as I would have liked, no. And I would be the first person to admit that. I think that primarily it was because of my preoccupation with the proscenium – that is really not what I deal with in stage production – and I think then it was not knowing how cinematic images work as well as I maybe know them now. Surprisingly, the play worked well for a lot of people – not as satisfying as it could have been, but again, that is part of the learning experience. The images that one had of the movies before, you check back to when you were a youth and went to the movies – John Wayne and those guys who were on the screen while black people at that time, twenty years ago, were always in menial roles. I remember the night that *The Harder They Come* opened in Kingston. There was a whole *spiritual* reawakening of the man – one could write a whole thesis on that movie, on what it has done – though it is sort of hard to record what it has done to the psyche of the man because it's not something that's tangible. You can't say up 10 points, up 20 points, but it has done remarkable things for the Jamaican spirit.

Q: Have you worked on any other screenplays since?

TR: No, because my experience has, by and large, been bad, financially; I would consider it almost foolhardy. There is another area that I think black people need to do *desperately* – as I had recommended to Mr. Hill to do – to set out guidelines for black people not necessarily how to proceed, but how *not* to proceed in terms of creative work. Because the story of *The Harder They Come* is about the levels of exploitation that were wreaked upon the artist and upon the society, which still continues in many ways, and people ask why through naivety, through inexperience, through not knowing, through not taking the trouble to find out. How do you sell a film? How do you sell a record? How do you sell a book? How do you market a book? One of the things I have set out to do – and I hope I have time to do it – is just to sort of *leave* little guidelines, so the person who is going to write a play in the year 1999 or 2000 doesn't make the stupid errors that I made in 1970 with *The Harder They Come* or with *Smile Orange* or with any of my work, because it *can* destroy the spirit almost completely. It can destroy the creativity and it can lessen the energies. It is something I'm going to do.

Q: You seem to have a thing about time. Do you have a sense of urgency about your work?

TR: Not really. I won't put it down until it's ready, because I know when I put it down I want it to last forever, so that it will not evaporate with the first ray of the sun. At this time, for example, *School's Out* – three of my plays published by Longmans – one is being studied at the university now, another one is going to the Caribbean Examination Council and these are major – for me – milestones, breakthroughs, in terms of the analysis, of the study of self. So really, I take time, a lot of time, lot of time. I am writing a new play now, a two-hander; I have no idea how it will go when it is done. But, you see, I have basic concepts and I think, as a black person, one needs to almost devote one's life to the upliftment of the black spirit. And today, I think one is being given some very harsh choices to make: bread or spirit, spirit or bread. You can't have both; you have one and you don't have the other. But no real urgency in finishing my work. When it is finished and I am happy, then it is done.

Q: What do think are some of the elements that shape good dramatic writing?

TR: I think one's structure has to be sound. I think one has to hold – well, this is very clichéd – to reflect the people in one's community, not so much yourself, because people, I think, are primarily intrigued by themselves and are constantly looking for solutions to their own problems – I'm mixing up things here, because the whole question of structure and shape and form is a very *technical* thing. I think for us in the Caribbean, the search for form, the search for structure the search for – I don't know if you saw *Old Story Time*… for me, it still falls between two schools structurally and in its form, because a lot of it is still stuck behind a proscenium, while a lot of it is flying in terms of African methods of communication. So there is still that dilemma, because we are a new people in a new setting, coming out of our African thing bastardized by European thoughts and influences, so there is all that confusion which is tending, most times, to erupt in my own mind as a playwright looking constantly for new form, new shape. But structure is something that I find is terribly important. A work has to have this very firm basis, very firm shape, form – it's almost something that I can hardly define, but it's something that I search for – and, again, I combine that with talking to the man, talking to the community, talking about problems that interest them and, again, *entertaining* the man – I mean that is almost the priority thing. When, see, a guy pays his $7 dollars to come to this space, he is paying you a lot of money to come to see what you have to say, and he needs to be satisfied in one form or the other. I'm being very vague, I think, but again, it's not really, form, structure, shape, it's the man.

Q: What about style, types of theatre? You work mostly with a proscenium.

TR: Been trying to break away from it, but, again, one is locked in the way one has to work. This little space here is very restricted in terms of what you *can* do with it. What you see is what you see: it is a box. And most of our spaces here, apart from the Ward Theatre and the Creative Arts Centre, are really just boxes, but one tries to make do within those confines to make things functional. *Old Story Time*, in fact, functions best in a big stadium, in a open, free space. That *is* maybe the most expansive that I have got, in terms of getting away from what I call the proscenium.

Q: Do you think there is a Caribbean style of theatre?

TR: Developing. I think we are still very much stuck in what we inherited out of England or Europe. You have asked me a question that a lot of people have been discussing, trying to say what we are going to be doing; I think all of us are searching – who live in this community – and out of our experience in this community will come that form, in time. But because of the heavy influence, whenever we think theatre, a lot of us think of flats and proscenium, and all of that. I think the new generation that is coming up, who have not been as heavily influenced as we have been, will find it easier to create this new thing. I think it is a probing into the dark. I do not think it is a conscious thing as "I'm going to do that" – for me it isn't, anyway. And as for the other guys whose work I have seen and been seeing, some of them mystify me; I don't know if that is the new Caribbean theatre.

Q: Is it what is termed "roots theatre" or "reggae theatre" or "calypso theatre"?

TR: I don't know. I see with the theatre that there are two groupings – I won't call any names – and it is at the school [Jamaica School of Drama], where some guys are producing out of the mind – what I call "mind theatre" – which nobody goes to…

Q: Avant-garde?

TR: Might be avant-garde… not even experimental… it's befuddling.

I have been to a couple of plays at the school, for example, and I sit there for two hours and I leave absolutely befuddled. Maybe I am an idiot, but everybody else leaves there absolutely befuddled as well. I have spoken to a couple of guys there and said, "What are you doing?" They are into this thing of carrying the audience to some other level, and I don't know what that level is; it is based upon a lot of symbols. Symbols to me do not mean anything unless I know what the symbol is originally. Saying that putting six stones on this cross... means something, but I don't know if the six stones belong on a piece of wood – it doesn't mean a damn to me! Doesn't mean anything to anybody else either in that bloody audience, because they all yawn and want to leave.

Q: Errol Hill said something similar about some playwrights whose work tends to be too private, because theatre is a public art, that theatre cannot be private.

TR: I guess so. A lot of the new guys befuddle me; they don't explain anything to me; they don't communicate anything to me.

Q: They are private symbols.

TR: Yeah. And you can't ask me to pay seven dollars to see your private symbols. I don't know if *that* is Caribbean theatre.

Q: What do you think it should be? Maybe that is not a fair question.

TR: A bit. Each play that I write I try more and more to get closer to the man and to the community that I live in, and I am moving further and further away, hopefully, from Shakespeare, Molière and my earlier influences. Maybe in time I will get closer to... and wherever I reach might be regarded as Caribbean theatre. Do you follow what I mean? But I will not in any academic way predetermine what this is. I really don't know, to tell you the truth; I'm trying to find it.

Q: I would like to get your brief critical view on the work of some of your fellow contemporary playwrights: Errol John.

TR: Errol I admired; he hasn't done anything recently, which is a major tragedy. *Moon on a Rainbow Shawl* comes immediately to mind. I have not seen anything that he has done since. I admire the man for what he had done then; what he has been doing since I don't know. I think he is a great talent.

Q: Slade Hopkinson.

TR: Oh, Lord! Slade is another major talent. Unfortunately, Slade got ill. Slade would, for me, have been a *major* acting force in this world. I have seen him act about twice, once was at the Ward in a Shakespeare play. I mean, an explosive talent. The other time was only about ten minutes. He came to rehearse a play that I had written and he had only rehearsed it for about a half an hour and he couldn't continue, unfortunately, because he was sick.

Q: Alwin Bully.
TR: I have read some of Alwin's work; I haven't seen enough to be critical – or to give a good value judgement of it. I saw one rehearsal he was having, when I was in Dominica. I was very impressed by the rehearsal. I don't know what it turned out to be.
Q: Stafford Harrison.
TR: I haven't seen anything for such a long while. Again, impossible to give a meaningful comment because it has been *years* that I haven't seen anything of his done.
Q: What did you think of the things that you saw by him?
TR: Interesting, interesting.
Q: Lennox Brown.
TR: Lennox – I met him many years ago… He hates my work, so maybe it is unfair to comment. He leaves me sort of cold, really, I have nothing with the man. Don't know his work, again, and the couple of things I have seen… I go by how my audience responds; are they willing to pay seven dollars to come in and watch this piece of work or are they going to walk out?
Q: Carmen Tipling.
TR: The thing about Carmen is that I am sorry she is *not* writing or doesn't spend as much time as she should writing, because Carmen has a nice talent there. I would hope that she would devote more time and energy to writing rather than – well, she has to make a living – but good, good talent, really has.
Q: Dennis Scott.
TR: Dennis, as a writer, mystifies me. A lot of his work mystifies me; I don't understand it. The things like *Dog*, I didn't see, I read – mystifies me.
Q: What did you think of *Echo in the Bone*?
TR: That I rather enjoyed. I enjoyed the production; I thought it was a nice piece of work, really did. I have a lot of regard for Dennis's talent, some things he does work very well, some things don't. I guess it's like anybody else, but a good mind. I think Dennis's strongest thing, that I have the most regard for, is that if I give Dennis a script to read for me, his assessments have been bloody accurate and bloody good. I really have a tremendous amount of regard for him in that sense.
Q: Michael Abbensetts.
TR: The only thing that I really know of Michael's is *Sweet Talk*, that I know well, I have seen it done a couple of times. Again, it would be unfair to make a judgement without knowing the man's work as totally as I should – and I really don't.
Q: Mustapha Matura.
TR: Mustapha's curious. I'm not certain how well I get into his work

– I'm not certain. I have seen a couple of things, I saw *Rum 'n Coca Cola*; it worked very well in Trinidad. Was I over-keen on it? I don't know. I gather he is doing very well. I think I have read a couple of other things which I quite enjoyed. Again, I am fudging rather than coming out in a positive or negative way.

Q: Roderick Walcott.

TR: Roderick Walcott. Different *style*. To me, it is north pole-south pole – to me. That sort of style has its – I don't know – I mustn't say anything, to tell you the truth, without being able to justify completely whatever I say. Who else?

Q: Derek Walcott.

TR: Oh, I have a lot of regard for Derek, primarily as a poet. I think he is an incredible poet. As a playwright I don't know; I wouldn't say he is a brilliant playwright in the same way I say he is a brilliant poet. I have seen a fair amount of Derek's things; the thing I liked best was *Ti-Jean*, great sense of joy I found in that. I like his poetry better, put it that way.

Q: Why?

TR: I guess I don't find that his plays as complete as I do his poems. I find his poetry fascinating. Who else?

Q: Slade Hopkinson feels that Derek Walcott is our Shakespeare in the Caribbean.

TR: We don't really need a Shakespeare in the Caribbean, you know… Yes, we do! What am I saying? Oh, yeah. It depends on how… Shakespeare wrote really for the man down the road, you know. Shakespeare wrote for the man down the road and I write for the man down the road. Shakespeare really did. Derek, yeah, a poet – excellence.

Q: He has been criticized for allowing his intellectualism to block his art…

TR: That's possibly right.

Q: Another criticism is that a lot of his plays are based on models of classic plays from the past, that the only time when he has really freed himself up and let his imagination flow freely was with *Ti-Jean*.

TR: Which is the one I like. I find – if I can put it into words – in some of the plays the drama doesn't take control of the play. Does that make sense? The drama doesn't run away, doesn't take the play away as totally as it should. *Ti-Jean* I found totally enjoyable.

Q: What did you think of *Dream on Monkey Mountain*?

TR: I enjoyed it. The symbols were clearer in that; solid; one of his better, but I prefer *Ti-Jean*.

Q: Do you work in any other forms?

TR: No. I am trying some TV things, but, I don't think so. Plays.

Q: Have you ever written any poetry?

TR: One – one poem.

Q: How close do you place yourself to the socio-cultural changes in Jamaican society and in other parts of the Caribbean?

TR: Am I in tune with them?

Q: Well, judging from your plays you seem to very much in touch with what is going on around you. I don't know how long ago you wrote *Old Story Time*, but when I read it, it seemed very timely.

TR: *Old Story Time* was started in 1967 or thereabouts; it was started a *long* time ago. *Old Story Time* really is – people see it twelve times. The most amazing thing was a man from the Philippines came here, and he says: (*imitates accent*) "I been in the island three weeks an' I see *Old Story Time* three times. I stay in island two more weeks I see *Old Story Time* two more times." It's *amazing* how much that play affects so many people – people who you would think would be *least* affected by it. A lot of reality is in it; in many ways it is my own life story, in terms of some of the hazards I had to face as a poor black person growing up – a lot of naivety and innocence – into a harsh, cruel world. In a way I am quite into what is happening, but normally from a very personal point of view. I try to keep in tune, try and find out – yeah – I try to breathe it. I try. Sometimes you miss a lot; but you can't know everything.

Q: How do you view Black theatre in America and how would you compare it to Caribbean theatre?

TR: That's a difficult question. One, I have not been to America for a *long* time to really sit down and watch any Black theatre, as such. The person who I was vaguely in touch with years ago was Ed Bullins, and I have sort of lost touch with now. I really am out of touch with Black plays and Black playwrights.

Q: What inspires you to create a piece of work?

TR: That is a damn hard question to answer. There is a need within me to write; it gives me pleasure, for one thing, to complete it; a sort of compulsion, almost. And it is not so much *what* inspires for me, it is not so much inspiration as the search for clarity, how to make the damn thoughts function. It is not so much inspiration, it is sitting on my ass to make it work, to make it live – be *alive*. I hate things to be boring. I may not have answered well because I don't really know. I have been doing it for so long that I could not think of myself not doing it, or doing anything else – although I have terrible problems with work sometimes, not being able to get it together.

Q: Do you get release and enjoyment from writing?

TR: When I get it out. When I have solved the problems. But right now I have about four or five thoughts stashed away in my head, and I know I need to write, it is just a matter of finding the time; I am working on something now. When I finish that, I select the next problem and try and solve it.

Q: How do you select, how does an idea come to you?

TR: A germ might just come to you, a speck of dust, a thought and I let it settle in the head for a while, forget it; if it is still there and erupts in another six months, you give it another thought for another six months, make it rest. And then, one day you say you are going to work on that – like this thing that I am working on was just a *germ* of an idea – and now I have explored it I have what would be two good hours on one theme, one thought. Invariably, something comes to you that intrigues you, says "why?" Like this thing that I am working on now is really an examination of what has been happening in this country for about ten years, and, again, about the choices that we have to make between bread and spirit.

Q: How would you like to be remembered: as a playwright or as an artist?

TR: That's a hard question; I have never thought about that.

Q: Let us put it another way. In the beginning, when you said to yourself that you wanted to write or to be an artist, what was the inner drive within you? Was it that you wanted to make some grand statement or to leave your artistic mark on the world?

TR: Not really. Because I am fortunate that I – unlike most other playwrights – am a very well equipped actor and could earn my living in broadcasting, as an actor or as a director, yet I really gave up the acting thing, gave up the broadcasting thing and settled on the most difficult of all the forms – which is the playwriting form. I don't even know why… there is something there that makes… I don't really know, Mr. Stephenson. There is something that drives me on to do it because I know I can't stop doing it; and I don't do it for the money; it is because I know I need to. I must. I haven't examined it, I just go ahead and do it.

Q: So, for your contribution, how would you like to be remembered as an artist?

TR: I have never thought about dying… (*Laughs*)

Q: Not necessarily dying, but, I mean, there might come a time in your life here when you have said what you had to say.

TR: No, sir! I always have new thoughts to explore. I can't answer that one, I really don't know what to say. I guess my preoccupation is with today and what I am doing, because the pleasures that I am getting, I am getting them *now*.

Q: You said earlier that you hoped that your plays will last forever.

TR: Oh, I know they will. I think they will be an absolutely valid document a hundred years from now in terms of accuracy and reflecting the lifestyle of 1980, 1990, 2000. Maybe for that, yeah. I regard them as very, absolutely *accurate* documents of the times and I guess that would be enough, actually. Yeah, yeah. Because one of the major weaknesses of our lives – all our lives – is that we have nothing that we can look back at and say: "Oh, yeah, that guy did that, that's what it was like." It is like we are each starting each day, each life, as if there was no prior life and that means that our growth and our development is hampered because we are always reinventing the wheel.

End Notes

1. David Edgecombe – see interview with Alwin Bully note 8.
2. Charlie Hyatt (1931-2008) was a notable Jamaican comedian, actor in films and drama and broadcaster. He was a regular star of the annual Jamaican pantomime. From 1960-1974 he lived and worked in the UK, then returned to Jamaica, where he headed JBC's drama department. He appeared in the film *Cool Runnings* (1993) and wrote a well-received autobiography, *When me Was a Boy* (Kingston: Institute of Jamaica, 1989). See<http://www.guardian.co.uk/news/2007/feb/24/guardianobituaries. television>
3. Leonie Forbes is a distinguished Jamaican actress, broadcaster, producer and lecturer. She began work in the Jamaican pantomime in the 1950s, was awarded a scholarship to RADA in 1960 and worked for a time in theatre in the UK, and Australia before returning to Jamaica and working for the JBC. She has appeared in over twenty films. Her autobiography, *Leonie: Her Autobiography, Leonie Forbes as Told to Mervyn Morris* appeared in Jamaica in 2012 (LMH Publishing). See <http://jamaica-gleaner.com/gleaner/20080330/out/out1.html>.
4. Yvonne Brewster is a Jamaican stage director, writer and editor, one of the founders of The Barn Theatre in 1965, Theatre 77 and Barn Theatre 77. In the 1980s she came to the UK where she still lives. She co-founded the Talawa Theatre in 1985. Her memoir, *The Undertaker's Daughter: The Colourful Life of a Theatre Director* (Arcadia Books) appeared in 2004.
5. Greta Bourke Fowler and Henry Fowler, see Errol Hill interview, note 18.
6. Ranny Williams (1912-1980), Randolph Samuel Williams or Maas Ran, was a Jamaican actor and producer who began his professional career in 1929, performing in a vaudeville group organised by Marcus Garvey at Edelweiss Park in 1930. He was a stalwart of the Ward Theatre and performed in many of the annual Jamaican pantomimes. He regularly performed with Louise Bennett in Jamaica, and performed

in the UK, USA and elsewhere in the Caribbean. See Bennett & Bennett, *The Jamaican Theatre* (2011), pp. 328-331, and <http://www.ltmpantomime. com/pages/History/rannywilliamsbio.html>

7. Louise Bennett – see Errol Hill interview, note 7.
8. Noel Vaz – see Errol Hill interview, note 4.
9. Orford St John, see Errol Hill interview, note 21
10. Ed. (Bim) Lewis is a Jamaican comedian and theatre producer who appeared in *The Harder They Come* (1972)
11. Ernest M. Cupidon was a Jamaican comedian (noted as a female impersonator) and actor, a man of colour who played an important role in breaking down race and colour barriers in the Jamaican theatre in the late 1920s. He worked with Marcus Garvey and Ranny Williams. He adapted several of H.G. De Lisser's novels for the stage.
12. Perry Henzell (1936-2006) was a Jamaican film director and novelist, whose *The Harder They Come* (1972) was an epochal Caribbean film. A second planned film "No Place Like Home" never appeared when funding ran out. He published a novel, *Power Game*, in 1982. He was a white Jamaican who came from a privileged plantocratic heritage, which he rejected. He was a social activist campaigning for prison reform. See <http://www.guardian.co.uk/news/2006/dec/04/guardian obituaries.obituaries1>.

DENNIS SCOTT
(1939-1991)

Dennis Scott earned a First Class degree in English from the University of the West Indies in 1970 and a Drama in Education diploma from the University of Newcastle-upon-Tyne in 1973. He taught at Jamaica College from 1971 until 1976 and was the first director of the Jamaica School of Drama between 1977 and 1983. He was a distinguished and adventurous theatre director.

In 1983 he was visiting Professor of Directing at the Yale School of Drama, and he remained there to become Acting Chairman, Playwriting in 1984 and Co-chairman, Directing in 1986. From 1984 until 1991 he was a consultant to the Playwriting-in-Residence Program at the Juilliard Theatre Center. He was a Director for many years at the National Playwriting Conference in New London, Connecticut.

His plays include: *Breakfast with a Witch* (1963); *The Caged* (nd); *The Crime of Anabel Campbell* (1970); *Terminus* (1976); *An Echo in the Bone* (1977); *Dog* (1978); *Sir Gawain and the Green Knight* (1978) and *Live and Direct from Babylon*. His work as a director and teacher is widely acknowledged as being one of the major influences on the direction of Caribbean theatre today.

Scott was one of the most significant poets of the early post-independence period in Jamaica, and his first published collection, *Uncle Time* (1973), is marked by an effective literary use of the vernacular. His other collections include *Dreadwalk* (1982) and *Strategies* (1989). *After-Image*, is a posthumous collection of Scott's poetry, edited by his friend and fellow poet, Mervyn Morris (Peepal Tree Press). Scott was also at one time editor of *Caribbean Quarterly*. He was the recipient of many awards, including a Musgrave Silver Medal for achievement in poetry from the Institute of Jamaica.

Dennis Scott was a dancer with National Dance Theatre company of Jamaica. His role as Lester Tibideaux on the former television series, *The Cosby Show* gave him wide visibility to American audiences.

The First International Dennis Scott Conference on Caribbean Theatre was held from June 12-14, 2003, at the Edna Manley College for the Visual and Performing Arts. The conference was focused on assessing the state of Caribbean theatre; paying homage to, and critically assessing Scott's influence; proposing new directions and dimensions for Caribbean theatre and examining its reach and influence in world theatre.

As part of its Emancipation Day celebrations, the Trinidad Theatre Workshop (TTW) performed *An Echo in the Bone* 9-12 August 2012. It is one of the best known and studied Caribbean plays, taught at many universities, including Yale. Told through music, dance and narrative, with a mix of humour, the play is a story of a family that encourages the audience to reflect on its collective heritage.

DENNIS SCOTT

Kingston, Jamaica, 9 February, 1982

Q: There are some people who believe that you have not allowed yourself to develop to the maximum of your ability as a playwright. How do you feel about that?

DENNIS SCOTT: What are their reasons?

Q: That if you had directed less, you'd have written more.

DS: No, that is an explanation... What's in the work says that there is further to go, as there always is. Which distance could have been gone if I had not done other things? I am only being very playful in attempting to answer the question at all; I am not sure whether the question is worth answering in its own terms. I don't know, for example, whether there is some arbitrary scale on which one measures the work of a man. And can you say that man has reached the whatever, X on the scale, but not Y?

Q: Well, I think that they are referring mostly to the numbers of plays written, where one could see a development.

DS: Oh, that's all right. I am – and this is said with great deliberate arrogance – a poet, a playwright, a teacher, a director, an administrator. I have been an actor and a dancer – I don't count those any more – and I am very good in the things that I now do. It seems to me that life is terribly short and what I am trying to do is to pack it full of a number of skills; all these skills are involved with sharing, with encouraging people to share ideas about the universe – right or wrong ideas. In any one, or all, or more of some of these areas, certainly one wishes one's output had been more, is more, intends to be more, but I really am not terribly interested in evaluations which say, if you produce more in any one field or less in any one field – that is an impertinence which I don't deal with at all.

Q: I don't think it is an impertinence; more the respect that one has for a particular artist.

DS: A more respectful way of responding would be to say: What have you done in these areas and what commonality of interest and concern links whatever little or more that one has achieved in these areas? And I am being less than playful, now. That kind of critical judgement seems to me essentially unhelpful. I don't resent it, I simply don't care to make it part of my – the arbitration on my work, on my life...

Q: It shouldn't, but people can say anything they like; you are the one who, ultimately...

DS: No, it is a dangerous position to adopt. I would imagine, you know, Olly, if you start trying to measure achievement or quality of work in terms of the quantity of work – what a curious way of evaluating experience or creativity.

Q: Yes, well, isn't that a western way of looking at things?

DS: Is it really?

Q: I am asking you.

DS: I have never thought of it in those terms.

Q: When I say the west I always think in terms of the United States because they have the biggest influence in the west. Right? Do you agree?

DS: Certainly the second part, yeah, and certainly from your experience, the first part, yeah.

Q: OK. And the way a lot of things are assessed in the United States is always on the matter of productivity. You could be a good poet or whatever, but people always tend to say, well, if this is a good poet they want to find out more about this poet, to see more of his work to assess the poet's quality as a poet. Which, with what you were saying, is unfair because ultimately the quantity does not matter.

DS: No, I am saying something different and, perhaps, more useful than that. Which is that my own experience is that important things that have happened to me are measurable, but are not quantifiable; they happened in different sizes, and one short story or one novel or one poem or one play or one production may, in fact, change one's whole way of looking at reality and oneself. And maybe that is the important question to ask: How useful for other people has been whatever people have achieved? Rather than how much have they done.

Q: With the qualitative measure they are also using a quantitative measure.

DS: Yes, I understand this and regret it all. Pity.

Q: Do you consider yourself more of a poet than a playwright or a poet of the theatre?

DS: I think they are two different *kinds* of activity: One, the theatre is intensely collaborative, the other one is intensely private. This says nothing at all about the potential effect of either, or about the value of either to myself or to others; but I do think they are different activities and I am very glad that I *want* to do both. I am very glad that I have both those media to talk about the world and myself; I don't know which one I am more. Which one do *you* think I am more, from what you know?

Q: More effective as?

DS: Two questions: Which one am I more effective as, and which one am I, in my *tendencies* to create, more of?

Q: OK., this brings us back to my original question concerning your output as a playwright. I have seen more of your poetry than I have of your plays; it has nothing to do with the power of either form. For me, I think you are equally effective in both.

DS: That's interesting. I have never been able to get that response. Yes, that's interesting. I am glad you answered that fairly honestly.

Q: In the case, say, of Derek Walcott, I find his poetry more effective than his plays. I think he is more of a poet than a playwright – not that he isn't a good playwright, he is an excellent playwright, but I think his power lies mostly in his poetry.

DS: His craft as a poet is more developed, certainly, and surer.

Q: Considering the time that you spend directing, and your administrative position at the School of Drama, do you find yourself placing more emphasis on other aspects of theatre, rather than writing; and when do you find time to write?

DS: Taking it in the reverse order, I find time to write – which is a private occupation – when my family are asleep and my day's commitments at my job and to other people are more or less resolved and completed; that time is mine, I am free to play in that time. My job as an administrator keeps me in touch with the practical problems and the day-to-day momentary pains and pleasures of students and teachers who are focusing their energies on the business of defining professionalism and craft and the business of learning to recognize in what *appears* new, things that are old, tired and well worn... so that is no time wasted whatsoever. That feeds back into my own creative energies. Thirdly, as a primary creator, that is, as a playwright, I find that my work with actors keeps me in touch with needs that playwrights very often forget – that your job as a playwright is to tell a story as clearly as you can and to make that story *playable* by other people, presentable by other people, and therefore to make that story contained in itself, to be *coherent* in itself and to present a view of the world that you wish others to at least consider seriously, if not agree with. So, that feeds back into the other areas of my work and my life, in the same way as playing the role of a husband or a father feeds my perceptions of what it is to be human in the day-to-day problems and pleasures, just as an ordinary human being, not an artist at all. There is no compartmentalisation necessary or possible.

Q: How many plays have you written to date?

DS: To date, I think I have six or seven one-act plays that I am not ashamed of; there are one or two that I am and I don't want them to be used or looked at. And two full-length plays of which I am quite proud: *Echo In The Bone* [premiered 1974] and *Dog* [premiered 1978]; I am working on a play now that is supposed to be completed by summer, a two-hander for four characters – a play for two men and two women written for one man and one woman, which ought to be interesting.

Q: I read a draft of *Dog*, which you had shown me some years ago; it seemed a little confusing to me when I read it. How was it received in Jamaica? I understand it got favourable reviews. Did it have a wide response in terms of audiences?

DS: The numbers of people who saw it was comparatively small. The number of people who see work here tends to be small, I believe, unless one is talking about work that, A), can run for a long stretch in a small house, and, B), is quality work. So, no, I don't think it has had wide acclaim at all. I think it is, however, in the minds of many people who have seen it, an interesting and useful piece of work and worth remembering and, perhaps, talking about. It is interesting because its central metaphor or metaphors are very original; they haven't been done here before as far as I know; and it is interesting because it is a very theatrical piece; it is useful because it says something – I think politically, with a capital P – politically interesting and useful; also, because it explores the capacity of theatre to extend itself into forms that are not conventional, that is, not statistically normal, not very frequently used. And it useful, also, because it demonstrates – in at least two of the productions – the fact that for a play to happen – as people have said from time to time – all you really need is some actors, an empty space and an audience.

Q: That was how it was done?

DS: That was how it was done at least twice.

Q: How do you see the present state of theatre in Jamaica?

DS: I am very glad that, very stubbornly, we keep saying to each other: "I don't care or maybe understand what you are doing, but this is what I want to do." It provides a situation in which, at a given moment, the School of Drama can be presenting, with a budget of $200, a play by a Trinidadian playwright, Victor Questel[1] [*Sufferer* (1981)], while Trevor Rhone's *Old Story Time* goes into its 400th performance at a hotel venue; while two or three indigenous Jamaican comedy-dramas attract fairly respectable audiences for fairly long runs; while the annual LTM [Little Theatre Movement] pantomime – an indigenous folk-fantasy, romantic musical – attracts *huge* crowds, sold-out performances for virtually every one of the seven or eight [weekly] performances for a three-month period; while another group does Molière, *The Imaginary Invalid*, at the Little Theatre, sometimes for audiences of school children. It means that we are retaining our options and refusing to exclude the possibilities that theatre contains for each of us; it means that some of the choices may be wrong, some may be right, but at least the options are kept open – which is one of the freedoms that I personally demand of people, that they retain their options and allow me to retain mine.

Q: How do you see the present state of Caribbean theatre?

DS: Perhaps historically, it is possible to assert that amongst our governments there is a kind of attitude to art, culture, in each of our countries, that has tended to dictate the levels of achievement within that country in the arts – and the levels of respectability which are offered to the arts, or the way communities in those countries see the arts – and that there is a wide spectrum throughout the Caribbean – the English-speaking Caribbean, certainly – of these attitudes. We see governmental interest, disinterest – sometimes governmental interest but no real knowledge of how to implement, how to create policy that will help the arts to grow, to prosper. Sometimes interest but no money with which to assist the artist to grow and assist the arts to flower; sometimes no interest and a great deal of money. I think that this is, perhaps, the situation now, in my clumsy view of it. I think that the artists themselves, in each of the countries, whatever the condition and whatever the respectability of the arts in that country, are enormously energetic and *hugely* receptive to any chances of growth that they receive. I think they [artists] are inhibited from growth when they are inhibited by lack of finances, for one – by a certain ignorance of the possibility of turning their hands to *make* fashion, of *using* what appears to be economic disadvantage and creating a *style* that works for them; they are inhibited by the essential inertia of most people and the difficulty people experience – generally, all of us – in dealing with change and movements that involve change. They are inhibited, perhaps, also, by the gaps between the islands, all that water that prevents us from coming together as often as we should and want to, to talk about our common concerns, to exchange our work, to look at each other's work, to talk about what we are doing, and by dialogue to arrive at some clear understanding of what and why we are doing things. I think we are inhibited, also, by the lack of scripts and that is very often a basic economic reality now – the disadvantage of the lack of publication of scripts that makes it hard to even see work on paper much less in performance. I think we are inhibited, also, by the failure – and I use the word a little too heavily, I know – of planners to see CARIFESTA as anything other than momentary circuses in which people don't get a chance to see or to share enough. I think the whole business of CARIFESTA, as people have been saying this last year, needs to be very carefully re-evaluated, and different strategies for sharing information and culture brought into existence. I think that one of the advantages is that recently, within the last five years, for the first time there has developed in Jamaica – who cares where it exists as long as it exists – a centre for the arts, including theatre, that is a geographical point of reference, where experiment and documentation and an attempt to find the truth of the crafts can continue with the Cultural Training Centre.

I think one of the next stages of the development of the CTC and for all four schools, certainly for the School of Drama, is that the kind of work that goes on within those premises gets extended into the rest of the island and into the rest of the Caribbean, so that we are not creating a museum or a place where everybody has to come to, but creating a centre which can energize the cultural life of the community. Some of this work has already begun. Recently there was formed the Graduate Theatre Company, which is an Inter-American Foundation funding, a small company of teacher-actors, teacher-directors whose mandate is a three-part programme: one, to take theatre to schools in the rural areas of Jamaica, and, two, to work with communities outside of the urban areas on developing, on creating theatrical forms that work for the community, that *talk* about the community and its problems, that *celebrates* the community and offer, perhaps, solutions to some of its problems. Thirdly, to create a repertory season of two or three plays which can be presented in the urban area first and then taken on tour to the rural areas. This is a *large* step, a huge step in taking the work of the School of Drama, for example, outside of the small urban area of Kingston into Jamaica and hopefully, on a much longer term plan, to the rest of the Caribbean.

Q: What do you think about the more recent crop of Jamaican playwrights?

DS: I think we are learning right now, to manipulate tone so as to hold audiences by a reflection of their concerns, and by challenges to the areas of taboo and by dealing, however superficially, with the immediate concerns of the community-at-large. I think this is a learning period for many of the new playwrights, and that's all right; I mean, you don't develop a craft or an art overnight. Again, there are a whole lot of things going on. There is somebody like Stafford Harrison, who, having flashed in the pan for a couple of years and shown that he had a lot of talent and energy, has now gone abroad to consolidate that talent and to build it further, on a foundation of very formal kinds of learning. Whether or not he returns home, if something has happened or will have happened in his head and in his heart, that is bound, I think, to make his work stronger, more secure, more *morally* centred, that is, more directed towards presenting a view of the world to which a vast number of people can relate, whatever their initial ideological persuasions may be. Simultaneously, Trevor Rhone continues to work, experimenting – he did a production recently which I directed, which failed economically and lost him a lot of money – for which he blames me and my direction, I think – but it was a very interesting experiment, his first entry into the field of writing and producing a musical. Well worth doing, I hope he finally comes to realize. Simultaneously, there are people who are working in the field, writing now, who are toying with the superficialities of Jamaican life and the social order; they are writing social comedy and comedy of manners – nothing wrong with that at all. Comedy of manners, by its nature, is very often a very superficial form, but it is one of the ways of dealing with the realities of now. The great comedies of manners retain their ability to comment on human nature in general, the mediocre ones are evanescent – that's all right – historically.

Q: What do you think of contemporary Caribbean writing, generally, and playwriting, specifically?

DS: I think one very important thing has happened in the last couple decades and that is, that the playwrights are almost without exception – none that I can think offhand – very much in touch with what is happening. It has become very, very rare, indeed, to find a playwright in the West Indies who is not attempting to deal with the situation of the Caribbean now, and that I think is an important step. There is the problem – a dual problem, perhaps – in bringing the work to the stage: one, is that the impulse to go commercial; to make the material commercially viable and successful tends to militate against preparatory work being done by the playwright, or the playwright and director, or the playwright, director and actors, so that the work rarely achieves its potential. And I know a lot half-assed work gets *done* very quickly – and, is sometimes, very commercially successful – that should *not* be done, that is a discredit to the work of the people who are involved. Simultaneously, there is work that is attempting to push the boundaries of the craft further, of the profession further, that by its very nature cannot be hugely commercial in its impulse, cannot rely on mass media for approval; it cannot rely on mass appeal for its perpetuation or its commercial success, so that it tends to have smaller audiences, to have shorter runs and because there is very little, if any, publication, is very inaccessible; which does not allow the people who should be looking at it and evaluating it and talking about it seriously to see it – that is, specifically, the people who live in the groves of academe, the critics – the *serious* critics very seldom write in the press – and the people who are deeply interested in theatre in all the areas of the Caribbean and that, perhaps, is the dual problem facing playwrights in the Caribbean right now – two sides of the same coin.

Q: Derek Walcott has said that one of the problems that he has found with the recent set of writers is a lack of discipline and laziness towards their craft. How do you feel about that?

DS: I think whatever those words mean for Derek, I would take them as rough ways of saying something that I too believe, but might we say it in this way: until quite recently there was scarcely enough attention paid to the fact that people in the arts, people in theatre, need to be intelligent as well as talented. By intelligent I mean need to be very sensitive to language and its nuances; need to be very aware of what has been done before so that, for instance, they don't pretend that they are breaking new ground when they are actually building on a very long and important tradition; need to be aware of the logistics of the business so they can administer their own work and its commercial uses; need to be responsible for their own work and its success or failure – which means that you are a professional and you do what you have committed to do come hell or high water, whether you are doing it for free or for money; need to be able to feel themselves *accountable* to the societies they spring from, and that requires a lot of conceptualization sometimes, that balancing of the needs of the self against the needs of the audience – audience with a capital "A" – all that's what I mean by intelligence. I know, until quite recently, these elements of intelligence were not among the qualities that theatre artists were supposed to have; you're supposed to have talent only, and good voice or a presentable person onstage. I find that this in itself is boring and insufficient, and makes for bad work at all levels; this is changing I think gradually but surely.

Q: In terms of conceptual theatre…

DS: What does that mean?

Q: The ideas of "roots theatre", "reggae theatre" or "calypso theatre" that have been floating around for the past several years – what do you think about them?

DS: Again, I think about a matrix of responsibilities and interest. In any given situation there is the audience, there are the makers of the work, there are the economic interests operating and dictating the parameters within which both can function. In any given situation there is also the idea that the work is offering to its audience a view of the world, whether it is a huge view of man in the universe or a specifically small view of the labourer in his current situation. Given the specific situation, then, a play will demand the use of a number of possible theatrical devices – tools which range from drumming to dance, to singing, to orchestrated music, to elaborate technological backup, to incredible lighting systems, to huge casts, to two-man casts, to arena-type staging, to proscenium arch staging. The work and what the people want to say with the work, and what the audience want to hear, all determine, it seems to me, what that work finally is as a finished production. So, when people talk about conceptual theatre, I tend to go a little bit blank; I want to know – instead of what do you believe theatre should be – I want to know what play are you talking about, to whom are you going to present this play, under what conditions, why, and with what effect? And that dictates what the theatre is, what the concept is.

Q: I would like to ask you a more personal question: Do you write slowly or quickly?

DS: I do a hell of a lot of preparatory work and notes and schematization and structuring, and then I write very, very fast indeed. *Echo* was written in two weeks, *Dog* was written in one week, finally.

Q: When do you write best, in the morning, midday or late at night? I find that many writers like to write early in the morning.

DS: Whenever I can. Because I insist on seeing the various roles I play socially as complementary, I can switch from one to the other with comparative ease; it makes no difference. Although, of course, there comes a point when you need to sit down and say, "Okay, I must not be interrupted for a while" – for a day or a week or four weeks – "and I must actually do the work, now, and finish it."

Q: What inspires you to create a piece of work?

DS: I have an image in my head sometimes – in response to that kind of question – of a creature who is irritated – and soothed – in various ways by a texture of experience simultaneously at different levels, through various senses, and that creature, processing these experiences that are coming in full-tilt, at enormous speed – simultaneously, constantly – produces a kind of response that is an attempt to define, redefine the creature's self in terms of all these experiences that are happening to it (I don't know if that makes any kind of sense) so, that, finally, when the level of irritation becomes great enough or constant enough – it varies from person to person and time to time – what is excreted, what is resultant, is an artifact in whatever art form it is that one is accustomed to work in, or one attempts to define oneself and the world in that artifact, which is a result of the irritation.

Q: How does a poem and a play come for you?

DS: A poem comes, for me, very, very sharply; the level of irritation ascends a level or two and a very immediate experience hooks into other things that I am feeling, thinking, sensing, remembering, and that makes a poem start to happen. Recently, I was on a train passing through a very rocky part of Connecticut, and it was very cold and there was frost on one shaded rock wall near the train and the image came together in my head that there are places in people, certainly in myself, that the sun doesn't hit, that love and affection and familial warmth doesn't get to, and those places are always bare, and nothing grows there – they are very *terrible* places – and that, it is in those places, perhaps, that one hides and is most cruel, places that are secure from the healing warmth of human contact. And that poem started to happen at *that* specific moment when that image concretized.

A play happens in a very different way; a play happens for me with a series of images that may or may not be overtly connected – that is connected in some kind of narrative line – but that begin to hook up with one another and to create a story between themselves, so that finally a story evolves and from that story the play grows. So, for example, the play I am working on now began with a number of very separate images; one is a woman who is teaching her man to deliver her child, a rehearsal for the birth of her child; another image was of a man who needs to know, jealously, what a couple are doing and asking the descriptive assistance of a girl in explaining to him what they are doing, so his jealousy can be either fed or exacerbated. These images and others started to come together in a kind of narrative and finally, the play that I am about to write, I think, is about a relationship between people who contract to each other informally, father-daughter, man-woman, lover, her possible lover with the other man. So, essentially, the images start to hook to each other and create a story, and I find out what that story is and then find out what that story means to me and then find out how to make that story mean something clearly to somebody else.

I think the commonality in my perceptions that produces two different kinds of art forms is that in both cases – that of poem and that of play – I begin by seeing an event, images of something happening... frequently something happening, always that something happening to someone, and frequently something happening to that person *for* someone – overt physical behaviours.

Q: How do you view the socio-political situation in Jamaica at the present time?

DS: Not necessarily with any sort of importance or validity to me – I think people *feel* that they are happier and better off now, so therefore they *are* in curious kinds of ways both, because it encourages them to *be* better off and to find ways of being better off – and, in terms of their psychological health, because they are then less distrustful of each other and of themselves. I think that the strategies that any government of a country like this must employ are essentially similar.

We have a choice constantly of working with, and being friendly with, either nonaligned countries and/or, when they differ, with Third World countries and/or, when they differ, with a place like Cuba, *or* of tying to the Western Imperial powers… I think the names of the game may change, but, basically, we are deciding constantly: who will help us more and destroy us more slowly?

Q: How do you see that affecting the cultural aspect of the country?

DS: In a funny kind of way – and this maybe a pretty dumb response to make – in the decades during which I have been politically fairly sensitive to what's going on around, I have yet to see a moment in which the innate energy and sensibility of Caribbean peoples has been affected in any major way by transitions of government or transitions of a particular allegiance – world powers or whatever. I think there is within us a core instinct of survival and impulse to create that – no matter what the surrounding political, socioeconomic situation may be – keeps proposing new strategies for survival, new strategies for commitment to ourselves and this is really our hope and our health: that they can't beat us on those grounds. People keep creating, creating in new ways, constantly, without blinking an eye, as a matter of course. And, really, when it comes to the artist in this region, and I do believe in this very strongly, that the moment's politics or the moment's crisis and the moment's catastrophe finally, is just that – the moment's. We continue to engage with ourselves healthily, no matter what happens.

Q: "Healthily" is the key word there. Do you see within that creativity a growth?

DS: There is a growth in the sense that continually we are exploring, we are finding out things that we didn't know we knew before – or actually didn't know. We are finding out things that were found out before and we're now recognizing afresh. Each generation learns *again* to be black, to be creative, to be self-reliant, to be strong, to survive. It's a constant *battle* and a constant process of change and growth, and as each generation becomes… middle-aged, as the case may be, the new generation goes through the same process and learns again to be strong. There's no problem. We survive.

Q: How closely do you remain connected to other cultural activities around, and how closely do you place yourself to social movements in Jamaica and in other parts of the Caribbean?

DS: This is a kind of lazy answer, but somewhere in it lies a focused response. By the time the late '60s early '70s came around, I, personally, had gone through a process of realizing, looking around me and seeing people wake up to being black and committed and nationalistic and so forth and so on and, simultaneously, realizing that because of various elements in my own life and upbringing, I had been through that process without noticing it, and that it was not a problem area for me, an area for possible potential public discourse. I was black, I was a mongrel; I had, I felt, accessible to me, all that human beings can and have done, and it was not an area of potential concern.

Simultaneously, I began to realize there is this necessary constant for people to discover themselves – and sometimes very painfully – and to tell everybody about that discovery – sometimes very painfully for everybody else – and that you just have to live with that fact. Just about that same time, too, I think I must have begun to realize that part of this is an education – to encourage people to go through that process, however painful, and to come out of that process with as little pain – residual pain – as possible, for themselves or others. So that, by the time the '60s, '70s came around, I felt very easy inside my own skin. I have fairly clear, fairly discernible and describable political views. I'm aware of the ironies which are involved in the differences between some of my views and some aspects of my lifestyle, and those ironies I regard as an intrinsic part of *myself* and I accept them fairly happily.

Q: Are those ironies of yourself or of this culture?

DS: I think it's both, but I was being intensely, perhaps, personal on this for a moment. I think many people are in this same situation, and that from *within* that awareness of irony and from *within* that conviction that I belong here and I wish to stay here, it is necessary and possible for me to do what I do best, that is, teach and work in theatre, so that somebody else can benefit in some way from what I have learnt personally and professionally. It is a very selfish kind of attitude and one which I value for its very selfishness; it produces pleasure in me and it has a certain utilitarian, and, perhaps, quantitative and measurable use to this society.

To return to part of your earlier question. It does seem to be important that artists keep in touch with what other artists are doing all the time. Not judging, but to share, to find supportiveness in them, to offer support to what they are doing, to engage in dialogue as a result, to learn better how to be (A) person, (B) artist, both of which are impossible ideals but worth trying for.

Q: Why do you think it is impossible?

DS: Well, ideals are by their nature goals that one sets, which one is aware and one is, perhaps, too human, too fallible to ever reach, but which are worth attempting. I mean, it is a way of organizing your life so that you have some goal, some objective which you regard as important, at least to yourself.

Q: Coming back to the question I asked you earlier about "Roots theatre",

I put the same question to Stafford Harrison, some years ago – this was late '76 – and he said that the idea of a roots theatre in Jamaica would not happen until roots people started writing their own work for the theatre. In this instance, he was speaking specifically of Rastafari. What are your feelings on this?

DS: Series of different responses – hopefully collective. The ironies, I hope, remain intact in everybody's head that, among the so-called roots people, there are those who are driving very expensive American cars, wearing dark glasses, tams and locks, and I am not judging in my answer to say that when you talk about roots people you're also talking about these – so is the statement therefore applicable to them too, would be one of my questions – a little ironically and pleasantly. Another response is that blanket statements about what people should be writing or should be creating I tend to find boring, personally uninteresting and personally useless, since they seem to me to fall into the category of proscription and things that proscribe what a free individual must do – when those actions do not affect the well being of others very directly – seem to me dangerous and essentially fascistic. Third response is that since that kind of statement used to be made – and I am sure I have made it at sometime myself in some form or the other, too – a lot has changed and the needs of the society, the needs of roots people, perhaps, can no longer be simplistically stated in terms of the ideals of Rasta or the ideals of any other singular group. A fourth response is, perhaps, that attempts to create art that speaks only to a select group, a group which is select because of its particular set of beliefs – political, religious or whatever – seems to me less useful than art that deals with the quality of a man's life... A good play by a Rasta will be a good play not because it is by a Rasta or because it speaks to Rastas, but because it defines as honestly as possible the relationship between a certain set of beliefs and another set of beliefs and tries to be truthful about the values that are worth keeping, retaining, in both those areas of belief – and that's why it is a good play. Which seems to me to rule out the possibility of labelling things as "roots" or "Rasta" or what-the-hell have you – I hope.

Q: What are your feelings on Black Theatre in America and how would you compare it to Caribbean theatre?

DS: I haven't seen that much Black theatre in recent years or even read much. If we are talking – as we probably are not – about Black Broadway musicals, musical revivals, and so on, then I don't think that's an important area to talk about. But we are talking about the work of people like Steve Carter...[2] In each case these generic terms are so tricky – Black theatre, I mean. Steve Carter comes out of a particular generation and a particular kind of historical experience in which the Blacks, after the pains of the '60s and early '70s, were beginning to try and reshape their ways of looking at themselves in terms of the white world that was obviously going to win – that was clear by the '70s. Then that's one kind of black theatre and I think it is a valuable kind of – I know I'm not going to get trapped into trying to evaluate it – that *certainly* is one of the inevitable responses to that situation – especially when we talk about a playwright whose roots are in the Caribbean. Talking about Baraka and Black Arts[3] and we're talking about a man who's saying we are *not* to try and deal with existing *in* this white culture, we are simply saying it invalid for our experience; we have stuff that we can build our own lives on as Blacks and we had better think very carefully about segregating ourselves politically, economically, socially, culturally and making our own lives worthwhile for ourselves, equally valuable, equally inevitable *long* after the rhetoric of the '60s and '70s have disappeared.

I saw a piece in New York, last time, it was about a young teenage killer – NEC [Negro Ensemble Company] did it – Charles Fuller's play [*A Soldier's Play* (1982)]. We are talking about an immediate response to urban contemporary situations and an attempt to evaluate what happens in those situations in terms of social and economic pressures operating within the white culture in which the black culture is encapsulated. Again, inevitable and valuable, it seems to me. This is not answering your question.

Q: Getting close. Take your time.

DS: Comparison. In North America, the Blacks seem to me to be writing about a number of things that affect them; attempting to come to terms with their experience of what it is like to be black in a white world. Here [in Jamaica], we seem to be attempting to come to terms with what it is like to be ourselves, to be Third World, developing people, impoverished, mostly black – or various shades of black – culturally very strong at root, but, superficially, very much at the mercy of the technology of a non-black set of civilizations. I think that is just as valuable and just as necessary and inevitable for us.

I think the major difference is clearly that we have never been a minority here and that therefore the culture that sometimes binds us or appears to bind us is never felt as being undefeatable. It is never felt as being unconquerable or as absolutely alien to us, because we are a set of creole societies and it is both our weakness, because it provides us with a lot of dangerous options sometimes, and our strength, because it provides us with a lot very exciting possibilities for further growth and for exploration.

Q: You used the phrase "creole society". There has always been, it seems to me, this very moot contention of people attempting to define just what the Caribbean is. Is defined solely on the basis of colour or sociocultural and economic terms? I would like for you to elaborate on that for me a little.

DS: If I were to be stupid enough to attempt to define creole, I'd probably say something like: The resultant of two cultures whose value systems are essentially different and, therefore, whose cultural patterns are essentially different and the degree of the creolization is immaterial. The moment you get those two forces happening, then you get a vector happening, then a new entity, a new *way* of dealing, a new *kind* of society is created which should be better or worse or same as either of the two, but which is essentially *different*, and, can never be regarded as either one or the other – if I were silly enough to attempt to define creole.

Q: Yes, but the conflict lies in the fact that there are a lot of people who do not see it as a creole society, but more a black African society, because of numbers.

DS: Unfortunately, numbers do not validate experience. A number of people living in the same tenement yard cannot be said to belong to a part of a country which is, after a while, separate from them, because their interaction in the yard, their moment-to-moment dealings with each other and their situation in the yard creates a dynamic of experience and change, of people in the process of change. That makes them never again the same as the people who lived in this other part of the country or that other part of the country or that part of the city – they belong to each other.

Maybe what I am trying to say is that the creolization process has one very strange – and for many people, I do believe – terrifying effect; it makes it essential that one recognizes the fact that we belong to each other because we share, we are the consequence of the same process of change and a confluence of energies This can be very terrifying because it then forces you to attempt to absorb into your concept of self the fact that the man over there, who is a different colour from you, but who has lived here fifty years longer than you have been alive, and who has shared the same experiences as you have shared while you were alive, belongs here, too, and is a part of your community. Therefore, you then have to deal with issues like: "How can he a part of that community if he is white and I am black?" or "he is black and I am white." And it's a very, very terrifying phenomenon for a lot of people. It has been observed, I think in the last few years, by a number of writers, some of them educationalists at the university here – and it is a *very* interesting question, very interesting phenomenon. If you sit down and try to deal with it squarely it faces you with all kinds of ironies and self-contradictions. How can you talk about a motto like "Out Of Many One People" when the culture so often says that the Syrians, the Lebanese, the Chinese, the East Indians are, in fact, *not* a part of our culture, that their behaviour patterns have no place in our lives. It produces a peculiar kind of – at its worst – illness, at its best, sense of humour.

Q: And, for dramatists, fantastic theatre.

D.S. (*Laughter*)

Q: I would like to get your response to the work of a number of your fellow contemporary Caribbean playwrights. Errol John, for instance.

DS: I haven't seen anything he has done recently; the last thing I saw by him were screenplays, which were for a different medium and different kind of audience. *Moon on a Rainbow Shawl* is still one of the very important Caribbean pieces; recently watching a very new Caribbean play, someone said to me, "Boy, the structure of *Moon* continues to happen in Caribbean plays." I think they are right: about people wanting to leave, to escape and in doing so, in saving themselves, damaging other people. Good play.

Q: Slade Hopkinson.

DS: I wish that Slade was able to be working with West Indian companies. I directed *Sala* [1974], and directed *Summer Dread* [1976], his play about revolution, he was very much – is very much – in tune with what was happening – the last time when I saw him here; the craft was growing by leaps and bounds. He was beginning to work in theatrical images rather than in language only. He began, for me, by being a very, very verbal playwright who made his characters talk a lot. Increasingly, it seemed to me, he was learning to make his characters *do*, interestingly, in front of us, which I thought was good.

On Slade, still. This is *no way* at all an indulgent comment. But, it seems to me that creative artists like that *leave* behind them a kind of influence that is *very* difficult to measure People who have seen Slade as an actor, who have seen him operate as a playwright and sometimes as a director, have learnt from the quality of his work something – I am speaking for myself – certainly about the possibility of excellence, about the necessity to attempt the ideal. That is maybe, finally – I don't know – more important to individuals, certainly – and maybe through the multiple effects to a lot of people – than saying he wrote the great West Indian play or he wrote a lot of plays.

I remember seeing him in Trinidad do Beckett's *Krapp's Last Tape*. I saw him do *Lear*, in Jamaica, worked with him on *The Long Vacation* (*Summer Dread*); there is a quality of integrity about the work, always, that is very persuasive and, perhaps, has helped a lot of people, consciously or not, to validate their belief and the possibility of doing good work – which, after all, is what counts.

Q: Alwin Bully.

DS: I think that Alwin suffers from not having anybody around to look over his shoulder and say, "That is crappy, do something about it," or, "That is very good, you know that you're trying something new." He is his own editor, his own critic, his own director, his own playwright, sometimes his own actor and I think it is a very dangerous situation for anybody to be in. Walcott's work suffered for a long time because he was in that kind of situation, too, where he himself was the sole arbiter and his own critic of his own creative work. It is not an enviable position for any artist; you need somebody who can challenge what you are doing intelligently and approve of what you are doing intelligently, and, finally say to you: "This is what you are doing. Now, would you decide whether you really want to do this." I think Alwin suffers from that. *Enormous* talent and terrific energy and he is very accountable for his society and to his society, which is something I praise very highly, but I wish he had people around him who could talk with him constantly about the work, monitor his progress and his growth.

Q: Stafford Harrison.

DS: He was, when I lost personal contact with him, a spoilt brat suffering a lot of disadvantages from being a middle-class dropout who had opted for social responsibility and political sensitivity. A great talent. Great deal of talent. And a very *daring* kind of talent which I value very highly indeed. But, a little too careless in his dealings with other people and this is, in my book, unforgivable. I hope that being a minority abroad has helped to sober his instinct for selfishness.

Q: Lennox Brown.

DS: I think he has an *extremely* inventive head. And, by inventive, in his case, I mean a preoccupation with form and a willingness to experiment, to play with form – that is comparatively rare in the Caribbean sensibility. I think, also, that because of his comparative isolation as an individual – if I recall him correctly – and as an artist, and as a black artist, and as a black expatriate Caribbean artist, he is in a very – in some ways – enviable position of being able to view from a certain aesthetic distance both the Caribbean and his immediate environment. And aligned with his concern for craft, for form and structure and his innate understanding of the West Indian creole sensibility, it makes for a body of very interesting work indeed. I wish it were more available to us here. Very interesting work, which I would love to see more of it done in the West Indies. I wish he would come home occasionally, too, so that he could be *fed* more by what is happening freshly here, and he could feed into our system what he has learnt abroad more directly than he can from that tremendous distance.

Q: Carmen Tipling.

DS: She has, as far as I know, one one-act play, *During Lunchtime They Had the Revolution* [1969], and *Straight Man* [1974], about illegal immigrants in New York, *The Skeleton Inside* [1977], about what happened at the beginning of the transition to socialism and into social unrest. I think her craft grew in the course of those three works; she has an innate humaneness and understanding of the problems people face when they attempt to respond truly to their situation in spite of what their heads tell them should be happening. She is concerned, it seems to me, with the ironies implicit in any movement towards change, change of location and milieu or change of political ideology, and that is what all her three plays focus on. I think that if she had continued to write she would have become a very, very valuable playwright, not because of her concern for form – she hasn't, she's very much a traditionalist in her formal skills – but because she views the contemporary situation from the point of view of a slightly distant and very sympathetic observer and that is certainly one of the points of view that I would like us all to keep, I would like the society to keep intact for all our uses – that ability to look at *intensely* violent processes of change in the individual and in the society from a little bit of a distance, so as to say: "This is what is being lost, this is what is being gained, this is the irony implicit in the situation." I think she also has an interestingly non-gender aligned attitude in her plays; her male and her female characters are equally sensitively defined. And the point of view of the plays has nothing to do with who is winning the war between the sexes, it has to do with who is winning the war between head and heart, which is a useful kind of battle to observe, I think.

Q: Michael Abbensetts.

DS: The only work, really, of his I know is *Sweet Talk* [1973]; that is the only thing I really know. I thought it was wordy and that structurally it fell down in the second half, and that the characters did not seem to move to complete the arc of their action satisfyingly. I thought he had a great facility with delineating the interaction that happens intraculturally and interculturally; that his subject matter was potentially very exciting – the clash of cultures is always intrinsically useful and interesting – and that he was a little romantic, that is, his characters seemed to me at that time not to be as fully fleshed as I wanted; it seemed a little romanticized in terms of near caricature in some places, in terms of the ease at which they arrived at decisions. I wasn't sure – in retrospect – whether he was really writing comedy, and that has implications in form, and for attitudes towards the world, or whether he was writing social drama or comedy-drama. I think maybe he wanted to write social drama and was being pulled towards writing comedy.

Q: The plays of his that I have seen seem to have a tragi-comic quality to them.

DS: His head is doing one thing and his heart is really wanting to go another way; it makes for an uneasy meeting of forms. Have you found that, structurally, he provides problems constantly?

Q: Yes.

DS: Maybe that's the reason.

Q: Mustapha Matura.

DS: The school is about to do *Rum an' Coca Cola* [1976], as a student production. The final eight minutes of the play is incredible. Somebody must have gotten in the way of his craft and not told him how difficult it would be to play – and if you are an audience to receive – a murder, a suicide, a breakup between friends, a realization that one friend has murdered somebody dear to the other friend and so on, in the course of eight minutes. It hovers, if not actually arrives at melodrama, which is a great pity because the first three-fifths of the play is very, very exciting indeed, very carefully crafted. I know most of his other stuff – maybe that is a constant problem with him. I have thought seriously enough about it for some time; his control of the resolution of the dramas tends to slip and he goes off into melodrama – that is action which intrinsically interests either because of its violence or because of its intensity of emotion, but which it is not prepared for and which does not resolve our sense of what the characters and the play are really about.

Q: Edgar White.

DS: A wild talent. Edgar has *no* concern for form whatsoever; he wants to tell a story and whatever form that comes out in he is happy with and I think this is both a strength and a weakness. It is a strength because it makes him tell a story which is very strong, very clear, very interesting, with very intensely *feeling* and intensely behaving characters. It is a weakness because the arc of the action of the play, that line that leads us emotionally and intellectually from the postulate – this is the situation he leads the people into – to the end, the completion of the action, this is what happened to them finally and this is why it happened. That line gets blurred and swings out of control very often in the course of the play. So that, finally, I arrive at the end of his plays with a sense of great many important and *very* interesting things having happened, but not a sense of the *total* experience being *meaningful* to me and capable of being dealt with emotionally and intellectually by me as a whole. I keep seeing the parts instead of the whole. With Edgar that is a great pity, because he has such a talent for creating interesting characters, people behaving believably in difficult situations – and such a sense of music in language. He modulates the Caribbean language into very strange kinds of poetry, strange in the sense of evocative, subliminally affective, surprising, shocking and convincing.

Q: Roderick Walcott.

DS: Last time I saw Roderick, he was completing, or about to complete, a final term as a cultural officer in St. Lucia. I got the impression that he was a man who had disciplined his creative instincts to the point where they were no longer free to play, and this is not on the basis of his work – I didn't see any in St. Lucia then, two years ago – but on the basis of the man, and therefore it is, perhaps, quite untenable as a critical statement. The early Roderick I thought interested in action and less in language – in a way that Derek was never. Derek has always seemed to be more interested in language and what it exposes, what it reveals about character and the ironies with the character, contradictions with the character. Roderick has always been more interested, it seems to me, in action and social conflicts, so that what is revealed are the dangers to human feeling and not the ironies in feeling. There is no way of saying this other than crudely. I wish that they did not know each other existed, and then Roderick might have been free to play and to grow more fully in *his* area of interest, concerned with action and social conflict.

Q: Derek Walcott.

DS: Word drunk, like many of his early exemplars – Dylan Thomas, for example. Incredibly fertile sense of comedic situation, incredibly fertile ability to create characters who are just this side of the believable and who are very, very strange and eccentric indeed, in one way or another; incredible ability to document their character qualities through and in the language they use, and of having a very clear ability to invent music for their voices, so that they speak what seems on the surface the same kind of language, but speak it so very differently they become very, very clear to the audience. Extremely, totally committed to the Caribbean situation, its paradoxes, its problems; very much a creole animal, committed exquisitely in poetry and prose to that area of experience, making a lot of mileage out of the contradictions and the pains and the pleasures of being a creole animal. I wish he had had more monitors and had not had – it's a strength and weakness – a company, and because he wrote for that company he could write very clearly what he wanted to write, because he had nobody to say to him, "Pull away from that. No, as director, I am telling you that the playwright is indulging himself." Because of this the playwright loses a lot of ground, from time to time, and becomes very self-indulgent. He did things that a playwright should not have been allowed to do. Which is a pity. He remains still one of the most impressive people, one of the most useful and interesting artists in our artistic community; he is a very enviable talent, very large talent.

Q: Slade Hopkinson regards him as our Shakespeare.

DS: If you find it necessary to create that kind of analogy I guess that's possible, yes. I prefer to regard him as a Walcott. *Sui generis* – one of its kind.

Q: How do you compare the two brothers?

DS: Derek has a lot of daring; Roderick doesn't. Like all comparisons of that kind this is harmful, damaging and contemptuous, and it is not meant to be any of the three.

Q: Well, you certainly hear less of Roderick. I don't know whether Derek has overshadowed him or whether that is because of exposure or talent or what have you.

DS: He is a very pleasant person in a way that Derek could never be accused of being. Derek is deliberately, raucously abrasive – and placatory, loving and hostile, simultaneously himself. With considerably more formality, with considerably more respect for one's own personal space, with less daring, Roderick seems smaller; he does not, as Derek does, intrude himself on your awareness and this is both his loss and his gain. Derek cannot be avoided, which is nice.

Q: What happens to people who graduate from CTC? Do they see theatre as a practical and viable place to work in on a fairly full-time basis?

DS: Perhaps fifty percent go into teaching, or go back into a phase of teaching, a couple go into cultural work in the field and/or into cultural administration. Jamaica's infrastructure of cultural development agencies permits that kind of professionalism. I would say roughly a fifth or a sixth attempt full time professionalism, and this means freelancing, skanking, scrunting, but working in mass media, radio or sometimes combining the two, meaning teacher-actor, teacher-director. It is all comparatively new so far. But then we have had only seventy graduates in the last three years and thirty of those have been accumulated over the course of the years when the school was a part-time school.

Q: When was it a part-time school?

DS: It became a full-time school five and a half years ago.

Q: How many of the graduates have migrated?

DS: My last check was three years ago – there are either eight or ten abroad.

Q: Doing theatre abroad?

DS: Not necessarily theatre. Three are students, one is a nurse, one is a teacher, one or two have married and settled down and sensibly avoided all attempts at creative activity.

Q: The reason I asked that question was because someone raised the question with me about what your graduates did with their diploma. Whether it enabled them to get a job in the mainstream jobs market.

DS: The students are very clear as to the problems. We have hassled the system for enough years so that they understand the difficulties – whether of going into what appears to be the security of the classroom or of hustling out there in the field as a freelance theatre professional, or combining the two. So, there is very little naivety left among us as to the risks.

Q: Is theatre being viewed in a more professional light in Jamaica, now than, say, six years ago?

DS: An unconditional yes. That is, people are attempting more honestly and harder than before to carry out the task to which they commit themselves; and are being paid more than they were ten years ago – *when* they are being paid. And producers tend to be honouring their verbal or written contracts more than they did ten years ago; and audiences are providing them with more respect and more of a sense of being a professional than they did ten years ago; and the media are making more use of them than they did ten years ago – so, yes.

Q: Are there any kinds of union being formed within the theatre here?

DS: No, there are not. And I am not sure whether that is not a good thing. There is a concept that hooked into my head a few years ago which I keep remembering. An anthropologist defined the two kinds of contract one may have with other people as, firstly, the kind that you write down and the law says you must honour, and then the kind that the participants in the community make informally – and those are quite as strong. The post-industrial, high-technology civilizations of today operate in terms of the former, ones that are formal, written and protected by law; so-called primitive – certainly pre-industrial societies – tend to operate by the latter. I suspect that our preference, because of our nature as a people, is towards the latter – informal contracts. And you find people like Trevor Rhone, who *never* writes a contract with anybody, he is very punctilious about paying people, but paying them what he has verbally promised to pay them, come hell or high water. But, that's the latter. A lot of people who attempt the former fall back on their faces.

Q: Are there any kind of associations for writers?

DS: No, no associations still. That solitary art which is made even more solitary by the fact that nobody tries to help you develop your work.

Q: How have you managed to function under such conditions? You are regarded as one of the few major writers who have remained in the Caribbean and not taken flight.

DS: I wish I could take credit for that fact. My wife has a career which is rooted here – in communications. I would hate to have to try and bring up my children in just about any other place you can name; I love my jobs and I find them intensely creative and exciting and constantly self-revelatory. I play with my poetry in privacy, I collaborate with artists, some very high calibre colleagues on the staff and those artists outside I choose to work with from time to time. I very often get free trips to the high technology civilization up north, where I am required to do *nothing* at all except play in the theatre creatively and usefully, and for the most part, successfully – a free holiday to do what I love best. I am intensely concerned and increasingly involved with the educational systems and methodologies that the Caribbean needs. What have I got to complain of? I'd be silly to leave.

But I am cushioned and one pays the price. In order to be able to teach and function in an atmosphere that is deeply concerned with craft in the profession, I pay my dues by being an administrator. By the end of the week I shall have attended three plus three plus two plus two and a half – twelve hours of meetings, policy-deciding meetings. Boring meetings, with minutes to be taken, action for follow-up. One pays one's dues. I am, also, concerned annually with making out the budget for the school. Making a budget for a government organization is one of life's larger nightmares, particularly when the government in question has no money. There is no risk but there are dues to be paid. I pay them.

Q: As someone who seems to be a veritable fixture at the Eugene O'Neill Playwrights Conference, do you see much hope for West Indian theatre or West Indian playwrights getting a greater reception in the United States?

DS: Yes. Two things have happened recently. One is that Lloyd Richard has included Derek Walcott in this year's winterfest, and being the Artistic Director of Yale Rep and Dean of the School of Drama, he included Derek's *Beef, No Chicken* [1981], in this year's four play repertory going on right now. The other thing is that the CARIBUSTE TIE has decided at a meeting in December to do two things: one, is to print – not publish – for dissemination among the regional theatres in America and their artistic directors, six Caribbean plays at no cost to anybody, for familiarization; and, two, to agitate among those regional theatres and their meetings, for greater exposure, greater interest in whatever the Caribbean has to offer in terms of theatre which might interest those theatres. It will take time before the effects starts to leak through, but I think these are two very major things that have happened.

Q: Do you see CARIBUSTE as something that has a big future for theatre in the Caribbean?

DS: Yes, I do. Precisely because it is a non-governmental, very informal kind of association of people with coinciding interests. Those interests being: One, the sharing of expertise, talent, insights and energies between the two areas, the Caribbean and the US. Two, the ability to access from each other from those areas – which may not mean sharing, it may mean simply taking sometimes – that's cool. So, yes, CARIBUSTE is important. Low key, low profile and very important in a lot of curious ways.

Q: What would you say to young aspiring writer or any would-be artist in Jamaica, today?

DS: I say two things, really. One is that I know a lot about some things and nothing at all about other things. Information which I have – and we both have the time – you are welcome to, because I owe to everybody around me to give what I can to others who want it, when they want it, if they want it. And the other thing is, if everybody tells you that you mustn't do this and you want to, go ahead, and if you have it in you, you will do it, and if you don't, you won't; and if you don't want, don't bother; don't waste your time or mine because life is very short.

Q: How would you like to be seen in the continuum of art in the Caribbean?

DS: As somebody who played incessantly and enthusiastically and found out some things that are worth recalling in notes on the process.

End Notes

1. Victor Questel (1949-1982) was a Trinidadian poet, dramatist and critic. His plays included *De Doctor, He Dead* (1974); *Sufferer*; *Improv*, a ritual drama, revised version of *Sufferer* and *One Man and His Dog* (1984).
2. Horace E. "Steve" Carter (1929-) is an African American playwright of Caribbean heritage who wrote a trilogy of plays about Caribbeans in the USA: *Eden* (1978); *Nevis Mountain Dew* and *Dame Lorraine*.
3. Amiri Baraka: see interview with Lennox Brown, note 4.

CARMEN E. TIPLING
(1943-)

Carmen Tipling grew up in Kingston, and attended the Central Branch Primary and Kingston Technical High School. She studied for her degree at the University of Missouri. She worked in New York and Los Angeles before returning to Jamaica. Among her myriad of working experiences, during the late '60s (1969-1973) she worked at the Warner Bros. Entertainment Group of Companies as a motion picture and TV researcher where she worked with a team in the research department, researching scripts for television shows and future movies, in addition to collaborating with producers, and set designers.

In Jamaica, she was director of Communications Consultants Ltd. for nineteen years (1981-2000) where she supervised the implementation of public relations programmes on behalf of local, regional and international companies and organizations. She worked for more than six years with the Jamaica Information Service where she carried out the government of Jamaica's mandate to merge the JIS with JAMPRESS, a public-sector media house and upgraded the performance of the new entity. She is currently a public relations consultant at the Jamaica National Building Society from October 2011 until the present. Prior to that she was corporate communications executive with the company from February 2007.

Her plays include: *During Lunch They Had the Revolution, a one-act play* (1969), published in *Three Caribbean Plays*, edited by Errol Hill, (Longman, London, 1979) also in *The Whistling Bird*, edited by Elaine Campbell and Pierette Frickey. Her other plays include *The Skeleton Inside!* and *Stowaway* (c. 1972).

CARMEN TIPLING

11 May, 1981

Q: What got you started writing?

CARMEN TIPLING: When I was at the University of Missouri in my sophomore year, I was an English language major, and one of the optional courses was a course in theatre, which had no particular meaning to me at the time. But I signed up for it, and it consisted of designing and making sets – ham and eggs sort of thing. And, so I saw theatre for what could really be regarded as its most *unglamorous* side: putting up sets, pulling the curtain, doing the lights, and all the various things that happen backstage. But there's a magic to that because although the reviewers and the audience only see the people before the sets, you know that without you those people could not be the stars (*Slight chuckle*): if you didn't put the right piece of set or prop in place, the show couldn't go on. And I became fascinated by the theatre from that experience; for the first time I really understood what it was that happens in terms of teamwork: the people backstage, the people offstage, the audience, that sort of thing.

The next semester I took a course in playwriting and I wrote my first play, a very, very stupid play, really. It was the first time I had gotten into the business of writing – crisis, conflict, resolution, that sort of thing. The name of the play was *The Delicately Wounded*. It wasn't a very good play but it was a beginning. And for me it started a relationship with the theatre department at the university and I began to take other drama courses. I never took acting because I never thought of myself as an actor; I saw myself as somebody who could work in theatre. And probably one of the nicest things that could ever have happened to me during that four-year period happened in the year I graduated when I received what was regarded as a top theatre award, an award which was usually given to someone who had majored in theatre. I was an English major but I got the coveted Washburne Theatre Award for the simple reason that I was the only person on campus who had worked on productions, written a play, directed a play, produced a play, acted in a play, and reviewed plays. The whole concept of the award was commitment to theatre, and the professors thought that I was committed. An English major getting the top award in the drama department (*laughs*). It was unheard of! A lot of my friends screwed on me! (Laughs)

Q: How did you feel about the whole art of writing? Did you see yourself as a novelist, a journalist or a dramatist?

CT: I knew that I was going to be a writer from the time I was about nine years old. I was going to Central Branch Primary School in Kingston, and I wrote – for me this is an historic moment in my life – a composition about an imaginary journey. It was one of those rainy days when not too many children had come to school and not too many teachers either. So the teachers combined several classes to make little groups of people – and a teacher, Herbert Neita – I'll never forget this guy – helped me decide my direction in life. (I met him years later after I'd come back from the university, and I said to him, "Mr. Neita, I don't think you will even *remember* me, but I want you to know that you had something very, very significant to do with *what* I am right *now*.") So I wrote a composition, and it started out with the fact that it was a rainy day and the story involved being on some island. I went through a great adventure until there was a crisis and I wasn't able to cope with the crisis, broke down in tears, and suddenly felt my mother shaking me and *waking* me up! Because I'd fallen asleep on a rainy day, reading a book. (*Chuckles*) Mr. Neita thought this was rather clever for somebody in fourth grade and within the next week I was transferred out of fourth grade to sixth grade. And I think I spent about two and a half years in sixth class before I passed scholarship. Trapped into the system at that level. Well, it was a very good experience, because, what really came out of it was the fact that I'd written this composition which showed a certain command of the English language and an imagination. I'd gone to the Jamaica Junior Centre and read and read and read and read. The composition was a milestone in my life, because it changed my thinking. I was moved out of a class of people whom I considered my contemporaries and kicked into a higher class – people I had to catch up with. My parents decided I should take private lessons, and so I took private lessons with a lady named Miss Leslie on Brentford Road in Kingston. And if I was ahead of my time in terms of age and class, taking the private lessons made it even worse in that I advanced very quickly; things really started to excite me.

It was then too that Mr. Neita asked me: What did I want to be, and I said, I want to be a teacher – because every other person in my family at that time was a teacher. And he said: "You have a flair for language, you should become a journalist, a writer." So, I went home and I told my parents that I was going to be a journalist, a writer. I was from a typical Jamaican family – six kids, mother and father. My mother said, "You can be anything you want to be," and that was my cue. My father didn't try to discourage me, you know, but him just tell me: "Writer, journalist... you are going to starve."

Q: Was your father a teacher?

CT: No. My father worked for the Jamaica Omnibus Service.

Q: And what did your mother do?

CT: Housewife with six kids – what else can you be?

Q: You said you came from a family, background of teachers. Did they have any influence on you in terms of books?

CT: I had great admiration for books. My father was a great reader, yeah. *He* influenced me in terms of reading. He read every single cowboy book in paperback that you could ever think of and every single war story that was ever done in paperback. I mean, there were always a lot of books in the house. I read *The Norman Conquests* [this seems unlikely to refer to Alan Ayckbourn's 1973 trilogy] and *Forever Amber* [a blockbuster romance by Kathleen Windsor, 1944] and all the whodunit books while I was still in primary school. Before I went to high school I had read through Shakespeare and all the material that one had to read to take the Jamaica Local Examination. I had a *feeling*, right there in primary school, for story line and dramatic conflict.

Eventually I went to Kingston Technical [High] School. This was to prepare me to go out into the system and become a civil servant. In a way I think that was probably the best thing that could have happened to me. If I'd have gone to another kind of school I don't know if I would have ended up going into journalism and taking the sort of route that I've taken. I'm very glad that I went to Kingston Technical because it made certain things very, very clear. I found that I could not only take shorthand, typing, and bookkeeping, I could also take history, geography, language, and literature.

In fact, the teacher who taught me English language and literature was teaching me to read Shakespeare plays and certain kinds of novels and poetry and *that was already a part of me*. So I wanted a little bit more than what was being said in the average classroom. In fact, although my contemporaries elected me prefect every year, I was regarded as a nuisance and there were occasions on which I was kicked out of the classroom.

Q: As a nuisance?

CT: As a nuisance. Teachers didn't take kindly to me because I would say things like, *We haven't reached that chapter yet*, or, *That's not what we're talking about*. And there was *one* teacher in particular – she and I have become very good friends *after* the fact. In fact the last time she was in New York, she came to my office and said to my boss,

"You know, I must tell you that Carmen was one of my most unusual students. You know how many times I kicked her out of my class?" After the fact she tells me that it would be unfair to the rest of the students to accommodate all my questions, so sometimes it was better to send me to the library to go and read something else. Very true.

Q: Were you in any way influenced by West Indian writers?

CT: You couldn't say that I was influenced by West Indian writers in the *early* stage of my life, except for the fact that I'd read Vic Reid's *New Day* [1949], which was one of the books that my father had read; that was probably the only Jamaican book I'd read at that stage of my life that had a bad word in it. Naipaul, I knew about; I'd read *Spotlight* [founded by Evon Blake – V.S. Reid was one of the contributors] magazine with people's poetry and stuff like that. But I couldn't say that I was necessarily influenced, because at that stage of my life I don't think I was aware enough to be influenced by anybody. After I'd been to university I became aware of *American black writers*, and it took me a while before I became aware of them. I went to university in the midwest, at a stage which was *very* formative, in the middle of the Civil Rights movement, and I started reading people like Richard Wright and James Baldwin. I'm talking about 1961 to '65, that era in America. In my first year of going to university I worked in a laundry, sorting laundry; my sophomore year, I worked in the dining room; my junior year, I worked in the library, and that was my beginning of understanding a lot of things. Working in the library I had access to *all* the books before the rest of people who wanted to come in to borrow them, and I could *insist* that certain books came back in the library so I could have access to it myself. But, I think I discovered not only American literature, European literature and, would you believe, a very nice representative sample of West Indian literature in an American university in the midwest. And *that's* when I seriously started to understand *my own country*.

Q: People like who?

CT: Well, not in terms of Jamaica specifically. People like Naipaul, I read during that period, and there were papers and articles and stuff written by sundry people. Rex Nettleford, for example, was represented all over the place; Norman Girvan – I often saw stuff of his come through sundry publications. And Derek Walcott.

Q: What of Derek Walcott's did you read, his poetry?

CT: His poetry mainly – and some of his plays; years later I would see these plays being performed in Los Angeles, when I lived there.

Q: How did you feel about his poetry?

CT: Well, I'm not a poetic person myself, although I think that poetry is a word exercise that I put myself through. People who write poetry

I've great admiration for, for people like Dennis Scott and Mervyn Morris. There're a lot of other Jamaican poets whom I like but I don't think I've read their works that extensively to articulate about it.

Q: So, this period in college was when you started to get your eye-opener towards American literature and Black American literature?

CT: Well, this period was when my eyes just simply opened! I mean, seventeen years old: and coming from Jamaica, and one is not really equipped to deal with the great society. This was the year of Kennedy, there was a whole new frontier movement in America and the Civil Rights movement. Didn't understand all the ramifications of the Civil Rights movement when I was a freshman, but by the time I was a junior I *knew* what was going on.

I started to read very extensively. One found oneself in a position where one didn't have to read just one daily newspaper, you can read ten, twenty, twenty-five – you're in a university situation and the papers were there – magazines and so on. And you'd get a whole new different feeling, not only for what was happening in the society.

Q: During that period, the time when people like Dr. King and Malcolm X were at full blast, did you become angered by the mood of America?

CT: Well, when you're in the midwest, you get the news filtered from coast to coast, and Martin Luther King was a personage in the midwest, there's no question about it, and the Civil Rights movement and marches were very evident in the midwest. I remember marching in a little town, called Quincy, Illinois, and I was one of about 20 black people in this march and there were probably about 2,000 white people who marched for Civil Rights. The whole idea of the march was based on the fact that Quincy, Illinois was the site of the Lincoln-Douglas debate [A series of 7 debates between Lincoln and Senator Stephen Douglas in 1858 on slavery].

Q: Who are some of your favourite writers?

CT: Some of my favourite writers in terms of playwriting: Pinter, Chekhov, some American playwriters, too – modern-day guys, I like Neil Simon and Paddy Cheyevsky.

Q: What about Jamaican writers?

CT: Well, of Jamaican writers, I'd say that Dennis Scott's work I like, and I've read Mervyn Morris's stuff, and Trevor Rhone, in terms of performance for stage, very good.

Q: Do you read a lot of novels?

CT: Yeah, quite a bit. I've always had the feeling that you should read everything that comes along whether it's good, bad or indifferent.

Q: What do you think of Derek Walcott and his work and its influence?

CT: I like his stuff. What I find very impressive about him is that when you're on the east coast of America, the midwest or west coast, you're always likely to run across something about Walcott and his works, whether it's his poetry in *The New Yorker* – or to find out that one of his plays are being performed at some place like the Mark Taper Forum in LA. I've seen *Dream on Monkey Mountain* done very, very professionally in Los Angeles. I was really very, very impressed with the theme and the whole feeling for the play.

Q: There are two writers who I could say compare with him; there's Slade Hopkinson and a Trinidadian playwright Lennox Brown.

CT: I've heard of Lennox Brown, I've not read any of his stuff, but Slade's work I'm very familiar with. I worked on a production of his called *Sala*, which was done by Dennis Scott at the Barn Theatre in Kingston [1972]. In fact, that play excited me into going to Guyana; when I went, having seen *Sala*, Guyana had meaning for me. The whole feeling of the vastness of the country when you fly over it; and the cultural attitudes of the people, whether they're Amerindians or Blacks or East Indians

Q: What do you think of theatre in Jamaica and its development?

CT: A very wide question... Right now I think theatre in Jamaica is very, very vibrant. I mean, there're a lot of plays being done and that's very good. At one time there was a limitation on where you could put on a play, and I think people are overcoming this limitation and they're not just relying on the availability of the Creative Arts Centre or Little Theatre or some place like that but have stepped out and been *creating* places where people can go to see plays. There are some young people in Jamaica now who are writing, and the material might not be as polished as some of the material that's been done before by people like Trevor Rhone or Dennis Scott, but at least something is happening and that's the important thing. Because out of the wealth of productions that are going on we evolve the better ones, and I think the people who are writing and acting will have developed some sort of measurement of what's good and what's not good. There's a tendency on the part of some producers, playwrights to assume that the audience just wants to come to the theatre to laugh and therefore one finds that there are more comedies being done. But I think that Jamaican audiences are subtle enough that you don't really have to just give them broad comedy all the time; they can take a dramatic play or what some people call a "serious play", as well as the comedy.

Q: Do you consider yourself a Jamaican playwright, West Indian playwright or just a playwright? Some people hate to be labelled.

CT: Well, I am not even sure if I consider myself a playwright (*Laughs*). I guess I could be called a Jamaican playwright, being Jamaican and the fact that the themes that I've explored and the plays that I've written are about Jamaicans; most of them have taken place in Jamaica.

Or even if they take place in North America, they are about the Jamaican situation and Jamaicans who find themselves in a North American situation. So, I guess it wouldn't be too far out to say: Jamaican playwright. But I really don't consider myself as such, but if I were described as such it wouldn't offend me.

Q: So most of the plays so far have come out of the Jamaican experience?

CT: Not just the Jamaican experience in terms of living in Jamaica, but a wider Jamaican experience. For instance, *Straight Man* [197?], is a play about Jamaicans caught up in the US as illegal aliens. *Skeleton Inside!* [1975] deals with a definite Jamaican situation and the whole feeling for an acceptance of change, whether it's political or economic or developmental change.

Q: Yeah, I saw that play and I liked the way you managed to cover a lot of ground in terms of the social and political aspects of a certain time in Jamaica.

CT: The play was written in '75; and I'd been walking around with the idea – it was when I went back to live in Jamaica in 1973 – that there was a slightly different Jamaica than the Jamaica that I left in '66, '67. When I say different, I mean people were a lot more politically conscious and some infrastructure type of development had taken place: there were more apartment houses, an emphasis on small business and people getting into business and stuff like that. It seemed a whole new era for development in Jamaica, and it occurred to me that on the one hand people were talking about the colonial past and on another hand people were talking about change and development. My concern was how are we prepared to deal with these changes – such as a change that asks that children graduated from high school give two years voluntary service to the government – and don't really get a salary as such but are paid a gratuity or something like that; government creating certain incentives for business and some people being able to take advantage of it and some people not; or having to face up to certain economic restrictions in society: will they be prepared to deal with them? So, for instance, *Skeleton* addressed itself to the Fisher family – which was taking a small unit to indicate what was happening in the larger society – where the family was in terms of being arrested for exporting foreign exchange out of Jamaica, or dealing with a strike at a factory or making a decision whether you want to join the job corp. All this happening in Jamaica in 1975 made it very, very simple and very possible to write a play like *The Skeleton Inside!*, where you take a look at somebody and how if all the things were stripped away, all you have is this skeletal structure, and fear is internal to some extent, and trying to say that one has to face the fact that change is constant and therefore one should be prepared to deal with it. Well, in a way, that was what I was trying to say in *Skeleton*.

Q: What do you think of the development of theatre in the Caribbean at large? And, if you want me to narrow it down, I will say, the English speaking Caribbean. But you can take the whole thing – the whole movement of the theatre.

CT: I'm probably not too familiar with *all* that is being done in the Caribbean in terms of theatre; I've read collections of other people's works and I've seen plays in Trinidad and in Barbados. I know one playwright-actor who's in Antigua and people in Guyana and places like that. But I really don't have a *feeling* for what is Caribbean theatre. The last CARIFESTA was in Jamaica; I saw some of the work and heard some of the poetry; as a region, if we take it regionally, I think it's impressive. But literature is something that takes time to amass. Maybe one of the reasons why we don't – why *I* can't see – a total picture of Caribbean theatre is that nobody has yet helped to focus it by compiling larger volumes of Caribbean plays, poetry and so on. There're small volumes – Longman's did a volume in '79 called *Three Caribbean Plays*, which was projected at high schools. And there've been other collections that I have heard of but I've not read. I know they're productions out there in those islands, where people do go and see plays, but I really don't have a good feeling for how extensive it is or exciting it is and what sort of cultural feeling of the Caribbean is being expressed.

Q: Well, I spoke with one young playwright from the Eastern Caribbean, and he was arguing the need for the Caribbean theatre to come together. His model was something like CARIFESTA, except you don't have to wait every four years to do it, but have regular connections. His idea was that one island would deal with dance for one year, another with theatre or whatever, but at the same time the plays are touring throughout the Caribbean, so that everybody is getting to see them.

CT: What would be really great for the Caribbean – to establish more communication for people who are in drama – would be to have an annual playwright's conference. I think the idea has actually been started, because under the umbrella of The Eugene O'Neill Theatre [New York], a conference was held earlier on this year – I think it was in February, in... the Virgin Islands. And I know that Dennis Scott was involved in it and Jim Nelson [theatre and TV director active in 1970s], from Jamaica, went. But I think for this conference to continue it needs support from the governments or foundations and private sector organizations; and it could be rotated from island to island each year. That would establish some focus. Give people who are in the business of writing plays, producing plays, directing plays, acting in plays an opportunity to get the feeling of the history of drama in the Caribbean, what's happening right now and, hopefully, to see some sort of future to it.

Q: Yeah. The only thing that bothers me is that a lot of times governments pay lip service to the cultural arts when it's the last thing on their priority list.

CT: That might seem a little bit harsh, in that any struggling society has to do all the basics – house, clothe and feed – and then something like drama becomes a frill in terms of financial support. Well, this doesn't mean that the people who are involved in drama and want to make a contribution in terms of cultural expression to their particular island should stop making these requests.

Q: But don't corporate organizations in the islands, offer grants to cultural organizations?

CT: Well, I think we're coming to the stage in the Caribbean where more and more private sector organizations *will* take an interest in the cultural development, whether it's music, dance, or theatre of their particular country. One multinational organization in Jamaica – and I mention them because they've supported drama – have always made a contribution to the Jamaica Festival's drama prizes. I know a bank in Jamaica which has clearly stated that it wants to support Jamaican artists in our theatres – as well as making scholarship grants and things like that. And I think eventually we might see something evolving where more and more private-sector *Jamaican* companies will come out and support different sectors of the arts. [...] First, it was a simple production playbook or ad in the *Gleaner* or *Daily News* or *Star* taken out by an organization in support of a production, which means real funds are being spent, but not necessarily tremendous sums.

Q: Because of the state of literacy in the Caribbean, do you think theatre can reach a bigger audience than fiction – and that, because of its immediacy, it stands a better chance of getting across?

CT: But the real reason for theatre having the tremendous impact that it does on a larger segment of the society is the fact that it's oral and visual, and we are still locked in a very oral tradition. Not many people in Jamaica would buy a copy of a play and sit down and read it; more people would go and see a play, but there're still a lot of people there – we almost have to take the play to them, because going to see a play still seems a very esoteric thing on some levels. But I tell you where it differs: when a play is put on at the Ward Theatre[1] by the old Bim and Bam team,[2] thousands of people go to see it, because it has immediate appeal to them. They actually have a feeling for what they're going to see, and I would almost equate that kind of theatre to the sort of original Shakespearean sort of theatrical situation. Thousands of people, whether they live out of town or in Kingston, they would get together and take a minibus and come into town to go to the annual Pantomime,[3] to this serious annual event. The feeling for theatre – not just for the one show here or once a year for the annual Pantomime – has to be generated further into the society. But there is also a limitation in terms of numbers of people because a lot of theatre venues in Jamaica are small. Most of the places house probably a hundred, hundred and fifty, hundred and sixty people per show, and for some people the prices for some of the shows are a little bit steep, though prices at some place like the Ward Theatre are usually not as steep.

Q: Yeah. It's been my observation – from the short periods that I've been there and observed – that in Jamaica theatre is still a metropolitan, Kingston type of thing. What about travelling theatre?

CT: There has been an attempt to take more plays out of town. Ed Wallace[4] has been very instrumental –and I'm not using Ed Wallace to say that he's the only person that has done it, but I think he's probably done it more consistently than anybody else in the last three years. There is somebody else, Claude Clark,[5] who's also doing the same thing, where he produces a show in Kingston, it runs for a certain length of time and then he makes a circuit with it: Port Antonio, Ocho Rios, Montego Bay and I think even probably as far as Savanna la Mar. I could be wrong but I think he has been to other parts of Jamaica. This is ideal, but it also has its limitations, in that you can only take the play to venues where you have the facility to perform the play; you need a stage and lights and seats and all the very basic things. I know there've been attempts to do open-air theatre, but not every little town in Jamaica or even every major sort of township has the facility to do it. Some places you can always use the high school auditorium, but you might have problems getting permission, transportation problems to get there; you can't overnight, you have to turn around after ending the play and drive back to Kingston; these logistics create the limitation.

Q: Can you comment on what is happening at the Creative Arts Centre with respect to its goal of producing professionally trained people in all the arts, but specifically in theatre. I've heard the argument that they're turning out well-trained people, with a piece of paper saying they have graduated and they're qualified, but there's no place to go. Is the level of professionalism that is being attempted possible? Is it work in the day and theatre at night? Stafford Harrison told me that a lot of people feel that since they have this piece of paper it can enable them to get a job, not necessarily in the theatre, but a 9 to 5.

CT: This is a dilemma that we have to face up to right now within Jamaica, in that theatre, whether it's writing, directing, acting, is still a hobby, a part-time occupation. There're very few people who have been able to sustain themselves *totally* and not do anything else. Many of the students go to school [the Creative Arts Centre] on a daily basis from 8:30 to 4:30, take structured courses, participate in a four year programme, and they graduate and they can act and they understand all the nuances of experimental theatre and so on and so forth, but where do they go from there? That's what your question asked. The next thing is to develop the kind of theatrical situation in which these people can find real jobs. But I don't know which comes first at this point. We can't have a professional theatre until you develop the people who are on the way to being professionals, an audience willing to come to support it, and the theatre in which to perform. This makes what's happening in Jamaica now almost seem like a launching pad, in that the number of venues are increasing, more students are coming out of the school of drama with very good training and background, more people are writing, more people are going to the theatre, and I think that given a little bit of time these elements will come together and result in a professional theatre, where professionals in the theatre can see it as a full-time occupation.

Q: As part of this same drive towards professionalism, I understand that they're trying to establish some kind of actors' union in Jamaica.

CT: That's logical. (*Laughs*) That had to come, because people, whether performing or doing the lights or working backstage are doing it on a part-time basis, and their monetary rewards are out of kilter with other part-time jobs. The cost of putting on a production is sky high right now, with inflation and so on. People participating in a production are giving very good performances, doing very good work and therefore are asking for better remuneration; and this has to be so, there's no question about it. You perform five nights a week in a production to full houses, there's usually some sort of good income. And whilst I've not heard any specific complaints, there've always been smatterings of complaints about people who are not properly paid for their performance; it happens all the time – it happens here. I don't know if a union is being conceived solely on that premise, for better pay or to ensure that certain standards are maintained and to protect actors and production people, so that guarding against the menace of poor safety standards also adds to the professionalising of the whole theatre structure. So I can see why there is a feeling that there's a need for one, or why one is being started.

Q: Ironically, as we're speaking about the problems there with theatre, people I've talked to elsewhere in the region point to Jamaica and say Jamaica is where it's happening. Again, it seems as if the smaller islands look to Jamaica for an example.

CT: Yeah, well, the pace is being set by Jamaica when it comes to theatre in the Caribbean right now. What you describe as problems I would like to see as part of the growing pains of creating a strong, unified professional theatre.

Q: Do you see yourself getting involved in this sort of activity when you go back home?

CT: Oh, yeah. I'm going back to Jamaica. I've been living in New York for about three and a half years and it's time to leave. I have plans to continue to work in theatre, whether it's in terms of writing or assisting with productions or promotions, and even make some contribution towards some of the things that will increase the level of professionalism, and looking forward to doing some real work.

Q: You're not one of those people who got tired of the amateurism of how things were being done or the haphazard nonchalance of the way people go about business, and left for that reason?

CT: No, not at all, not at all. Because I was involved with theatre on the West coast when I lived in California, and I'd been on the fringes of a few theatre groups here in New York, and I've seen a lot of Broadway stuff. And when I make the comparison between what is a Broadway show with millions of dollars support to it, and ones that are Off-Broadway shows with thousands of dollars to support them, and the real Off-Off-Broadway show put together with a few thousand dollars, in the final analysis it's not the venue, it's not the amount of money supporting the production, but the production itself. And I have come to realize that the *quality* of productions that we Jamaicans have, the performance on stage, the logistics behind the stage – as inadequate as they might seem in some cases – is as high as you will see in one of the best Broadway shows here. I don't think that I'm being too overenthusiastic about the Jamaican situation. I've seen plays here that live through two or three performances and then they're off the boards because the chemistry wasn't there or the show was just simply *bad*. And I've seen small, very ambitious productions in Jamaica which *work* and there is a magic on stage, there's a level of energy and enthusiasm that you don't find in a lot of theatre here.

Q: Talking to Stafford Harrison, who has had the opportunity to write for a Broadway show, he said that what was most important was *learning* the whole machinery and seeing how it worked, because he felt that we in the Third World are always engrossed by the idea of product as opposed to process, and he was interested in seeing process more than product.

CT: Well, the theatre situation here in the USA is very complicated. When you go backstage behind the performance, whether it's with your guilds and your unions – you're an electrician, you can't move a chair because it has all these restrictions; with the backers who put up the money for the show, wanting to get more profits; with the producer himself, director, lighting director, the this director, the that director, the actors themselves with their agents and contract – there're a lot of elements that come together here, where in our Jamaican situation, sometimes writer, producer, director, backer is one and the same person. You have a cast of five, you have three stagehands and you have a production. And so emphasis is very much placed on production, what you see on stage. And maybe that's good for now – maybe that's good for now.

Q: I've been hearing people talk about calypso theatre, or roots theatre, or indigenous theatre – the idea of theatre by the people for the people. How do you feel about that approach as opposed to the more establishment type of theatre?

CT: However you look at it, whatever level you look at it, it's still by the people for the people. If you're gonna make distinctions between the peoples, then that's different. Roots theatre – on the west coast they call it street theatre – has its place in the scheme of things. And there will be those people who feel that rather than do a play about a family in Trench Town, then you should probably get the family in Trench Town to do the play for themselves, which is the feeling that one gets when you talk about roots theatre. But whereas somebody else looks at this family and sees the dramatic elements in their situation, the family don't see it as dramatic, they see it as normal everyday living, because they have not made the separation between reality and drama in terms of how their lives are being mirrored. Somebody outside can take it from a slice-of-life basis and project it to a larger group of people, so there's that. But I must mention there's this theatre group that was developed, being taught by Honor Ford Smith, called *Sistren*,[6] a very, very nice group who I find very, very interesting. It was a programme that came out of the school of drama to do some work with the crash programme workers and they wrote the material, they did improvisations based on certain situations, and developed scenes, and they developed acts and moved into full-fledged production. I saw a rehearsal of a play that they were working on called *Belly Woman Bangarang* [1981]; it was just pure joy to watch those people work together. They were changing a scene, rewriting as the action evolved on stage, and doing it very, very well. It was like sitting in a theatre workshop at the Mark Taper Forum [a prestigious theatre in Los Angeles] with a group of people who regard themselves as very, very serious professional people. The interaction on stage was terrific. One person would set up the situation in terms of crisis and another person moved in, created the conflict and a third person came in to bring about some sort of resolution of this scene, back and forth, and within two tries the scene was rewritten. They had somebody to write it down and the lines learnt. But it was very interesting.

Q: I was talking to another playwright about Derek Walcott, and what this writer was doing with his work in theatre in the eastern Caribbean. Although he acknowledged being influenced by Walcott, he felt that Walcott was writing at too high a level for the people the plays were addressing, and that if Walcott could go one level lower, he would bring more people into his theatre, and then bring them up; because this was what this playwright was attempting with his theatre work in Dominica. I mentioned this to Derek Walcott and he dismissed it as a patronizing middle-class attitude and an insult to the audience's intelligence.

CT: I agree with Walcott. I feel that while you should strive to ensure that you are communicating to the audience, there is no need to talk down to them. Put it into the Jamaican context. On that basis, because the majority of the people in Jamaica speak patois, the only kind of play that you could write which would appeal to the majority is obviously a play which is done *totally* in patois. This is not necessarily so, because the same people who speak patois also understand what is regarded as standard or proper English, and if theatre is to entertain *and* educate, then I think you'd be doing the audience a disservice if you didn't give them the opportunity to grow by what is being presented on stage. You should relate to *both* our languages and not just patronize the audience. I agree with Walcott.

Q: Walcott's other feeling about writing for the theatre is that writing a script is not solely a stenographic matter – of recording speech in a literal way; that concerning the use of the language of the people, this language carries its own metaphor, but that if you take ordinary patois or street language... and heighten it to the level of theatre language, you get something more powerful and beautiful.

CT: That is true, but you can also take something out of its natural state and put it into an unnatural one – which is your proscenium arch, and you start to put in lights and costumes to depict the situation and eventually to articulate a language – and it can fall very flat.

You take some situation as it happened in real life and project it on stage and it can fizz or die. You have to take licence with it to make it work, to make it believable. Because in its natural state it was fine, alright? I'll accept it. But once you put it on stage you have brought in other elements to it, and in the telling of that dramatic situation you have to now restructure it so that it comes off to the audience as being dramatic. So I agree with him.

Q: Types of stages. Again, I was speaking to Walcott about this some years ago. He felt that we Caribbeans are essentially a daytime people; we don't really concern ourselves, as in the metropolitan areas, with evening theatre per se. And he felt that we could put theatre into the same outdoor, daytime context as carnival. This might be considered as experimental – but with the practical idea of putting on plays at times when people are most available to watch them, like on a Sunday morning.

CT: Then you're gonna come up against the church if you do it on a Sunday.

Q: Or a Saturday.

CT: Saturday is when you go to market and clean your house and get ready for church on Sunday and the next week.

Q: What about what he says about a theatre of bare essentials, writing for a bare stage because of the limitations we suffer from in the Caribbean in terms of theatre buildings and equipment?

CT: I could see, for example, on a Saturday, in any little Jamaican township – the market is in progress – I could see something like a flatbed truck, sides dropped down, with a troupe – a travelling troupe and this Saturday you appear at Coronation Market and the next Saturday you appear at Spanish Town Market and the following Saturday, you're at Linstead Market – and you have an instant audience. Your performances would have to be staged in such a manner that they're actually skits; you cannot do a 90-minute production; you might hold some people for the entire time that you're there, but most are busy going about their work and they'll probably pause for ten or a fifteen minutes to watch. So if the action on the back of the truck can be done in segments that are, indeed, almost like blackouts, if that can be done on that basis, it would be tremendous. I remember as a child growing up in Kingston, and going to market with my mother – Coronation Market in particular – and there was always some little excitement or activity in the general area of the market on a Saturday morning. Usually – and I'm not dating myself by telling you this – but there were two guys singing, one playing a little fiddle or banjo or something like that and the other guy singing, with tracts, and they'd sell them for threepence or sixpence. This is where one learnt new songs. I guess it was probably in the late days of ZQI, before RJR [Radio Jamaica Rediffusion] came into being.[7] I don't know how many records were being cut in Jamaica at that time, but one used to hear these guys singing in the streets. And I remember there's one song I know that stands out in my mind that I heard being sung out there – I don't know if it was ever recorded anywhere – but it was a song about being taken back to Ethiopia. You know:

"Take me back to Ethiopia/ lemme go mark out the burial spot/ No matter where/ I do not care/ I know I must be here/ to get my share/ of all the riches… in Ethiopia." [Erna Brodber credits these lyrics to Laurel Aitken,[7] but could it be Bongo Herman and Eric "Bingy Bunny" Lamont?] And the two guys who were singing the song were not necessarily Rastafarians. But that was an element of theatre in a marketplace. And your idea: going down there with performances to the people… takes some organization. And of course, you're talking about free theatre because you know there's no way that anybody would pay; in that marketplace one does not collect admission.

Q: Yeah, well, this is it, you bring your little tent and you close them in, and you say: "If you want to come in this tent give me a dollar." On another topic, there's a playwright from Montserrat, who's lived in the USA most of his life, young guy named Edgar White who told me he doesn't believe in writing historical plays per se. He might write something with a historical concerns but relate it to what is happening now.

CT: Oh, that's understandable. A lot of people do that.

Q: He doesn't believe in sticking to the historical facts, but using elements of a particular historic occurrence and making it alive now.

CT: As if it's happening right now. Oh, yeah, that's been done now for a time, and part of it is so you can take a certain licence to make things dramatic on stage – and to protect yourself from libel suits and things like that. For example, if one wanted to write a play about certain changes in Jamaica right now, but didn't want to make any allusions to persons living, the ideal thing would be to go and do some research – just a little bit of research – and identify another period in Jamaica's history when similar things were taking place and set your play at that time and deal with exactly what is happening. Taking a little licence with the history, yes. But then you can put it in period dress, dress of the times when long skirts were in, or miniskirts or whatever – the music of the time – maybe one or two known historic events that took place in the time so as to set the stage and go right ahead and make a statement.

Q: You wrote a novel.

CT: I guess it's presumptuous to call it a novel – I *have* a manuscript, I guess… (*Laughs*) "A New Broom". It's been knocking around in my briefcase for a few years now. It's about the rise and fall of a Jamaican politician, and it covers a period of changes in Jamaica, from pre-independence up to what can be regarded as modern times.

Q: You mentioned earlier that some things you had written as inventions in your novel actually came to pass. What are you going to do about that? Any amendments?

CT: No, it still holds. I think there was no magic in how I thought up those things. In this novel I talked about a youth corps organization in the country, and a job corps was created years later. There're a couple of other things, like I switched around some of the names of ministries of government as they exist in Jamaica, so as not to identify a particular ministry, and I found it interesting that after writing this, some of these very ministries were switched around and called the same thing that I had called them. (*Chuckles*)

Q: I remember reading something that Derek Walcott said about his generation of writers, that it came about at a very opportune time in that they were given the chance to create… to tell the story of a new world, to put names to things…

CT: Well, a very similar situation exists in *these* times in the Caribbean, because the process of change is still going on. I get the feeling that Walcott was probably talking about the switch or the evolution from colonialism to independence… and *that* evolutionary process is still going on. And we're at a stage – in most of the Caribbean islands – where the emphasis is on economic independence and therefore events and things happening in the society also need to be labelled and described and written down – chronicled not in terms of historical fact but in terms of the cultural psyche and the feelings and fears of the people.

Q: I was talking to Stafford Harrison, who said that he's intrigued by the idea of creating myth, our own mythology in the Caribbean, of exploring that. In other words, bringing forth a life which is there but untapped.

CT: I understand Stafford's thing about almost creating myth, though I'm not as mystical as Stafford. I'm more concerned with creating a vehicle which can express the tempo of the society as it goes through the changes. In other words, I'm willing to take *what is* and dramatize it.

Q: Do you consider yourself a healer or an educator in terms of your work?

CT: I don't consider myself a healer. Hopefully, I would hope that whatever I write educates to some extent.

Q: Do you think that theatre can heal?

CT: Oh, yeah. There's a whole cathartic process that can take place for various and sundry people in the audience. And I guess once you write a play, see it being performed and people responding, what you hope you have accomplished is that you have taken an event or situation and given it some focus – you've asked the audience to live through the experience with the characters on stage. And I'd be satisfied if any audience who sits and watches a play that I've written leaves the theatre feeling that they understand, have some level of understanding about what happened and why, and being reassured to some extent about their own situation – or challenged.

Q: What about the question of theatre that entertains or theatre that gives you something to think about?

CT: Well, you can achieve all of those things in one play. Even if it's a comedy, you can teach and somebody can be purged; laughter in comedy is cleansing; if it's a very dramatic piece – creates no laughter – it still does a bit of cleansing because it gives one pause, makes you stop and think and, hopefully, evaluate and learn something.

Q: I asked the same thing of Stafford [Harrison], and his response was that you can only be healed if you want to be healed. If you go to a doctor, the doctor has to examine you to see what is wrong with you, if you don't go to the doctor he can't help you.

CT: True. It's like there was a guy who asked Bob Marley in one of his last interviews how does he feel about whether people listen to his music, and Bob's response to that was terrific. He said: "Well, if them don't listen today, they might listen tomorrow."

Q: When you see your play produced and you get feedback from people pro and con, good and bad, how do you feel? Do you feel that the effort was worth while?

CT: Oh, yeah, I'll answer that by, telling you an experience I had outside of the Barn Theatre, about two weeks after *Skeleton Inside* had been playing. A gentleman I know (he's a manufacturer, he owns a factory and employs two hundred and fifty people or so) and he sat through the first half of the play and I saw him preparing to leave during the intermission, so I went over and said, "You're leaving already?" He says, "Carmen, to tell you the truth, I go through that shit *every day*! I can't sit and watch it, I will have to come back and see the rest of it another evening." (*Laughs*) So, I had obviously reached him.

Q: Do you ever want to write for the screen?

CT: Oh, yeah. I would always say it's a big thing out there to strive for, but it's very complicated. Not complicated in terms of writing a script per se, but complicated in terms of getting it through the stages where you can sit and watch it. Having a proper agent – that sort of complication – of your agent going to the right person. And of course, starting out, you run the vicious cycle of no track record and therefore you can't get a good agent and so on. But I've got friends out on the west coast who have been successful, starting from scratch, getting an agent, getting a script in, seeing it produced, doing a second one, doing a third one – but they work very hard. I don't think I work very hard at it.

Q: Why? Weren't you interested?

CT: Uh, no, it wasn't a lack of interest; I don't think what I was trying to write at the time was of the standard that would hit. Maybe I will try it again.

Q: To come back to what we were talking about earlier – about the creating of a mythology, specifically, a Jamaican mythology…

CT: Is the word really *create*? Rather than *identifying* and *clarifying*? Because some of the things we regard as myths – they're there, people talk about them… so it's more like crystallizing the thing, taking it out and saying this is how it evolved, this is what it means and you see how people respond to it in their daily lives.

Q: Yeah, you're right.

CT: From that point it's not creating but clarifying.

Q: I know that Walcott and his generation say, "We are the pioneers." But this other young writer, Alwin Bully, from the eastern Caribbean, also considers his generation as pioneers because they've picked up the baton from their older peers and are continuing it. Do you consider yourself a pioneer among West Indian writers?

CT: I probably see myself in about the third wave of a movement, because so far nothing that I have written has been necessarily different in terms of style and content from what other people are writing, so there is no pioneering in that respect. Part of a wave is probably a good way to put it, from the very fact that I am writing, but not pioneering in terms of breaking new ground.

Q: But do you see yourself as pioneering in the sense of being part of a group of people who are still trying to break that ground or of bringing forth a life that is still yet to be known to the world?

CT: Well, if you put it that way, maybe – but not really.

Q: Do you feel a total commitment to your work, to writing?

CT: I'm usually committed to anything I get involved in, whether it's writing or a job or a project. I have to feel it, believe it, to do it.

Q: I know one poet and playwright [Derek Walcott] saying that he could never write a novel because he can't believe that particular lie he's telling, he can believe much more in drama – theatre. How do you respond to that?

CT: Well, I don't see too much difference between it being a novel or a play, because I deal with the same elements in both. Now I'm not saying that they're the same, not for one second. Because with a play you create the dialogue and you set up scenes and the dialogue is what counts eventually – and the action on stage itself. But in a novel, there's the exposition with the same dramatic formula that can be applied to both. So, I don't find it very difficult to relate to writing a novel as against writing a play. Maybe this writer that you paraphrased is saying that what's in a novel is probably more difficult to deal with or he doesn't believe in it enough as against believing in a play because of the dramatic elements that are there. I would disagree because if the book is going to be good then there have to be a lot of dramatic elements in it; you're going to have your main plot, your subplot, your antagonist, your pivotal character and so on, and these same elements are in the play too. In the one there is action on the stage and in the other there's a whole heap of exposition which is almost like a narrator setting the stage and setting the scene, so I don't agree.

Q: What, Carmen, would you ultimately like to have as your legacy, in terms of your work?

CT: You mean, legacy in terms of something I leave behind?

Q: Right. How would you like to be seen?

CT: Oh, you're dealing with the footprints in the sands of time thing? Which is a terrible phrase, because the waves will come in and wash it all away! (*Laughs*)

Q: How would you like to be remembered as an artist? You have championed other areas of endeavour, but specifically as an artist.

CT: I'd like to be seen as somebody, a playwright, who tried to be honest. I said, tried. That's it.

End Notes

1. The Ward Theatre was built in 1912 by Charles James Ward, Custos of Kingston, who presented it to the Mayor and Council of the City of Kingston. It is the third Theatre to stand on the same site since 1775. The first was the Kingston Theatre which was destroyed by fire and the second was the Theatre Royal which was destroyed in the 1907 earthquake. The Ward was in its earliest years a theatre mainly attended by white Jamaicans, and mostly featured British touring companies and Shakespeare productions. It became a theatre for all Jamaican people with the founding of the Little Theatre Movement and the annual pantomime beginning in 1941.
2. Bim and Bam were a very popular Jamaican comic duo who began performing in the 1940s. In the 1960s, they toured with the ska singer Derrick Morgan. See <http://bimandbamcomedy.blogspot.co.uk/>
3. The Annual Pantomime initiated by the Little Theatre Movement in 1941, was the beginnings of an authentic Jamaican theatre, involving Louise Bennett, Ranny Williams, Greta and Henry Fowler, Barbara Gloudon, Trevor Rhone and others. See <http://www.ltmpantomime.com/>

4. Ed Wallace is a Jamaican theatre producer and writer of more than thirty popular plays and the designer of the entertainment website www.bestseatinthe housejm.com.
5. Claude Clarke helped to set up the space for the Jamaican Barn Theatre 77.
6. Honor Ford Smith and Sistren: see interview with Errol Hill, note 36.
7. See Horace Leslie Galbraith — "The 'Radio Man' and sound system innovator" <http://www.jamaicaobserver.com/entertainment/Galbraith _7681311>
8. Erna Brodber, "Black Consciousness in Popular Music in Jamaica in the '60s and '70s", in *New West Indian Guide/ Nieuwe West-Indische Gids* 61 (1987), no: 3/4, Leiden, 145-160

DEREK ALTON WALCOTT
(1930-)

Derek Walcott and his twin brother, Roderick, were born to Warwick and Alix Walcott in Castries, St Lucia. His father was an artist who died when Walcott was very young. His mother who was a teacher, born in St Maarten, was a well-read woman who taught her children the love of poetry.

He was educated at St Mary's College, Castries, and received a scholarship to the University College of the West Indies in Kingston, Jamaica (now the University of the West Indies), where he studied French, Latin and Spanish.

In 1950 Walcott founded the St Lucia Arts Guild, for which he wrote his first play, *Henri Christophe*, performed in the same year. In 1953 Walcott moved to Trinidad and from 1953 to 1957 he worked as a teacher at schools on several Caribbean islands. He then started his career as a journalist, writing features for the Jamaican weekly newspaper *Public Opinion* and features and drama criticism for the *Trinidad Guardian*. Between 1958-59 he studied theatre in New York.

As a poet Walcott made his debut at the age of eighteen with *Twenty-five Poems* (1948), which was privately printed. His international recognition as a poet came with *In a Green Night: Poems 1948-60* (1962) followed by *Selected Poems* (1964); *The Castaway and Other Poems* (1965); *The Gulf and Other Poems* (1969); *Another Life* (1973); *Sea Grapes* (1976); *The Star-Apple Kingdom* (1980); *Selected Poetry* (1981); *The Fortunate Traveller* (1982); *Midsummer* (1984); *Collected Poems 1948-84* (1986); *The Arkansas Testament* (1987); *Omeros* (1990); *Poems 1965-1980* (1993); *Bounty* (1997); *Tiepolo's Hound* (2000); *The Prodigal* (2004) and *White Egrets* (2010).

From 1959 to 1971 Walcott was the founding director of the Little Carib Theatre – later the Trinidad Theatre Workshop, for which he wrote many of his earlier plays. His *Dream on Monkey Mountain* was commissioned originally by the British Royal Shakespeare Company in the late 1960s but was produced finally in the USA by the Negro Ensemble Company and broadcast on television.

Walcott's plays include: *Cry for a Leader* (1950); *Henri Christophe* (1950); *Robin and Andrea* (1950); *Senza Alcun Sospetto* (1950); *The Price of Mercy* (1951); *Three Assassins* (1951); *Harry Dernier* (1952); *The Charlatan* (1954); *Crossroads* (1954); *The Sea at Dauphin* (1954); *The Golden Lions* (1956); *The Wine of the County* (1956); *Ti-Jean and His Brothers* (1957); *Drums and Colours* (1958); *Jourmard* (1959); *Malcauchon* (1959); *Dream on Monkey Mountain* (1967); *Franklin* (1969); *In a Fine Castle* (1970); *The Joker of Seville* (1974, with Galt McDermott); *O, Babylon!* (1976); *Remembrance* (1977); *The Snow*

Queen (1977); *Pantomime* (1978); *Marie Laveau* (1979, with G. McDermott); *The Isle is Full of Noises* (1982); *Beef, No Chicken* (1985); *The Odyssey: A Stage Version* (1993); *The Haitian Trilogy* (2002); *Steel,* a musical (2005), with Galt McDermot.

His published plays include: *Henri Christophe: A Chronicle in Seven Scenes* (Bridgetown: Advocate, 1950); *Harry Dernier* (Bridgetown, Barbados Advocate, 1952); *The Sea at Dauphin* (Port of Spain: Extra-Mural Department, 1954); *Ione: A Play with Music* (Kingston: Extra-Mural Department, UCWI, 1957); *Ti-Jean: A Play in One Act* (Jamaica: Extra-Mural Department, 1957); *Joumard or a Comedy to the Last Minute* (UWI: Extra-Mural Department, n.d.); *Dream on Monkey Mountain and Other Plays* (New York, Farrar, Straus, Giroux, 1970); *The Joker of Seville & O Babylon!* (New York, Farrar, Straus, Giroux, 1978); *Remembrance & Pantomime: Two Plays* (New York, Farrar, Straus, Giroux, 1986); *Three Plays: The Last Carnival, Beef, No Chicken, A Branch of the Blue Nile* (New York, Farrar, Straus, Giroux, 1986); *The Odyssey: A Stage Version* (New York, Farrar, Straus, Giroux, 1993); *Moonchild* (London: Faber, 2011).

In addition to his collaborations with Galt McDermott, Walcott has worked with Paul Simon on the Broadway musical, *The Capeman*, in 1998, that starred Puerto Rican pop star, Mark Anthony.

His nonfiction work includes *What the Twilight Says* (1998), a collection of his essays, including "The Muse of History", and *The Antilles: Fragments of Epic Memory* (New York, Farrar, Straus, Giroux, 1993).

More recently, a stage reading presentation of *Moon-Child* (*Ti-Jean in Concert*) a musical reworking of *Ti-Jean and His Brothers,* was performed at the American Academy in Rome, April 4, 2011 with music by Ronald "Boo" Hinkson and André Tanker. Another staged reading was presented at Essex University's Lakeside Theatre in the U.K. in May 2011. A production of his full-length play *Pantomime* was staged at that university in October 2012. In 2013 Walcott produced his latest play *O Starry Starry Night* at the Lakeside Theatre and at Samaan's Park in Choc, Castries in St Lucia.

Derek Walcott, who was awarded the Nobel Prize for Literature in 1992, is widely known as a consistent traveller throughout his life, continuously studying the conflict between the heritage of European and Caribbean culture, from slavery to independence. While he has lived most of his life in Trinidad, he has worked as a professor of poetry at the University of Boston, and dividing his time between Trinidad and the USA

DEREK WALCOTT

Q: From the experience you've had of having plays produced here, how do you view the emergence and the development of Caribbean theatre in North America – to be more specific, New York City?

DW: Well, I haven't had as many plays produced in New York as I have in Los Angeles. I've had three plays done on the coast: *Dream on Monkey Mountain*, *In a Fine Castle* and *Charlatan*. I've had two done in New York. [*Dream* and *Ti Jean*] But that really wasn't a West Indian experience, because I was the only West Indian in the productions. I don't think there is anything much happening in terms of Caribbean theatre on the coast. But I'm beginning to become more aware of a generation on the East coast – a sort of second generation – whose roots are here either because the family has migrated or because they have come for a visit and stayed. They put down roots in New York, and they want to develop an expression through theatre of whatever culture –and this applies to Haitians, Cubans, Puerto Ricans, and so on.

I think there's going to be very soon a recognition and an awareness of not only Caribbean theatre but also of Caribbean literature, and the two would naturally be simultaneous. I don't think that America has paid enough attention to what has come out of the Caribbean in terms of the novel. There is an impressive body of writing that has come out of such a small area. They're now beginning to pay attention to the people who are the best novelists and poets in the whole world now, in my opinion – writers like Marquez, Borges, Neruda, Fuentes – people like that.

Now the body of Caribbean literature in the theatre, I think, is still minuscule. And I think the reason for that is that there is not enough encouragement given to the development of the Caribbean actor and dancer in his or her native island. For instance, the Cuban ballet [*Ballet Nacional de Cuba*] is a world renowned company that is supported by the Cuban government. The Jamaican ballet company [National Dance Theatre Company of Jamaica], that Rex Nettleford runs, is very strongly supported as part of the national identity by the Jamaican government. But that's not true of most of the large Caribbean territories.

This is bound to be crippling for the actor in the Caribbean because he needs the space and some kind of monetary support to express himself. And that should, I think, definitely, however small, come from the state. But, there can be a balance between what can be written by the playwrights in the Caribbean itself and what can be performed by the Caribbean actors in New York. Now it's very good for these actors to be in New York because if you live in the Caribbean, in a small island, there is a great tendency to develop an inflated opinion of one's own talent. You have to be in a testing situation where you have to be as professional as the writer is when he submits his plays to professional producers. So the ultimate goal would be to have the Caribbean writer develop his plays in his native territory and performed by groups there in a professional interpretation. And that is what I think is going to happen. But I think that the only way it can really flourish is if the governments pay more attention and give subsidies to the development of the native talent in the territories themselves.

I think too, though, that what is needed is a Caribbean company performing in New York, just as they would perform at home but as professionals, without being inhibited by and at the same time without becoming Americanized, without submerging themselves within the idea of being an American actor or an American writer.

What I believe in is the idea of a company; I think a company should flourish on its native soil, just like the Berliner Ensemble is in Berlin or the Royal Shakespeare Company is in London. So I'm not urging that individual talent migrate from the country of its origin, but, since it has to happen, that talent should move into a competitive situation of quality so that it can emerge and be recognized. The ideal, of course – and this is something that I have spent eighteen years trying to do – is to return to the native country and build a theatre company in which nobody is superior in terms of the talent: the actor is equal to the writer, the designer is equal to the actor. That can only exist as a domestic situation: you cannot wholly export a complete company because then you're not functioning out of your roots.

Q: What similarities or dissimilarities do you see between Afro-American and Caribbean theatre? Do you see any aesthetic distinctions?

DW: I think Afro-American theatre – just to answer your question very simply – comes out of protest. It is a violent reaction to untenable conditions. I'm saying that, as theatre, it detonates. I think that for a long time the theatre of the Afro-American is going to be a theatre that comes out of his own anger and desire, a rage for justice and revenge; it is a sort of catharsis. Now that does not make it any stronger as theatre than Caribbean theatre. Caribbean theatre has all the same reasons for the anger, but our memory is not the same kind. It is not a close anger of a recent personal humiliation but of a more abstract sense of general injustice. That makes for a different kind of sensibility, a different kind of theatre, subtler, more clinical in its examination of a colonial condition. The battle is closer, and nearer victory for the Afro-American; the battle in the Caribbean is more bewildering because there are Blacks in power doing the same things, in many cases, as the white man did. So it's more of an internal struggle in the Caribbean to resolve those injustices.

In addition to that, the education of the Afro-American and the education of the Caribbean – not just black, any Caribbean person – is a different colonial condition. The African black here has, as I said, a direct conflict, an open battle to fight. He knows the enemy. Our crippling condition in the Caribbean is that we still have a kind of love-hatred relationship with the colonial past. And we have to confess and deal with that love and the hatred that make us ex-Englishmen or ex-Frenchmen or ex-whatever. That is one very big difference there. The Afro-American is an *American*, and when he gets up and says, "I have my rights, I am an American," he is an American. But our assertions of ourselves as West Indians or as Jamaicans or whatever is not yet defined. It's in a way more private and less polemical a condition. We can distance ourselves because we have been through that a little longer, we're a little older – there's been more *time* behind us than the Afro-American. In fact, a lot of intellectuals of the Black Power movement came out of the Caribbean. And the only reason that they could come out of the Caribbean is because they had that distance; they had both the metropolitan experience of being Black – people like Frantz Fanon, or C.L.R. James, or Aimé Césaire, who had been to Paris or Washington – and the ability to go back and write about it with a clinical anger that could write manifestoes.

Q: What is your reaction to some of the Caribbean dramatists who have had exposure in the New York or North American theatre community – Errol John, for example – compared to some of the more contemporary Black-American writers like Amiri Baraka,[1] Ed Bullins,[2] Lonne Elder,[3] Richard Wesley[4]?

DW: These Black-American writers that you mention have one very good thing in their favour, and that is they have behind them a body of people – actors, directors, producers, within their race – willing to express whatever their plays mean. What stultifies and cripples in the Caribbean is the absence of that machine. So what you find is a lot of people having to give up writing plays because they can't get them done. I have, for instance, done a lot of plays with the Trinidad Theatre Workshop but the bulk of them have been *my* plays because

I have a company and I'm a writer. You almost have to create your own company in the Caribbean to get your own plays done. And any playwright who keeps getting his plays produced is bound to improve technically because, just as an actor learns by doing, so does a playwright, even if his next play is a flop. That accessibility to a theatre, to an audience, is another thing that differentiates the Caribbean playwright from the Afro-American playwright. That is one of the tragedies of Caribbean playwrights at home. I know people who have four, five, six plays that are unproduced – the total amount of unproduced plays in the Caribbean must be very, very large, and God knows how many are good.

Q: I asked the same question of some African-American playwrights, and they said that African-American writers were angrier, and that West Indian writers weren't angry enough, that the West Indian writer tends to write about things that are not, say, immediately concerned with racism, with Black people in the diaspora.

DW: Well, you see, I don't think that a West Indian gets up in the morning, saying, "I am black." There is not an American Black who doesn't get up in the morning and think, even subliminally, "I am black and I have to face the day." They get up in the morning with the feeling that something's going to happen to them that week that will make them realize that they are black and disadvantaged in this country, that certain things will happen to them simply because they are black. That goes on in this country *still*. It does not happen in the Caribbean. One does not get up in the morning and say, "Jesus Christ, I am black and some mother is going to be out for my ass today!" And that's the difference. And because the Caribbean writer does not wake up in the morning with that kind of burden, he has the advantage of being able to develop a sense of universal anger, a certain perspective on the conditions of the Black or any Third World disadvantaged race. One of the reasons why Caribbean plays are so banal – so many plays are just jokes, comedies, or backyard farces – is because that problem, the weight of being Black, does not exist for them; there's no fight against "The Man", against a visible oppressor. If anything, the Caribbean tendency is toward a *political* anger rather than a *personal* anger – towards a socialist or a Marxist perspective. You can't help but be leftist in the Caribbean if you're a writer – you have no choice, really. Not that you don't have any choice...

Q: What makes you say that?

DW: Because of the poverty, of the violent contrast between the rich and the poor. And anybody with a simple sense of justice realizes that the system in the Caribbean is unjust for the majority of the people. So that kind of anger is there. It may occasionally come out in satire, but the people who simply write backyard farces or comedies have just not developed the universality that would require them to look at not only their little island but the whole Caribbean, and then beyond the Caribbean to America.

Q: I would think that the work of Lennox Brown has a tendency to be more universal, even though he deals almost exclusively with Caribbean themes, don't you agree?

DW: Lennox's experiences – of being Black in Canada – do have that necessary balance between his country, Trinidad, and the rest of the world. One of the worst things that can happen to a Caribbean playwright is to stay only in the Caribbean, to close his eyes and not realize that where he's at is not all it's all about.

Q: Steve Carter[5] said he felt that the West Indian writers he's met made more use of the language than Black-American writers, who have a tendency to be more concise. He wondered whether this was because of differences in their educational experience. Garland Thompson,[6] of the Frank Silvera Writers Workshop, felt that young black American writers do not have a good sense of the use of metaphor and that Caribbean writers make greater use of the resources of language. For instance, he calls Lennox Brown a "wordsmith". What do you feel about that?

DW: You can take a generalized view, but, you see, it takes a certain talent, a certain genius within the language. You take any language, any argot, any street language, any peasant language, any dialect, and heighten it. Refine it. Select it. Make it a powerful theatre language. I don't think O'Neill did it – I think it's very wooden in O'Neill. But Tennessee Williams' melodic instinct is Southern. It's both Southern and feminine, in a sense. Now, that man is one of the linguistic geniuses in the theatre, in the sense that he has his own melody; even though his melody is Southern, he is easily a universal writer. The tone of the individual comes through the general argot, the speech of the region he comes from. The same with Synge or Beckett or Pinter.

To make a distinction between the conciseness of language in the Black-American and the ebullience of language in the Caribbean is unimportant. A Black-American writer can take the language of the street and heighten it to a powerful and beautiful work of art, regardless of the subject. A lot of people believe that theatre speech is just speech, which it is not. Theatre speech is a selection, like a poem, a selection of a whole body of speech; it is not purely stenographic.

The instinct of a revolutionary theatre – in this instance, Black-American theatre – is to be realistic; therefore, the inclination is to have a stenographic vocabulary – to pick up the jargon of the street, the fast, decoratively abusive rhythm. You know, "motherfucker," and all that sort of thing; it sounds realistic, but it fades. But if one got *beneath* it, picked up the rhythm of Black speech, one could write a speech that would be the equivalent in language to anything from *Henry IV*. That would true of either the Caribbean or the United States.

The difference is we lean back more on our words; our predisposition is toward a rhetorical, demonstrative, elaborate speech. Our rhythms are different. We don't have catatonic rhythms, we don't have percussive rhythms. We have a leisurely rhythm in our way of life. Over here it's a fast beat. It's the difference between, say, jazz and the languidness of reggae and calypso. Jazz is percussive, hard-to-the-point, it darts in and out. But we lean back on the music and we lean back on writing in the same way. Nobody's going to call jazz superior to reggae or calypso; they are each art forms in their own ways.

Q: Do you believe that there is misinformation and misunderstanding between English-speaking and Spanish-speaking peoples of the Caribbean?

DW: Yes, because a lot of us are brought up in the English experience and, we have a certain contempt, just as the Englishman had a contempt for anyone non-English. An Englishman made this remark: Africa starts at Calais, in other words, anything outside of England was inhabited by "niggers". And we, brought up as Englishmen, tend to think of Spaniards as inferior – we still have residues of prejudice. I that a lot of that still remains in the Caribbean. People are even suspicious of Venezuelans in Trinidad, although Trinidad has a greater affinity for the Spanish.

Again, it is always the individual genius that makes a culture recognized. If you read a writer like Marquez, you become proud to be a part of the experience of the Caribbean because he writes for you. I understand what he's talking about and it's fantastically done. So I'm sharing the experience of being Latin. A writer like Marquez can annihilate, by his genius, can eradicate any residue of prejudice. That genius could come out of Puerto Rico as it came out of Colombia. One of the tragedies is that the Caribbean is riddled with a lot of inferior prejudices: prejudices against the East Indian, against the Chinese, etc.

If a Trinidadian wanted to understand the composite culture of Trinidad, he would have to understand East Indian culture, African culture, Chinese culture, and Spanish culture. It's like being locked in a single room with a bunch of people for a week: you're bound to understand them eventually, you're bound to get somewhere. A Trinidadian is bound to be Chinese-Trinidadian-Indian – and that's what makes him a West Indian. But these prejudices are exploited by politics all the time. That is what is very tragic. I don't want to go into the politics and the fragmentation of the Caribbean, I don't want to get into that.

When people say that Caribbean writers are less angry, one of the things you have to be aware of is the fact that, as Caribbean people, our daily experience is multiracial and non-threatening. We meet white people, talk to them without any sense of anger, hostility, or hatred. Not because we have been brainwashed but because our conditions are not *tense* conditions; we do not require you to reassert your individuality as a human being. That is not true of the Afro-American, because the only people his internment or ghetto situation has allowed him to meet are his own people. He's locked into only his experience within his own race. Naturally, in this situation, there's bound to be detonation – anger, violence – even in the writing.

The other thing is the tragic and bitter situation of, and the *contempt* for the education of the black man in America, the idea that if he's educated maybe he'll start to think, and if he starts to think the white majority will be in a lot of trouble. It's OK if he gets violent, because they always have more cops. Now this indifference – which is a deliberate indifference – toward educating Blacks, naturally has made the Black himself contemptuous of education, so that education is looked at, in some ways, even among black intellectuals, as being a white thing.

What the black American has to stop doing is his "own thing". He's got to do not just "his thing", but *everything*. Look what has happened to the theatre now: you have black shows, but the same segregation. Whether it's the black man saying, "We doin' our shows, we can do it better than the white man, we dance better, we sing better", or whether it was the black exploitation pictures of ten years ago. They may be doing black musicals, but the segregation is still there. While the black man is entertaining himself on stage, the white man is looking on and saying, "Yeah, you dance very well, nigger." What's the difference between what he says now and what he said seventy, eighty years ago? And *that's* the trap. So you can't really say that there's much happening in terms of the development of Black theatre. Blacks are getting more work because there are more musicals, but that isn't doing anything specifically in terms of developing Black theatre. In the Caribbean, people say, "We take you on your *talent* not on your *colour*."

Q: You mentioned earlier the influence of Carnival on theatre. What are some of the influences that caused you to become a writer?

DW: I used to write as a child. My mother, who was a teacher, encouraged me to write. My father wrote, too, and they had an amateur theatre group. There was a certain ambience at home. People of my generation, like George Lamming and V.S. Naipaul, had – and all Caribbean writers still have it – this fantastic opportunity of articulating a people on paper or on the stage for the first time. Before that, tradition was still inside him. But, on the other hand, everything around him was totally new, unnamed, and waiting for him to name it and you couldn't get a better start than that. The elation of beginning a theatre, with new language and a new people, is a hell of a – nobody can cover the Caribbean in his own lifetime.

Q: How many plays have you written so far?

DW: I must have written about a dozen full-length plays and about four one-acters, not to mention those that I've torn up.

Q: I've heard it said that if you had not been so involved with the Trinidad Theatre Workshop, that you could have produced a greater body of work. Do you think this is true?

DW: No, I don't think so; on the contrary I have quite a lot of plays written *because* I had to turn out work for them. There are a lot of plays that I've done down there that are only known down there. What happens normally to a professional playwright is that he writes one play which may be a hit, and then that's it. The next one is going to be looked at extremely hard... when it comes out. The critics jump on it and say, "No more" and he's crippled. Now, if you have your own company, it's a different situation. In fact, I was writing, in many cases, with a particular actor in mind. By the time one play has had a short run, you're moving on to the next one. Now, if I had not had a company, I would have one play, maybe, and be trying to get it done by somebody in New York. Unless, say, that play is a big hit, then I'm stuck with that play for several years, following it around till it becomes a movie, in the normal course of events. Look at the number of playwrights who have had one hit and can't come back and do theatre.

Q: It's interesting that you have had your work successfully produced in New York, and yet you have remained faithful to the Caribbean and not completely transplanted yourself.

DW: Well, I was writing for a company that was very, very good. In many cases, the actors are as good as any actors I've worked with up here. And sometimes, in their own language, better, actually, because they knew what I was talking about. The plays that were being done by my company in Trinidad were taken up by professional producers here, by regional theatres – not Broadway.

Q: Have you ever thought of writing novels or have you ever written a novel?

DW: I wrote a novel a long time ago; it was terrible; I was too young; I was awful. I can't write novels.

Q: Why is that?

DW: Well, you have to believe the lie you're creating; any form of art is a lie. It's artificial, really. And I can't believe the fiction of that kind of fiction. I mean, I can't write: "John got up and went... and next day ..." because I can't believe it myself. But I can believe a play.

Q: That applies to short stories as well?

DW: Yes, any narrative fiction. I'm doing a book, though, which is an autobiographical book. [This is "American without America", never published but used in Bruce King's *Derek Walcott: A Caribbean Life*, OUP, 2000] That's OK because it happened. But generally, the talents required for plays and novels are different.

Q: In what respect? Where does that distinction lie?

DW: I think a novelist could make a good scenarist for a film and not necessarily a good playwright, because, if you're a playwright, your head is full of a moment: if you place somebody in a room, you have that whole room in your head and that person is there. So you have assumed, as a playwright, the whole geography of that moment, the whole background, the time, etc. The novelist progresses in a different manner; the novelist *accrues* that knowledge sentence by sentence. A lot of writers I know who are trying to write plays have a hard time getting characters in and out of a room. And that's never a real playwright's problem because he knows why the people come in and why they go out. And for that same reason, I think, a playwright who decides he can write a novel may write it in such a way that when he makes somebody enter a room it is a theatrical entrance as opposed to a normal day-to-day casual entrance. Playwrights writing a novel can be very theatrical, and a novel is not theatrical.

Q: I recall one playwright saying that a play calls for precision, whereas a novel is more diffuse – you can go on and on.

DW: I have to disagree. I think that the novelist explores sentence by sentence; he builds life as he goes along. A playwright does the same thing line by line but he doesn't know that he's doing it. He starts off with people and stays with people; the surroundings are in his head. The characters in a novel cannot exist without geography. I can't think of any novelist-playwrights, really, off the top of my head. Shaw... Oh, I think people can try to write both – I suppose I could write a passable novel but I don't think I would believe in it.

Q: Where do you think Caribbean literature and theatre is going?

DW: Caribbean literature is dried up in terms of the novel and that's very sad. I think that a lot of novelists of my generation are going through a transitional period and will re-emerge. It's sort of like menopause, a shift in focus. It may be that because they are living outside the Caribbean, they are somewhat out of touch with their native countries. I think that, once they get more closely in touch, they will reassess their experience, and re-emerge with a deeper knowledge of the Caribbean. A writer like Naipaul, for instance, who *does* stay in touch, continues to get better and better.

The theatre, I think, is in very, very serious trouble, simply because it's ignored. Trying to make a government understand that when you say water, or you say lights, or you say roads and you say sewers, then in that same breath you have to think art. We have picked up the English attitude toward art; art is a hobby. That is the worst thing that has happened to us, for me, in terms of the English. If we were Latins, it would not have happened. Because for the Latin, life and art are the same: self-expression and whatever surrounds you – that's in the Latin sensibility. It's in the African sensibility too. But, in the Caribbean, "necessities" are given priority, not realizing *this* necessity: that a man cannot live without art. And then, of course, we have all those deceiving things that look like massive artistic expression, like Carnival or festivals or the natural ebullience and talent of all Caribbean peoples for music and dancing. Although these are certainly of great value, they are really entertainments, which keep people contented as far as governments are concerned. In terms of a policy, in terms of a individual artist, there's nothing like that that happens. There should be only one attitude, and that is for the development of individual talent.

Q: But there seems to be such a great wealth of natural raw talent in the Caribbean. I see it in Jamaica every day. We should be able to channel that talent.

DW: Exactly. I mean, everybody has got to be trained. If Botticelli is studying under some master, he's taking a course like everybody else, he's qualifying. He's getting a degree under a Renaissance master; he's an apprentice, and it's as formal an occupation as engineering or anything else. Nobody can be an artist without years of discipline, either self-discipline or apprenticing yourself to someone. But we are an ebullient, easy-seeming people, and we have instant explosions of entertainment that passes for art. But these are ephemeral things.

Q: It has been said, by some in the Caribbean, that you have a tendency to be too classical in terms of your references, and these are foreign to the Caribbean.

DW: I don't think that they are foreign. I can't be responsible for the education I've had, and in fact I have educated myself beyond the education I have had. Nobody would look at an English writer and say, "I think you know a little too much about Homer and Horace." Just because I'm a "nigger", I don't see any why anybody should tell me, "You shouldn't know that much." If I appear to be arrogant, well, that's unfortunate. But I think that, as poets, we have no responsibility to the reader at all. None. All you have is a responsibility to the poem. And if you're not lying and the associations come to you naturally when you write, then you can't fake it and say, "I have a responsibility to try to put aside my intelligence or my knowledge because many people are illiterate." When I say illiterate, I mean not formally educated. People don't delight in the fact that they can't understand, people *want* to educate themselves. I don't use my work to educate people. That's like saying you shouldn't read so and so because it's European or whatever; that's bullshit. I think it's ignorance to say that.

But what *is* the responsibility of any writer toward his own country is to be true to the inner voice of his people, of his race, of his experience; to catch the true tone of the language he's working in. The language I'm working in – the one I was born with and speak with – is English and that comes out of another older experience. I may be from St Lucia, but I write in English and that makes me a poet who writes in English. I'm not an Englishman but I write in English. What one doesn't want to do is put on an artificial tone as if one were speaking like an Englishman.

Q: Who are some of your favourite Caribbean writers – novelists, playwrights, poets?

DW: Well, I'll tell you – this is going to sound very arrogant – I think that the bulk of Caribbean poetry that I know is very self-indulgent and very weak. Very lazy. It's lazy to say, "I'm Black, that's the only thing I write about and you must understand how I've been a slave or a colonial..." A writer can't be lazy. You have to use your imagination. If you have a bright-blue sea and a red bougainvillea and a nice, white cloud passing, it's not enough to put that down. It's like painting by numbers. So there isn't much Caribbean poetry that I really have great respect for. By Caribbean poetry, I would include not only the English-speaking Caribbean but any experience that I consider to be Caribbean. I consider Marquez to be a great Caribbean poet even if he writes in prose. And take a writer like Aimé Césaire – he's a great poet. Césaire is by no means a lazy poet. And there's *new* laziness emerging which comes out of the protest poetry of the young black poets, which is the easiest thing to do. To get up and say, "I don't *need* to know anything about technique, I don't need to know what makes a poem work, I am speaking to you as a black man and you don't understand me." Well, that's junk, and that's going to disappear in two days. People *dismiss* the idea because, they say, verse is structure and verse is formality and, "I don't need it because I'm liberated and a New World person." That's junk.

Q: I found that too, here in America among black American poets.

DW: Absolutely. It's not only true of Blacks but it's true of a lot of young American writers who believe that, for instance, a writer like William Carlos Williams is the best model they could have. They feel that Williams wrote in short lines just what he thought, very simply. All poets admire Williams because, structurally, he's so technically exact. But if you try to teach that to black or white young Americans and you show them that their model of casualness and ease is a highly structured technician, then you're in trouble because they don't believe it. But it is because the attitude toward art as work has been so amateurish that so much Caribbean poetry is so bad. By comparison, I look good.

Q: So, who are some of your favourite Caribbean writers?

DW: Well, I like Martin Carter,[7] when he's not too rhetorical; I like a lot of Eddie Brathwaite,[8] when he's not being too embroidered. Who else?

Q: What about Mervyn Morris?[9]

DW: Yes, I like Mervyn, who is reticent, unambitious – I like the modesty of Mervyn Morris, I admire it.

Q: What about Slade Hopkinson or Dennis Scott?

DW: I don't want to pass judgment on them yet. I think that Dennis Scott is certainly a powerful poet; he's working his way out of the entanglements of his own art, and when he wiggles out of that, with a burst of some kind of clarity, he'll have another kind of fullness. He has a powerful imagination.

Q: And Slade? What do you feel about his work?

DW: I haven't seen any of Slade's recent poetry. But, you see, all of us are going through a whole crisis of language and personality, which may never be resolved in our time. But the process of trying to resolve it is what makes the poetry. So if it comes out anguished and tormented and unclear, it's a result of the search. It's just that the search has to be exact.

Q: Who are some of your favourite novelists and playwrights?

DW: I think that the remarkable thing about the English-speaking Caribbean is the body of very, very fine novels and short fiction. Because there have been, easily, twenty very readable, very good novels written. I'm not talking about the works of one particular writer, like, say, Naipaul. But most West Indian novelists have written one or two very good novels, so we have a body of novels that is very, very respectable. That has been our real flowering. Ezra Pound said something a long time ago: that poetry has to be at least as well written as prose. Now, our prose writers have a tremendous sense of structure. But when we approach poems in the Caribbean we feel, well, you don't need all of that. That's what leads to disaster in most cases, because we depend on our belief that our sense of structure will come out of just being ourselves, but you can't wake up one morning and say, "I'm going to write a poem, right." The most transient thing in poetry is sincerity.

Q: Would you agree that most artists are, or should be, regarded as the visionaries in their society?

DW: Remarkably enough, I would say that the Caribbean writer is gaining tremendous respect at home from the people. I think the indifference and the callousness comes from the people in power, people in charge who do not know, for instance, that all our writers are in exile. A lot of them are broke, and the government couldn't care less if they die. It would not be true, I think, of a Latin American writer – it's better to be shot for your beliefs than to be treated as somebody who doesn't matter. It's not the indifference from the people who understand what he says, but the fact that there's no acknowledgment of his worth, of his presence, of his necessity – the need for him in the society.

People know who the writers are, and the average man on the street will say, "Yes, you are Naipaul the writer, you are Walcott the writer," and greet you with an affection that is separate from the way they would greet a politician. But what is the point of that if a writer has to be in some foreign city when he would really prefer to be back home, if he could find a place there. And if he contradicts the government, and the government is fascist or a dictatorship, a writer would prefer to be shot for his beliefs than to be ignored. Indifference is the worst thing.

I'll make a bitter remark: I think I've seen two generations wasted in my theatre in Trinidad. I've been there for eighteen years. That country has tremendous opportunity and wealth, but has *no* attitude toward art. None. So somebody who's eighteen years old, I cannot sincerely encourage to become a dancer, or any kind of artist, in his own country. I would not say now, out of my own experience in Trinidad in particular, "OK, you become a writer, you become a painter, you stay in Trinidad." I could not honestly tell him to remain. And that's not how I saw things happening when I began eighteen years ago. I would have imagined that by this time one would have been aware that people don't just spring up out of the ground and wait like flowers to be held and nursed. Not that you have to be pampered but you have to feel you're necessary. Nobody wants favours, but you want to be in a climate that allows you to function. It's ironic that I am treated with – I don't know – anything you want to call it – in America, than I am in the Caribbean. Most ironic, because my life was aimed in the other direction and now I have to change.

Q: Why do you think that those in power care so little that the writers feel they have to go abroad?

DW: Well, you see, the people who are in power are of the same generation as the writers, or a little older, so they haven't changed. Why should they have a different attitude? When I talk to younger people, younger writers, younger revolutionaries, younger Blacks, they say they have no wish to migrate. Their revolution, if they would only look at it, is an expression of their *art*, not an expression of violence. It is a wish to express a spirit of a people in art work, not in the blowing-up of buildings. That is the drive inside the Caribbean now. It's not violent, it is creative. There is no enemy. Most people believe that the enemy is something outside; whereas what is going on is just a desire to utter and to articulate and to *shape*. The thing is creative not destructive.

But when you have people who don't understand that, then you get despair. The next stage is somebody saying, "What the hell am I doing anyway? Let me get a job in a bank, screw the revolution; what am I trying to be an artist for?" I mean to say a country like Trinidad doesn't have a *single* good art gallery, a *single* good museum, a *single* theatre – a place that has billions of dollars? No, man. It's not a culture. No matter how much you tell me about Carnival. You're selling yourself.

Q: Can you tell me about the beginnings of indigenous theatre in the Eastern Caribbean?

DW: In St Lucia, there's the St Lucia Arts Guild, which was started by the late Maurice Mason[10] and myself, which later my brother, Roderick, took over. That still exists. My brother has written a lot of plays for them, and so have I. There's a young writer named Stanley French[11] who has come out of that group. After I left the country, my brother tried to do a combination of classical and contemporary pieces, including West Indian plays. There's also a young writer in Dominica, named Alwin Bully, who's doing a lot of work there. In Trinidad, there's The Company of Players, but it does very sporadic productions. It was formed right after the war with Errol Hill, and there's another playwright, Freddie Kissoon, who now has his own company [The Strolling Players, founded 1957]. And, of course, Errol Hill, who wrote *Man Better Man* [premiered 1957], went on to Dartmouth where he is now head of the drama department. The Whitehall Players, I think, was the first name of the group; later, I think, it became The Company of Five; Errol John and Errol Hill were in that company. Around that time, Errol John wrote *The Tout* [premiered 1949]. Later he went to England, became an actor, and also won the Observer Prize for his play *Moon on a Rainbow Shawl* [1958].

In Trinidad, the groups that did the most technically satisfactory productions were The Phoenix and The Trinidad Dramatic Society, both of which consisted of expatriates. The Trinidad Dramatic Society was headed by Dagmar Butt, who had theatrical experience, and her husband, Hugh, who I think had also done professional acting or some repertory acting in the provinces.[12] Some of the work they did was modelled on the London West End productions, with very few black actors. I don't know whether that was deliberate; but I think they just did the material they knew how to do. I can still remember that a black actor on stage in that kind of production was very rare, but it may have been just the material.

There is also the Trinidad Theatre Workshop, which was begun in 1959, and which I left in 1976. Then there's a group in the south, in which one of the active people is James Lee Wah[13]; one of the actors in that group is a man who is in the film *Bim*, Ralph Maraj.[14] Errol Hill has written about a schoolmaster named Roberts, who used to write popular farces in the '30s or '40s that evidently had large audiences. In terms of roots, or folk drama, Hill's the schoolmaster-playwright who recognized the need for indigenous theatre.

But I'm not aware of any far-reaching development in the theatre. Of course the powerful thing is still calypso and carnival, which is oral theatre, anyway, and has a very dramatic narrative quality. This was more of a movement in music than in straight theatre. The theatre there came out of an already existing, sophisticated form. All of us knew we had to write something that would come out of Carnival, a free-form kind of expression. Errol John, for instance, wrote one of the first true roots, backyard plays of any quality, *Moon on a Rainbow Shawl*.

Now in Guyana, for instance, there is a theatre group called The Theatre Guild, which is pretty old and has had some very good actors. But, while they had a theatre building, they didn't really have a permanent company; I don't think they ever formed one. So they had a theatre without a repertory company.[15]

In other parts of the Caribbean, other aspects of the arts were developed more fully. Trinidad for music; definitely Jamaica for a much stronger theatre and stronger painting; the novel in Guyana, with Edgar Mittelholzer, Wilson Harris, Jan Carew, Denis Williams – I can't think of anybody else off the top of my head now – but that's four novelists from a country that size. When I say that size, I mean in population not in scale.

Q: I was always under the impression that Trinidad was the place that produced the bulk of the playwrights.

DW: No. I think more plays of merit have been written in Jamaica, and that would include the recent pantomimes. They should stop being called pantomimes and just be called musicals – Jamaican musicals. This has been going on for about the last fifteen years.[16]

Q: Do you know much about Haiti or Cuba?

DW: No, only hearsay. You see, you have problems like immigration, customs, currency, things like that. For instance, there has never been, to my knowledge, a trip made by a St Lucian troupe. I would like to have had a troupe of actors come from Martinique to St Lucia. It's about five minutes flying time and about four or five hours by boat. They're very, very close – you can see one island from the other. If, for instance, somebody wised up to the idea that if you write a play in French patois – say, a Dominican playwright like Bully – you could have an audience that would include much of the Southern Caribbean: Dominica, St Lucia, Martinique, Guadeloupe, without even going as far as Haiti. The same thing could be done in terms of Cuba and the Spanish Caribbean. I don't know how much it would really be understood in places like Trinidad, and so on.

Q: Well, aren't the Spanish regarded as the Latin aspect of the Caribbean?

DW: Yes, but that's a lot of crap. It's crap because there's really no difference. We have been trained to think of each other as cultural curiosities. As English "niggers", for instance, our sensibilities were not allowed to include exuberance. Enthusiasm is a vice, the English do not like enthusiasm. They consider it to be amateurish and immature. Now that is our thing – an ebullience, a joy, which comes out in Carnival, which is a Latin aspect. But although a Bajan [Barbadian], for instance, has been brought up with a certain English reticence, it's really not true that there is any difference between a Black Barbadian and a Puerto Rican as a West Indian – everything adheres to the same experience.

There's almost a double audience for every playwright because there are many situations that are bilingual in the Caribbean. I'm not sure a Curaçao audience would not understand a fair amount of English and I'm not sure that that's not true of Suriname too. I'm talking now about a kind of Caribbean street audience. I would think that you could perform an English play in Caracas, for instance, and a Venezuelan audience would understand it.

The whole Caribbean is multi-tiered. You could translate a Jamaican play, for instance, into Spanish, and that experience would be immediately recognized by any Puerto Rican *barrio* person or any ghetto person in Cuba – anywhere in our part of the world.

Q: I was reading a review of a play from Martinique called *Choses* [by Joseph Alpha, see Bully, n. 22, p. 109] in the CARIFESTA issue of the *Arts Review*. There were no sets or costumes or anything. The emphasis was on body movement and the language was Creole. The reviewer, Yvonne Webber, said it was nevertheless understood by the audience. However, she speculated whether such a play could be done in Jamaica because she felt that Jamaican actors would not be uninhibited enough to use their bodies in that way.

DW: The Jamaican actor has been brought up in the English tradition, which is pure voice – just depending on your voice and not your body. Jamaicans are not public dancers, like Trinidadians, for instance. I know what she means, but what does one do? If I translated a play of mine into patois I'd have to teach actors how to perform it. It would be very difficult for a full-length play but you could begin with small pieces, which could be carried around and performed in two languages. Translation is the biggest necessity in the Caribbean now.

Q: Well, you did that with *The Sea at Dauphin* [premiered 1954].

DW: Well, what I did there was to translate from a French Creole to an English Creole. Plays from Puerto Rico and Cuba must exist and we never see any translated work. The whole opening up of Latin American literature in translation is a hell of a thing. I was just knocked out by Gabriel Garcia Marquez's last book, *Autumn of the Patriarch* [1975].

Q: I've noticed there are some West Indians who don't regard themselves as West Indians but rather as "Caribbean". It's very seldom that you hear a Puerto Rican or even a Cuban calling himself West Indian. I know there are some people who prefer to use the term "Caribbean" because it sounds more progressive, because "West Indian" is more colonial. What's your view?

DW: It doesn't matter what you call yourself, but whether you admit there is one cultural experience that speaks different languages called the Caribbean. The Cuban revolution is a most significant thing that has happened since emancipation in the Caribbean. Now whatever that means, there has to be an awareness of the cultural significance of that revolution for the rest of the Caribbean. I'm not saying that every country has to follow the model of the Cuban revolution because that's not necessary. I'm a socialist, and I would like to see that. I think every writer in the Caribbean is bound to be socialist. You can't help it, you see too much poverty not to be. You cannot come out of a place like the Caribbean and wind up a conservative. Even a man like V.S. Naipaul, who appears to be conservative, is, at the core, revolutionary. His criticism is cynicism, the need for upheaval, for change – to stop getting on like fake white men and stop imitating and get off your ass and stop calling yourselves pretty and not doing a fart about it. That kind of thing, that's revolutionary. It's disciplinary, anyway.

This affects the theatre too. For instance, throughout my writing life I have known one truth, and that is, we can't afford sets, we cannot afford changes of scenery. So that has made me write in a way that does not need anything. I've always tried to write the kind of play you could perform on a Sunday morning in an open crowd, with natural light. We don't even have to go by the concept of darkness, which is what the theatre has traditionally used. We have no winter, we have no darkness in the Caribbean. We have a daylight and we have night. We don't have that artificial darkness that cities create. Our fun, our theatre fun, our performances are day things. Carnival is a day thing. Our entertainments are broad daylight entertainments, not after-work-with-artificial-light type of thing. I'm not talking about clubs and all that, I'm talking about mass entertainment. So therefore the kind of theatre that comes out of that is a theatre that does not need lights and scenery – illusion – just as in the Elizabethan experience or the Greek experience of performing in the day – a primal theatre.

But for a long time our theatre has been done as if we lived abroad. Now, I am very much in favour of a fully-equipped theatre; I either want a bare theatre or a totally equipped theatre – there's no in between. When I did *The Seagull* [July, 1975 at the Little Carib, Port of Spain], it was disastrous technically – I could not handle the scene changes. It's four different sets of scenery, both inside and outside. I didn't have the machinery; I could have done it bare but I did it proscenium; and the fact that I did it proscenium screwed up the whole production. And if you do technically bad Chekhov it's going to be terrible; the props are very important in Chekhov – if you're doing it picture-frame style.

Jamaican theatre, I think, has been crippled by presenting pantomime [the traditional Jamaican musical] in a certain British-expatriate framework. That has led to a lot of very bad writing in Jamaican theatre. There are a lot of people who are writing expressionist plays whose style is almost out of date in terms of what is going on now in the wider theatre world. But for many Jamaican playwrights it is a breakaway into a bare-rooted, unencumbered theatre. Jamaica has had a kind of arrested development because of that picture-frame, winter, expatriate type of theatre. You had to put on a tie to see a show, just as if you were in New York or in the London West End.

Q: That's another thing I wanted to touch on: the expatriate experience. Was it out of that experience that grassroots theatre emerged, when indigenous writers began to create their own work?

DW: I think it depends on the playwrights you're talking about. I grew up with poverty one step outside my house, next door, all around, the yard and so on. When we talk about grassroots, we're talking about poverty – plus, of course, language and ebullience. But I think a playwright cannot get away with just being grassroots. He has to use his education and his intelligence. If [Tennessee] Williams writes American dialect – Williams is a great playwright – he is still using his intelligence. If Synge writes Irish dialect, he's using his.

Now if you're talking about written theatre, there was none. What we had was oral theatre, the dramatization of experience that took place, and takes place still, in the Caribbean, on the streets.. For instance, a fight or quarrel in the Caribbean, as you know, is a very elaborate business, with a beginning, a middle and an end. Sometimes *several* endings. Somebody doesn't just say, "Fuck you, buddy," and he's gone. This thing has to be staged to the point where there are exchanges

– it's very African. Somebody must be allowed to cuss and the other guy must be allowed to cuss back – whether it's women or men. The whole pattern has a one-two-three development – a threat, a fight, a reconciliation – but it always aims towards a theatrical conclusion. You have people performing in the streets attracting audiences. This is true of the entire Caribbean – your arena is in your backyard. I have seen a quarrel go on for a day: a neighbour will start quarrelling at six o'clock in the morning and this thing isn't finishing until six o'clock at night, with plenty theatre – doors slamming – I mean, the whole thing is a production! (*Laughs*) With a rest for lunch break!

The language that is closest to its roots is in poetry. The most sophisticated poet may be closest to the roots of the language because he understands its natural rhythms. Lorca is a surrealist poet but look at the great Spanish dramas he wrote about peasants; he knows the language of the people is the poetry of the people.

For instance, in Dennis Scott's last play, *Echo in the Bone*, the Pocomania[17] theme is essential; it is the dynamo of the play. Possession is a theme in Caribbean roots theatre; you see it in *Dream on Monkey Mountain* or in Errol Hill's play *Dance Bongo* [premiered 1965]. This is a primal, powerful, ritualistic experience which comes out of dance and religion. When I was a boy, for example, there used to be a sort of Black Mas' with the Devil going around town in a big red robe made of sacking, horns, and a pitchfork, followed by a lot of little imps with their bodies coated with molasses – Jab-Jab[18]. I didn't realize until I grew up how African that was. You don't have that in Jamaica?

Q: No, but we have a Devil in John Canoe[19]. John Canoe is like a miniature version of Carnival – you have some of those same characters appearing. We know that its roots are African. In Jamaica it started at Christmas when slaves got the day off, dressed up, imitated the master, and danced around the different plantations.

DW: In St Lucia, every year, there was a mas' in Castries, in which the lead role was played by a man called Flavier. He was called Flavier Jab or Flavier the Devil. I don't know if any other Caribbean island has this – it came out of our Catholic tradition – but the more I think about it the more fantastic it is. You know what it's like – it's like the mas', the passion play, in Oberammergau, Germany, where they re-enact the Crucifixion. It's a big pageant. So this man played the Devil – he had the beard and the whole thing. His theatre was the whole town. So imagine this man getting up on Boxing Day – he wouldn't emerge on Christmas Day because Christmas is too holy. He could choose to walk on *any* street in the town, followed by imps with pitchforks. He could *chase* anybody he wanted to, demand money from anyone, smear anybody with molasses! He and the other "actors" would take a street corner and enact the resurrection, but as a Black Mass because of the Devil. And there'd be a Lucifer, and a fellow called Cizo or Ciwo. He was a tall, thin Black guy; I remember them clearly. And he would rebel like Lucifer and the Devil would kill him and the audience would be all around them on the streets. Then he would strut and pose and behave like the Devil – beautiful.

When Flavier stopped playing that role, people would criticize the performance of the man who succeeded him. The fellow had to be damn good to try to beat Flavier. I remember when, as boys, my brother and I – or any child leaving home to go downtown – used to ask on what street the Devil was. Sometimes you turned the corner you would hear this chant: "*Woi! Woi! Oui diable la!*" Which means, "Oh! Oh! Here's the Devil!" There were some fantastic responses. Terrific. Now these were invented responses, not coming out of the church. They would say: "*Voi blo bo moi ca boui le!*" "Throw water on me, I'm burning!" I put some of this in *Ti-Jean*. It's beautiful when you remember it, but I was so scared then that I didn't realize how beautiful it was. You hear that chant down the end of a long street; you just hear, "*Voi blo bo moi ca boui le!*" Over the whole town! Man, you didn't go down *that* street, you just headed somewhere else or you stayed in, and if he was coming up your street you closed the shutters – it was terrifying.

Q: John Canoe had the same effect in Jamaica, but it's dying out now. But you have men who have been doing the *Kumina* dance and John Canoe for *years*. It's the same sort of fear as the Devil Mas': when you hear John Canoe coming, you run! The masqueraders would crack their whips, chip their machetes on the ground, dance, demanding money.

DW: And the whole town is the theatre, right? Now for his performances, the audience would throw money to Flavier Jab. Someone would walk in his direction, maybe some dignified civil servant going to have Boxing Day lunch. And Flavier Jab would come up to him and the man would be so embarrassed that he would *have* to pay, or he would turn another corner. But if he didn't pay, the fellow had the right to do *anything*! He could take molasses and put it on your clothes. Now, mark you, Flavier was like a base stealer in baseball if he did this. (*He gets up to demonstrate*) Flavier is walking here – imagine that you are playing this role. First of all, you're coming up a main street and you're walking with a pitchfork, you're weaving, and kids are following you. When you stop, they stop. Now if he just said, "Um!", the kids would *pelt* down the road. So that every gesture that this man did, even if he just did... (*Mimes a gesture then claps his hands*) They're gone. So you see the dynamism in that kind of thing?

I did *Ti-Jean* in the round for the first time in St Croix in a little theatre there. When I made the Devil character walk around the theatre and made the audience pick up the responses, it was exactly like the Devil Mas'. You can keep doing that until the whole audience becomes possessed. Part of Caribbean theatre, really, which is very difficult for us to know what to do about it as playwrights – or anybody – is possession. Possession in terms of, say, Shango,[20] in terms of Carnival, in terms of the kind of participation on the part of the audience that I'm talking about. When we get close to that audience, we begin to realize that we can start to have a theatre in which the audience responds in the same way that the audience responds to any ritual, like Shango or Pocomania or Carnival and so on. But there's a long way to go in terms of that. Some of that happened in my play *The Joker of Seville*: the audience came back time after time and began to know the songs and the jokes. There should be more poets writing for the theatre, developing the ritualistic, semi-liturgical, aspect. We shouldn't have novelist-playwrights; we should develop poet-playwrights. And choreographer-playwrights. Right now, we're going in a direction in which we have playwrights writing for Western audiences and there ain't no Western audience which knows how to respond to shouts from another culture – giving things back and forth. That's a conflict that can go on. And of course it's difficult to write a play which can produce possession in the audience because it takes a long time to build it. You have to build up to a point of a kind of catatonia, like a religious revival meeting. But I believe that that is the kind of force that we need to develop. That is roots theatre – and it has always been there. But I think we will continue to write two kinds of plays; the fusion will take a little time.

Q: It's like being bilingual. You said there were two types of theatre. You're talking about the formal, European-style theatre as well as…

DW: Yes – not really. But not as language. I don't think that the language, either in English or in French, is really a problem; the instinct for the theatre is the same. But it can never be just ritual. In dance, yes, but you see, even in formal dance there's a point at which a dancer has to stop – even when the piece is finished. The people are cleansed and it's over. Whereas in Shango, it goes on for days, or in Carnival it goes on for days. But that's the difference between ritual and art. You have to decide what you are doing – whether you want to involve people to the point where they leap up, come onstage, and participate – which is damn hard to do if it doesn't happen – like Carnival, over hours or days. And you're working in a confined space. But you can still get it, still formalize it to the point where it can be present, but participation is difficult to achieve.

Q: It would be more natural for a theatre in the round.

DW: Yes. As soon as you have a door and a ticket and people dressing up to go into a building, you're making a social statement. Whereas if you have a ring and multiple entrances, everybody's equal. As long as we continue to build theatres in the Caribbean that are very gimcrack imitations of the proscenium stage, we will continue to have social divisions in the theatre. It takes a long time to correct that; it did not happen with the Trinidad Theatre Workshop. And one gets the usual accusation by the pseudo-super-Blacks, who tell you, for instance, that you don't know anything about black people although you've lived all your blasted life among poor, black people whom you see catching ass, and you're catching ass yourself. You know the kind of person I mean. His Afro is bigger than yours...

Q: Blacker-than-thou.

DW: So you've got that kind of criticism. And then you've got, in both poetry and playwriting, a lot of fake ass-licking of poor, black people. For instance, the Better Village [Best Village] project in Trinidad[21] is a total waste of money and time; that is an example of government trying to form a grassroots theatre by bringing people from villages all over the country and putting them onstage to perform with microphones. They have to run up to the microphones, talk their lines, and run back. So, I mean, there's no shape; it can't work on that basis because, no matter who you are, if you're acting you have to develop certain skills. I mean, Flavier, as a mime and as a man who sent out vibrations on that one day, controlled a bigger audience, a bigger area than Laurence Olivier.[22] That man had a whole people on a syllable, on the sound of his voice. Flavier was not just a man who put on a devil's costume and then went boo and frightened people; he had to have something inside him which told him how to turn and time and make children run. That man was an actor. And he played that role year after year in the same bloody way that the Kabuki people play: one actor plays a role for the rest of his life.

Thank God, I recognized the power of the mas' early enough. There are some things that I have to say that sound like flattery. But I'm talking about what happened, okay? So, if I mention myself, it's not anything to do with modesty or immodesty. When we did *The Joker* [*of Seville*, premiered 1976] in Trinidad, we did it with bleachers and the stage all around – just like when you go to a cockfight. That's not a new idea, everybody's had that idea. We sold oranges, we played music, we had coffee, so that it was like a Sunday morning social gathering. Now if you look at the text of this play, it says, bam-bam, Venice, Naples, so on and so on. Everybody who looked at that play didn't touch it because they see it as proscenium, with velvets [curtains] and changes of scenery. It's costing money in their minds. Now when we did it in the round with the bleachers, the man who was the director of the Royal Shakespeare Company said: "Derek, you have done what Brecht tried to do for twenty years." He came to that show and saw people participating in the action, laughing, singing back, on a Sunday morning, just as if they were in a movie – no, something better than a movie. And when he told me that, I said, well, I knew it wasn't *I* who had done it, but I knew it had to be done – but that's the difference between framing that experience in a Brechtian production and allowing the kind of thing that Brecht spoke about to happen. It wasn't really my achievement; this is how the theatre can work, should work, and *did* work like hell. If you do that, you have the immediate and the same kind of freedom Shakespeare had, or a Kabuki playwright had. You just say, "Fuck it – a mountain." You don't even have to say, as you do to a Western actor, "Imagine there's a mountain." You don't have to imagine the mountain, it's a mountain, for us. We haven't seen what we're supposed to be missing. That makes for a poetic theatre.

The crippling thing for us, too, is that we are spending money in ways – I have done it myself – that are expensive attempts to reproduce theatre in the Western or metropolitan style. I've written plays like that, too. But I did do a play, *Remembrance* [1977], in the round, without any walls, etc. And when it's done here [it was in fact performed as a workshop, non-commercial staging in the small Other Stage theatre in 1979, see King, *Derek Walcott: A Caribbean Life*, p. 374], I'm sure it's going to have a suggestion of solidity – it's not going to be in the round. I don't know how much will be lost; it will have another dimension.

Q: In Errol Hill's book, *The Trinidad Carnival: Mandate for a National Theatre*, he talks about carnival and calypso as the natural starting-points for Caribbean theatre.

DW: Very often a calypso is not presented just as a calypso. Sometimes you get sketches around the calypso, which are enacted and sung like any opera. There could be a musical theatre coming out of that.

There are a lot of things that have become the rule in western, or Theatre with a capital T, that do not necessarily apply to Third World countries. The fact that a westerner has to catch a train to go back to his apartment means that the theatre must exist between eight and ten o'clock. Any play which goes beyond that is in trouble. We, however, are prepared to see carnival for two days. That makes the whole idea of performing an epic possible. The idea of concision and economy – which affects dialogue, which affects concepts, which affects *everything* – may not necessarily be the best thing for us.

Q: I've heard people say that though they've seen a definite move on your part toward the use of dialect, that you've tended to the obscure.

DW: In what way?

Q: In terms of your images and references – that might be foreign to the Caribbean.

DW: I don't think so. People can choose to limit themselves by reading poetry that's nationalistic in its parameters. But anybody who seriously reads poetry will take into account the entire range of world poetry. If these references are obscure to people, those people are incompletely educated. If I make a reference to, say, a Greek myth or something out of English history, that comes out of a whole body of knowledge. I don't consider that obscure. If they think the writing style itself is obscure, that's another story. But in terms of references – what people call classical references – I have as much a heritage of English poetry in the Caribbean as they have in England – or anywhere else.

Q: Yes, you were saying earlier that you can't be responsible for the education you've had. Many regard you as one of the finest writers in the Caribbean. Do you consider yourself a writer, period, or a Caribbean or Third World writer?

DW: Well, to be considered one of the finest writers in the Caribbean is not a great compliment because the bulk of Caribbean poetry, and a lot of Caribbean writing, is lazy, I think. Mainly because of provincialism and nationalism, the merit of local writers' work tends to be exaggerated – unless you're measured against any other writer in any other part of the world. Because, I mean, you can narrow that down to being called the best writer in Tobago or some rock off St Lucia. And that's the whole danger of making statements like that. It's not easy to be a writer, but it's not very hard to be considered a good Caribbean writer. A lot of young writers in the Caribbean – or even writers with reputations – are content to settle for that kind of description. But if you go by published poets, it's a very small number.

Q: You are considered by many people, to be the "dean" of West Indian poets and playwrights. How do you feel about that?

DW: The same way. First of all, I don't think we have that kind of hierarchy going in the Caribbean, which is a good thing. Second, the fact is you realize you know nothing about the art of playwriting when you begin another play. I mean, every time you begin a new play you annihilate what you knew in the previous one; you really learn nothing from – sincerely – the last play, because the new one always has different problems. So, the acquisition of this sort of title simply because of age doesn't impress me. I feel equally ignorant about theatre – or even more so – at 51 than I did when I had the confidence of youth. I suppose you could say I have many plays published. But, for instance, my brother Roderick has written as many plays as I have, and he's my age, so he's equally entitled to being called the dean of Caribbean writers. And I have a good publisher who prints my plays and poetry. It's impossible for a young Caribbean writer to send a play to a publisher and have it published unless it has a major production here – which doesn't even guarantee the sales of the play. I mean, there is a lot of energy now in playwriting in the Caribbean and a lot of people are doing work. But I still say that unless the playwrights get tested in a bigger arena, a judgment that is made in Trinidad or Jamaica is not a significant judgment, really.

Q: You've had a significant influence on younger poets, playwrights, and, I'm sure, even novelists. In some there is an undeniable respect, bordering even on awe. Perhaps, this also gives rise to very unawestruck forms of criticism. One younger playwright said that your writing, especially your plays, such as *Dream on Monkey Mountain*, was "too sophisticated for the average Caribbean man", and he feels that if you're talking about building a theatre audience you should start at a lower level and work up – without dropping standards to please the audience. He classifies your work as "the holy theatre" as opposed to the work of someone like Freddie Kissoon, whose theatre he calls "bacchanalian theatre." That's one. The other, a young Jamaican Rastafarian playwright, feels that you are too "intellectual" for your own purposes, and for your audiences, that you stand in the way of your work. What's your response to that?

DW: First of all, I find all of those criticisms very outdated, very anaemic in feeling, dangerous to themselves – not to me or to an audience. Populism is the nastiest trap an artist can get into; it's a political trap – it's worse than a political trap – it's an aesthetic deceit to try to write for who you think the masses are. Well, of course, it is obviously a pretentious statement. I haven't got the contempt for the masses that they have. If I write something that is difficult, I'm writing as I've always done. When I wrote *Dream on Monkey Mountain*, I imagined that it would be played to an audience of people walking the streets in Castries. And at some performances they wanted to see it again, so we had to have an instant matinee. You're talking about people coming into a theatre – a town hall – and you're talking about having a truck going around town saying that there'll be another performance of this very abstruse, esoteric, symbolic kind of play – and people coming in and wanting to see it again. And you can say, okay, it's the-native-son-comes-home, but people don't go *back* to the theatre for that reason. So, whenever a writer says you have to be popular, that writer is talking from a feeling of superiority. Those people who appear to be wishing to help the masses are really in a way the enemy of the masses because what they're saying is that the public has a limited intelligence and that the imagination and perception of the public, say, in the Caribbean, is inferior to the perception of the public, say, in the period of Shakespeare, or the classical Greek period.

If one of those critics went to Sophocles and said, "We have a lot of slaves in the audience and you've got to write down to them", we wouldn't have had the Greek theatre. If you said the same thing about Shakespeare's audience, the same thing would have happened. So, I mean, this phoney socialism is a deceit, and a betrayal of a writer's imagination, and it is really an attempt on the artist's part to popularize himself, not to educate but to limit the receptivity of an audience. I think the emotional impact of a great work of art is universal, has nothing to do with education, ultimately.

I'm doing a play now that is a comedy set in a restaurant in Couva, Trinidad [*Beef, No Chicken*, premiered 1981], a country restaurant, using the language and the characters of the people there. I am trying to make out of that as high a theatre speech as possible. The confusion that arises in the mind of a writer who makes that kind of criticism is that he thinks that if he sticks to the cliché, the work is recognizable. And that has been the bane of West Indian theatre – and it dates so fast. The *audience* gets tired of it more quickly. There's no audience that doesn't want to be challenged.

Q: When you say high theatre speech, are you referring to, for instance, the panman character in *Pantomime* [premiered 1978]? I've heard the criticism that that character was you, that a panman wouldn't speak like that.

DW: Well, that's ridiculous. I mean, that is nonsense. I remember going to see a friend in a suburb of Kingston, a rich friend. I remember when the chauffeur was driving, that by the time we got past the gate and had turned the corner, the man had said three sentences of ordinary conversation that were fantastic in terms of the economy of their poetry, in terms of what they were saying. I'm not bothered, at this stage of my life, about people who talk about low characters and high characters. Because implicit in that criticism is a social contempt for the very people they say they want to entertain. In other words, when you hear somebody say, "A panman doesn't talk like that", that person is a middle-class critic, believing that there's a kind of exoticism in the speech of a pan man, and that it is a speech that has its limits. That person knows nothing about language and knows nothing about his own language. The instinct behind that kind of panman talk is a poetic instinct; the instinct of that language is metaphorical; the instinct of that language is to be as descriptive as possible, and that's the same instinct as a poem. Now, therefore, you're denying a panman or a fisherman or a chauffeur that instinct for language. That instinct is stronger in them than it is in the middle class. I mean, nobody talks consistently like Pinter, nobody talks like Beckett, nobody talks like the porter in *Macbeth*, nobody talks like Mad Tom in *King Lear*, otherwise they'd all be poets.

The theatre *is* artificial speech; what is true about it is that it comes out of an organic impulse in the language to heighten itself. I hate to hear that kind of a remark because it puts you on the defensive, and that is the banality of the Caribbean that Naipaul is always attacking. It's very tired, that kind of criticism; it's jaded, it's immature, it's infantile.

Q: I've heard it said, though, that when your play *Dream on Monkey Mountain* was presented in Dominica, the audience couldn't understand the metaphors, the similes, the symbols.

DW: First of all, if they're not understanding it, the blame has to be on one person, me. If I am writing incomprehensibly – now if that is the charge –

Q: No, this was –

DW: No, it's okay. If it's a charge about being an incoherent writer –

Q: No, this was also said about Shakespeare plays that were presented there, too.

DW: No, no, no, it's okay. To make that criticism, to say, "This is incoherent as writing", that maybe my metaphors, my language are incoherent or obscure or self-indulgent, that's different. Now if that's the criticism, let the man say that. That's all right. But if someone, some West Indian, is saying that his own people cannot comprehend metaphor, that's an insult. It is really a middle-class insult, not to me, but to the audience. And very often people confuse clarity with monosyllables.

You see, if that criticism were applied to a Spanish writer – if you told Marquez or Fuentes or Borges – you cannot write like this because someone in the mountains isn't going to understand you, or some man on the street in Argentina or Colombia isn't understanding you – that would be laughable. That's this whole phoney, middle-class, intellectual Black romance with illiteracy.

Q: Well, this person is a teacher who's found the same problem in teaching high school students poetry; he has to start from very basic concepts and work up.

DW: You see, he's wrong, he's *completely* wrong. When I went to school – and I was taught beautifully – what I was given was the best poets in the language. I wasn't given some creep from Tunapuna who was writing a poem about hibiscus. I wasn't insulted as a pupil. Therefore, a lot of the writers who have come out of my generation were never treated as people who had an inferior intelligence. That is what's happening in the Caribbean now – people are treating students as if they were inferior, just like that professor who wrote in the *Harvard Review*,[23] who says that Negroes have smaller brains – these are racist positions. They're not even infuriating any more because they're so widespread. Nor is it even frightening, because individual talent will always survive that criticism; the tougher the criticism, the stronger the talent becomes. I'm not talking about me, I'm talking about some child, some genius of a child, who has to endure sitting in a schoolroom, hearing some banality about palm trees and fishing boats and being black and beautiful, and is made to feel that unless his intelligence stays on that level, then he is some sort of show-off, that he has some sort of dislocated imagination. That is crippling, that is dangerous. It's true from the evidence of the university that the level of education all over the Caribbean has dropped. The students are the victims of people you have to call populists. They're the residue of middle-aged Black Power people, really, who have seen themselves as victims. There are a lot of people teaching who are embittered about being black in the Caribbean – they're talking from bitterness. Nobody quite knows what they want, but I know what they seem to want: to hide their education and their experience because it has been warped. They are ashamed of it; it's as if they want to say to the younger generation, "Don't let what happened to us happen to you." But you cannot have a situation – any situation – where knowledge is restricted; that's totalitarian. And I don't care if it's Black or if it's Russian or whatever. That's no different from a regime that insists on limiting the imagination. It's fascist, really.

Q: Do you see that attitude growing in the Caribbean or do you think it's dissipating?

DW: I think that the standard of knowledge in the universities and in the schools is shocking, and it's caused by nationalism.

Q: In the Caribbean – more specifically, Jamaica – there seems to be a trend toward a populist attitude to the arts or politics. Certain standards have diminished. You're talking about universities but I'm talking about the society in general.

DW: I think the confusion that has happened is a natural confusion. For instance, some of the political leaders in the Caribbean have been educated abroad – in America, England, and so on – and in addition have gone to colleges and universities in the Caribbean. Now that is an "elite class" in terms of their education, because of the privileges they've had. They come back and they see a mass of people and they do the wrong thing: they apply technique – *dialectic* if you want – to use their kind of language that they have imported – to a people who really haven't changed in their values, in their family life, or their desires. We have divided ourselves so stupidly into two polarities: you're either capitalist or you're socialist and never in between is there any kind of political philosophy *based* on the atavistic experience of childhood and the traditions of the place you've grown up in.

So, you come roaring in with reform. You say, "All right, things are going to change and everybody's going to get an opportunity," and so on. And therefore you are given to *leaning* on communist or socialist doctrines that have moved you. You come in and you want very rapidly to make everyone in the society equal. But, again, you see, some people don't join the society – they remain, very, very banally, in large houses, with expensive cars. They may wear the kind of uniform that looks proletarian or they may make *statements* about being proletarian, but, really, they are still elitists. The person who has this proletarian exterior will take his language and *coarsen* it and make sure he develops a manner of addressing the mass of people in a language that he *thinks* they want to hear. That's the first betrayal right there, because when he goes back and sits and relaxes and *reads* – whether he reads Isaiah Berlin or he reads Bernard Shaw – he becomes a private person again in his living room. Whether you have a white colonial or a black colonial, you still have the busha [overseer] and the man in the fields. Now this man who goes out and *plays* the man in the fields is still the busha. So, the more he says, "We're going to have an equal society, we're going to have a society in which everybody has an opportunity", the more he contradicts himself by making sure that his speech is ungrammatical, that his conduct, his manner, his bearing, looks as ordinary as anyone else's, although he knows damn well that, in the mind of every person there, the wish is still for his son or daughter to become a doctor or a lawyer. In the usual pattern of people who have been through all the different conditions of degradation – whether it's slavery, colonialism, the chaos of independence – we'll still take imported patterns to apply. Now this seems to anyone outside the Caribbean, so predictable, so common, that I don't know why it continues to amaze us, why we are fooled by it.

If you take the high school in St Lucia, for instance, which used to be elitist, and says it's not going to be that any more, that education is going to be available to every child, that's fine. If you can intensify the education, bring it to a higher level, that's okay. But you see, with nationalism comes all those dangers of self-denial that are really limits imposed on people. You can see it in Bishop[24], you can see it in a way in Odlum[25], you can see it in Manley[26] – you can see it in every *one* of the two kinds of language being spoken, and that is a deceit. The newspapers remain eloquent. Caribbean journalism is excellent – most of it – because nobody writes a *Gleaner* [Jamaica] editorial or *Gleaner* column in the language of the politician. The last bastion, of eloquence and clarity remains the press, and, of course, some of the media. But even in the media, if you interview a politician or you hear a politician being interviewed, that man makes sure that his tone, his inflection is such that he appeals to the gut level rather than to the intelligence of the people; and that is the whole morass that we're into. And if you stretch that to the writer, who gets deceived into thinking that he has to do the same thing as the politician is doing, then you have no use for such a writer. Because that writer would, tomorrow morning, if a tyrant took over, change his tie to suit the tyranny. He's a sucker, really.

Q: At this point in your life, how do you feel as an artist travelling between the Caribbean and places like the United States, Britain – do you feel torn or do you feel reconciled to having to do this to make a living?

DW: Well, what tears me up is absence from my family – I mean, absence from my daughters – my son is here now – that tears me up a lot. You see, the parent may miss his children more than the children miss him, and they may understand whatever sacrifices are made much more easily than the parent thinks. You're attached to your children and your country, your parents and your country. But the reality is that by being here I can do more for them. As far as Trinidad is concerned, I miss it, but at the same time I have a quarrel with, a hatred for the corruption of standards, the decline, the rapid decline, of honesty. There is a rip-off mentality, a boomtown mind. Every time I go back it takes me less than a day to get into a rage about some taxi driver, some guy in a shop, somebody trying to rip me off for three times what I should pay. Now that's the kind of hatred that I don't associate with the people, but with certain aspects of the economy. I don't really feel, ultimately, that a country can be so corrupted in its soul purely because of economics. I think an upheaval, a revolution, a cleansing is inevitable. So this situation comes to the point where it explodes, and then values are reassessed. If you could look at it historically, you could say, "Well, if any upheaval starts to happen in Trinidad because of this ripping-off of people, then they damn well deserve it and something good will come out of it."

In terms of the arts, I feel rewarded more when a play of mine is done in Trinidad than in New York, for all kinds of reasons – not only because of the locale, the accent, but also because of the quality of the acting. I'm not saying that there are better actors in Trinidad than in New York but that the whole banality of economics in the theatre in New York compared to the really alive creativity that can happen in a good production in Trinidad, with good actors, is more rewarding for me. And things are becoming much more professional in Trinidad in terms of money. So, I don't really feel torn; I think the balance, as a matter of fact, has become greater as I've gotten older. I've been lucky – I've had my plays done both in Trinidad and the States. The big thing for a writer is to be able to make a living from his work.

Q: Do you feel lonely as a writer? Because sometimes you sound disenchanted.

DW: You mean as a Caribbean writer in the States?

Q: As a writer.

DW: No, it's a condition, not a loneliness.

Q: I don't mean lonely in the sense of being alone when you write but –

DW: – not being among colleagues, other people?

Q: Yes.

DW: No, because, you see, I've always had the theatre and that's a great community, the theatre. You live with a play, with actors, a new family every time, so it's very rewarding. In terms of the poetry, well, that's an occupation that nobody can help you with. What I am still – after all these years – infuriated about is neglect. That, and also a kind of dependence, that says: The government do everything. But, the thing that irritates me most as a teacher is to come across any kind of smugness in an artist – either a mature artist who has a reputation, or a young artist who feels ten times better than he should feel. This is a patriotic anger; I don't mind if some idiot in New York or London feels he's the greatest thing that ever hit town, but when I see a young West Indian or a West Indian with a reputation *believing* smugly in his talent, then I get a patriotic anger that is very severe. The same with painting. When I go back to Trinidad and see terrible painting, I don't laugh at it, I get mad. I have the same fury about my own work when it's bad. I just have a creative hostility against people who I think can do better but don't practice. We don't practice the arts in the Caribbean, we do them: a man will paint and he'll frame his picture tomorrow and try to sell it. The phase between learning and performing is missing. That's also true of a lot of actors. When they do a play, and they're a knockout, you hear people say, "Well, boy, I saw that play on Broadway and I saw that play in London, I'm telling you, you were as good as… that kind of crap. That whole tiring discipline, that apprenticeship that is agony, we're skipping. We're skipping from learning to stardom, and that you really have to keep attacking.

And it's true of the practice of poetry, too, because half these poets who publish poems, their own little booklets and so on, have jumped. They're Trinidad poets or Jamaican poets or West Indian poets, and they have this terrible advantage of being black. Because they're black they have the attitude that they can put out what they want, and just skip all the craftsmanship that poetry requires. And that is part of this quasi-independent spirit.

Q: What voice do you prefer to be heard in, that of the poet or the playwright?

DW: Well, the poems are not really mine when they're finished. I mean, they're there but I don't really own them any more – honestly; what is yours is the play. Because if you make anything that comes alive it's a different sort of thing. And it's consoling and interesting and challenging to have all these various people involved in your work. The whole effort is shared by the twenty, thirty people, and that is, in a way, more rewarding emotionally – whereas a poem is not emotionally rewarding because you can never feel anything about what you've written. You may feel some kind of pride, but you can't enjoy your own poems, whereas you can enjoy the creation of a play. With a poem you're by yourself and then after it's gone it's not yours any more. There's no real satisfaction in a poem for me.

Q: That seems strange for a writer who's considered primarily a poet.

DW: Well, no. It would be a very vain man who'd enjoy his own poetry. But you can enjoy your own play because, really, it's not only you doing it. An actor does an interpretation and shares in the delight of what you make – it's terrific.

Q: Would you say that the poet has less value in the twentieth century than he might have had at an earlier time?

DW: No, no. I think the hit list of poets shows that society recognizes that an idea is worse than a weapon. The more totalitarianism increases, the more ideas are repressed. So, on the contrary, I think that the responsibility of poetry has increased in the twentieth century. The conscience of poets has intensified and therefore we can do more – all totalitarian regimes know that, and we have God knows how many fascist regimes, how many empires of fascism now.

Q: Do you find your writing easier or more difficult as you grow older? Do you find your ideas to be simpler or more grand in scale?

DW: To try to answer that as honestly as I can – I would hope that I would not write if I thought that the poetry was becoming predictable or mechanical. In other words, if people began to say, "Oh, yeah, well, that's Walcott," and so on, or I began to think, myself, that whatever talent I had was becoming – regardless of my increasing reputation – predictable, I would stop writing, as hard as it would be, and I'm quite serious about that. A piece of engineering that is continually exciting is the theatre; that's where you have to keep in condition much more so, in a sense, because there's already enough poetry in the world. In every century what is added to the volume of world-poetry is a very small number of poems, ultimately. And you can't expect that any one poem of yours – well, not that you can't hope – that any one thing you write will last in the memory of mankind. Whereas a play has, in a sense, a built-in ephemeralness and you work within that, so you're working within a medium that is subject to tastes, subject to vacillations in an audience and so on, and that creates more energy – not ambition – but just more physical energy than poetry. So if I didn't write poems or never wrote another poem, I don't think I'd be that distressed. I think if I found myself writing plays that didn't get better with every new one, I would be very, very unhappy.

Q: So your first love is drama?

DW: Well, the love that you have for poetry has nothing to do with you. I suppose if I didn't write poetry I would still love it, so it's a privilege to have tried to write it. The theatre, as I've said, is such a shared thing that it's very beautiful when it happens. Poetry cannot be shared, it's unshareable. Even if you read a poem to someone or you read it in public, you're really just reading aloud to yourself and the audience is just eavesdropping on your monologue. You can't read to anyone, you can't read a poem to anyone, really, though it's very pleasant to be in an auditorium letting people hear you, whereas being in the theatre brings with it immense and complicated and maddening problems. Until the play is achieved in the production, you don't know that you love it. It's only after that you say, "Well, yes, I love the experience of going through that." But in the course of doing it, you don't; you hate it.

Q: I've heard one writer say that he writes not to entertain but to heal.

DW: Who said that? That's very pretentious. (*Laughs*) I don't think even Jesus said that.

Q: He feels that the world needs healing.

DW: Well, a writer can't heal the world.

Q: He thinks that there are too many entertainers out there and that the world is sick and needs to be healed.

DW: Well, if that's a playwright, then, I'm not going.

Q: He's a poet.

DW: Oh, well. (*Chuckles*) I don't know how a poem can heal. A poem can do great things, it can change a man subtly. You can look at the world as a poet and be in very profound anguish about it or you can have a kind of sublime resignation about it. But in terms of it's doing something miraculous for the condition of man, that's religion. The confusion between poetry and religion is an old one; I mean, you can call Jesus a poet, if you see what I'm saying. To set out to heal in a poem, I think, is a little pretentious.

Q: Have any younger writers had any influence on you?

DW: Influence? Younger writers? My God! No, I don't think so. You see, you have to allow a man of fifty a certain irascibility and I hope a young writer will have some irascibility when he is my age. If there were a young writer who was someone of startling genius, I would not in any way feel astonished that such a thing happened in the Caribbean, because I expect it to happen. I think that we are just at the beginning of Caribbean writing and that there's going to be a succession of explosions of some genius in certain areas – in *all* the areas, painting and so forth. It's inevitable, it will happen. Talking from my irascibility, I can't see any, *now*. I'm annoyed that I don't see any in poetry – maybe there's somebody who would say, "Well, if you saw it you wouldn't recognize it." Okay. But I would recognize it in playwriting. Let's say I can't recognize it in poetry – although I *doubt* that – or in painting. And this irascibility, this refusal, this stubbornness, comes from the intense apprenticeship period that every artist of any self-respect *knows* he must go through. I see a lot of facility, I see a lot of glibness, I see a lot of posturing, and a lot of naming of oneself as X or Y. And it angers me because if I had to show the work of some of these people to some of the people I know in this city, it would be dismissed as regional, provincial, dated. I don't think, necessarily, that we're in a downward period and that my generation was the peak of writing. I don't think, for instance, that Naipaul's prose style is the end of Caribbean literature and that *nothing* like that will happen *again* in terms of that kind of prose. But to say that I see it, say, in someone in his thirties, no, I don't. I don't see a Marquez. I teach a lot in universities in the United States, and it is maddening to know that *most* of the students painting or writing poetry, and so on, were they in the Caribbean, would have immense reputations. Some of that stuff I see on the pavement of New York I see hung in galleries in the Caribbean, and I find it very hard to take that at fifty, you know, I find that hard to take. I've always resisted this idea of having fame and that's why I like the Caribbean, because I'm nobody there, really; they know my name and they know my work, but when I'm there it's me. I have no big fame. I mean, crowds don't part when I walk down Frederick Street; no cops have to go ahead of me or stuff like that. I don't have to wear dark glasses – you don't have to chase me for an autograph.

Q: It seems that a lot of writers, in particular Naipaul, write from a place of cynicism. A younger writer told me that he's become more cynical and he thinks that's healthy. Do you write from a place of cynicism, feel yourself to be cynical?

DW: Cynical? No. I am angry, I'm not cynical. I cherish my anger; I think it's a holy thing. But I'm not in despair and I don't have contempt for the place I come from. I don't have contempt for people; I have contempt for manipulators, but they don't affect my love of my people. You see, cynicism is a substitute for the TB of the nineteenth century; it's a disease, too. In the old days poets got TB and died young. It can be a posture, an affectation. Despair is very romantic. It's very healthy to be satirical, even nasty about your own society. If you can make your society look ridiculous in its pretensions, that's healthy. But the source of that is not cynicism. I mean, you can't call Moliere a cynical writer.

Q: What do you think are the reasons for Naipaul's apparent cynicism? And what do you think about his position on the Third World and the Caribbean?

DW: Inevitably any interview leads to Naipaul – justifiably, because of his reputation. But I have dried up about Naipaul; I am just very tired of Naipaul.

Q: *I've* never heard you say anything about Naipaul; I've heard you make remarks like "very Naipaulian" or "that's a Naipaulian stand". But I don't know what your position –

DW: Oh, I see. I just think it's a tragedy that his books are infected by a kind of – I don't know what you can call it – they're racist, really. He's become a racist and that's a tragedy for a great imagination.

Q: Once, in an interview with Sharon Ciccarelli, you said:

> There is no one among my contemporaries whom I wish to apprentice myself to. If I were aware of some epic, some ancestral masterpiece, then I would perhaps regard that as masterwork. But the fact remains, the masterpieces of the language in which I work are from a white literary history. That must not prevent me from mastering the language. It is not a matter if subservience, it's a matter of dominating. One becomes a master, one doesn't become a slave.[27]

I wonder if you could elucidate that statement. I think there are many things that can be interpreted from that.

DW: Well, I hope not; I found it pretty eloquent. I think it's the same thing we've been talking about all afternoon: what's cherishable in this world in terms of art is very, very small. What is true, unquestionable, about genius – whether it's a Dante or a Shakespeare or whoever – is that the body of that work is small. The major activity of man is destroying his fellow man and what is preserved can be put into – metaphorically – one room in a very large house. At a certain age you make selections about what you should and should not bother to read; and half of what is called literature is rubbish, really, or is egotistical, egocentric, or tribal. And those things that are unquestionably universal are very, very few. If a man devotes himself to those things within his own language, it will take him his own lifetime to do it.

Even if I did say that there are not many such universal works, your life isn't long enough to be able to take in all of these things; but you should try to take them in.

The reality is that there's *no* memory in our race and you cannot force a man to remember what he doesn't know. We do not know the Swahili epics, we do not know the Nigerian cosmology or mythology – that is gone, we don't have it. This effort of romanticizing a past that has never been remembered is futile. Someone might say, "You're trying to deny your African heritage." You know, the reality of it is we have no such memory of an African heritage and it's artificial to impose it on people who are already African.

The areas that are important to a civilization today, in terms of achievement or survival, are increasingly technological. Now, we may not have that in the Caribbean but it would be equally absurd for us to dismiss the idea of technological development at the cost of some nostalgia about being a pastoral people who were taken away five, four, three hundred years ago from a past that may not have been as pastoral as we would like to think. All of that, I think creates confusion, but I believe that we are a very gifted people, who have been through a lot and are resolving what we are; I really believe that. I find increasing confidence in West Indians in terms of *knowing* who they are, despite economic deprivation, despite political corruption.

End Notes

1. Amiri Baraka: see interview with Lennox Brown, note 4.
2. Ed Bullins: see interview with Mustapha Matura, note 2.
3. Lonne Elder (1927-1996) was an African American playwright and filmscript writer, whose work includes the play *Ceremonies in Dark Old Men* (1969) and the script for the film *Sounder* (1972) based on William H. Armstrong's novel of that name.
4. Richard Wesley (1945-) is an African American playwright and filmscript writer whose plays include *The Black Terror* (1971) *The Mighty Gents* (1978) *The Talented Tenth* (1989).
5. Steve Carter: see interview with Dennis Scott, note 2.
6. Garland Thompson is an African American playwright whose plays include: *Incantations or the Incarnation of Reverend Goode Black Dresse; Papa Bee on the D Train* (1972); and *Sisyphus and the Blue-Eyed Cyclops.*
7. At the time of the interview, Derek Walcott may probably only have been familiar with Martin Carter's work up to *Poems of Resistance*

(1954); *Poems of Succession*, exploring a more oblique voice was published in the year of the interview, 1977.

8. At the time of the interview Kamau Brathwaite had published *The Arrivants* (1973) trilogy; *Other Exiles* (1975); *Black + Blues* (1976). *Mother Poem* (1977) was published in the year of the interview.
9. At the time of the interview Mervyn Morris had published only his first collection, *The Pond* (London: New Beacon, 1973).
10. Maurice Mason was a nationalist politician in the St Lucian National Labour Movement and co-founder of the St Lucian Arts Guild.
11. Stanley French (1937-2010) was a significant St Lucian playwright whose work included *The Rape of Fair Helen* (1962); *The Interview*; *Ballad of a Man and Dog* (1970?); *The Light and the Dark* (c. 1971); *No Rain No Play* (1972); *Under a Sky of Incense* (1977). See <http://caribbeanbookblog. wordpress.com/2010/11/11/st-lucian-playwright-stanley-french-is-dead/>
12. Dagmar (and Hugh) Butt was a RADA trained English theatre director who worked with the Whitehall Players in Trinidad. She directed Errol Hill in the lead part in J.B. Priestley's *An Inspector Calls* in 1951.
13. James Lee Wah: see interview with Errol Hill, note 10.
14. Ralph Maraj is a prolific Trinidadian playwright, actor and director, and more recently a politician and, since his party's defeat, a newspaper columnist. His plays include *The Missing File*; *The Broken Bridge* (1985); *Cynthia Sweetness* (1981); *Cynthia's Marriage* (1985); *Flowers of the Nation* (1987); *The Hardest Hard* (1983); *The Heart of Laura* (1981); *I Want to Stay with You* (1982); *In the Office* (1983); *The Last Competition* (1973); *Lovers and Warriors* (1983); *Oh Prime Minister!* (1990); *Poison* (1975); *Retreat-Return* (1978); *The Saint* (1984); *Sea Mystery* (1985); *There Comes a Freedom* (1981); *The Undefeated* (1983); *Under The Sapodilla Tree* (1980); *Wake it Up*, musical (1979); *Easy in the Ashes* (1985); *The Saint* (1984). Ralph Maraj acted in the Trinidadian feature film *Bim* (1975).
15. On the Theatre Guild of Guyana see Frank Thomasson, *A History of Theatre in Guyana*, 1800-2000 (London: Hansib, 2010).
16. On the Jamaican pantomime, see interview with Carmen Tipling, note 3.
17. Pocomania or more properly pukumina is an African Jamaican religion dating from the early nineteenth century, part of the African revival, despised by the respectable and rooted in the rural and urban poor, involving drumming and possession. An early treatment in drama was Una Marson's play of that name, performed in 1938.
18. Jab-Jab, literally "Diable Diable", from French Creole are the devils who carry whips at Carnival. See Errol Hill, *The Trinidad Carnival: A Mandate for a National Theatre* (University of Texas Press, 1972), pp. 87-90.

19. John Canoe or Jonkunnu were a group of masqueraders in Jamaica that come around Christmastime. See Sylvia Wynter, "*Jonkonnu* in Jamaica: Towards the Interpretation of Folk Dance as a Cultural Process," *Jamaica Journal*, 4/2 (1970).
20. Shango was the popular name by which the Orisha chapelles in Trinidad tended to be known. Shango was only one of the pantheon of Yoruba derived gods worshipped in the chapelles. Divine possession could be by any of the gods, male or female.
21. The Best Village project was the brainchild of Eric William's PNM in the 1960s and '70s. At it's best it could be seen as a nation-building exercise in village democracy and the encouragement of grass-roots culture; more realistically it was locked into party patronage, excluding Indian Trinidadians, and ensuring African Trinidadian votes and a backwards looking folksiness. See Micheline Critchlow et al, *Globalization and the Post-Creole Imagination: Notes on Fleeing the Plantation* (Duke University Press, 2009).
22. Sir Laurence Olivier (1907-1989) was the most famous English Shakespearean actor of his day.
23. The reference is to Professor Arthur Jensen, "How Much Can We Boost IQ and Scholastic Achievement?", an attack on head-start programs designed to improve the educational standards of African American children on the grounds that the reasons for lower IQ scores were mainly genetic.
24. Maurice Bishop (1944-1983) was the prime minister of revolutionary Grenada after the overthrow of the Eric Gairy government. He was murdered by the faction of the New Jewel Movement led by Bernard Coard and others. Criticism of Bishop focused on his tendency to pursue a popularism that echoed the pattern of the "hero and the crowd".
25. George Odlum (1934-2003) was a radical St Lucian politician whose support for Cuba, for the New Jewel Movement in Grenada and his anti-imperialism brought him into conflict with the USA who may well have pressured for his sacking as a deputy prime minister in 1981.
26. Michael Manley (1924-1997) was the one-time socialist prime minister of Jamaica (1972-1980) whose government was destabilised by CIA support for the conservative opposition, who returned to power in 1989, his wings much clipped by the IMF's neo-liberal structural adjustment programmes.
27. Sharon Ciccarelli's interview in *Chant of Saints*, an anthology edited by Michael Harper and Robert B. Stepto, University of Illinois Press was reprinted in *Conversations with Derek Walcott*, Ed William Baer (Jackson: University Press of Mississippi, 1996).

RODERICK ALDEN WALCOTT
(1930-2000)

Roderick Walcott was the twin brother of Derek, born to Warwick and Alix Walcott in Castries, St Lucia. His father was an artist who died when Walcott was very young. His mother who was a teacher, born in St Maarten, was a well-read woman who taught her children the love of poetry.

He was educated at St Mary's College, Castries. Even while at college, Walcott crossed class and colour boundaries with his involvement in steelband. He led the Turks steel band, which is acknowledged as one of the pioneers of St Lucian carnival.

From 1951 to 1967, Walcott headed the St Lucia Arts Guild; the group presented the best of international and regional drama to local audiences. For the first five years he was involved in direction; from 1956 onwards he began writing plays for the group.

Popularly known as "Roddy", Walcott was highly respected throughout the English-speaking Caribbean as a playwright, screenwriter, painter, theatre director, costume and set designer, song lyricist and literary editor.

In 1968, Walcott and his family moved to Canada, where he studied theatre arts at York University in Toronto from 1969-1973. He returned to St Lucia in the late '70s to become the island's first Director of Culture from 1977-1980.

He represented St Lucia at international cultural conferences and headed delegations to CARIFESTA in 1972 (Guyana) and 1979 (Cuba). He returned to Montreal, Canada in 1980, but visited St Lucia periodically to produce his plays.

His now-famous musical, *The Banjo Man,* originally banned at the behest of the Vicar-General of the Catholic church in St Lucia in 1958, was staged by St Lucia at CARIFESTA in 1972 to huge acclaim. The play was part of a trilogy that included *Chanson Marianne* (1974) and *Romiel et Violette* (1979). These plays featured the local flower festivals of La Rose and La Marguerite. His collaboration for many years with Charles Cadet produced many folk songs that have now become St Lucian standards.

A listing of his work includes seventeen dramas, eight musicals and two screenplays. These include: *The Harrowing of Benjy* (1958); *Shrove Tuesday March* (1956); *The Banjo Man* (1958); *A Flight of Sparrows* (1958); *The Education of Alphie* (1960); *The Expatriates* (1962); *Field of Honour* (nd); *The Trouble with Albino Joe* (1966); *Malfinis!* (1967); *Cul de Sac* (nd). Other plays include *Chanson Mariane; The Devil at Christmas; Cassian and Capricorn or The Creole Drummer Boy; Columbus and Guarionex; Conte Mabouya or The Guitarman's song; I'll remember Clifford; The Devil in Love; The legend of Tom Fool* (a musical comedy); *Poucette or The Devil with Love; Sugar Ray* (a screenplay);

Sweet Like Sugar – a musical; *The Prowess of Ti-Jean* (based on the novel by Zane Grey); *Voyage of the Heart or Let them Call it Jazz : a play*; *The Wonderful World of Brother Rabbit*. See <www.mowlac.org/.../1-St%20Lucia-%20Roderick%20Walcott%20En...> for the Roderick Walcott documentary heritage at the UWI Open Campus library in St Lucia.

His published plays include *The Harrowing of Benjy*; *Malfinis!*; *Shrove Tuesday March*; *A Flight of Sparrows*; *The Trouble with Albino Joe*; and *The Banjo Man*, all published in the UWI Extra Mural series, Trinidad. His trilogy of plays, *The Benjy Trilogy* (Kingston: Ian Randle Publishers, 2000) was launched at the Department of Culture.

He, like his twin brother, Derek, was a painter; a one-man exhibition of his work was presented in 1978 in St Lucia.

In 1976, he was awarded the Order of the British Empire (OBE) for outstanding theatrical work in St Lucia. In 2000, he was awarded the Saint Lucia Medal of Honour (Gold) "for eminent and outstanding contribution to the Literary and Performing Arts". In the same year, he given the Joseph Devaux Lifetime Achievement Award at the annual M&C Fine Arts Awards.

Roderick Walcott's play, *The Harrowing of Benjy,* a one-act comedy, reportedly has the distinction of being the most staged play in the English-speaking Caribbean. He is regarded as one of the founders of modern Caribbean theatre.

RODERICK WALCOTT

Canada, Thursday, 28 October, 1982

Q: As one who contributed to the beginnings of the contemporary theatre movement in the English-speaking Caribbean, what do you think of the present state of theatre there?

RODERICK WALCOTT: The theatre there has gone through what we can call a social and political change. In other words, what happened, say, from the period of the '50s when I began – I continued a theatrical company after my brother formed it in 1950 – is that we passed through a historical phase in Caribbean and St Lucian history where theatre was part of a middle-class society, which had been brought up on a European, literature-oriented kind of theatre. It was done through things like speech nights in schools and so on. In most of the Caribbean the drama that we went through was of that kind. What has happened between then and now – we've had the whole political scene of independence, but before that there was the independence movement, which in the '50s began to be reflected in theatre, especially inspired by the work of Errol Hill, who, ironically, had a British Council Scholarship, and came down quite versed in Shakespeare and so on, but felt that we needed our own theatre. And from that period on, when Hill influenced Derek and myself, we went through the business of finding our own folkways and finding our own culture and then writing about it.

Since then the changes in the Caribbean have been social and political. From the time of independence we have had the idea of what you'd call a kind of *new popular culture,* of musics, mostly influenced from Jamaica, with a different kind of religion, and this has made the area a little more homogenous, which might or might not be what you'd call "good" for the writer who wants to identify with his island or with his community, and as a Caribbean writer. In other words, he would have his own St Lucian, Grenadian identity, but his work would still be Caribbean, from the shared experience, the history and whatever. So, you have that change from what you'd call an "out-of-the-colonial" kind of experience into a new kind of sociology and politics… And here you have the argument with the younger people, etc., about whether politics should be part of the artist's work or not.

Q: What did you mean by a new kind of religion. Has theatre been affected by changes there?

RW: Yes. In other words – whether it's Christian or not – as part of the changes in culture we've been getting into in the Caribbean area, it is felt that rather than the religion we've been accustomed to, whether you want to call it Roman Catholic, middle class or Protestant, the whole idea is that theatre should spring from the roots of the culture rather than from the Sunday morning kind of Presbyterian or Catholic meeting, which comes from outside of our cultural ambience. That is more or less the kind of feeling you have now and it's felt a lot by the younger type of religious leaders, that there should be a stronger Caribbean cultural element in how we interpret our religious beliefs – as Christians even.

Q: Do you mean like Rastafari?

RW: Well, the Rastafarian influence has been strong because of that kind of philosophy. Whether people feel the whole Ethiopian-African-Abyssinian source of it in the '30s etc., etc., was right or wrong, people feel that philosophically there's some kind of truth in the idea that a man should worship according to his cultural bent. If an artist goes into his cultural beliefs and then he goes further into his religious beliefs, he may realize that, hey, something is missing in the form of worship for a Caribbean person, rather than as a person whose religion has been imposed on him, with a European style and content and manner of worshipping. For instance, there's a distinct difference in Christianity between how the Blacks worship in the States from how the Whites worship, and that hasn't really happened in the Caribbean, except for sects in small areas. It's a kind of a turning of the wheel in the sense that we're going back to the old medieval kind of thing about using drama as a didactic form of teaching religion in the churches as a form both of art and worship – which is a good possibility for the writers and for the priests.

Q: What is your feeling about the quality of writing in drama, fiction and poetry that is coming out of the Caribbean today?

RW: That is a difficult question because my reading is, in a sense, limited because of my workload, and because I haven't got my hands on too much of the work because of a lack of publishing opportunities for these people... so that you can't make comparisons. Whereas in the '60s Errol Hill started the Caribbean Plays series[1] and you could see what others were writing, unfortunately it has been discontinued, so you can't get a good comparison with the material being written today. I don't want to be hard but I find the material a little less exciting than the '50s, in the sense that – when you take a cross section of different kinds of plays – it seems everybody might be thinking in the same way now, because of that whole influence of the political surge, but in those days, to me, there was more of a variety. You had a play like *The Creatures*, [Cicely Waite-Smith,[2] 1966] which was a kind of a light fantasy, you had Errol Hill doing the steelband type of indigenous plays like *Man Better Man*, [1957] you had Samuel Hillary[3] writing *Chippy*, [1961] and, of course, in St Lucia, you had that kind of stylized Creole kind of folk drama. I saw more of a variety, and the *joie de vivre* – which made it so Caribbean – is kind of lost.

What I'm getting a little afraid of – this whole business around sociological issues – how long do these things really last? But then, right now there's a dearth of what you'd call "giant" playwrights in the world, since Beckett and a few others did some bright stuff. But how many truly great playwrights are there around now? Not very many. I mean, a few in Europe, perhaps, and, of course, Tennessee Williams, but I think he's on the decline. The States has a few promising young guys and so on; England has a lot of competent guys, but I'm talking about great playwrights, you know, to assess the philosophy of the times or the feeling of the times on that kind of cosmic scale.

On the Caribbean level, now, we're talking about social issues, politics, socialism, the whole Rastafarian wave, and so on. If you balance in a lot of the music – which is really the cultural lifeblood of the people – that's where you see a lot of things happening, a lot of exciting things. The Caribbean has always been exciting for music, because its cross-cultural – it's probably the richest area in the world for diversified music. In the theatre, what happens is that a lot of material is coming out of experiences in England or in the United States, just like the revolutionary period of the black writers in New York, and you get a whole batch of that kind of work – good, competent and so on, but really, after a few of these, where are they going? Do you see what I'm getting at, what I am saying? This is how I view my theatre – very seriously, in terms of what you'd call endurance or longevity. A lot of Ibsen is not any use now, really, I mean, other than as a sociological curiosity. Strindberg will last because Strindberg is talking about man and woman, the essence of sex and that basic kind of conflict that will always ring a bell. If you deal with aspects of man and God, man and man, man and woman, man and philosophy – which are basic for all plays – if you want to start writing on that kind of level, you read good stuff… Now, some might say that's not important, ask you why you have to struggle so hard to show your work as a Caribbean writer at a high level, like the Latin Americans have done with the quality of their novels. If somebody asks that, I'd say, Well, first of all, every human being wants to be individual, he wants to be heard and have his own voice. But he also wants to identify with something, a society of some kind… but he shouldn't get into a situation where the Englishman can do it better than he… but once he's on a footing with his own folk material and he knows about it, he studies it, he gets down into it and knows the basic things about what life is about, he's bound to succeed *in a way*. He might be not a good *writer* – O'Neill wasn't really a good writer but he had his finger on the pulse of life – that's very important. So we can get a writer who really can't write poetically or his language is not so good, but if he's thinking deeply, the language is going to come out well in some kind of way.

Now, the other way – in which I have been influenced, which I think is a good way – is the way Derek started as a poet. Derek and his gifts as far as language was concerned made me and our theatre. I always feel that poetic language is very important in the theatre. In other words, you go into the theatre and the language you hear must *ring*. It must be something you do not hear on the street; it must have a quality about it – that's why you work so hard on the language, plus the fact that it must have a rhythm. These two things are extremely important in order to have some kind of individual identity as a playwright. And your rhythm differs depending on whether you're in the States, in Latin America, or in the Caribbean. If you really study writing, or you really study the music and you really want to have an individual rhythm – which is *ingrained*, incidentally – you have to dig deep to find it, to bring it out. And the work – you must orchestrate, it must have an overall rhythm and it must *sound*, because it's not a novel, it's a play, so it must ring. When the people come out of the theatre they must still hear an echo of what was happening in there, and that goes with the voices and the images. That's why *Dream on Monkey Mountain* was so good, because apart from the rhythm of the verse, it has an echoing quality in what is being said.

My problem – and I've tried to curtail it by using a different method of writing – is that I *overstate* – which is a very common problem with West Indians talking – their overstating of things and so on and so on. So, a lot of drafts and a lot of rewriting – the best writing is rewriting, and I've met a lot of guys, especially in St Lucia, whose work will not get better because they refuse to *rewrite*.

Q: Your brother feels that many of the present group of young writers in the Caribbean lack a sense of discipline, with a tendency towards laziness.

RW: Yes, a very good point.

Q: Errol Hill feels that the present wave of writers also lack a true foundation in dramaturgy.

RW: You see, we're going through a period now – like you're going to get a lot of bad reggae composers in Jamaica because that's the wave and the guys are on the wave. The same thing is happening in writing. If you come from a small island, imagine the advantage in it – it's also a disadvantage – for the one writer, say, in Carriacou [an island dependency of Grenada with a population of around 5,000], if he's a playwright, he has an identity as *the* Carriacou playwright. Now, that can be bad for the guy, because he feels: "OK, I'm the best writer in Carriacou", and probably there's a little adulation around him, so he's not disciplined enough in his work. Secondly, there's a strong tendency, whether it is in sport or whatever, as long as they have a gift, they feel that's it. They don't sit down and work on it and really improve on their talents.

Q: Big fish in a small pond mentality.

RW: That's right. Now, what happens, too, is you go to the writers' conferences – like I went to one in the Caribbean and I got my blows or a little tension from this guy. I'll give you a little example. There was this young guy who's in film – I don't have to mention names – but he was doing this improv, and then he was doing a series of things for Trinidad television. He said, "Man, this thing came so easy… these actors were improvising and then you go back and write down the script and then you take out that… man, no problem at all!" So I told him, "But didn't you have to at least edit it and go through it and revise it?" He started to get angry, because I was getting down to the core of the thing. He was trying to tell me: "Oh, you just put the thing on tape and just push it through and the thing was a marvellous success." But I was trying to prove to him the whole importance of *editing*, which a writer has to do for himself and then it has to go through the whole editing process. Because, tell me what you want, I don't care *what* kind of improvisation you do, nobody is that brilliant that everybody is saying one brilliant line after another, or making up some lines which aren't clichéd. So it was all a farce to me. Then he started talking about, "Oh, all you guys talking about art; what is art?" He started to knock art. Now, the whole question about art – OK, arty-farty, whatever you call it – we understand that – but when you get down to art it's *working* – whether you're a screenwriter, whether you're a playwright – it's getting down and fixing the damned thing. And that's the laziness Derek and Errol are talking about, or the background that young writers need. They don't want any background because they've cut away their history. They expect to just start afresh, some of them – I'm not knocking them, really. Some of these guys would sit down – like some Carib would do in a ritual – and hunger and thirst – and then they see the light, and then they write down the stuff, right? But how many guys can really do that? That is what a writer like [William] Blake might do, who do that once in a lifetime, and these guys like Blake had the training anyhow because they were writing in the English tradition. But these guys smoke a grass, grow their beard and then they're a writer, they're a poet. They just sit down and they write good plays and so on – that's crap. I don't care what anybody says but you have to go through the same discipline, fixing your stuff, seeing where your weaknesses are and trying to get over it.

Now, I'm going through another phase now. I've always found plotting and writing relatively easy because of the environment I grew up in when I was young. My aunt was an extremely good folk storyteller; I met a lot of people who very good *raconteurs* including the actors in my group. My additional experience was in doctoring a lot of scripts, doing a lot of adaptations and script work before I really became a playwright – which sort of came by accident in the sense that I took over the company as a director. It was nearly six years before I started writing so I have a very good foundation in theatre, you know, in directing.

Q: When did you first start to write?

RW: I started writing in '56 and I started directing in 1951. So that I had about five years experience in staging plays before I started writing, and I only started writing because the company didn't have a writer. We had Derek, then he left…

Q: So Derek started writing before you then?

RW: Oh, yes. Derek started writing at eleven years old. He was a born writer; he used to write poems at school and so on. I remember the first experience was when they put him on a stage and they made him recite his first poem and he said: "Now what is about Christmas …" – or something – "…and we saw the masquerade/ and I gave them a lemonade …" or some kind of thing like that. But we had good encouragement, too; the headmaster was so thrilled by his poem that he put him to stand up on the stage and recite it. My mother and my father were artists, all that kind of thing – a good environment.

So, as I said, I went into playwriting. Now, usually with your first piece, especially if you felt inspired to write it, whether you have the experience or not, the first play is usually fairly easy to write, even though structurally it might not be that good. The freshness, the vivacity, the *life* you get, you put that down and it just goes. It's when you start writing the second, the third and the fourth that you realize there're problems. I didn't have *that* real trouble because I had known all that before; but my first play was relatively easy. This was *Benjy* [*The Harrowing of Benjy,* premiered 1956]. Another thing which could have spoilt me very badly was that it was a terrific success. It's probably the most produced play in the history of Caribbean theatre. But the point is, after that I went through the whole structure of my writing – my main problem being the thing about overwriting – through directing, constantly, directing great plays, meeting people like Errol Hill, reading Derek's work, and these things helped to structure my work. I started to get into what you call the "skeleton" or the "anatomy" of writing – which I only read about just a few years ago – because I said, "Look, my work really needs pulling up," because my plays were always a little too long. So I started to restrict myself, limiting my pages of writing and getting what I had to say within a limited time period, and also going back and going through the whole socio-history of each character, doing the thing in a real anatomical detail. After I'd do that hard work – which is really grinding work – you jot down your ideas for each page, and the ideas come in by and by, and then you start linking the plot through metaphor and then you're doing the stage, the setting, how you're presenting it to an audience. You're putting it within a structural frame and identifying how that operates. What, to me, was best about going to York University [Toronto] was studying design – which I used to do before, because I used to do drafting and I could paint and draw, etc. – I'm not being arrogant – but that was one of the best things I got from York – stage design. So when I write a play I design it as well… I talked of orchestration before, which means the way that the metaphors, the characterization, the colour, even the symbols, all work together. You do a good complete job *before* you write it down – which I didn't used to do before. I would do it in the second or third rewrite, but now I do it before the first writing. It usually takes about three drafts and I do it in three colours, blue or green and yellow and then white, so when it reaches the white it looks nice, it looks white and fresh, you know what I mean? (*Amused.*) I have a little quirk which is I like to use a new ribbon with each new draft so it keeps looking fresh, because you read it over like hell! Sometimes you read it over too much; you have to be distant from it and leave it for about two weeks and then come back to it. So that is really how I work.

Q: What are your thoughts on the concept of "Caribbean theatre" – that is to say, a theatre movement that addresses a unique Caribbean voice? What of such concepts as "reggae theatre", "roots theatre" and "calypso theatre" – what are your feelings about those?

RW: I think giving it those several kinds of indigenous names is kind of dangerous. I think Caribbean theatre goes through a process and I am hoping – I don't want to pontificate – that the kind of work that I do, has a sound groundwork in my culture, the area in which I live, all the folkforms that I am aware of, the behaviour of the people – whether it's their geography, their history and their problems as human beings within that kind of area. Yet I also find that you don't isolate yourself, you make yourself heard in a world community, on an international stage. People would say, "Yes, that work is Caribbean" – but the thing is, on that international stage you cannot *really* say that a dance from India is better than a dance from Africa, and this is the whole core of the thing. Take the best dance executed by the best folk-people in India – they have had thousands of years of training there, so it's almost beyond criticism – and take the African child who dances and becomes a Watutsi dancer, if he performs on a stage with a Indian dancer, we see the diversity in the world and the height that man can achieve. And you cannot say that this dance is better than that dance. I don't care how much you say that opera is better than the best kind of singing you might get in the Congo, or that the best kind of drumming you can get is *less* than a piece conducted by Stokowski. So that while I agree with identifying theatre with an area – though, incidentally, that is not so popular now in the sense that we're going through a kind of homogenising thing in which we're saying we're not Caribbean, we're people from Africa, we're identifying with somewhere else as if we are misplaced people etc., – in the same way as we can't dispense with the concept of the individuality of the human being, we can't get away from nationality. So, I think, that it is very possible to have what is called a "Caribbean theatre" – and it must be called "Caribbean". I don't like the idea of a "West Indian" theatre, because it is political and it is Anglo, though with the barriers of language, the problem is we don't know all that much of what is happening in Martinique or in Spanish theatre – which might be very close to what we are doing – but the point is the identity is there.

There is a problem, though, in wanting to be recognized. You say, "OK, I am a Caribbean playwright, and I want to be heard in Europe and Australia and the Western World." But you still have, unfortunately, a problem with being put down in those areas – *you* know the problem, whether it's colour or whatever. In things like film, on a world level, the Caribbean is not really considered as an artistic entity; it is a struggling small area in which they have some guys doing art. Now, as for recognition as a *movement*, that will only come when the artists per se are identified by literary critics over a historical period or when the activity of the theatre is recorded in some way – and, unfortunately, I think a lot keeps getting lost. That is why my pulpit now is film, that something must be done about film or else we'll be another decade behind. I've tried to tell other Caribbean artists that – not to mention names – who think I am mad, you know. But that's a way to be heard on a world level, in film.

Theatre is OK for itself, it's OK for books, for communal activity, it's OK for four-year festivals, for people seeing what you're doing, but a lot gets lost along the way. A lot gets lost. There's a lot of frustration in people not being able to be published, there's a lot of frustration in writers not getting their work staged, not being able to work with theatre companies and all those kinds of things. And there's a very serious job for the critics to keep analysing what's valuable – whether it's one book out of a hundred on a university shelf, it's still some kind of significant thing. I mean, let's be realistic, and don't imagine that Caribbean theatre is now something that is big in the world; it's really not – and not because it can't be, but because people don't want to recognize it as such yet.

Q: Your brother feels that not many writers in the Caribbean have had the quality test of going abroad to the metropolitan areas such as New York City or London, and really being tested.

RW: Even then you have the problem of the indigenous material, and how it translates from one area into another. The people you're writing for in the Caribbean, a lot of them can't read, that's a basic problem, some of them can half-read and those that can read don't care enough. But when the play makes a transition or translation from the folk material onto another level there's a problem; you still want to do it in Creole, you want the guy to speak in Creole, or speak in a kind of respectable broken English – thinking in Creole and carrying that over into English – because you're writing about that kind of peasant level a lot of the time. But then how to get that carry-over into the bigger market of the United States if you don't want to lose your identity? Tomorrow, I could turn around and write on episode for *Fame*, as any competent writer could do. But if you don't want to do that, or you do it as a part-time thing – it's like painting; you paint a picture for a guy because he likes a scenic picture of St Lucia, that's your bread money, but the real stuff you want to paint, which might not sell, you hang in your own drawing room or give to an admirer; these are two different kinds of things. It's the same kind of problem you have with writing indigenous material – once you believe in it – and going for crossover, which people like Naipaul have done fairly well, considerably well, in his case, but he has abandoned whatever kind of identity he had. He's dropped part of himself, if you want to put it that way. Writing indigenous material you get the hassle, especially if it's plays, of getting published. The printing of plays is a limited field, anyhow, a limited market. They say: "Oh, this material is too Caribbean; it won't sell on the market." That's a big problem you have. So what the guys do, you have to write like Abbensetts, taking the material into an English context. Of course, he's the urban kind of writer. The closest that you can get to that, so that the North Americans understand it, is to do the kind of Mexican film that is pastoral, sort of lyrical material; that kind of thing they understand – early Steinbeck kind of thing. But when it gets down to the real thing – the forest, the drums – some guy says, "Why are you giving me this boogoo-boogoo stuff?"

What's good about the States is the vigour, the energy and the muscle in the place, the fact that the melting pot is, in a way, encouraged, but it's limited. They really tell you, "OK, we'll encourage you, but you will have to stop there." Do you see what I'm getting at? Like they did with the Blacks and cinema. A community has to have political clout and be strong to be acknowledged – like the Cubans in Florida. But that's why the States is so rich; it will always have material because it comes from here, there... Look how they grabbed the stuff from Jamaica; they're trying to milk reggae now – and Jamaica won't get as much as it should. And that is the *biggest* fight in the whole thing, the war I have, as far as a Third World person is concerned, the way they drain us, man, of our material, of our culture and how delicate it is and how they break it up, they pull it out and they take what they can and then they just dump it – that whole kind of *waste*, you know what I mean?

Q: It's pretty much like slavery.

RW: It is, yes. You're taking out material, now; you're not taking out goods anymore, you're taking out brains; the most brilliant people who were in St Lucia and so on, are right here in Canada and England, you know. The raw material that Europe and North America took out of the Caribbean – it might be limited in depth – but a lot *was* taken out, and there's a lot deposited in libraries all over the area.

But there's another problem in the Caribbean now, that the western side of the Caribbean is being denied. There's the whole question of not being pure African but Afro-European, which a lot of people don't want to hear now. A lot of idiots are saying, "Oh, we shouldn't think about Shakespeare; Shakespeare is a bad influence," and all that crap. He's still the greatest writer in English, right? Of course, there's the counter-argument to that – it isn't really a counter-argument, but a different perspective – from Eddy Brathwaite.[4] There's the comparisons, now, in terms of a Walcott-Brathwaite thing. With a lot of the younger writers, it's more Brathwaite-Walcott, in terms of identification, because of where Brathwaite is coming from – from jazz and ethnicity and that kind of thing. He's saying: You must see that first, then you can go and read the English tradition.[5]

Q: This is the debate about whether the Caribbean is an African or a Creole society.

RW: It's creolized. That's the whole essence of it.

Q: Now, I know a lot of people who will debate that tooth and nail, because the predominant race happens to be Black or African.

RW: No, it's not the skin, it's the blood! That, to me is the difference, because there's a lot of problems between the black Caribbean man and the black African. Now I'm not being anti-African because I'm very African in terms of the way I feel. But I *am* talking about the way the African thinks about the Caribbean, the guy who's trying to identify with Africa. Because, man, there's a lot of sea between us, you know, and it is what is *left* that you have to work with. What was left was memory of your forefathers and what had been transplanted; it's a whole mixture, a whole hybrid. Now, a lot of people used to accept that there was a kind of middle-class pride in being Creole or being coloured – with the negative that they looked down on the person who was usually blacker than you, and because they were either the maid or the butler – the class aspect of it. In other words, they have not yet cut out that English stratification thing. So that whilst in Brazil, you are proud whether you are very black or even white and both very Creole – which is, of course, a good thing about Brazil. But in the Caribbean – well, not in St Lucia, for sure – there's no real white guy coming from a French Creole family who behaves as if he is essentially a St Lucian Creole, a black-thinking-white-skinned person – that's rare in St Lucia, still. There are very few.

Q: Could you explain that?

RW: Yes. Because the white French Creoles who are in St Lucia are very few in number, very powerful; they marry within the group, they either own big businesses or big estates and they never mixed in any cultural way with rest of the population. They send their children to study in England. But there wasn't such a big problem with the "coloured" Creoles, as there was between "coloured" and Black in Haiti during the revolution where the Blacks and Coloureds were at war. Haiti was French, too, like St Lucia, but there was even more of stratification there, like Jamaica, especially in the disparity between the rich and the poor. In St Lucia, it was less so, because the plantocracy tended to merge a little more; many of these guys had black mistresses and children by them, and these children enjoyed some privileges; they'd send them to college [high school], leave them land. So that you had, also, a lot of coloured people with medium-sized estates, so that things sort of levelled out. But you never had an extreme black-white or extreme rich-poor tension, you know. And this was unlike Grenada, which had a very prejudiced coloured middle class. There was a larger population of what you'd call "high coloured" people with brown hair – you know that type? – a lot of them in Grenada. When I went there I was really surprised at the disparity; that's why Gairy got in and did so much, and that's why I think there is extreme socialism in Grenada now, because of that very strong disparity between the brown middle class and the Blacks.

Q: You said that you *think* African; how did you come to terms with your own identity?

RW: Well, I didn't have too much of a problem, because what I had was two white grandfathers and two black grandmothers, third generation. I didn't know my grandparents; one was Dutch, in St Maarten, that's my mother's side and one was in St Lucia. In a sense it was a little unusual; this white Barbadian guy married a black woman and he had five "coloured" children – something like me – from which my father came. When I was younger, I went through the whole mill of feeling I was better than some others because I was of a lighter complexion and had a more privileged situation. But as soon as I started realizing that what was being told me was wrong, I didn't really have any sort of severe problem, but I had to go through the whole motion of understanding myself.

Q: How old were you then?

RW: I would say I was early teens – quite young.

Q: In some of Derek's earlier poems, it seems he was wrangling with that same question. "A Far Cry From Africa"[6] was one such, I believe.

RW: Yes, yes. There are more like that in his early Jamaica poems; there is one called "My Audacious Self"[7]; there is a lot of complexion stuff in that Jamaican period. I went through the whole social thing where people of my "type" were always saying: "Why does Roddy have those kind of friends?" I had a steel band, I was in Carnival and my best friends were people of that kind; you're talking about lower-class people, as well as boys in college who were not fair. As I was growing up I realized that the blacker people were a bit more underprivileged than I, and that people were taking offence at the fact that I had a lot of darker friends. But then I had it fairly easy, because I had the drama group. I had the opportunity to mix with people from the kind of class that my mother used to sew for, the people who owned stores or who were in an upper position in the civil service, but I found that these guys had *nothing*, really, and I was always looking for values, in terms of the steel band, the plays, the drama. I always hung around gifted people or people that I admired, people who I could work with, people that excited me or people that I enjoyed. It was the best part of my life when I ran the steel band and the theatre company between the mid '50s to mid '60s. That was a beautiful time in my life.

Q: Were you in any way affected by the Black Power Movement?

RW: No, I was very much for it, as a matter of fact, but that's a time when it didn't affect me at all; I felt *no* kind of skin difference or anything, I was very strong in it. As a matter of fact, I left St Lucia just when it was emerging. That was '68. Stokely Carmichael was just getting into the political scene, and you got a lot of knocks in the Caribbean then. I came up here (to Canada). I realized at an early stage why people like Rap Brown had to do what they did, and I got more militant when I came to Canada because I realized what Canada – I saw underneath the skin, sort of thing – was about. It never really fooled me. From an early stage I already had a built-in thing, before I even came up here, against being star-struck by North America. I never was. I came here realizing I had to stay here for a certain amount of time – as you'd say: "Get something from the white man and then go back" – which was becoming an expert in my field and then going back and doing it. The sad thing was having to come back here [Canada] because of my children's education. I really don't want to be here, but it's a period which I just have to go through because I feel the sacrifice is necessary.

Q: Do you write now from your present experiences here, in Canada, or is it still from experiences of back home?

RW: It has to be from of home. I'd never write in a North American context. I might have to do it for bread, but to become what you would call a St Lucian-Canadian and write in a St Lucian-Canadian context – I really could never do that, never write a play, for instance, about the experience of a St Lucian family in Canada and their problems – like *A Raisin in the Sun* [Lorraine Hansberry, 1959]. There's so much stuff already written from that kind of experience, I could never write a play like that.

There's also the additional experience, which you haven't asked about, but I think I should mention, of the opportunity I had, as most writers don't, of being a cultural administrator. When I became the first Director of Culture, in St Lucia, on a three year government contract, it was virgin territory. I had the task of setting up this thing, making it respectable and have some quality. What was good about it was that the country was really ready for it – it already had a background of some artistic merit in the theatre work that had been done – Derek's work with the Art's Guild and so on. So I went in as a respected person who had some sort of weight in the community. I did whatever was possible in that time. Having to go to conferences and weigh the whole situation, not only of the writer but the whole society in a global context, gave me an additional dimension as a cultural agent within that field. I saw it from inside and out. Going into a job with people looking to you for direction was quite a challenge.

I remember Rex (Nettleford)[8] saying "Why should your posts down there be called 'Directors of Culture'; it sounds so authoritarian." In a sense, I agree with him, but it's at the stage when a lot of these people need that kind of direction. And that whole question of the artist as teacher – which is not in the European or North American style – is an additional responsibility, an additional *weight* on the artist. You have two types of approach: Derek, for one, doesn't work like that; he says, "This is my work, I'm not making a bridge for me to link up with you, but this is what I see and this is how I am presenting it on the level I want to achieve, whether you understand it or not. This is my work and it must be respected on the level that it is." And a lot of it is probably not understood by a lot of the people in the area it was written for. It's not his fault; it's an uncompromising thing which is what you'd call artistic integrity.

Q: He says he can't make any excuse for his education.

RW: Well, that's a kind of Derek remark. He's at the stage where the tendency now is to write simpler, and it's even better work. *Another Life* – it's quite simple, you know, compared to the complexities of his earlier work where he wanted to show how bright he was. He was showing, in a way, what he could do; he was going through the phase of showing the white man he could write as well as him – which is, in a way, the problem with the West Indian artist – you have to prove yourself. I know a lot of guys who have it bad.

Q: Isn't it because you really have no choice but to do that in order to get onto the first rung, so to speak?

RW: Yes, yes. But he was doing it, I think, a little too much in the sense that he was writing more for outside than for himself or for his community. He doesn't necessarily have to write for his community, but from a sincere inward thing, which is what he's doing now, because he's matured. And I know his work very closely, so I can see the change. I took a long time before I read *Another Life* [1973], because I didn't have a copy of it and I was very busy; I remember his second wife asking me: "Have you read *Another Life*?" I said, "No, I haven't read it yet." She said, "*Roderick*!" She was really shocked. When I sat back and read *Another Life*, the first thing that hit me – and I am very good on first impressions when I read something – I was surprised at the simplicity and it was good, it was really good. But it was *so simple*, I said, "What's happening here? He's going through another phase," which was really true.

Q: Another life.

RW: Yes, that's right. (*Laughs.*) On that score, I am not writing to be completely didactic and saying: "This work is written for my people" – that kind of patriotic zeal, or the kind of socialistic writer who's going to boil it down for you – I do that in a sense…

Q: Do you think that attitude is condescending and insulting to the people that you're addressing?

RW: Well, it's not necessarily insulting – but you want to meet them. You want to say the same thing but you want to say it simply and effectively. Sometimes you really can't do it. I had a problem with *Cul-de-sac* [1981], in that sense. The woman in it is a very wise person – I am talking about an uneducated wise person, who had to say some very profound things but I couldn't have her say it, because the French creole in St Lucia has gone to a stage now where it's limited, because it is no longer practised by people who think heavily enough – it's on a conversational level – so if a creole person in the country says something wise, people can't understand it. I remember once, this university professor, expert in Creole, who told me that one of his greatest experiences was picking up a lady from the heights of the country in his car and giving her a lift and conversing with her in Creole, and he said it was a fantastic experience. It is an unwritten language, eh? But she was like a sophisticate, speaking an earth-language, but she was so wise and the way she spoke – the retention of the Creole sounded like a kind of French – not making French better than African – but a lot of the words have been lost, the weightier words, or what you'd call the "big words" in English, are getting depleted in Creole, which is what they still use in the countryside, especially among the very old people. I don't have the knowledge of that anymore to turn this into theatre, and the younger people, without too much Creole, will not understand it either.

Q: A similar thing exists in Jamaica, because you find that the older people in the countryside speak an early type of Jamaican patois using words that are not used today.

RW: In Jamaica, too, there's a tendency to use a kind of ancient English, which comes as a nice surprise to people here (in Canada). They tell me a word like "virago", which is a very rare English word, is a common word in Jamaica. It's a biblical thing plus a very good English grounding.

Q: You'll find that, also, in the Rastafarian way of speaking.

RW: That's right, very strong biblical thing. That is what is especially great about black people – they have a natural gift for language. Look how many languages there are in Africa, and that gift for improvisation … So the language in our writing is extremely important. Now, what can kill it – the same point that Derek and Errol have made – is the laziness of just running into cliché when you write a play – you don't want to really study the linguistics of the thing. It's not just that one character talks differently from another, but the rhythm, the kinds of words he uses, etc., that give it immediately a Caribbean identity – and that is getting lost, because the guys are not working enough.

Q: Who were some of the writers that influenced you?

RW: I have a very mixed-up influence, eh? When I was small I read a lot of the right books. And I am not saying that in a pompous way, but when I started to love writing, I had a couple [of] very good teachers who used to teach poetry. They would explain the poem; you went through the "Rhyme of the Ancient Mariner" – things that you used to find in school books – just the whole tone, the whole beauty of the words was essentially something which we have always loved. St Lucians have a way – not only St Lucians, but all Caribbean people – a tendency to spout oratory, write in a florid language, even the politicians – and there would be jokes about that. In Trinidad, there's the whole "Robber Talk"[9] kind-of-thing, using decorative fine language, as if from the Elizabethan period of English.

When I went to college, I hated it, because everything was imposed on you and you had no kind of outlet. Shakespeare was very badly taught because it was done by rote, so you never really enjoyed it. English history was dry; I nearly lost my taste for literature, especially Shakespeare, during that period in college when I had to do it for exams. What sustained me at the time was reading a lot of novels, and this is where I got nurtured on Hemingway, Steinbeck, Sinclair Lewis, Faulkner – that whole rich period of American writing in the 1930s. How I got into the *theatre*, now, was kind of an accident. I was always very light-headed and didn't know what I wanted to do, very troublesome, very funny, comical, while Derek was always serious. We are completely opposite in that way. We had the same taste and the same sense of direction – which I didn't then know; I didn't know I was that way inclined at all, because Derek was always towering. I was in the shadow. I used to counteract that psychologically by either just being funny or just not giving a damn – which really drove my mother nuts! I never got serious until after I left college, because the whole time it was just the steelband I was interested in.

My first experience with the theatre, I was playing the spider in *Little Miss Muffet*, and I was *terrified*; I was actually shivering and crying. The next experience I remember was hearing a piano at a rehearsal and the whole conviviality of the thing, someone rehearsing a song. I said, "Hey, this thing sounds great, man!" So I used to hang around. At that time Derek used to write plays for the college; one or two plays, kind of melodrama, and I started to get into the groove. I gradually got so interested that I told him, "Why not write something about the Haitian revolution, because you write poetry so well; do something on a grand scale" – and that's how he wrote *Henri Christophe* [1949].

I forgot to tell you that when we were small we used to draw a lot of comics, go to a lot of films and gradually we used to write our movies. We used to do that a lot. I didn't realize then that I was creative, I just used to do the damn thing, and I used to do a hell of a lot more than Derek, because he used to take his time if he was going to write a movie. Now, we used to have actors and everything, just like Hollywood. I remember I had a guy called Rod Ronson, who was really Humphrey Bogart, and I wrote a whole *Casablanca* [Michael Curtiz, 1942] thing called *Leipzig* with this guy called Rod Ronson. We used to do the drawings in frames and we would call friends in to see it. That was in my early college days. I didn't realize, really, that this was my field. I actually used to be a director when I was writing, and the first day I realized what I wanted to be in life was when Derek and the leading actor had a row – he, in fact, is now my brother-in-law – and that broke up the whole production of *Christophe*, and I had to go and patch up the damn thing. The first day that I sat in that theatre – it was in an elementary school – and saw these actors and tried to move them around to see what I wanted – whether it was good, bad or indifferent – I realized then that was my goal in life: to be a director. And directing is what I still really like. And after nursing people into writing for the stage, I gradually decided to do my own writing. But I used to write a lot of plots before, so it was really ingrained – and I didn't know.

The writer who really hit me – I remember saying that in Jamaica, and people were amazed because they thought it was kind of uncanny – was Christopher Marlowe. The first time I read *Tamberlaine* [1587], it was like I had taken speed or something! I didn't realize that such language existed, man. That man was a fantastic guy, you know. In fact, he inspired Shakespeare. When I read *Tamberlaine*, I said, "Oh, my God, how can a man write like that?" My second year of directing, I did *Dr. Faustus* [Marlowe c. 1593]; I trimmed it; I did *The Duchess of Malfi* [John Webster, c. 1613], and took out a lot of the comic parts and ran it as a pretty straight play. I left out some minor characters and it didn't really hurt the play. Elizabethan plays have a lot of subplots, a lot of unnecessary characters. That's how I learnt; it was groundwork that I did for myself – which a lot of guys don't do today. So when I'm writing a play all this is somewhere in the back of my head, so I can jump from one thing into the other because of the diverse experience that I have had.

I was lucky, too, when I was younger, to have done drafting – survey drafting – which is very precise. This helped so much with my stage design work with sets and so on. Actually, I don't do enough of that. Costuming was my real forte; I think I got that – apart from my graphic experience – from my father who was a very good water colourist and my mother is a very good seamstress; she has a lot of taste in designing clothes. I used to design costumes for my band every year; I still usually do it every year for the band at home.

You see, people get amazed about somebody like Geoffrey Holder,[10] they say, "How is it that this man is so good? The man is a painter, the man is a designer, the man can dance, the man is a writer." But that happens in the Caribbean so often. I think it has a lot to do with our creolization – and the fact, of course, that when you're running a group in the theatre you have to design, direct, stage manage – every damn thing yourself. It's a strain, too, because sometimes my talents pull against one another; I don't paint enough, I don't design enough – that kind of thing.

Q: Is it just coincidence that both Derek and yourself paint?

RW: It's a multi-talented thing that we got from our father. The kind of poetry he used to write was the sort of Robert Herrick [English lyric poet, 1591-1674] kind of romantic thing or – what was popular at the time – ditties for skits. His real talent was in watercolouring. He used to order for the library – as an assistant voluntary librarian – books from England which I used to read. A lot of the books got burnt in the '48 fire. He ordered some huge books on English watercolour painters for the library and he had some of these for himself. He had a book on the woodcuts of Albrecht Durer, who was Germany's greatest etcher. We just used to go through these books as kids. He also had a big Victrola, and he used to order these heavy 78s and we used to skylark with these things – well, he was by then dead a long time – just throwing them around in the house. That kind of bookish atmosphere was very helpful, so in a way I was informed from a lot of different directions. Although the opportunities now are greater, in that people can go and study for the arts, and they have a lot of workshops coming in and out of the country, they have festivals, they have a lot of information coming in, but back then a lot of people would not have had that kind of environment – it's not putting people down – it's just noting the opportunity of being in that kind of ambience. And, as Derek has said, and I feel it too, we share the same legacy of my father dying when we were one-year-olds, the feeling that we had to continue his work. That might be sentimental, but it's something that has sort of pushed me, you know.

I think, too, that music has a very strong part in my work. You see it a lot in *The Banjo Man* [1958/1971]. I've been, in a way, a frustrated musician from the fact that I used to play in a steelband and ran one. I never really read music, but I'm a good percussionist. And the whole thing about the coming together of the writing and wanting to have been a musician – it's difficult to explain because it is a kind of subconscious thing – but it has something to do with the question of rhythmic values and jazz. In the early stages, it can be best be seen in something like [*The Trouble with*] *Albino Joe*, [1966] which you might not have read – and this is an aspect of my work which I have to develop a little more: working that whole jazz orientation into my work – the idea of abstract, experimental work with language and music, which is a thing I have neglected. But I hope that in the drafting of my next play it will come out, and will extend into the next development in which music, whether it goes in a reggae direction or into what might be called a "Creole-jazz" idiom – is where I would like the play to go – keeping the theatre, of course, but you're talking about "it" as an undercurrent in the work and having "it" as a theme. The next play that I write will have a musical theme. And that's what I encouraged Derek to do a lot in the early stages – before he even started writing musicals.

That's another reason why I am very proud to be a Caribbean person, because the music is exciting, man, and it influences the world over every period. I mean, look at the amount of music that is written on the basic samba beat, the best pop music is based on samba material, you know. The changes that are coming about now, are really through a lot of Caribbeans playing in the United States.

Q: Disco for one is like an uptempoed reggae.

RW: Oh, yes. A lot of disco, too, is like a road march in Trinidad, you know: *kenna-ketta, kenna-ketta, kenna-ketta*. The beat superimposes itself, and it's done that over the entire *world*, and people can't understand *why*. And they still try to disrespect it by saying it is not as good as classical music and that kind of crap, but it's a music of the people that has taken over the world.

Q: How would you compare the directions yourself and Derek have taken since the early years with the St Lucia Arts Guild?

RW: Well, first of all, Derek and I don't compare work at all.

Q: I meant in terms of your individual growth, the directions you have each taken.

RW: I see what you mean. Derek started as a poet, then to writing plays. I got interested in directing and together we discovered a lot through what Errol Hill was telling us – there was a union as such, there. Then Derek broke off and went to Jamaica, so we were separated, though we used to correspond quite often. I, of course, used to pour myself out; Derek would either not write or not say much. He might not say it, but I think I was a very strong early influence on him in his choice of material, because I would always comment on whatever play he wrote. I used to read his material as soon as he sent it and he sent me a lot of material for the Arts Guild. When he wrote plays like *Ti-Jean* and *Sea at Dauphin*, in that early period, we were fairly close, though I hadn't started writing yet. Our main influence was film, because we hardly used to see plays, and I think we developed – if it wasn't an early gift – a very strong discriminating attitude towards what was good acting and what was not, especially watching those villains in the movies and how good those guys were. Anyhow, we transposed that into our taste in directing and our own plays. When he left for Jamaica and started writing on his own, and I started writing, my first two plays were *Benjy* [*The Harrowing of Benjy*] and the steelband play, *Shrove Tuesday March* [premiered 1956]. I was trying to get a laugh from the audience, trying to make people recognize their own thing. That was a nice time.

I think after that we went into what was a more serious kind of period, where the work started to gain recognition *and* more seriousness – with *The Sea at Dauphin*. After Derek had used classical-type material in *Christophe*, [*Henri Christophe: A Chronicle*, 1950] and then in *The Sea at Dauphin*, where he used both indigenous material and his poetry, we realized the success in joining the two. When he wrote *Ione* [1957], for Errol Hill's Federal Theatre Company's first production, Derek made it very stylized and Graeco-African, in a sense, about a battle between two families in St Lucia for land. Grand kind of thing with a lot of ethnic stuff, like the woman who was a sort of witch who could see into the future. It was the Helen and Paris theme – St Lucia was called "The Helen of the West Indies".

Derek's work tended to run into two areas, one in which he used the experience of the native – to put it very simplistically – in his environment – *Malcauchon*, *Dream* [*Dream on Monkey Mountain*], etc. – which, to me, was vibrant, terrific stuff – the stuff I really liked, and that goes well on stage. The other area is one that focuses on the expatriate (or the colonial) in a negative kind of experience – most of the time in conflict with the native environment: *The Charlatan*, [1954/1973] *The Countess Quinine* [announced in 1956, but seemingly never performed or published] – these are white protagonists within a Caribbean environment, and to me these plays didn't come off as well. There are a lot of plays he has not published yet, because he realizes the deficiencies in them. There is *Franklin*, [A Tale of the Islands, premiered 1973], *The District Officer*, [no evidence it was ever performed] which he wrote in Jamaica – it is a T.S. Eliot kind of a play, a drawing room play in which this black district officer is in a white community outside of Castries, and he's trying to be white.

Q: Errol Hill argues that when Derek is not modelling his work on some other great play and lets his own imagination "loose", that is when his plays work best, like *Ti-Jean*, for example.

RW: I'm still a little disappointed in *Ti-Jean*. I have a Ti-Jean play, *The Prowess of Ti-Jean* [unpublished, no evidence of performance[11]], but it is not constructed to make it an ethnic play. I wrote the play as a kind of movie using the Ti-Jean heroic theme, different in a lot of ways from Derek's *Ti-Jean*, but using the same traditional character and putting it in a kind of adventure. But you are right in the sense that he writes his ethnic material better, and that's what I was pointing out. *The Sea at Dauphin*, *Malcauchon* – there's only one that differs from that, actually, and that is *The Joker of Seville* [premiered 1974], which is in a kind of classical mode, and which is his only adaptation. It is a sort of jump-back to *Christophe*, where he goes into the sophistication of the English literary kind of mould, although using it in a Trinidadian context.

Where we differed and where our directions sort of changed, is when he wrote the article on "The Muse of History",[12] where he knocks anthropological pursuits in writing and makes fun of indigenous writing, in a way. He and I sort of fall apart there. I know what Errol Hill is talking about – it is the imaginative part of the folk material, changed into the poetry and the splendour of language. I think that's where Derek's strength is, that's where he differs from any writer in drama outside of his world. If you saw *Dream* performed with a Japanese play or an English play, you would see that they were three culturally distinct plays, in the mode that I'm talking about. Take Peter Shaffer's play *The Royal Hunt of the Sun* [1964], and imagine a really good Latin American poet-playwright taking that same material and writing it. Although *The Royal Hunt of the Sun* is good – you can imagine what the Latin American guy would do with it. The kind of writer Lorca was in terms of the theatre is the kind of writer that I think Derek is. Some parts of his work tend to be pappy, whereas I think mine is not because I am dealing with material that I am a part of, the indigenous material. I am not as good a poet as Derek – I'll never be, because of our talents – but in terms of the concepts and the dramaturgy I don't think there is any very great difference there. What I'm saying is that it's in terms of the vision, the whole thing of being a poet – a born poet – or a writer like I am who has to do the struggling into the ethnicity, the mythology of the material, and what you have to dump or preserve, etc., that is where I think the difference lies.

For instance, there's his philosophy of the Adamic man[13] and his thing about the great writers of the New World – people like Whitman and so on – and saying that you cannot keep falling back on slavery, on your history, on your indigenous thing, saying that you have to get over this, not necessarily forget it, but you have to get over it at some stage – this is in rough what he is talking about. What I keep saying is that I can't for one minute believe the history is over, in the sense that man's inhumanity to man will keep recurring, because history still has a very strong influence on the Caribbean, and that's because a lot of them don't even understand what happened. I think that our history should be rewritten – that's the didactic part I am talking about as a writer – to write our history as seen from *our* point of view – which is what *Cul-de-sac* [1981] is about.

You see, I don't know where Derek is going to head, but I know exactly where I am going. I, for instance, have plays I know I will never write, but I have at least twenty-four plays – and I'm not kidding – that I have to write. And I might get through – if I live that long – maybe six or seven. If I see that I'm going to go fairly soon I'm just going to pick out the best and try to write them fast.

There's the kind of discipline of knowing exactly where I want to be. I think if somebody were analyse my work – especially if I were to write a little more – they would be able to see some kind of strain [direction] quite clearly, I think.

Q: I'm going to read you two quotes from two different writers – Errol Hill and Dennis Scott, both comparing yours and Derek's work. Errol Hill says:

> "...Derek has a poetic vision and Roddy has a theatrical vision... I think Roddy is farther along the way of developing folkforms than Derek... Derek will always take the folk and try and merge with the so-called universal... and he has a marvellous ability to take those classical plays to find parallel situations in the West Indian experience. That is what I think is the technique he uses... Roddy gives me the feeling of being much more in touch with the reality of the folkforms, that when he writes about them he is writing straight from the heart and is writing without the encumbrance of trying to find a poetic metaphor for what he is saying. So, on the one hand, Roddy becomes far more accessible than Derek, but on the other, Derek's plays, when he succeeds, will have more depth and more meaning because he is writing at different levels." [See interview with Errol Hill, p. 163]

RW: I think that is fairly correct. What I don't have and what Derek has, which you see a lot in a great writer – and we have to face it that he is, right? It's true he is my brother and we are twins and we're very close – but I sometimes stand back and say, "Well, if I were reading this guy and I didn't know anything about him, would

I think he is that good." First of all, he has a strong sense of acute irony, a very sharp tongue in his pen, he can bite; I don't have that bite. Brecht had it and a lot of great writers have that strong sense of irony. Also, when he writes he writes as a world playwright – I mean, this is where you have to go if you have a reputation, and that can make it ethereal, so to speak, which is the voice of the poet. In my development – though I think I am getting a lot more into metaphor, and so on – I think I will eventually write poetry…

Q: You have never written poetry?

RW: No. But I think I will eventually, but I am not so sure when. I might write it when I'm much older. Probably it's because of Derek being there, you know. If I go and put out a book of poetry now, what the hell is going to happen? They're going to say, "That's crap, man, I though Roddy could write poetry," that kind of thing. And say what you want, there is always that thing at the back of a writer's mind, like myself as a dramatist, that the playwright is considered to be a kind of a hack, and he will never get the dignity that a poet has. A poet, like a composer, draws that kind of awe, for putting words together in a abstract form. I've always admired composers – and that's another field I'd like to get into because I think I can do something there. I've done a little composing, too. To write poetry – and write good poetry – takes sweat, strain, discipline. It's like cricket: take Sir Garfield Sobers,[14] you *see* how things come easily to the man, but it meant working and disciplining himself and getting *better* at some things that he hadn't done, like bowling fast, and so on. Derek is the same. There are guys who have talent, but to get somewhere they have to plod and work hard; I have to plod if I'm going to get better. That's why my favourite parable is one about the three talents.

But there is little difference between Derek and I, in the sense of being multi-talented. I have a little more talent in that broader sense than him, but his writing is so much *bigger* than the other talents that I have. But I feel that I'm developing every time that I write, that I'm not putting out material because I have to or just hacking it out. My next stage I think is working on the questions of place and time. With the theatre you can break and divide time; with place, now, that is where the poetic thing starts to come in; it is starting work with what we learnt from folklore, and from film. In film when a scene is set among rocks, you see a depressing scene. The play I'm writing now is about Mabouya Valley, an area in St Lucia where peasants live. Their concepts of things are different in the Valley, but to get that sense of place in the theatre, it has to come from the words used in the scene. You'll see it in *Cul-de-sac*, and you'll see it in the next play I'm writing.

I'm discovering all the time and discovery is nice. I'm very religious; I don't think that my talent is mine, my talent is from God, and that's the way I see it. I remember writing Derek about that…

Q: How does he feel about that?

RW: I don't know how he feels, really. But I believe that he knows that his talent isn't really his – but I really feel that way because I get surprised like hell when I'm writing! When I write something and it's good or I get out of a hole into something which is better than I thought I had, or, I'm looking at something and I say, "Hey, you could put that in there", and it immediately becomes a metaphor, gives it an additional dimension – do you see what I'm saying? And that's what you should feel when you come out of a good film or a good play. There is so much that you have to do for an audience: the words are ringing, the words are going together with the design of the play and the setting and the characters – that's Shakespeare, you know – so much is involved in one thing. That's why I was so glad the first thing I learnt was from Elizabethan theatre; so much is happening there, man. When I was young I used to say, "But how the hell did they produce this thing?" Because there's so much in it. And it's not only in Shakespeare, it's in Webster, it's in Marlowe – and these are the people we will have to start going back to, because they write about the *same* thing as we have in the Caribbean – whether it's Voodoo, whether it's the pantheistic aspect of what water means outside of being water, and how that relates to your *scene*, whether it's a soft scene, or hard in terms of texture and all that kind of thing. Very important, man. And Derek just has it like that because he's a poet, but I have to work on it. Actually, a lot of the stuff that he does, he doesn't understand. Say he gets a concept and he gets two metaphors working, but these two metaphors working are *so* good that they solidify and crystallize and become a third concept and ambiguity sets in, and it becomes a form with different colorations. Do you see where we are? I'm talking too much.

Q: Oh, no, not at all.

RW: But this is what writing is about – really good writing. You can read a piece and it doesn't seem to say much, but the thing has so much power and depth. I remember as a kid reading *Portrait of the Artist as a Young Man*, by James Joyce – that was the time that I started reading a little heavier stuff, after I got off Steinbeck. When I started reading Joyce I was still a bit too young and there are things that will happen to you if you start reading a writer who is too heavy and reading him at too young an age – you can get a lot of bad feedback. *Portrait of the Artist as a Young Man* is an Irish story so there is the very strong thing about sin, redemption, hell and so on. And I put down the book and couldn't read it anymore because it was too strong. The same thing happened when I was reading Dostoyevski; I read Dostoyevski much too young. I was trying to read *Crime and Punishment*; Dostoyevski is a great novelist, but that man is *grim*. *Bleak* stuff, man! That's why Dickens, to me, is better, because Dickens has all the sense of humour, it's very colourful. But Dostoyevski is Russia, *bleak*, *heavy*... oh, it's a little too much to take. (Laughs)

Q: I'm going to read you the other quote, this one is by Dennis Scott: He says:

> "The early Roderick, I thought, was interested in action and less in language in a way that Derek was never. Derek has always seemed to be more interested in language and what it exposes, what it reveals about character and the ironies with the character, contradictions with the character. Roderick has always been more interested, it seems to me, in action and social conflicts so that what is revealed is the dangers to human feeling and not the ironies in feeling. There is no way of saying this other than crudely: I wish that they did not know each other existed and then Roderick might have been free to play and grow more fully in his area of interest concerned with action and social conflict." [See interview with Dennis Scott, above, p. 277]

RW: Well, Scott's thing is a little more limited than Errol's, because Errol has really studied us; Errol grew up with us, in a sense. Action – right; social conflict – for a period. And he's talking about my early work, too. That was the time when I hadn't really identified with myself, my culture and where I was. And, it's true about being outside of each other. I don't know if it would have worked that well, in that I might have taken another direction in which I might not have grown – because I think Derek's work makes me grow even though I just read it. I think the similarity, and where Derek grew, was the time when we both wrote very humanistic themes: man's inhumanity to man, and stressed the colonial and the class thing, etc. The second play that I wrote, *Shrove Tuesday March* [1956], had the same theme as Derek's *Malcauchon* [premiered 1957], which Derek wrote afterwards. Now, this is not saying anything about influence, but it's saying how the two minds were going in the same direction without consulting or talking to each other.

Basically, as people, he's tough and I'm soft, I'm very soft. He *feels* deeply because he's a poet, with his rancour and anger and powerful kind of reaction, whereas I would suffer in silence... There's a good comparison in the four artists St Lucia produced during that period, four important artists: Derek, myself, a painter called Dunstan St Omer[15] whom he called "Gregorias" in *Another Life* – and Garth St Omer[16] – Garth and Dunstan are not related, though they have the same surname.

Garth is now a professor at UCLA. His first work was *Syrop*,[17] but the rest of his work has gotten very intellectual... Dunstan and I work somewhat alike, and Garth and Derek are similar.

With Garth and Derek it's the alienation of the intellectual artist looking from the outside at his people, whereas Dunstan's painting and my kind of writing come from the native kind of artist growing up with his people, with that kind of energy. I think that Dunstan and I are very similar there.

Garth has a strange kind of development. His first work, which is a lyrical kind of work called *Syrop*, about a wharf boy – is very St Lucian, very well written. Now, what he has done was change from that into a very personal kind of style which is very Camus, very existential. His last novel, [*J, Black Bam and the Masqueraders,* 1972] which he wrote about seven years ago – and he is still trying to write a new one – merged those two forms when he made use of the concept of the traditional masquerade. Both Derek and Garth suffered from the fact that they could not communicate with their society because they were put on a pedestal, and they have felt intellectually estranged. Garth's response was even more bitter, because he didn't have the intellectual friends that Derek had. Derek, as a young literary young lion in those days, was wined and dined by people in the community, the architects, the heads of department, the cocktail society circuit. Garth came from a very poor family, got into the Arts Guild, did a little acting, did a little writing for the theatre, but basically he was a novelist – he's really a natural novelist.

Q: How old is he?

RW: Garth is around the same age as us – early fifties. All of us are the same age. So that kind of alienation: not getting scholarships – Derek didn't go to Oxford, when he was younger; he was recommended for Oxford, but there was a problem and they didn't send him. There is a bitterness in their work which does not exist with Dunstan and I. They matured early and you might even say that while Dunstan and I have a kind of an African concept of life, Garth and Derek have a kind of a European concept. That is being very simplistic and probably very crude, but, in a sense, that is how they developed. You see, we developed from the roots while they developed from the English tradition. That's more or less it in a way.

Q: What inspires you to write?

RW: The fact that I know have material to write and to finish. I have a list of plays that I have to write, and I just do them one after the other. My working routine is difficult, in the sense that I don't work daily like Derek does. I should have more output, really. A lot of my early work was written with too much padding, too much overwriting, so my work got slowed down in that way. I tend to be a late-nighter, I can't work mornings. The other thing that kept me back was that I was in a regular job so I had to write on weekends. Now, Hemingway used it – it's called the "writer's bluff" – about trying to face a typewriter in the morning – I always rewrite the last page I wrote; it gets me back in the groove; and then there is so much already prepared as far as writing the next stage is concerned that I am able to go straight into it. The preparation part is the new way that I'm writing; it makes it very smooth – I'm starting to wonder if it isn't making it a little too easy for me. The *content* is what I am starting to get a little worried about, that the content might be too light, too thin. One day I might do a page or two and another day I might do five pages; but the page or two might be equivalent to six because I might write a page three times and then go back and read it. Then the final page that I write for the day, I type it over the next day.

Q: Do you see much hope for West Indian theatre developing in Canada, particularly in Toronto?

RW: I don't know. I know that it will have a place as a kind of an ethnic curiosity. Then, to organize a company on the kind of level, say, that you probably get in the States – of a grant given every year, regularly, like The Negro Ensemble Company, etc. – to have that happen in Canada? You have, first of all, a problem with the society itself, and the Black community which has a lot of complexities. Artists pass through, some don't have any real ideals as far as Black theatre is concerned. It's gotten into a mercenary commercial kind of thing as well. A guy will act in a play for you and you pay him his bucks and he does his work and he's gone, so we don't have a repertory company where you can see a choice of plays and the actors develop by doing several different roles. The ideal kind of theatre, to me, would be for a fellow to be doing Athol Fugard, doing Derek, doing a Black writer from England and the best material at the highest level. That's the way it's going to really ring true. But it's the internal infrastructure and that access to grants, and having a following – a lot of complexities that make it difficult.

Q: You had a play produced in Toronto. How well did it go?

RW: I opened the first Black theatre Canada production with *Malfinis*, yes. It went OK. But I had a problem with the producer and we had a tiff. I think she (the producer) pulled back on publicizing it, and when the attendance was starting to grow, the run was over. But it was a production I was quite satisfied with. One thing I didn't like, but couldn't help, was that we had to take a guy who we had to try very hard within a short space of time to get him to lose his North American accent – in a St Lucian play – and it was difficult.

But outside of that, I had a chance to work in an old church and the design was the thing that I liked about that *Malfinis* production. The stage had a lot of height, so I built steps and it looked like a hangman's gibbet – it was a two-level stage. For dance, we designed the whole floor, and we used eerie lighting. It was a nice production. It got good reviews from the two critics who saw it. The only bad panning I got in a review – and I haven't had many reviews, unfortunately – was by some Guyanese guy – a brother West Indian. I talked to him before the play, and he asked me, "How much of the material did you use from the original recorded material?" Because it was a piece based on an actual murder trial that happened in St Lucia. But the idiot didn't realize that it was a fantasy, because I set the play in purgatory *after* the trial. And the man had the brass to write – and I wanted to answer him – that I had actually used the authentic recorded material. In other words, I was just a kind of instrument; it was really bad, you know, the man downgraded my material by saying that.

Q: Maybe it was because he didn't really understand what he was seeing.

RW: Yes, probably. The only thing that the Canadian reviewer didn't like was "the choice of material." He found the material so "indigenous" – that's the only thing. He was saying that we should choose a kind of Canadianised thing – you know, the usual crap. What's bad about here, now, is that they're tightening up, they're closing ranks. You can't get Council grants like before. I got one once. They tell you that your material has to be Canadian in some way.

Q: I would like to get your candid and critical reaction to some of the following Caribbean playwrights…

RW: That's kind of rough. You're making me put down people – I don't like doing that to my peers… (*Laughs*)

Q: You're not putting them down, you're merely giving a critical commentary. Errol John.

RW: Errol John. I know Errol John had about three plays, his first early plays I found strong but very crude. And when I say crude, I mean in the sense that they were good work but sort of crudely done. Crudeness, I think, is the word for it; not making the material evolve into something more. That's his very early work. *Moon on a Rainbow Shawl* I think it was influenced by the American theatre, especially since he had just directed *Member of the Wedding* – Carson McCullers has a kind of influence on him there. That is not derogatory. I think the play, because of its newness, its new environment – I think it's a bit of an overrated play. Now, that might sound hard, but when I read *Moon on a Rainbow Shawl*, I liked it; I liked the concept of the metaphor in it, but there was nothing after the metaphor for me. It had a nice atmospheric environment, about people's dreams, where they want to go and the reality of life – a very American concept. And the play has a design concept which works beautifully theatrically. I would have liked to have seen him develop into something; unfortunately he went into films and I think got screwed up somewhere; maybe he got frustrated. But, I'm still a little amazed at people thinking it is such a great play. I never saw it staged, I read it, and maybe I'll have another concept when I see it on stage.

Q: Lennox Brown.

RW: I think Brown is a theatre man, definitely. He understands theatre, but I'm missing something in Brown. In other words, I haven't read a play of Brown's yet that I am really satisfied with as a piece. I have read some one-acters and pieces of that nature – I don't know if *A Ballet Behind the Bridge* [1972] gives me an unfair bias towards his work, because I have not read a lot of his material. What I have read, there is something nice about his imagery and some of his concepts; I don't find the language particularly exciting, different or deep. There was one play of his that I read and I wanted to do – two of them, actually – one had a back-to-Africa concept, *The Throne in an Autumn Room* [1979], that's a nice play, nice title, nice concept… I find him a soft writer, which is good, I think he has a delicacy which is fine and that's what a lot of West Indian writers still don't have.

For instance, supposing, tomorrow, you got a fellow like Oscar Wilde writing in the Caribbean. He's writing about West Indian society – with the wit and brilliance of Wilde – let's say that happens – but he has come from an upper class, semi-white or white social group. Are we going to say that man is writing crap or that he is not Caribbean? If he is a good writer he's going to reflect something Caribbean – and different to Wilde if he's a really good writer – mannerisms, etc., would differ; the gossip between the upper class, the whole creolization thing would be different from an English Edwardian drawing room conversation. What right would we have we to say, "Oh, the man has no Africanisms in him…" and the man is a brilliant writer? I mean, you just have to accept the man as being a good Caribbean playwright. And that's where Derek gets knocked sometimes, which is unfair, I find.

Q: Slade Hopkinson.

RW: Slade, I find, is more of a novelist. I think Slade would have made a very good novelist. I found his work a bit muddled, psychologically confused, etc. I find the same thing with Dennis Scott's early work – at least the two that I know – *Terminus* [1964] and *The Caged* [1961]. I don't know of Dennis's later work and I don't know Slade's later work. But, for instance, last year we read something Slade sent to the Third World Players in Ottawa. It was about this man in Guyana, who is teaching in a native community of Amerindians, and he has some problem with his wife and his mistress. Actually, I think Slade was trying to deal with the whole novelist thing about the corruption and strain of blood and the miscegenation thing, that kind of concept. There's this lack of completion that I find in a lot of his plays; probably I haven't read the right ones.

Q: Alwin Bully.

RW: I don't know Bully's work that well, unfortunately. I was supposed to get a copy of *Nite Box* and I haven't. I think there is a magnificent thing that could happen with Dominican musical theatre. But, I think, with Bully's concept – which is popular theatre – giving the masses what they want – a little bit of action, a little bit of song – a musical concept which he calls "Calypso theatre" – something could happen, because I think he is a very talented guy, especially as a theatre director; as a writer, I can't really say. I mean, he's the best thing that has happened to Dominica for a while – but you remember the thing I was telling you about Carriacou?

Q: Trevor Rhone.

RW: Rhone, I think, is a brilliant or very bright kind of Wildean person that we were talking about. Not putting him down. I think he's what you could call the "Neil Simon of the Caribbean".[18] Rhone keeps telling us – and probably selling himself short – "I'm not the heavy kind of playwright like you guys; I am Trevor Rhone writing for my people." I don't know whether it's a sham or what, but that's the impression that he gives us or has given me. I have never met Rhone for long, I meet him, we say "hi" and then he moves on – probably gives a talk somewhere. But of the material that I know that he has written and I have read, I find, first of all, he's a very good comic writer, but I think he has to be very careful with his situation: with cliché, North American sophistication, that kind of thing. He's in a area where a lot of theatre is going, he's right there – kind of a Noel Coward person, you might say. *The Harder They Come*, to me, was a very pleasant surprise, because I didn't know he had that kind of thing going for him, and I think that was a damn good job. I think West Indian cinema could have really begun if we had the wherewithal. I think Rhone could have developed there. I saw *Old Story Time*, in Nassau, when I went there to a conference, and I was a little disappointed in it. He was still doing it in a pantomime kind of way. But I think as far as the others and Rhone is concerned, I've been more satisfied with Rhone – in other words, having his finger on a kind of worldliness in theatre and feeling the pulse for laughter, sadness. But how much further does Rhone want to go or is he satisfied where he is – prepared to do like Neil Simon is doing now, which is staying in a bloody rut, turning out the cornbeef stuff?

Q: Michael Abbensetts.

RW: I only know one play of his, which I think was very well structured and done well. But, there again, I'm thinking about Abbensetts's development – if he's going to be writing at fifty or sixty – if he's going to be turning out Abbensetts material as sociology – or whether it's going to get any heavier. How is he going to turn? That's just from the one play that I've seen and that was *Sweet Talk* [1973].

Q: Mustapha Matura.

RW: I don't know his work at all.

Q: Errol Hill.

RW: Errol Hill was a good playwright. In fact, Errol Hill has four or five plays which he can put out as a representative body of work. He is very good with strong, telling language – sharp, spikey, rhythmic. I think we might have got a little more of that from him. He's very good on plot and atmosphere, etc. I don't think *The Ping Pong* [1958] was so good but it's a nice little situation piece. We did most of Errol Hill's work, you know; we didn't do *Man Better Man* [1957] – a lot of which I felt was dressing, but it was good folk theatre. What I like most, though, is *Dance Bongo* [1965]. Derek thinks it's fakey poetry, but it works, every time that play is staged it works, because it has an echo. It's his best play I think.

Q: Quite separate from the theatre, what is your opinion of V.S. Naipaul's development and direction, to date?

RW: There, again, my lack of reading. Others look upon him as what you call "a developed colonial" or a man who's sort of turned against his – whatever they want to say – and I know what I disagree with Naipaul about, regarding *The Mimic Men*, and things like that. I think the Caribbean has developed a lot more than Naipaul is willing to accept. And there are ways in which Naipaul seems to justify the colonial conqueror – you know, the kind of approach which irritates and angers Third World people reading him.

But after he got out of the quaintness – and it's the quaintness which the British liked – that quaintness of *The Mystic Masseur* – he's a terrific analyst and a fantastic essayist and he uses his essay skills within the novel. His essays are really good, they really are. And let's face it, the man is heavy, in terms of his ability. But Naipaul's philosophy, as far as writing and culture are concerned, I find a bit unpleasant, to put it mildly.

What I am worried about – and I'm not reading enough Naipaul – is whether the praise he is getting is not more for his political and sociological stance than his ability as a writer – and that bothers me. You see, he's a new voice talking in a period when there aren't very many wise, analytical type of people like him. Looking at it from the other side, these non-West Indian, white intellectuals say, "But this man has a fantastic analytical mind, look at how he is so objective about his own country, the Third World. His apogee is Western Civilization." The thing is, are they being honest because they think Naipaul's work is great, or because they are sympathetic to his socio-political beliefs?

Now, we can also run into a racial prejudice thing, here. You know the old sort of fawning coolie thing that we used to talk about in the Caribbean, the Indian immigrant coming down to the Caribbean, with his "yes, sir," and "boss" and that kind of thing. We feel that Naipaul might be a resurgence of that in England with the English elite and publishers – that attitude of fawning which we don't like. But I think he's a good gadfly, because the man isn't talking crap. I mean, he might be biased and in certain parts extreme, but a lot of what the man is talking about, West Indians have to bloody well get up and face.

Q: Finally, what style of theatre would you like to see being developed in the Caribbean?

RW: Well, I always say around my style! (*Laughs*) There'd be development if the writers do more homework, if the writers do more self-criticism and don't allow everything to go to their heads when they have a one-shot play and their peers put them on a pedestal too early, or they go on a little course in Jamaica and feel that they're lions around the place. If they do their work seriously there'll be development – whether it's going to break off into something more Rasta-oriented or more in a roots kind of area – and this is talking very lightly and quickly over this whole thing – or whether it's going to go more into an amalgam of cultures, extending further than Derek and I – or whether it's going to go more Brathwaite. Because it's these influences from people like us that will make the next generation decide what they're going to do or how the theatre will develop. But I would say we need to preserve our identity as much as possible.

I remember a young talented guy telling me that he just wants to write plain-good-language kind of plays, that he has no kind of ethnic identity. But that doesn't have enough substance for me – in terms of the man being a certain person within a certain environment. He needs to see himself more clearly and what he writes should come out of that.

End Notes

1. See interview with Errol Hill, note 5.
2. Cicely Waite-Smith (Howland) (1910-1978) was an expatriate English woman, born in Canada, an actress, who married a Jamaican, who made a significant contribution to the development of the theatre in Jamaica in the 1940s to the 1960s. She was part of the Edna Manley Focus group and a friend of Roger Mais. Her plays included several staples of the early Caribbean repertory, and she was credited with writing one of the first plays, *The Creatures* (first performed 1943) that portrayed Jamaican working people in a dignified way. They include: *Storm Signal* (*Focus*, 1948); *The People Champion aka A Woman of the People* (c 1957); *The Wild Horse* (c. 1957); *The Ravishers* (1958); *Africa Sling Shot* (1957); *The Creatures* (1966); *Uncle Robert* (1967); *Return to Paradise* (1966); *The Impossible Situation* (1966) – all but the first four published in the UWI Extra Mural playscripts series. See Honor Ford Smith's introduction to *The Creatures* in *Mixed Company: Three Early Jamaican Plays* (London: Oberon Books, 2012).
3. Samuel Hillary (1939-) a Jamaican playwright, author of the popular play, *Chippy* (1966) and including: *Departure in the Dark*; *Geva Charlotte*; *The Kingstonian*; and *Merry Christmas Mr. Murphy*.
4. See Kamau Brathwaite, *"The African Presence in Caribbean Literature"*, in Roots (University of Michigan Press, 1986).
5. See such polarising essays as Pat Ismond, "Walcott Versus Brathwaite", *Caribbean Quarterly* 17, nos. 3-4 (September-December 1971).
6. "A Far Cry from Africa", *In a Green Night* (Cape, 1962), p. 18.
7. "My Audacious Self" – It's not clear what this refers to; no such poem is mentioned in King, *Derek Walcott: A Caribbean Life*.
8. Rex Nettleford (1933-2010) was the founder in 1963 of the National Dance Theatre Company of Jamaica. He was a choreographer and dancer, an important writer on Caribbean society and culture in *Roots and Rhythms: the Story of the Jamaican National Dance Theatre* (London: Deutsch, 1969); *Mirror, Mirror: Identity, Race and Protest in Jamaica* (Kingston: Sangster and Collins, 1970); *Inward Stretch, Outward Reach: Voice from the Caribbean* (MacMillan 1993); *Caribbean Cultural Identity: The Case of Jamaica* (Marcus Weiner, 2003). He was Vice-Chancellor of UWI Mona, Emeritus.
9. Robber Talk is a feature of the Trinidad Carnival in the figure of the Midnight Robber who challenges passers-by with hyperbolic and bombastic threats, couched in alliterative and often outrageously metaphoric language.
10. Geoffrey Holder, see interview with Mustapha Matura, note 7.

11. In the documentation for the Roderick Walcott collection housed at the UWI Open Campus Library in St Lucia, "The Prowess of Ti-Jean" is listed as a play and an unpublished novel, based on a novel by Zane Grey.
12. "The Muse of History" (1974), is collected in *What The Twilight Says: Essays* (London: Faber, 1998), pp. 36-64.
13. For Derek Walcott's Adamic man, see "The Muse of History", pp. 40-43 and poem "Crusoe's Journal", *The Castaway* (1965), p. 51.
14. Sir Garfield Sobers (1936-), the greatest West Indian/Barbadian cricketing all-rounder of all time: elegant batsman, left arm spin-bowler and seamer, and outstandingly athletic fielder.
15. Dunstan St Omer (1927-) is St Lucia's most celebrated artist. He worked as an art teacher and officer for arts education in the Ministry of Education from 1971 to 2000. In 2010 he was knighted. A deeply religious man, his most famous work includes murals painted in St Lucia's churches. See <http://arcthemagazine.com/arc/2012/03/dunstan-st-omer-the-artist-the-man-the-light-the-quintessential-st-lucian-artist/>
16. Garth St Omer (1930-) is St Lucia's foremost novelist, a literary modernist who explored existential themes and the deep roots of coloniality in the mentality of the Caribbean middle class in *A Room on the Hill* (1967); *Shades of Grey* (1968); *Nor Any Country* (1968) and *J–, Black Bam and the Masqueraders* (1972).
17. "Syrop", in *Introduction 2: Stories by New Writers* (London: Faber and Faber, 1964).
18. Neil Simon, (1927-) American writer of over thirty very popular and successful comedies from the 1960s to 2004, including *Barefoot in the Park* and *The Odd Couple*.

EDGAR NKOSI WHITE
(1947-)

Edgar White was born in Montserrat and came to the United States at the age of five; he resided in the Bronx, N.Y. In 1964, he enrolled in City College of New York and later transferred to New York University where he graduated in 1968. He was awarded a scholarship to attend Yale University's School of Drama where he remained for brief time.

As a young dramatist, White caught the eye of the late Joseph Papp, the artistic director of the New York Shakespeare Festival's Public Theatre, who produced White's first play, *The Mummer's Play,* in 1965. White had six more of his plays staged at the Public Theatre.

In 1970, White, along with director Rosemary Stewart started the Yardbird Theatre Company in New York and premiered his play *Ode to Charlie Parker* at Studio Rivbea, in SoHo, Manhattan, under the auspices of tenor saxophonist Sam Rivers as the company's producer and artistic director. His work was also championed by Ellen Stewart of Café La Mama who produced what White regarded as his most important play, *Lament for Rastafari*.

In 1975, White visited England when *Lament for Rastafari* was produced in London, directed by Rufus Collins. In 1981 *Les Femme Noires* was produced at the Keskidee Arts Centre. White remained in the UK for the next six years where his plays received world premières at such theatres as the Black Theatre Co-operative, Temba, Talawa, Umoja, Lumumba, the Keskidee, the Royal Court Theatre, as well as the Edinburgh Fringe Festival.

In 1987, *Lament for Rastafari* was produced at the Royal Dutch Institute in Amsterdam and in 1988 *Redemption Song* was performed at the Edinburgh Festival.

White is an accomplished poet and novelist, but he says, "I prefer the play more than the novel, because with a play you can hear your characters talk, you get the joy and sorrow of watching actors perform your words – for better or for worse – and, lastly, but very important, you get to witness an audience."

White is an adjunct professor at City College of New York where he teaches Humanities and Creative Writing. Between 2007-2009 he was Writer in Residence at the Institute for Research on the African Diaspora in the Americas and the Caribbean (IRADAC). His work is part of the National Theatre Black Archive of Great Britain (2010).

His articles appear regularly in *Monthly Review* magazine.

His plays include: *The Boot Dance; Burghers of Calais; Cathedral of Chartres; Count It All Joy; The Defense; Dija; The Figures at Chartres; Fun in Lethe, or, The Feast of Misrule; Ritual by Water; Ritual; The Rastafarian; Seigismundo's Tricycle: A Dialogue of Self and Soul; Redemption Song; The Pygmies and the Pyramid; Masada; Live from Galilee; Ghosts: The Scotsboro Boys; Count It All Joy; The*

Black Women; Black; Baba and the Tree of Life; Moon Dance Night; Song of Genji; Transformations: A Church Ritual; Tres Cepas; Trinity: The Long and Cheerful Road to Slavery; When Night Comes Day; La Gente; Lament for Rastafari; I, Marcus Garvey (and the Captivity of Babylon); Offering for Nightworld; Live From Galilee; Little Orfeo's Lay; Like Them That Dream The Life and Times of J. Walter Smintheus; Montserrat Still; The Children of the Volcano; Underneath (Fire a Come); Marion Anderson the Lady from Philadelphia (a musical performed at the National Black Theatre in Harlem in 2002); *The Rhila* (a performance piece written after a visit to Baghdad before the war and published on the Internet); *Trance* and *Come February Morning.*

His published work includes: *Underground: Four Plays* (William and Morrow, 1970); *The Crucificado: Two Plays* (William and Morrow, 1973); *Lament for Rastafari: Three Plays* (Marion Boyars, 1983); *The Nine Night: Two Plays* (Methuen, 1984); *Redemption Song and Other Plays* (Marion Boyars, 1986); *I Marcus Garvey* (Applause Theatre Books, 1989).

He has published three books for children, *Sati, The Rastafarian* (1973), *Omar at Christmas* (1974) and *The Children of Night* (1974 – all Lothrop and Shepard) and a novel, *The Rising* (Marion Boyars, 1988)

City College of New York have the largest collection of White's published work and he has made the College the final repository of the Edgar Nkosi White Papers. White is a member of New Dramatists.

According to Errol Hill, White's talent tends toward "the oblique, ironical statement, and he boldly alludes to other literatures and cultures in dealing symbolically with the dramatic tensions inherent in his work."

On being a writer, the playwright is blunt and to the point. "To become a writer is not a problem," he says, "Staying a writer is the problem."

EDGAR WHITE

8 January, 1976

Q: Let's take it from when you first came to this country, highlighting some of the more significant things that influenced you to write.

EDGAR WHITE: I was born in Montserrat, in 1947. I remember images of the island that were very real, very strong. But I came here [the USA] when I was about five, and slowly those images faded. I stayed with my aunt; she was working as a domestic, so I couldn't stay with her all the time. I had to room out with different people. I guess that had a strong influence on me insofar as I was never surrounded by anything permanent. I never stayed anywhere more than six months. By the time I got used to the architecture of a particular place, something happened and I moved. I see things as transitory, floating. I wasn't used to a situation which was stable. I felt strange going over to the homes of friends and seeing how families functioned – the jealousies, brother and sister – but yet they were there for each other. I always found that kind of thing strange.

First place where my aunt roomed me out, I stayed there for about a month. I was supposed to stay there permanently but I got into a fight with a boy who was making fun of my accent. I really had a bad accent, it was heavy. I guess the Montserrat thing is brogue, similar to the Jamaican thing – it's harsher. It's got a very heavy Irish influence. So anyway, I got into a fight – knocked out his front tooth – and they threw me out. This was like twelve-thirty at night. Call my aunt up, say: "Come get him." Packed my shit, had me out in the hallway standing there waiting for her. So, it was a weird thing – a classic scene: snowing outside – a preparation for the whole trip – the beginning of a lot of shit.

Then I had a peculiar experience staying with my aunt when she worked with these white people... I kind of relived that experience in *Omar At Christmas*, [New York: Lothrop, 1973] trying to get the sense of change, the radical change. She was from the old school which is a total domestic. I mean, total. That is to say, you clean the house, you cook the food, you take care of the children, everything. It's all one person. It's like the house in *Omar At Christmas*. It's under her rule. So she did this, and kept me there, in the back room. She didn't want them to know I was there. I don't know how long that was – couple of months – living in this little room off the kitchen. I could never make any noise because I wasn't supposed to be there. So it was kind of weird. We got away with it for a long time. Then, one day, I moved up to the Bronx. They let me stay with a West Indian family – Reverend Gerdie and his wife (I guess he influenced me for that character in *Tales of Anansi*). Stayed there kind of shortly, because they didn't have time to deal with me, to deal with a child. Every place that I went to was always to old people, elderly West Indians. I got to see a whole spectrum. After Reverend Gerdie, I went a few blocks up to Prospect Avenue and Boston Road.

Q: A lot of West Indians used to live around that area.

EW: Yeah, yeah. They did, but they were not in touch with each other too much. You don't know what your number is until somebody calls it to your attention. We never knew there were so many West Indians living up there. Next person I was staying with was the Rhodens – and that got me into the church. Church – entrance into theatre. Church has always been and, I guess, always will be, the symbol, the beginnings of theatre because of all the rituals and the mystery… It put into my mind a whole lot of equations, which later on you clarify. Later on those symbols relate to each other, because, sure as sometime, the church got hooked up with the law. Because of the same outfits, I guess – stayed in my mind. Whenever I thought of the church I thought of court – the judge's robe and shit.

I went to St. Augustine's Church on Boston Road. It was a very unusual church – I've just been writing about that – because the minister was a very active cat. He's become even more so. He's the Rev. Hawkins, and he got into politics. Now I'm living with the Rhodens; Mrs. Rhoden was in the church choir; her husband is the deacon. So I was in church *quite* a bit. She was also a very gifted musician – a singer and played the piano. She taught me my first scale, "C" scale, and I was turned off, really turned off, because of the associations – stay at home and music. The only musicians who I knew were those in the church, and, for the most part, they were faggots. It was interesting how that aligns itself, how cats go choose their little thing that they get it off in church. OK. Mrs. Rhoden was, as I say, very gifted; Mr. Rhoden was the West Indian cook – the cat who somewhere along the line learned how to cook and that was it. Total. Nothing more than that. No personality, no mind, nothing! I guess that was my introduction to men, the first strong man in my family thing, because before that it was just women.

Q: Heavy father figure?

EW: Yeah. His thing was just hit you, he'd just throw something at you, knock you down, slap you, throw you against the wall. I very seldom heard the cat talk. I was there for about two and a half years; she went crazy trying to deal with him. They were totally different people. And he'd tie her up. (I guess I'd have to say I had a very weird childhood.) He'd tie her up to a chair when he'd go out, and ask me to look after her. So she'd be sitting there in the middle of the living room tied up. It was a weird experience watching.

Q: How old were you?

EW: Ah, this was first grade, second grade, third grade. Then one time she just wandered out in the street. I felt this draught, the door was open – she was gone. She was out in the street walking around in her nightgown, just walking in the middle of the street.

By the time I guess I was about twelve I moved in with neighbours across the hall, which was the first contact I had with a second generation West Indian. Everybody else was just right from the islands. It was Marilyn and her mother. Marilyn was very sensitive. She was the first one that I knew of that read books. The only book that I had was the Bible, which everyone that I had come in contact with knew, including my aunt, who could read nothing else, but could sit down and read a Bible. Memorize damn near the whole thing... Marilyn influenced me as far as reading, as far as relaxing. Because up until this point, my only association was with my aunt – again the authority thing. She came on her days off to see me get my clothes and all that – that would be my report day. Inevitably I had fucked up, always, every week. There was never a week that I didn't fuck up somehow. She has this whip, she had a dog's leash, a leather dog's leash, and she tied it up with twine and that was her thing – she'd just come in there, she'd say, "O.K., take off your things. What did he do this week?" And we'd go at it. But Marilyn never did that.

Q: How old was Marilyn?

EW: Marilyn, she was younger, at the time she was in her thirties. Now Marilyn was paralysed. She had an accident when she was very young. She had difficulty walking, but that never stopped her. She worked every day, never complained. She was a very different kind of head, mainly because she believed in optimism. It's a weird psychological kind of a thing, because West Indians I had associated with were very cynical, very church-oriented, defeatist; it's hopeless but you must keep working anyway, just to keep in step.

Q: Calvinist ethic.

EW: Yeah, something like that. It's good for you to strain; man is going to come through life – very, very difficult, because this is not his paradise here. Definitely not his place. But yet he must work. It's just like the schoolmaster rapping you on the knuckles – basically it's good for you, that's why you must suffer. But Marilyn's philosophy was, "Life is what you make it. All that's going to be is just you." So, Marilyn had stopped reporting me. Up to this point what all these different things had done was to make me a nervous wreck. You put all that shit together and you have the formula for a very bright, very quiet kid, who don't get involved in too much – but just fucking crazy. That's why I know it so well – when I see that West Indian child in that whole thing where there is no father, there is no mother, there is an aunt, a grandmother, whatever. My mother was not allowed to see me either.

Q: She wasn't allowed?

EW: Right, right. What my mother had to do to see me was to see me in the park. And I never knew she was my mother. I was introduced to her three times and was never told. She was allowed to watch me; she had to sit on the other end and watch me as my aunt took me around...

Q: How come?

EW: Because my aunt felt that she was not capable of taking care of a child. That she would be a bad influence on me. My mother was raised to do nothing. Not cook, not do nothing. Just wear nice clothes and relax.

Q: Your aunt, that's your mother's older sister?

EW: Yeah, since my grandmother died my aunt took over the full scene. Went over and got me, and brought me over here to this land of opportunity and shit. So what I'm saying about being a nervous wreck, what it does is turn you into a little sneak. A polite, quiet, unobtrusive thief. 'Cause I used to rip everything off that I came into contact with. I got caught probably about three times in junior high school, stealing. You know, pocketbooks, money from their purses, shit like that... shit from the teacher. Everyone put their coats in the closet and you just go in, lock yourself in the closet and emerge later on with everybody's stuff.

Q: It was like a lark for you.

EW: It was a little more than that because it was a habitual thing, where I would rip off anything I saw. I mean, anything I saw, really... Don't know why but just... But what happened was, with Marilyn, she got me to kind of realize that what they had done to me was set me up. That was my first introduction to that. OK, twelve, thirteen, fourteen. That concept that it is possible people had set me up, that it wasn't an accident. That certain things happen as a result of other things; that my aunt set up the situation in such a way that I was always being reported on – that West Indian thing, I've seen it to be a pretty common thing. They never give their children money. Like if somebody gives you money for Christmas you're supposed to give it to your mother. It's this thing: "You don't have change in your pocket until you become a man." Consequently, they would hide everything from me. Everything. So I got into this thing of stealing and hiding stuff under my bed. There was a kind of need for that, just to know I have it, it's mine – God knows what I would do with it. Case in point: you rip off somebody's wallet, dumbest thing in the world that you can do is to save the shit that's in there – you take the money and you throw the wallet away. I would save the shit. I might take pictures or something like that out of there... and that was one of the main reasons why I got busted.

Q: You actually got busted?

EW: What they did – very, very slick. We had a hell of a dean... I went to junior high school... Hell of a dean, man. See they had all basically been trained in police work. So, the dean, Mr. Roberts, after the robbery, three days later, calls the whole class downstairs – just the boys. Three days after the robbery, when you figure that if they didn't catch you at three o'clock, and the day is over – right? Three days later they call you downstairs and the cat says, "OK, everybody open up your wallets." And bang! I got some pictures in there from this girl's wallet, and the girl says, "That's my pictures!" Bang! OK, you can imagine the situation. My aunt comes into the school; here's your son downstairs away from everybody else. He's in detention. That was one of the heavy things she never completely forgave me for. Never mind beatings and all that shit. "My son's a thief! You going end up in jail! That's a bad seed!" Apparently rumour had it that my father was in jail for some shit, so you know...

Q Your father was up here?

EW: No. Down there in Montserrat. So classic labels like that: "bad seed". He's never seen you, but you goin' end up like this cat anyway. Anyway, with Marilyn, all that shit ended. She started leaving shit around, she'd never put anything away. She'd leave money around, and I *didn't* take it. And I started to ease up. I had a heart murmur, that was another thing which they can hold over you. You have a heart murmur so you can't do anything. Don't run, don't do... You just have to be in the crib, kind of thing. But after I was with them for about a year, that shit started to go away, because it was just nerves. I got in the track team. I never told them. Later on in high school – on the swimming team. It was just a whole other psychological thing. I really started to come down, started to look around, started to relax. I used to read – I guess it was the first library I had seen. Marilyn didn't have that many – but interesting shit. And it just got me into another kind of a head with it.

I was always rebellious in school. Was always in trouble as far as sarcasm – that was my thing. The one who instigates things because he sets everybody to laughter by saying something sarcastic. I guess that was my weapon. I guess for the first time, man, you start to see a house, you see walls, you see a permanency. Like, this is my room in here; this is my bed. Then my aunt got hit by a car and bang! It was all over. She was in hospital for a long time, she couldn't take care of me. Anyway, she gets hit by a car, she gets up, doesn't take the car number or anything like that. Her head is bloody, and she's like: "Oh, I got to go and fix these people's food, because Mr. Bancroft is goin' be home from work soon." She goes, drags the shopping cart up into the elevator from the basement and then she falls out and gets a stroke. And my mother shows up on the scene for the first time, because now my aunt can't take care of me.

Q: Your mother was in this country all the time?

EW: Yeah, she was here all the time. All the time she was the figure that was moving around in the background, around the parks and zoos and the rest of the shit. When she was presented it was like: "Say hello to this lady…" "Hello, lady." But one day she knocked on the door: "I'm your mother and I'm here to take care of you." So that was the whole trip. I didn't know what the relationship was supposed to be. So we were friends. OK, nice woman – she is not going to harm me in any way. Like that. Then she started talking and going out, and she tried to find out what kind of person I was. Then my aunt came out of the hospital; I had to move in with her to help take care of her. And that also ended the stay with Marilyn and her mother. I moved in with my aunt – we went right back to the same shit again. It was like: "You been having much too much freedom! But now I'm going to bring you back …" to whatever it is that she wanted me to be – namely Andy White.

Q: What was Andy like?

EW: He was the one that went to school the way you were supposed to. A nice kid. Step by step, all the shit. Two things they wanted me to do was work in a bank – okay, can't do that – then a newspaper man. A newspaper man because of the fact that her employer's son was one of the chief whatevers on the *New York Times*. They wanted me to start off as a copyboy and work my way up, what-ever-the-hell. A journalist. Whatever they imagined that shit was about. By the time I got back with my aunt I was high school. I started to read. I found the Salvation Army was right downstairs from the crib – very, very lucky. They sold secondhand books for a nickel. So that was my thing. I got strung out on buying books. I used to go down there and read one thing; that would tell me about another thing and then I'd find that. I didn't know I wanted to write. Well, around sixteen or so I guess I did. I knew I wanted to write because essentially what had happened was that I had read everything. I had read everything – it was just like damn, OK, now what?

Q: When you say you read everything... You mean all the classics...?

EW: Yeah, everything, man. I mean, I had a hell of a reading thing. I'd do a book a day. Sometimes two. And then for things that would turn me on I'd go back to them – three times – gone back to them. My room at my aunt was nothing but books. I had a little, tiny room and they were all under the bed – everywhere – and that used to wipe her out because she couldn't understand what this shit was. "What is this?" She was never into that; nobody that she knew was into that. On the one hand it's good that he is literate and all this shit... but these books are taking me in a certain kind of way, because she could see the rebellion that was there. She probably felt that these books were instrumental in that. It was away from the church... She threw that shit out the window. Came home one day, found all my books gone. "I'll get rid of this, I'll stop this." She was a very weird woman... To everyone else she was very strong, very clean, she knew what she wanted to do. Again, there are many, many like her. She's more of the rule than the exception in terms of the West Indian woman who comes over here and gets their life together – clean – just day-to-day crawling through this whole labyrinth that they got worked out for you. She has raised a number of children. There's a lot of West Indian women who never had a husband, never have families of their own – that's just their thing. They raise other people's. And it was a curse – so far as: "You betray me if you don't come around and help me". See, the classic formula; from four years old I'm hearing it, over and over again: I raised so and so; I raised John, now John becomes a man, John don't help me; goes back to his mother; John helps his mother or his father or whatever – and he "betrayed me", over and over again. So I split home after I got out of school, after I graduated. Graduated from high school at sixteen and got out.

Q: You mean you ran away?

EW: Yeah. Graduated one day and left that night. Packed my shit up, left a note said I was alright, take care of yourself, you'll hear from me in a while – I was gone.

Q: Where did you go?

EW: I went running around the Village and then to upstate New York. Got out of contact.

Q: Talk about some of that – like the transitions you went through.

EW: I guess I was kind of lucky. As I have said, the pattern had been set from the time I had gotten here, of nothing permanent. So this moving around didn't upset me. I had no trouble dealing with it. I started taking notes of things. I really didn't sit down and concentrate on writing, but putting notes together on stuff, little sketches of shit. And I would travel with my duffle bag... But I was not nervous; it was pretty cool. You feel like it is possible, you could do it. There is no beast out there that can destroy you. Takes a little longer to find out that there really *are* beasts out there. Like when I went to Europe, same shit. I was off – zip! – to Europe and not knowing anything about where, how – just playing it by ear.

Q: How old were you when you made that trip?

EW: Seventeen.

Q: Were you writing then?

EW: No. My second trip to Europe I'm writing. I thought maybe I'd go over there and get something published. Because the image of Baldwin was strong in my head. I knew he had done it. I couldn't get anything published. Then, I didn't know Wright. When he was alive he wasn't as real a symbol to me as Baldwin was. Again, you find out a lot of things; there's no preparation for it. The only way that you learn situations and so forth is by studying a thing. Watching it, hearing it, seeing it. I never saw the characters in Europe on [American] TV – there was the guys with the bowler thing, all that. I knew them because they were stereotypes. The vast in-between I didn't know nothing about them – that everybody wasn't walking around like that, everyone was not driving a Rolls Royce, that the majority of the people over there was just scuffling. Through that I could come back here and look at the shit and see the same thing. I went over there and I didn't know the factory workers, the industrial north of England, which is exactly like the United States. It was then that I realized that it was a model to the United States, and, actually that's where the whole structure, the architecture of poverty and ghettos – that's where it began. When I went to Liverpool and saw how filthy that place was; people going around didn't know where the hell they were gonna sleep. Sleeping in the Salvation Army – and the way some of them places stank, and that constant feeling of cold.

Q: Were you ever in Paris?

EW: Uh-huh.

Q: Did you ever see the bidonville?

EW: Yeah and I wrote about it too. I wrote about the Algerian women with their children in their arms begging in the Metros. But it was still artistic for me. What I was looking at was the Left Bank. It was raggedy, it was poor people running around – but there were artists there. I was walking around like, "Oh...", thinking I was walking the same streets as all these other cats, you know, Hemingway, Eliot...

Q: You were going through a romantic kind of trip.

EW: Right, right. Because I remember I was heavy, heavy into it. I mean, I really got down on my knees and kissed the ground in Paris. I really felt it. It was a feeling of the impossible being done to have even gotten there. Okay, I'm on my way to being an artist. And I really felt as though I had hooked up with a whole historical thing. But after a while you listen to more, you get older and there is something which is working which has very little to do with you.

It's dangerous to write because you record whatever you've done and there's a lot of beauty in seeing – ego satisfaction – in seeing your own shit, somebody doing a piece that you wrote. But they don't tell you that it's dangerous and that you get to see yourself, and that it's there forever. All you can do is say: it's a portrait of a given time. And you will have to stand and rest on it. Like I always define the ironic humour of myself in that character, Pariah [*The Mummer's Play*, 1970]. There's a lot of shit there for me because by the time I had written that I had gotten way past that. Looking back on that character, trying to understand that head, because there were so many other guys that I knew who were doing the same thing. That Pariah has become a stock character. The lost fool in Europe looking around to be an artist. Running around, his drawers are ripped – he's got to sit like this (*crosses legs*) – but he's holding intellectual conversations. Sitting around talking... and I mean, if I were the one to play that, I could play that. Because I was aware of what was going on – speaking the literary thing anyway – they used to like to pick your brain kind-of-shit. For a while it's a good game, but if you going six or seven months, you can't play that game. Some people get hung-up and play ten years, twenty years! You go there and you are THE ONE. And then people get tired of you. You're not an American living in Paris. The longer you stay, it means you *need* to. At first, more and more people trying to tell you "Come on, come here, here is a good job." You relate stories about the kind of prejudices and cruelty that you have to endure over there: "Come here, where you will be respected for your mind". But it's not like that. There ain't no difference. They talk about you just like you ain't there. It's that kind of schizophrenic thing that can blow your mind sometimes. .

Q: Is that because of the language?

EW: No. They do it in French, they do it English – they just do it! It's a thing like this – you know when you go into a guidance counsellor or a doctor with your mother when you're small and the doctor is talking to you, and all of a sudden they stop talking to you and start talking to your mother? And they talk about "him"! "Him, the child so and so, he's really…" whatever. "This monkey can walk, talk, eat…" So they do that on you. The heaviest experience that I had was in Germany – because they are the best at it. The Germans are the most scientific. They, for me, are the farthest extent, *the* manifestation of the white man. The whole Teutonic head. Because they are scientists. Their total: "What have we here? How large is his head? How long is his dick? What are his tendencies?" They did that shit to me on trains – everywhere. People stand and point and look at you. It's always worst when you go to places where there are very few black people. Like where they had the Nazi trials…

Q: Nuremberg?

EW: Went to that place – there was nothing! There was nothing but monuments; a large coliseum there and just people walking around drugged. It looked like a small southern or midwestern town – the nothingness of day to day. There ain't no theatre, nothing. These kind of people are just hard working, industrious, go-to-work-everyday. But nothing as far as art. Nothing. The women got all the legends and myths right there; they've heard that niggers have tails. They ask you if you've got that – if they get to know you that well. You go into places that are more cosmopolitan like Stockholm, Sweden, the women dig you – women hit on you all over the place but yet they hate you, they resent you. That is catalogues of experience that you deal with only when you really want to. If you are there and you have some chick who is taking care of you, she's giving you pussy and she's cool, then you don't see all the other shit. You don't want to, so therefore you don't focus on it. If you focus on the fact that you've gotten out of the pit… that cools you out. Same kind of shit when I was in Ireland, when I was thinking about the whole beauty of the Irish thing for liberty. You need something to hook-up to – James Joyce, Yeats, all that kind of theatre, that kind of art…

Q: Was that one of the things that kept you going as a writer, that idea of divine inspiration?

EW: Yeah. To me it was something sacred. It really was something sacred. My introduction to it was never as a business. It wasn't as a thing like you fall into it because it's – damn, I ain't got no money, what if I did this thing… would it work? It always was I was turned on by cats like Joyce. Cats who were alone. The serious ones always seemed to be about something else. I didn't know exactly what it was, but it was that absolute, that kind of isolation. More and more I realized… it isn't so much because you want to, it's what's going to happen to you. If you put what's really in your head out there then you goin' be in trouble. If you put what you really see out there as opposed to something amusing, if you're not creating a tale, then you are going to be in trouble if you really talk about your life. How many people are allowed to really do their thing? It's a luxury that very, very few have. I didn't know what it was I was preparing for – I knew I was always interested in different segments of things. I was interested in languages because I was turned on to rhythms of language. I used to do a lot with language. That so much shit is weak is because they've killed the rhythms of everything. So jive. You become dead when you see something on the page totally meaningless to you – unless you find some way to redefine all the rhythms – and language gave me that. Like sometimes I would translate something from Greek, I'd put it into Greek first and then translate it into English in the same form it would be in Greek, and that would give me another way of looking... Everything which I've ever found, everything which I've ever got into has helped me. I didn't know *what* it was that I wanted to do, but it came to a point where I finally realized that rather than looking at what so and so did, rather than looking at what Eliot did, cats like Pound – that you don't have to try to imitate them. They weren't trying to do Shakespeare, and Shakespeare in his time wasn't trying to do Homer. Everybody was dealing with the emergence of his own life, whatever it is. But there ain't no precedent for it. There ain't no diagram that says this is what you do – dat, dat, dat. But eventually I kind of saw a hook-up.

Q: Were you first influenced by poets? You did say that when you started you started writing poetry.

EW: I wasn't *first* influenced by poets but I was reading poets. I was influenced by novels; and was first influenced by Dostoevsky. That was my heaviest cat that I ever got into. I liked him, I could deal with him. I don't know why it should have reached me up in the Bronx, but it did. I felt that he was real. And I like Tolstoy.

Q: Kafka, Camus?

EW: Yeah. Kafka, really funny you should mention that. Kafka in Europe – I guess I was slowly flipping out in Europe. I was learning. Took a lot of railroads and that does a lot of weird shit to you. Then you realize, goddamn, ain' nothing there and time starts to completely change in front of you. You start to see everything, all history, it's right in front of your eyes – you start looking back. Anyway, I dug Kafka. I tried to go to Czechoslovakia when I was on my way to find Nuremberg. But there was nothing to see in Czechoslovakia. It was too quick because I couldn't communicate with the people. Took a train and got out of there. But what I did see, that stuck in my mind, was the houses – the little gingerbread kind of shit, the strange kind of architecture – Gothic. I could see that cat's head, I could see Kafka's head much more. I could understand him, he had much more meaning to me after that, when I saw where he was writing from and how unreal it was. It was like a strange Hollywood set off them old Boris Karloff flicks – Bela Lugosi and them cats. And *here* there are people going around – how can I say this? They're living, reliving their mother's mother's mother's mother's life in the twentieth century. They're doing the same shit over and over again. And that's weird. They're doing it in a slightly different way but the insanity is still the same. What happened was a lot of shit came to me – that historical thing, that awareness thing that I'm living in the twentieth century but I'm not really living in the twentieth century – I'm living in the Sixteenth century, Seventeenth, Eighteenth, Nineteenth and Twentieth all of them at the same time. And it's a fairly simple thing to *say* it – till when you see it. That can be overwhelming. Because I began to relive rituals. I'm going back. I'm seeing slave ships. Here I am in Europe and I'm seeing slave ships in my head, and nobody said nothing about slave ships. But, you put it away, you go to sleep, whatever. You're born again, it's all there. It's just a matter of whether you want to deal with it. When I came back I was able to write some of that down, that whole experience. I've been to Europe four times; pretty much eighty-something per cent of that shit was gone from my head. I don't remember nothing. The question is: why? I don't know. Why does all that shit slip out of my head? I don't know.

Q: When was the last time that you were there?

EW: '63, '64. Had to get the hell out. And I ran and left my clothes. I was in Stockholm. And I've never been able to get back. That was very dangerous. As I said, all the shit is there *and* you want to deal with it, but sometimes you don't want to deal with it and you want to jump the frames. It's just like the movie thing, you go click, click, click. Okay, everything is in sequence, there's a sixteenth of a second between click, click, and all of a sudden you jump some frames and you're up here and you're seeing the shit and it's like: "Oh, no! This is too much! Too much shit! Wait a minute!" These motherfuckers are witches, they really are witches. Now how much of it is influenced by reading LeRoi Jones,[1] I don't know. You say, "Goddamn! These are other beasts. These people really do not like me." Not only that – their whole thing, the whole structure, whole architectural thing is really built off of me.

Q: You are talking about the European?

EW: Yeah, some kind of way – but also we are so *in touch* with them! So much inter-shit, man, that it blows your mind. And I'm glad that I came back to New York. Then a lot of other subtle changes started happening with me; a lot of people that I couldn't deal with any more; a lot of white contacts that I had were blown. I couldn't even *talk* to them no more. Just couldn't. And I got into writing. I really got into writing.

I guess too, around that period of isolation, I got into drugs. I had influences. This was a very important time for a lot of shit. A lot happening with the art thing – the East Village was the centre – a lot of the new poets, The Last Poets,[2] and the New Music. Two heavy influences. LeRoi Jones was living around St. Mark's Place, Archie Shepp[3] took over his crib. A lot was in the air. Lot of music was happening. Now the music made the same kind of brutal assault as the poetry. The music influenced the art. LeRoi's delivery became more like the jazz delivery. He was listening to 'Trane[4] a hell of a lot was what it was. Heroes. Archie Shepp would come over a lot to the crib where I was. And afterwards I was living next door to Dave Burrell,[5] who was a pianist. Now, I hadn't anything to do with music really, not since that early little thing with Mrs. Rhoden up in the Bronx – the first scale and I was turned off music. Didn't know what the hell it was all about as far as executing it. I liked listening to it. Listened to a lot of different shit. I thought that I could work on certain kinds of things that turned me on, but as far as executing it and what it was that people were doing, I didn't know. Dave was responsible for turning me on to a lot of music – hearing a lot of people. Sun Ra,[6] for example, lived across the street. Marion Brown[7] and Sunny Murray,[8] these. They got me listening to Cecil Taylor,[9] and seeing the way these people were using music in a whole other way that I had never thought about.

But though we had a certain mood in common, yet still the correlation, the hook-ups didn't happen. Didn't happen until, I guess, Sam Rivers,[10] who was the biggest influence on me musically in terms of seeing how there's no division between your life and your music – none. How it's just an extension. He gave me my first flute, Sam, just put it in my hand, said, "OK, see this flute? There's a hole here, blow on it here." Essentially letting me know, after a while, there are no short cuts. It would be nice if you could buy your way, teach your way, maybe read your way into a certain kind of awareness, but you can't. It's just a step by step thing you have to go deal with. How music and architecture are one, the way the forms flow; how essentially, its all the same – from something religious. Where all that shit goes back to – religion – how it all starts there and moves – the whole cosmology thing.

The first builders, the first architects, the masons, how they acknowledged breath control – all this. All the things that you take for granted were for centuries a very private, sacred business that was taught to a certain chosen few. Nigger got into the shit. Because there are mysteries in it. There are mysteries in scales. And that is the foundation. The scale is the foundation to music. If you don't have the foundation then you don't know where to go. That was a heavy concept for me. The mathematical thing you can multiply to infinity... but you've got to have that base to do it, like the base of the pyramid, otherwise you can keep on just making noise. So I began to try and apply this to my work, my life, my experiences.

Q: Apply what you learnt from music to your writing.

EW: Right. So, the more I got into music, the more I saw as far as architecture, as far as math. Went back over a lot shit that had frightened me initially, had turned me off. The question then became: why did it turn me off? Why? Because the way I was taught. Everything comes back. There were no accidents. Like the language. When they first give you the English language in school, they present it to you as a black child with: "Here is something else which you won't be able to do. Here's something else that's goin' to fuck you around." Just like math. Like it's something foreign.

Q: You actually studied architecture in college didn't you?

EW: Yeah. That came as a result of getting kicked out of the other school, at Yale, the drama school.

Q: How did you get to Yale? Was it a scholarship?

EW: Yeah. Yale gave me a scholarship because I was writing plays. That book *Underground* [1970], was already published.

Q: Didn't you go to Manhattan Community College also?

EW: Yeah, I'd done that first. Manhattan Community got me back in school. It was good for that. And then I got a writing scholarship to NYU – after I won a writing contest. I was working at the hospital.

Q: What year was that?

EW: This was sixty-something. This was in between the time I was going to Europe. At NYU I took courses and then I got a full curriculum going. After that I came out. I didn't graduate. Never graduated at any place 'cause I never stayed to get degrees. But through my writing – I was always writing – I got that book published; I sent a book up to Yale Drama school, and they said, OK, yeah, we'd love to have you. I went up there and it was a whole foreign experience to me. I'd never seen that kind of trip before. I'd never seen, here, in this country, that kind of comfortable class thing, that kind of intimidation which goes with letters – the Man of Letters. And the hatred – the hatred I'd never seen. Because there *was* a heavy fear. It was a thing that had to do with time, which had to do with darkness and lightness. It had to do with the fact that in the evening those shades came down, people could no longer define you, see your outline, see your face, and then you become just another one of the people on the street. And constantly being stopped by the police, having to show my school identification, all this kind of shit. But anyway, the opportunity for the first time became apparent, in that I saw how it was done, I saw how power was achieved. Yale taught me that. It gave me a thorough course on how one goes about conquering the world. It just don't happen. They give you the hook-up and the wherewithal to do that. They gave you the sources, because they are all interconnected. When they live there, so and so is your friend and he will hook you to your next thing, and the next guy, from there – and you keep it in the family. It's an international hook-up. You're not talking about no small regional thing, it's talking about the whole world. Talking about so and so class of so and so, and he helps you. He either helps you or he hurts you, and that's the way they perpetuate their thing. All that makes me go back to ask what is it that happens with them in childhood that didn't happen with me. Or vice versa. And then I see the whole system, the whole structure. You're talking about architecture and you're talking about forces, economic this and that. Very, very few people at Yale have ever had to struggle for anything. There were very few scholarship students, and even those who were there were middle class.

Q: Is that including blacks?

EW: Yeah, oh, yeah. *Only* blacks got scholarships up there in that class as far as paying full tuition kind-of-thing... It was frightening... you have to deal with the fact that you are afraid. When you go into something which is foreign and people who have power, you feel frightened and you set up certain defence mechanisms. My thing was always "no". It's what I do in every situation... I assume it is a kind of an arrogance. I choose not to deal with you – so I was always alone. They tried to figure out what the hell is he going to be... But I saw that what they did with all that vast machinery and the rest of the shit that they have. Still, they could not produce one thing. They could not produce somebody who's ingenious. Whatever it takes to be operative, they kill it, they defeat you when you first come in – by putting your head into the wrong fucking frame, and it's easy to do that.

The heaviest concept is that everything of any value in art, in the world of the mind, has happened already, has already passed, and so therefore your function is to analyse that, glorify that, learn it and do a parody of it. See what I'm saying? Knock it, do a parody of it, but never ever go into creating your own forms. And that's what they are pushing, that's what they are trying to become – a second-rate version of the British educational thing. The Old Vic repertory thing, you know, trying to do that. All that's cool for them Whities who are not going to do anything anyway, the vast majority of them.

They were gonna take over their father's houses, run their businesses, whatever. Those who were into theatre, they were gonna end up as critics. In the final analysis, what can you do with a Yale degree? Become a critic or a teacher. No one wrote.

Q: Anything with creative worth.

EW: Yeah, short sketches, and they'd sit around and discuss it for two hours. And it was: "You have done well, come on with us, we will help you. We'll make you a celebrity here." They hook you up and you've got your little room, and you move around that. Lot of students going around saying, "Oh, he's very bright." But it's dead. Because everybody that I'd ever seen up there was terrified of one thing, one beast, and that was New York. New York is so close and yet no one had gotten to New York. Everyone was up there to get *away* from New York. They didn't want to deal with it. It was too heavy! It was too many minds here – the antagonism of the whole thing. I already knew that, ultimately, my thing was about New York. My thing was trying to find out as much shit as I can. Try to learn as many different things. I didn't want to turn *anything* off.

One thing that became increasingly clear to me *there*, was the fact that what you had to do was to be able to *feel* people. If you can't do that, then you've failed. I don't give a fuck how much you know, I don't care how bright, how many languages – if you can't put your shit without apology, you're in trouble. The supreme test for me was put it in the community. Don't tell them no Yale nothing. When you put it on in a church, in a basement – people come in and check you out. And what started happening – they would look. And actors were terrified of that because it wasn't safe; you could get hurt, and feelings could get hurt. But we learnt a lot. I'm still riding-off of the shit I learned in New Haven. Basic shit about putting on a play on nothing. *Nothing*. Talking about no lights… We developed a thing where we used the basement of a church, put on the lights of the church – that would be the entrance to a scene. Click. The guy's come over and put on a light, and when the scene is over, turns the light off. All kinds of emergency shit that has been vital and indispensable to me ever since. You come to the city and you learn that all the shit they teach you up there is not for you, was never for you. You were never in the motherfucker when they put it together. You were not. They let me use Yale Repertory Theatre once – all its millions of lights and its gigantic stage, all the acoustics and all the rest of the shit where you have the advantage of countless cats who have passed through there and passed on their shit in terms of the technical thing. Is a monster. They have cats up there who design their ass off – incredible sketches, revolving stages and all kinds of shit.

Q: You never got into that aspect of theatre?
EW: Yeah.
Q: As an architect?
EW: That's what I wanted. I went up there and I saw it. All that was cool, but the thing is – in terms of resources – in actuality I don't have them resources and I'm not going to. I realized *that* when I came back here. Seldom was I going to be allowed to use revolving stages and all the rest, because there was no money out there. My biggest problem was how to do something with nothing. And they didn't teach you that. You're studying economics, world population and this and that but they don't teach you how to grow. But I did learn it in the community. And I got a lot of trouble from the school. They threw me out... because I was doing four plays.
Q: They threw you out of Yale?
EW: Four plays, man, a fucking year – full-length plays with actors from the school. I took every black actor in the drama school and made a company. You see, they have the whole thing stratified: first year, second year, third year, right? First year associate with first year, second year associate with second year, third year you can do something. I said I want everybody that's black to come on in the company and I'll find roles for you, I'll write you shit. And that's how I put it together. But they gave me a lot of static; said I brought prejudice into the school for the first time, that they were a family. They had them doing nothing. They had them holding spears. That's what they did with them niggers there – three years of learning craft to hold a spear. Play Shakespeare and stand up there being a guard. But it's good preparation for the theatre world later on, because that's what they do now. I think I learned that it is possible to put everything together in one – everything I'd been shown were separate disciplines.

That possibility came to me as: What if a cat could take everything and put it into his work. Like, what if he could use his knowledge of architectural principles together with the gift for sound, speech, rhythms and music too, to put it all together into one dynamic thing. There is a possibility of taking off the walls. The image in your house of structure – what is it that makes a room, that essentially defines a room? A door is the most essential with the walls – something to open and close and to separate yourself... Started to take away the divisions, open it up. If you extend it like a scale – move from "C" to the next scale which is "G" – take the wall away, make space infinite; it's that opening up thing. So, that's essentially what I've been trying to do. So the thing becomes: What if you don't write a play about just one thing? Which is a trap which so many people get trapped into. Whatever they do, it's about "dot". What if it ain't about "dot"?

"Dot" is there, but that's just one thing. What if you developed a concept of time which is total, which is complete, which isn't separated by "here we are living in the present" this and that. But there ain't no present because all your fears, all your history, all your mother's fears, is extended, so that time is completely dissolved. So if I'm going to tell a story of somebody doing something, an incident, an instance, I'm putting everything which surrounds it, all the implications so that it isn't just a one single dynamic thing anymore. It can be infinite, in a lot of things. The more you know, the more you can put in there. The more you know, the more the person in the audience sees something. The heavier the work is – if it's really designed like a jewel, if it is really designed to the infinite – the number of sides to it – then the more they get out of it. Those who really, really, know are tripping. Those who just halfway know – the only kind of association they've had was with TV or whatever – okay, they see something. Those who've never seen anything but know their people on the street – the pimps, people who are alive and deal with the street – they see something that's real. Then it should be able to survive time just like the pyramids. Should be able to travel insofar as everyone in the world should be able to appreciate *something* – in terms of the whole universe.

What I'm saying is, *therefore,* it is not about an elite group of people sitting up and digging your work in New York City. Communication that anybody anywhere in the world should be able to look at it and get something, if it's for real, if it really has something that's of worth and it's not just talking about 1960 or 1970, but people be able to come to it at any time and say "Yeah, right." It opens up a lot of things, but it puts a lot of pressure on you, too. That means you have to try and find something which is a determinant behind that which is meaningful. Then everybody and everything becomes symbols of something else heavier. Relate to it musically. It's like each scale is a part of another scale which is larger. There's always a larger scale… and the largest scale is an infinite – that is what they call a chromatic scale which just keeps repeating itself endlessly, multiplying, multiplying, multiplying. That's the universe. That's the whole fucking universe.

Hopefully, that's the point you get to… then you know you're cool, you know it's alright. Then it's hard for you to worry about the petty jealousies and shit. There're very few who really have some kind of worth, so that you remember it. That's the heaviest thing when you rap to somebody and they say "Yeah, I remember you." That's the only thing that kind of cools you out, otherwise you're trapped. You're trapped psychologically and it's a pretty bad trap, because it ages you and makes you very weary. It hurts you. […] If man today uses five, ten percent of his brain full-time, he is *heavy*! It's possible to go through New York City with the mentality of a five year old and not be strained. Follow signs, just go. Some cats' heads can't even use a telephone, you know that? There're cats who can't read but survive, man!

Q: Tell me more about some of the writers who influenced you in your work? Earlier you mentioned James Joyce and Dostoevsky.

EW: Yeah, Joyce was a heavy, heavy influence, throughout the years. The only book I took with me when I split home was Joyce's *Ulysses*. It was the only one I kept coming back to and finding some worth in it. Because the possibilities were limitless. The possibilities of stream of consciousness writing... because what you were looking at was the man's brain. The man was putting his brain out there for you, just diagramming it for you. And that hit me as the freest form – total freedom. But it's incumbent on *Ulysses* to do that. I mean, without stream of consciousness it ain't got nothing to say. It's nice to look into a man's mind, it's nice that that mind got something... the other thing is the cat never stopped learning. The constant learning. He was a big influence on me for that; for getting back at the style, the possibility of a personal style.

Q: Speaking of style and influence, I was looking at William Demby's[11] stuff and I noticed a resemblance between his style and yours.

EW: Demby had a big influence on me. Letting time open. I think he's going to even get better at it later on. There's the possibility of having simultaneous time in the novel, as a kind of opening, liberating thing. I saw it on the stage – it's even heavier. You can have action going on simultaneously where you show what happens with people's lives, *really*. What happens in people's lives is not bop, bop, bop, bop, but whang! Like if we did an outline of this house there'd be so much going on: a murder next door – which happened at the time when this cat and his woman were there – Puerto Ricans yelling in the backyard throwing shit out the window, babies running around the street, man with no shoes – everything is happening!

Q: Do you find living here a source of inspiration to write?

EW: Totally. Totally. I've done more writing here than I've done anywhere in the world. Why? I don't know. There's as much here you want to deal with. Lot of times you're horrified by it; it's too powerful. It's like a drug – you take a drug, it speeds up your consciousness and you go outside and you see everything happening at once. Sometimes it's too overpowering; sometimes it frightens you. Your brain cells short, because there's too much shit! I think that's what becomes insanity. But you *can* deal with it. I think the basic move for me is you start where you are. After all the things I've studied – places, books – basically I come back to start where I am – and you're constantly redefining where you are at a particular time. It's the only way that you can get any sense of balance. There is so much shit moving so quickly you lose contact with who you are.

I don't think you're in as much danger as in some place which is more remote, where there is silence around – the school situation is ideal for that. You begin to believe that you have the greater forces because you're constantly reading, writing... It's much more difficult to do that in something like this, which is moving zip, zip, zip – in which you are as much of a mask as everybody else out there. People are frightened of you, as you are of them – maybe more so. Because when they see me, they don't see eyes. There's possibly one person in this building who knows what I do, that I write, that I have books. He just comes across here sometimes... but for the most part they don't know me. So you can't hide behind your art when you're dealing with this kind of shit; you're out there on the street, as much a part of the painting as you are the painter. And it's dangerous. You can't come back and say, "They didn't tell me that in school, that you could get hurt. You have to run for it all the time. The landlord's breaking down the door because of the rent. There's all kinds of shit going on. The place can go up at any time – you can't get no insurance. Ain't nothing in this place guaranteed.

Q: Don't you ever want to move out of here?

EW: It would be nice, but like how? How could I do that?

Q: I've asked you this question before, but just for the record: Do you ever want to get a play on Broadway? Have a bestselling novel, lot of money, fame, etc.?

EW: It would be nice – doing something you enjoy doing, but I don't see too many possibilities. Most I can hope for is respect. Very seldom do they give you money, because you're presenting their selves to them so realistically, so truthfully and so uncommercially, it's hard for them to deal with it. It would be nice if I could be some place else, but then...

Q: But would you like that? Do you ever aspire to that?

EW: I really can't say. Any place else I doubt I would have the luxury. Where else could I have the luxury of working all day long? After studying all day long doing my music, it's going from that to my writing.

Q: Do you write continuously?

EW: Read. No, but I'm always getting something down – notes for something. It's all in symbols on posters on the wall – and I guess it won't mean anything to anyone else but me. But it's constantly that.

Q: Is that the way you research?

EW: Yeah, man. Essentially what I do is immerse in the environment.

That's the heaviest thing architecture has taught me, that you are what you live in. So I live in art. I live in what I'm working on whatever it is. The play that I'm doing now, I'm living in that play. And whenever I get lost – which is everyday – I look and see the shit on the wall, I see images of myself on the walls, and I say, "Yeah, I wrote that, wrote that and wrote that" and that feeds me some kind of energy and that gets me back into a writing thing.

I've never heard from other writers on this thing, but I know for myself you lose the ability to write; everytime you've written something you lose it. Just because you got through writing whatever, *tomorrow* I might not be able to *write*.

Q: Why is that?

EW: You may have a craft but if you don't do it… it's only of value when it's in motion. I'm a writer only when I'm writing. I'm constantly thinking… and I guess you get to a point where you can practice all the time. You can practice 24 hours a day, damn near, because I'm at a point now where I can practice without the instruments. I don't need the instruments in my hand. I can run it, running shit in my head. I can even do it in my sleep. I can do that with writing a lot of times. I can go to bed thinking of something and I work the whole shit out in my sleep. In the morning I wake up and I got the shit. It's possible to do that but you need to begin – like, you don't do a book *until* you sit down. Step one. Trigger them others out and, okay, it's on. Once you start that then the shit is firing. And, okay, a week, two weeks, three weeks, a year – it don't matter. As long as you keep coming back to that, you've never left the canvas. It's important that you don't leave the canvas – for me anyway. Once you leave it you're dead – it's over. And you begin to have doubts about that – I do. Constant doubts… if I'm not working.

Q: Are there any periods where you have long lapses, not writing?

EW: No. It really doesn't happen. It just happens that maybe I wouldn't be writing *that* thing. Like, I haven't really written a play in damn near three years.

Q: What were you writing?

EW: Novels. Novel, short story and abridgements of other plays.

Q: How many novels have you written?

EW: One. Well, two.

Q: They've not been published? [White's novel *The Rising* was published by Marion Boyars in 1988.]

EW: Right. You know, it came to a point where I said, "What the fuck am I writing more shit for?" These motherfuckers haven't seen half of the shit I've done! So let me deal with getting these plays out there … Now that's why the novel was good; it got me back into a thing.

Q: Which do you prefer, writing novels or plays?

EW: There ain't no prefer. I don't even deal with "like" no more… I guess I got a lot of this shit from studying karate and tai chi.

Q: You know karate?

EW: Yeah, man, one of my loves. Tai chi more. Very simple, slow, steady movement. Concentration essentially, that's what it's about: learning how to continue a motion without stopping flow. How when you create obstacles you create a wall, and you bang your head against it. When you get to the point where there's no wall, where you are liquid, you're water, you're sunlight, you're pure energy – can't nothing stop you. I love the novel because of the fact that it's so personal. Just for the fact that the cat can take the motherfucker home with him, sit down there and wherever I can get him alone, and he comes back – and if I've done my thing well he's gonna come back again. That's good for that, the novel is hip, but I can't see him – that's the drawback. I can't see the dude or the girl who bought the book. But I *can* see the audience, that's the trip with the play. I know immediately what my effect is. That gives you a lot of energy. It's like the church. That's why I love to use that ritualistic thing – why I love the drums, music, because it sets the whole thing, sets the audience out, takes the actors out, it sets every thing off into motion – and the drum is the heartbeat. And everything moves like that. And then people become suspended in time and that's what the audience gets like: sshh. You see them sort of relaxed and that's it, you know, OK, here we go.

The novel is a more solitary thing. You sit home by yourself doing something to a unknown something out there. Step by step you learn your way, you learn in progression. You learn you don't know where you're going. But step by step each thing turns into the next thing. It writes itself. It really does. The theatre is a trip. The theatre is a commercial thing, and you're not alone in the theatre. I've always found as long as I had a play on I was cool. There ain't no "better". I trip. I'm going to work hard running around trying to get actors together, but it's all a trip. I'll learn something from it no matter what the fuck I do, because I'll meet somebody that's going to check me out and help me to the next step.

Q: You've been called a genius. Many people say you're eccentric in certain ways. How do you feel about this? What is a genius?

EW: What I feel is that it is endless. That's what I feel. What I feel is that people try to hook you up and they feel they are giving you an honour, right? But at the same time they're kind of saying, "It's over for you." It's like, where can you go, really? I mean, you can reach a larger audience… but it ain't that! The only thing that they have afforded me is – and I think everybody's mad some kind of way –

they've allowed me to see possibilities. And possibilities to me are endless. Where I found myself is that point, psychologically, where I see that I can flow. I could grow endlessly. There is no object. What I'm trying to do is just move. Just move. That's all. Constantly. If God leaves me with my health and shit… the possibilities are endless. Because art is the only thing where you get better. There's a period of failure of nerve, there's a period of all kinds of psychological pressures on you which just turns you off. But like, man, the possibilities…

Q: Tell me something, Ed, is most of your writing semi-autobiographical, gatherings from your life experiences or just what's happening around?

EW: Right.

Q: Some people say that a lot of the things that you write is about yourself. But I've read read your work, and I've said, okay, but…

EW: But it's something else. I don't care how many experiences you've had that have been of interest, there's got to be more. And what I do is incorporate some of this and some of that. The most immediate things to me, of course, is from first-hand experience, but then there are other people who help me open up things. Whenever I start a thing, my equations the same: "What if?" That's how I start. All my work. What if a man… what if my father were to suddenly appear on the scene? Or somebody who had the power to completely change my life. What then? And then – zip! That triggers something and I'm off to the races and eventually it becomes *The Crucificado* [1973]. The heaviest problem to teach a person is how not to overwrite. How not to take some one thing and give a cat a monologue thirty minutes long! He gets up there, stands up, takes his dick out and then the play goes out the window.

I always try to let the need determine the form it's going to take. A lot of times I don't set out to do something, I let the form determine where it's going to go. It doesn't have to be a novel because of the way I'm going. After the first page or two, I hear a solitary voice. It's a thing getting your ears accustomed to voices, because if you don't hear them, then you can't do it. But then only when you write it are you free. Then only. Because if I don't do that then I'd be carrying that shit around in my head – all them people babbling, warring, and that shit can drive you crazy, man. Sometimes it's at the point where I can't walk the street– I'm walking the street and my focus gets all fucked up. The heaviest thing with yoga – what yoga means is to join the senses – what yoga does to you is after a while you just feel all your muscles, you just know where everything is. Where's my head? My head's up here. I feel my balance right down here in my pit. I'm cool. Seldom do you feel that. It's hard to feel that in the subway. Hard to feel joined. You feel sectioned. You don't feel balanced. You don't feel: "Here I am. Here's this. Here's this space, I'm cool." When you get so that you can do that, man, that's your freedom. It's very important that you get your first note – music has definitely taught me that. It's the same thing with all art. A lot of times your book is destroyed from note *one*, because if that don't go straight up, straight, straight on up into space then it's fucked up.

The first note, by the way, isn't "I". What it is is the title of your work, that's the first note. Some cats can work differently. Some cats work the other way around, after they get through they say, "I think I'll call this..." But for me it's always the first note. What am I doing? I'm doing "Ode to Charlie Parker" – that's what I'm doing. Okay, here I go ... The resonance of the first sound sets me off into a thing where I'm staying with it every single day until I'm through. Because I ain't never leavin' that canvas. I may be out in the street, I may be sitting down with you, but that's constantly bouncing around in my head so I don't lose it – and I can't lose the voices until I'm through. You lose the voices, you lose it. You say, "Goddamn, what happened, I don't hear nothin', where am I goin'?" You go out into the street and people help you... you got to get humble enough to accept their help. Cat comes up to you on the street, and does whatever, he borrows, whatever he does, but what he's *really* doing is saying, "Here, brother, here's the next scene." It's *there*. It's working it out for you. Can you deal with it? Can you get back home and say, "Yeah, okay, thank you." Lot of cats will leave off that shit, they keep looking for resolutions and shit in books. It ain't there. One time when they broke my window, I said, "Goddamn, what the fuck is this, man, I can't even concentrate!" But then noise started to seep in through the broken glass; I started to hear about five or six different kinds of music going on simultaneously and then I got it. I said, "What kind of art do you call this, man?" You call it tenement art that's what it is. It's tenement art in which so many experiences are happening at once. It's almost like God this shit out there and you say to yourself, "God knows how much shit is going on here." But anyway, it works. It works. You impose a certain kind of thing on it because of your craft, you try and keep it as authentic as you can. Again, you don't fight it, you don't create no walls. As long as you're resisting you're in trouble. Sometimes you're with a chick who's fat, and you say, "Goddamn, she's fat!" But you kinda *groove* with that! "This is a skinny girl, let me deal with this..." And you groove. You don't try to make Sharon out of Rita, you know, you just go. I really try to enjoy everything now more than I've ever done in my life before. I haven't gotten any more in terms of a monetary thing, but I guess I have the kind of ease which I have. I don't fight, I don't fight no more.

Q: So if not money, what's your incentive for writing? Is it something that has become second nature or is it something that you find as a continual driving need?

EW: No, that was two years ago. That was what was happening then. And that was a big danger. That was after I did [*The Life and Times of*] *J. Walter Smintheus* and *The Crucificado*...

Q: What was the problem there?

EW: I'd really felt that I had completed everything I could. That there was no place to go – you know, okay, what am I going to do? Just keep doing this act over and over again in terms of how I've got it now? Because people get you into a subtle psychological thing when they ask – "What you doing now, working on another play?" But it ain't that – it's heavier than that. You write, you do whatever, because you want more, you want to see through more. I ain't got it out yet. I know I ain't got it out. How can I have it out when the world is constantly moving? That's done for this, but here is what's happening today – and that takes me to the next step. It's a desire to see new stuff being out there. I find I really like people coming and telling me they saw something, they heard something. It's good – keeps me in contact. I keep seeing – like my strongest thing is faces, women – big influence on me. Like I have a lot of postcards, African shit – to keep images in front of me. Man, like I found out how heavy colour is... I just learned about reggae, man, just beginning to learn where that shit comes from – how it comes out of the church, and I didn't know it until I heard gospel music. You see it when you're ready. I'm just beginning to deal with colours, man. I'm gonna try as much as I can to have bright colours around me. When I'm going into a situation in which people I know are out to drain me – which is one of the heaviest things on you – I always go in colours. Red is one of my favourite shit to go out there – because it feeds me. I constantly want to find new shit which feeds you energy and keeps me going along. If I don't keep moving... there's nothing protecting me, I have no umbrellas over me, really. If I don't keep moving I'm going to perish. So I try to have as many influences around me as possible – positive influences. I guess that's affected my situation with women where I can't get hooked up with one woman. Can't do that. I find it to be a draining thing. I do better with three or four, five women... there's constantly new energies. Everything for me is supposed to be an entrance into a journey which is supposed to be for liberation. Ultimately, that's my goal. *That's* what it's all about – at the end of that tunnel out there – closer to the light. And if you can't do that then you're in a hell of a lot of trouble. You kill yourself, man. You're programmed to kill yourself. You have to. You're programmed to commit suicide.

Q: Did you ever find yourself in that kind of bag? I was asking you earlier if you were inspired by the romantic writers and the whole romanticist trip of writing...

EW: Yeah, and the whole suffering school. I went through a whole hell of a thing with that. But I guess in there you have to put Beckett; Beckett was a big influence on me for that. He is a classic in sustained pain. It's like: "While I'm dying, let me put this down", and it's a long death note. It's volumes and volumes... But it's got to be more than that...

I feel that you can appeal to a lot of people; you don't have to be commercial to do that. I feel like I can do my shit anywhere and have some people feel it; not to say that they're going to give you a hundred thousand dollars. But you've got to have that light in there somewhere, where they see characters... What my whole thing has been, *now* more than ever, is always about that sunlight coming into that somewhere. Somewhere in there there's got to be that sunlight feeding you energy, feeding you light, because it isn't just about a death thing. We couldn't have survived as long as we have feeling that. And we're a classic study, man, in a spiral, a upward thing. I'm going to do that. I like that. I like that.

Q: Someone was asking me how do we describe ourselves in terms of a Caribbean theatre? How do we define what a Caribbean writer is? Or what is Caribbean art? We've been influenced by many sources, but we're still thrust into a unique kind of situation.

EW: Yeah, we do still have something unique about us, and we're all very different. We *are* Caribbean writers but what is Caribbean? What is it essentially? There ain't no set definition. We're all coming from different experiences but yet we all are Caribbean writers... Caribbean-American, Caribbean-*British* – whatever the fuck. But what *is* ours? What language should we write in? We're writing in English – but what we do with it is to turn it around into something else. Jazz – what is jazz? Jazz is all the notes there in European music, every one of them, but we take it and do a whole other thing with it. That's what it's all about. We take the rhythms and we turn them around into something else, because it's an experience which is our own. They're ain't no land which is our own. The Caribbean ain't ours; we were *brought* there! Right? We don't *own* it. We had a ball there in addition to working our fucking asses off – dying like *flies*. But up to now it ain't ours... but yet there's a thing which is: we *belong* there. We belong there because we are comfortable in the environment because it's so similar to our home – our real home.

Q: Do you see yourself getting into writing something dealing with – you did "Scottsboro Boys" – early Black historical heroes?

EW: No.

Q: I know you have a thing about dealing with the past.

EW: That's it. Because there ain't no past. To do that is to *say* it's the past. No, no – what I would much prefer doing is dealing *within* the present. Doing the present tense – taking it back, taking it forward, taking it everywhere you want to go, but don't stay back there. Because to stay back there, you gotta keep trapped into a whole kind of dialogue of the period and it don't become African no more, it becomes *European*. Any hero. Toussaint. You end up with a costume ball. That's where you're going to take yourself. My thing is: no, it ain't dead. None of them cats is dead. They're all walking around. All the spirits is walking around. And we're carrying it perpetually. Everybody's here. Miss Ann[12] is here, the nanny is here, the slave master is here, you're here, we're all here. We keep changing roles. We go back to the Caribbean, we take over his house, we move into his crib, call it our own, we get somebody working for us for ten dollars or twelve dollars a week and we replace roles. But we keep the history, we keep the motherfucker constantly there. It's all historical. Everything is a historical piece. That's how I approach it. For me, what it's really all about is identification. To try to realize more and more from where to where, because only from the where do we see what is – what is now.

What I would like to do… is an international thing. I'd like to able to travel anywhere in the world… I'm going to gamble, though. You have to have the courage to gamble and play. You want to be a player? Let's play. What are you using as your chips? You're using knowledge, man. You're using your art, your skills, your hands – that's what you're putting out there. And I think that it's possible to gamble with that shit and cop the world. I think you can get all over the world without money but with your art, using it as your passport… The hardest thing is to get back home. They don't allow you to do that. It's always a luxury to go back to the island. Go home with no money, they don't want you in there, the nigger who gets up off the street here and says, "I was born in Montserrat, let me go back." I left there when I was five years old. You go back there with your pockets empty, and they don't want you! They want to know what you're going to do. "What are your plans, sir? What are your intentions?"

Q: It would be the same thing if you went back to Africa.

EW: Oh, yeah. You can't be just be-bopping back there. They won't let you do that. But you can with your art; the art will get you back there… as a god. You could possibly get back to that motherfucker as a god – as a god of a kind… Hey, man, I felt something in Jamaica… Shit, there was a kind of respect which I had from kids… take out your horn, you blow, they gather… it's possible, very possible.

Q: That's a nice thought, but what I hear from other Caribbean playwrights is the disrespect of Caribbean governments for the arts.

EW: So then, the heavy question is: Why is art so dangerous, man? Why do they turn it away? It ain't nothin', it ain't no threat, is it? You playin' with yourself, write some shit. Why should they worry? They don't like it to be around. And they are frightened of it, they're frightened of the power of theatre.

Q: At this point I'd like to discuss briefly some of your past work, say, from *Underground* and *The Crucificado*. Incidentally, what is AMDG?

EW: "To the greater glory of God – Ad Maeorum Deo Gratis." [Ad maiorem Dei gloriam]

Q: I remember you wrote it my copy of your book, and you never gave any explanation

EW: A lot of times I like it because that's what – I got into a long rap with Derek Walcott about that. That's how he signs a lot of his shit – from school. That's what they do to you in school.

Q: Talk about Derek a little, I didn't know you ever met him.

EW: Derek is… He's a bright cat, he's multi-talented; started off as a painter and went off into the writing. Important cat. He's important because he's an influence on a things – a lot of things in the islands. I think he's one of the best there is in the Caribbean islands, in terms of style. I think that there is a whole lot of segmented parts in him, but he went through a period of actually caring about people on all levels. I think he saw economics as a hell of a fact and has been able to deal with it in such a way that he's been able to make people respond; so that he isn't just writing political pamphlets… and the best of it is good. It's going to make a lot of other cats' jobs much easier… so it ain't *that* totally weird – of course it is still – to be a writer, an artist, a West Indian artist… because there ain't no respect for that shit. But he's been able to survive and he hasn't stopped. He ain't no young cat. But he's also been fortunate that they've afforded him a kind of luxury to travel – he gets to do work in England, he gets to do work in Paris, Sweden, that kind of thing; he has mobility, the same kind of mobility as Soyinka[13] – another cat who has influenced me.

Q: Wole Soyinka?

EW: Yeah. But it's hard to say where something ends and something begins, but I like him, I like Soyinka and I like Derek. I like Soyinka's [theatre] company more than I did Derek's when he came over here.

Q: What's the difference?

EW: Ah, difference in terms of allegiance and loyalty and all – tradition, I guess. Soyinka's company was absolutely and totally committed to Soyinka. That is to say, Soyinka could rouse his troupe at any hour of the day and night and have them work without complaint, without pause, that kind of shit. Unheard of. What actor can you go to and just pull him out of bed at three in the morning saying, "I want to do scene"? He gets and go and do it. Yeah, they respect him. They really respect him, they respect him as a spirit – kind of visionary spirit. And they're good – they're damn good. They're into what I dig in theatre, which is total. Here is the kind of theatre which I've always dreamt of. That is to say, to have a group of actors who are capable of doing *anything*... mime, pantomime, rhythms, capable of drumming, playing all kinds of shit but complete, complete... I love that. I'd love to have access to some stilt walkers, I'd love access to dudes who could do acrobatics, all kinds of shit, because that mesmerizes an audience... but I also love the way Derek uses poetry, I love his lyricism...

Q: I noticed that both you and Walcott have a similar way of using names which...

EW: Which names the character... he's very lucky, he developed that ear.

Q: Shakespeare used to do that, using a name for the character which *is* the character. In your case, names like Nicknack, Bagatelle... [in *The Burghers of Calais*].

EW: Right, right, all of that, all of that, but that's one level. The other level is – the heaviest thing – is the resonance of the sound, not so much what it means – this is a trick for those who know – but if you can get the rhythm of the sound of the name to mean that character, so that when you hear it – when you hear Gongora [in *The Crucificado*], you see something – the image in your head is of an awkward elephant-like kind of...

Q: Was *Lament For Rastafari* [premiered 1975] a transition from the other type of material that you were doing – going back to your West Indian roots?

EW: *Lament*, yeah, was a transitional thing in that the strength of it took me to certain places. *Lament* got me in union with certain people... and it was important because I didn't try to exploit it... as a result of that I got Rosanna Carter, I got Basil [Wallace], I got Lou [Ferguson], Arlene [Quiyou], as a result of that coming together. And its success opened my head to a whole other thing – which they can't teach you in school – namely to ask: why do you do your work? I went through things when I had plays on at the Shakespeare [New York Shakespeare Festival] and people walking around saying: "Oh, brilliant ..." but then it's over and the theatre is no longer yours; you come back there the next week and they got another set up. Another dude goes in the coliseum. It's over. And if you ain't been able to deal with that then you're going to get hurt. But what it does, the real important thing, what it's all about, is getting a union together, people together, like a church or whatever, but bringing a group of people and you form a circle. That was the first time I even used a circle – the circle warm-up thing. That was the heavy thing... I think Arlene popped, and Liz Van Dyke, she went out, she fainted. See, what the circle is is a spiritual union; we get together, we hold hands, that's all it is. You have the drum in the centre and I would usually walk around and play. If the people have a common force in them then they feel the energy passing from hand to hand. It's a contact, it's a heavy thing, man, because we don't touch each other. And the power was so overwhelming that a lot of people just really – I mean energy – how can you explain energy? How can you say you can damn near see it moving – it was a strong thing, man. We could have walked on water, man! I'm *telling* you, we could have done that shit after that because we were so together as *who* we are for that space of time. I think that was the most energy I'd ever seen in the theatre. It showed me potential, what the possibilities are. I've never lost contact with those people. I mean, here I am sitting down with you tonight in 1976, right? What happened was, you came popping in one day to help out – none of that would have happened if that initial *Lament* didn't happen. There wouldn't have been a second *Lament*, we wouldn't be sitting down here now as we are tight, close, whatever – you know? That's the power of theatre. That's happened with every play that I've ever done insofar as the people come together and, like, we stay together, we influence each other even more. ...[Ed] Bullins has been a hell of an influence on writers and it would blow your mind to the extent when you see how many cats are trying to copy him.

Q: Similarly with Baraka.

EW: Yeah, but Bullins is a better writer than Baraka.

Q: Do you think so?

EW: Yeah, um-hm, for theatre, yeah. I really do. Because I don't think Baraka can write a play, really. I mean, the length of play that he really can do is a one act. He can't do nothing more than a one act, anything else he just extends over a period of time, but in terms of really dealing with characters, really clearly defining different people ... that's not his concern. His concern is to get an essay-like statement across. Bullins is more concerned with the architectural thing than LeRoi [Jones] (Amiri Baraka). And Bullins has been much more influential because his style seems easier, his naturalistic thing, seems easier at first until you try to do it, and all you find is a whole lot of repetitions of the same thing. You find tons of cats writing his shit. His basic situation thing: bar rooms, action in one room ... and they can't do it as well, man, there're very few cats can pull it off!

Q: He's criticized Lennox Brown for not being able to write plays about the ghetto. From what you know of Lennox Brown…

EW: I don't know much of Lennox Brown, so I can't make any statement about Lennox's work more than what I've seen, just the two plays. And from that I'd say the cat's sharp, he's got a mind, he's got an ear. I don't know how much he really knows about the American black character though. I don't think he really knows that cat… He's primarily a Caribbean writer whose experiences are mainly British oriented and is kind of a social critic after being here. Watching it is one thing. It's like reporting in a laboratory certain series of – but he ain't here, really… but that's only from what I've seen.

Q: He writes all the time, continuously.

EW: Yeah, I get that feeling; he works.

Q: You mentioned that you were once interested in existentialism?

EW: Yeah, that has been an influence. Now my thing is, I dig life. I mean, ultimately, I've got to say I dig life and all of the shit that goes along with it because that's what it's essentially all about. The existential writers turn me off because of the fact that they don't deal with life, they deal with one space, one wall, one thing…

Q: What *do* existential writers deal with?

EW: They deal with *existence*. And basically, the existential school has to do with the futility of existence. That's a very important thing. It's important in that it deals with life-death relationships, but yet they don't go nowhere with it.

Q: Cynical, pessimistic?

EW: Ain't goin' nowhere. Essentially, what they say is: "I'm dead, it is dead, we are dead…"

Q: You're talking about people like Sartre?

EW: Sartre, Camus…

Q: Dostoevski…

EW: I think Dostoevski they *made* into existentialist; they put him into the school. Because I think he was coming from something else.

Q: Did you ever read his short story "The Dream of the Ridiculous Man" [1877]?

EW: Ah, yeah, quickly. The short stories I dig. *Notes from the Underground* really turned me on. But most of the existentialist writers – they're into futility and they don't want to deal with life, and that turns me off. There're very few that can do it with a sense of humour. And, basically, I really do believe in such things as health and lack of it in perspective… Certain cats are just into grotesquery and shit. And grotesque is cool as a thing, because it's life, but you don't just dwell on it – and not for its own sake. I know there're cats who go up and cut shit up on stage and whatnot – happenings kind of thing – blood, cut up a goat, for shock. I saw it in Europe, too. You find the artists really going through a heavy trip of: "I'm tired of this whole playing with myself." They get tired of themselves. It was there that for the first time I ran into the kind of peculiar disease where you get sick of your own intelligence. I've never felt that before. Sick of being bright. Used to being so bright that you bore yourself. I mean, I got a lot of ideas for shit but I mean, I wasn't really turned on. I did find it. Some people do. [William] Demby found something to do over there for ten years. I guess a lot has to do with where you are.

Q: How do you see contemporary black writers – novelists, dramatists and non-fiction writers – how do they affect you?

EW: Well, I thank anybody who can give me something to go on with, who has the light. Sometimes you can tell people have a light for you, you can feel it on the page.

Q: Who have you had that from?

EW: I guess I got to say – before Demby, Demby was much later – the first black writer who had any kind of effect on me was Ralph Ellison. I was in high school and the teacher said – a white teacher – "You should really read this, *The Invisible Man* [1952]." I said: "Ain't that a movie?" She said, "No, not that *Invisible Man*, Ellison's *Invisible Man*. And I got it, man, and it blew my mind, in terms of what he did, the way he dealt with time and everything, psychological time, every fucking thing he broke down in there – style. He put a whole lot of different sections together; you can see that it wasn't just one work... because there are certain structures that are put together like a play. He tried to get into the social thing with the Communist party and whatnot – he took it a step further. He took it a step further than just social analysis and put it in a weird Kafkaesque kind of thing. His heaviest metaphor was that operating room where they try to take the nigger's rhythm away from him; hooked him up on the couch and tried to literally take his rhythm away from him with this machine. And then I came to the question of: "Well, wow, where can a cat go beyond that?" Once you done that much... and I was looking to him for some more things and it wasn't there, because the man who had written that was someone else. Ellison was my teacher at NYU, that man is not the cat who wrote *The Invisible Man*.

Q: What's he like?

EW: He was very conservative, very black bourgeois. You come to certain periods where you have to deal with something, so either you make a transition or you might have failure of nerve, or you say: "I can't do no more in this." He learned how to deal with this thing by coming into the whole system, becoming the man of letters; he got several book awards, he started making speeches about the American novel, how he considers himself a part of the great thing from Hawthorne and Edgar Allen Poe. I keep saying you're not a writer until you are writing. But he influenced me a great deal.

So, you were asking me how these writers affect me. I say, if there's a light you take it, you take the warmth from that. You don't get discouraged, you don't ask, "Who's he married to, is it a white woman now? Is he moving to…" I take the best I can. You get your feelings hurt and you stop, you run into a wall! It's not about the wall, it's about light. God knows who I'm going to be ten, fifteen years from now. So I just deal with the work. Right now I feel we're going through a lot of cycles, we just keep repeating cycles. We go back over the Renaissance, we do the same things over again, we have to prove ourselves all over again every ten years and then we go into a period of complete illiteracy and then we come back with a mediocre novelist and make whatever for a minute – rather than saying, "Oh, well, listen, we did that 1930." But it's cool. It's all cool because it's all running on some kind of middle. The main thing is not to get hung up in time. You *are* living in 1976 and not 1936.

Q: I want to get into some your published work. Richard Harrier, who wrote the forward to *Underground* says: "The most sophisticated of the plays is *Fun in Lethe*." I'd like your comment.

EW: I haven't read it since it was published. Well, that's how he feels. I guess he says that because of the structure of the play… I took a form which I used to call "The Feast of Misrule". It's a literary form. What I'm essentially saying is the clown is an honourable clown. In Italian theatre they got him in different kinds of coloured suits. That's how I saw the cat, running around Europe – he's in exile, man, he knows he's in exile. He keeps trying to make contact with all these different forces; he loves nobody – what can he do with that? He uses and he's being used. It ends with the fellow on the train coming out of there, saying that he's passed the night without incident, solitary, without incident; he's looking at all these grey industrial towns… It's that desolation that I was trying to get at.

Q: I'm quoting from Harrier, again, just to get your comment. He says: "Perhaps the play with largest range of focus is *The Burghers of Calais*. Here the writer is closest to his fellow victims, but also ready to place them in the broadest stream of the human race."

EW: I guess what he meant there is the fact that it's a play within a play, where the writer appears as an actor. It puts him right there in the drug prison with the rest of them. It's difficult, because a lot of times when you read it you don't realize that you've got two sets of realities to deal with. Not only are you going back into the 1930s, but then you've got to come out into the world of Lexington, Kentucky, drug prison too. Here are some junkies, ex-offenders, putting on something, and how do they feel about this play, how do they feel about the actor-writer? Because he's there and he's doing his whole thing, he's controlling it by way of the Speaker, but yet he's a prisoner there and they don't like him because he's still got his art. He's still a prisoner but he's got his art which makes him aloof from the rest of the gang. Every time I've done that play I've learnt some shit.

Q: *The Scottsboro Boys*, that was taken from a true case. Charlie Fuller[16] did a play on the same case... but he kept close to the real thing...

EW: But the reason Fuller did was because he got it from here. Fuller has been dead into my work for about five years now – I know that for a fact because he's told me. I had never seen him before that. But that's his thing. He won't do the many-levelled thing or surrealistic thing that I do; his thing is the historical thing. He likes historical black characters

Q: You don't.

EW: No, man, I only like them – as I said before – in relation to the present. It's heavier, you see, the effect is heavier. It is heavier if you are not writing about a *case*, when you write about a case there's a distance. When you write about some outrage which has happened in history there's a distance; when you put yourself in there you get a whole *other* thing happening. You can do all that *plus*. You can get all the historical data out there but yet you get something else happening, you get another dimension because now you have made it real. So therefore you can see yourself walking around in that drug prison; in addition to telling this tale, you can tell the tale of the drug-ridden man... there are about three different levels you can have happening. You can make the indictment much more piercing because of the fact that you don't take the role of: "Oh, here's another case of how poor people have been whipped." But when you take it and play with it on so many different levels and you laugh and you mock them – that is black comedy! And I think your effect is much fiercer. And it ain't no one-dimensional thing.

Q: What about film, have you ever thought about doing screenplays?

EW: Yeah, yeah. I have done some, but having run into a lot of walls and people not wanting to take a chance, or telling you how they want to reinterpret your work, takes you out. For example – perfect kind of thing – anybody who would do that kind of play, *Scottsboro Boys* or *Burghers*, would say, "That's beautiful, but let's not call it "Burghers"; nobody knows what the hell that's about; that's a piece of sculpture by Rodin with a whole bunch of people hooked together by chains, that's not important."

Q: And you got that title from that sculpture?

EW: From that specific work in which a group of cats are linked together. But the thing that turned me on about it was each character in that thing was different… a group of people chained together but yet each character was totally distinct in pain, and the movements of their hands, the detail work, incredible detail. So that turned me on, and I did it because it put a resonance in my head and I knew that I wanted to do that. Let me see Bagatelle's mother… Let me think about this white chick who lied on these cats, who brought all these cats so much grief for so many years – what was she really about? She was just a dumb Southern Belle; what was she wearing? She had to be wearing the shit out of the stores at that period, she had to be dealing with JC Penny and the whole fucking trip that they had down there, the bargain-sale-thing, the flower-print dress and the yellow hat… so that set off a whole – she was *real* for me!

Q: Harrier says of *The Mummer's Play* that "It comes straight at you like a song." I notice you use a lot of symbolism in your work. In "The Wonderfulle Yeare," the spelling of the title is symbolic.

EW: Yeah, I wanted to take people's heads into that, make them think about the Year of the Plague… the Black Death. Because I like the way they use the word "Wonderfulle" for it – anything which is incredible.

Q: How old were you when you did that?

EW: I couldn't have been no more than twenty-three.

Q: Were you still in that romantic phase?

EW: Ah, yeah, I was coming out of it. I was much more cynical, much more cynical. It's interesting because a lot of stuff was happening – time was a very heavy thing. You come to a certain awareness… Certain things I can't get published now. I was lucky at that period that they were out there. They put them out then.

Q: You said you did two novels?

EW: Yeah, this [*The Rising*] is the second one, the first one I'm not going to do anything with it all except use as ideas for other stuff.

Q: Do you think you can get it sold?

EW: Get it published? Yeah, man, I think that if you are determined enough to do it, yeah.

Q: And understand the market.

EW: Well, understanding the market is one thing … the market changes…

Q: Have you ever thought of just whipping out something like a *Jaws* [Steven Spielberg film, 1975], something that would make you a million dollars so that you could just kick back and write the more serious work?

EW: I've talked a lot about knocking something out and then sitting back and… yeah, it would be nice. No, it scares me, man, for the very simple reason I don't know what happens to your head after that. You see what I mean? It would be nice to believe you could do something like that and then ease off and say, "Well, *now* let me return…" I don't think it works like that. I think it's damn hard to just write one – if you write one, why not write two? And that's the problem. There ain't no stopping it and there ain't no return. Another thing that I think is hard to know – something turns you on, man, to make you create, and it's a light that I've been lucky to have. A lot of times I say, "Damn, I wonder what my next thing is I'm about to go into?" Sshh! Something happens… I'm out here, my mind says, sshhh! It moves, it moves. If I fuck up, I think that light goes out. Like a jet on a stove it goes out. And if it goes out I don't know how to light it again. If I knew some way… if I shot, if I snorted, if I drank – I don't know no formula for it. You see what I'm saying? If you fuck up and you let that light go out I don't know no way of putting that light back on again. Psychologists, everybody, have been trying to figure out what the fuck it is that makes somebody creative…

Q: Which brings me to another question, which is not a very original one, about the revolutionary and the artist. An artist as a visionary is one step removed from a revolutionary who is the person who actually puts the thing into action.

EW: Yeah, well, all that's hip, but it's just a matter of what you need to use psychologically to move you. A revolutionary, he has to think "I have to think that I am one step removed from the artist, I'm out here in the actual pragmatic world."

Q: Is he actually thinking in those terms?

EW: Yeah, he probably does. I mean, a lot of cats do. I know it's necessary for a lot of cats. I think more probably critics seem to think that of people who are out there doing. "Well, what am I now, am I one step removed from the revolution?" It's the critic who sits down and says, "You know what so and so did here?" "You know what Malcolm did over here?" It's just whatever you need to get you moving, man. I think guns and books, man. They sell the guns, they make the guns; you go out there; you could hurt yourself, you could blow yourself up, you can kill somebody. I don't think you can get as much effect from a gun as you can from getting your work out there; getting it out there so that it stays, so that it travels all over the world and has some validity to people much later on. It's a hell of a thing twenty years later somebody takes your book and you could be an influence for something in another country thousands and thousands of miles away – and it's *outlawed*! It is as outlawed twenty years from now in Africa as it is when you wrote it here! The revolutionary is good, I think he *is* the artist – I think they're one and the same. It's just a matter of using different weapons at a particular time.

Q: Tell me about why Charlie Parker is so important to you?

EW: Well, he was surely rewriting, restructuring music, restructuring chords, the use of chord structure, progressions… the same way Debussy and any of them cats were doing at the time. The real danger is the fact that he's alone. It makes a big difference – it's a different thing to be out there in a symphony orchestra, sitting up there with something written out and that's your umbrella there. It's another thing when a cat gets up there alone and creates, makes something flow, putting it together in his head. But it means nothing until much later on unless it gets recorded and it's documented – that's the thing, that documentation. And it has validity twenty, thirty years. That's the test, that's the test. Bird done made it. Ain't no question about that. He won. He won while he was alive and he won after that. It still stands up as *heavy*!

Q: Has anyone ever written a play about him [*Ode to Charlie Parker*, premiered 1973] besides yourself?

EW: Sure. Some white boys. Commercial though. They all get into it.

Q: I mean more serious stuff.

EW: No. Because you can't, you almost can't. It's almost taboo. Something about it which is of itself so… exploitative. The tendency is to rip it off because his life had just so much happening in it that it's difficult to do it and not get into the women involved – that kind of shit – and get away from the music. Woody King has been talking about doing my play. Okay, what he would like to do is have much more music in it and get away from what it is I'm trying to say. Because what I'm doing, again, is not about one thing, it ain't about Charlie Parker *only*. It ain't about "Here's the Life and Times of Charlie Parker", it's about the whole era, the whole renaissance, writers, everybody, because they're all in one character – one character. And don't deal with it in terms of a past thing, again, but deal with it as the present. Don't open with: here we are sitting down in the 1930s, 1940s, 1950s. Deal with 1970s. Take it *back*, have some cats sitting in a park now; they're talking about their lives right now, and then from that comes out these spirits and then the characters dissolve and it ends right back in the present where you are.

That's why it's hard to get a film like that… because they want to know what is it about, what can we sell? "We like your ideas, we like all ten of your ideas, let's have *one* of them and put that out there." The average cat can't deal with ten at a time, you can shortcircuit his brain, so let's clean your work up. That's what they'll do in the cutting room, man, even if they let you shoot it the way you want to, but what they do in cutting the flick… boop! Put these frames together and you got a whole new flick. When you come and you're sitting down for the screening you say, "What? We didn't even shoot it like that!" That's what they can do and you can't do nothing about it because the cat done put up the money on it entirely. Once the film is done, it's done; you've signed a contract; it's their film – what you goin' to do? Go burn the film? They own it. If somebody gave you a hundred and twenty-five thousand dollars, you tell them, "Here, man, go ahead, please, go, take my script! Do whatever you want to do, make 'Alice In Wonderland' out of it if you want to!" It's hard. It's hard. But that's not to deny the power of film or to say that it's an irrelevant medium or anything like that.

End Notes

1. LeRoi Jones, see Amiri Baraka, interview with Lennox Brown, note 4.
2. The Last Poets were a group of African American poets and musicians formed in 1968. They made a number of LP albums in the 1970s including *The Last Poets* (1970); *This is Madness* (1971); *Chastisement* (1973); *At Last* (1974); *Delights of the Garden* (1977).
3. Archie Shepp (1937-) is a tenor saxophonist who bridged the tonal freedom of the "New Thing" with a compositional gift drawn from Duke Ellington in such fine albums as *Four For Trane* (1964); *On This Night* (1965); *Fire Music* (1965); *Mama Too Tight* (1966). In the 1960s and 70s, Shepp was a highly politicised figure in the Black Power arts movement and author of the plays *The Communist* (1965) and *Lady Day: A Musical Tragedy* (1972).
4. John Coltrane (1926-1967) was the outstanding saxophonist of the 1960s whose modal harmonic explorations changed the shape of jazz, and whose quartet of McCoy Tyner, Jimmy Garrison and Elvin Jones produced some of the very greatest music of the 20th century, including *A Love Supreme* (1965).
5. Dave Burrell (1940-) is an outstanding African American jazz pianist who has worked with Archie Shepp, Marion Brown, David Murray and as a solo artist. His most celebrated recording is probably *Windward Passages* (1979).
6. Sun Ra (1914-1993) was a highly innovative and theatric bandleader, pianist, composer and record producer, a pioneer of Afro-futurism whose Arkestra offered listeners a different cosmic reality – from Saturn. Some of his best albums include *Jazz in Silhouette*, *The Heliocentric Worlds of Sun Ra* and *The Magic City*. See John F. Szwed, *Space Is the*

Place: The Lives and Times of Sun Ra. (New York: Da Capo Press, 1998).

7. Marion Brown (1931-2010) was an African American jazz alto saxophonist, who played with Archie Shepp, John Coltrane and led his own group. He made several fine albums such as *Three for Shepp* (1966), *Afternoon of a Georgia Faun* (1970) and *Gichee Recollections* (1973).
8. Sunny Murray (1936) was the foremost pioneer of a free-form jazz drumming style. He was central to bands led by Albert Ayler and Cecil Taylor.
9. Cecil Taylor (1929-) is the most important innovator in jazz piano since Art Tatum. His percussive style brought the jazz tradition into a connection with contemporary classical music. Taylor's epoch-changing albums at the time of the interview included *Nefertiti, the Beautiful One Has Come* (1962); *Unit Structures* (1966) and *Cecil Taylor Unit* (1978) and *3 Phasis* (1978)
10. Sam Rivers (1923-2011) was a multi-instrumentalist reed player and flautist who was a fine composer and mentor to the post-Coltrane generation through his jazz loft, Studio Rivbea, in the 1970s in New York.
11. William Demby (1922-2013) is an African American novelist who lived in Rome for many years. His novels included *Beetlecreek* (1950); *The Catacombs* (1965); *Love Story Black* (1978) and *Blueboy* (1979).
12. Miss Ann – the female counterpart to Mr Charlie – the imperious white woman, or the black woman acting white.
13. Wole Soyinka (1934-) is the Nigerian playwright and poet, awarded the Nobel prize in 1986, and author of such plays, at the time of the interview, as *The Swamp Dwellers; The Lion and the Jewel; The Trials of Brother Jero; A Dance of the Forests; The Strong Breed; Before the Blackout; Kongi's Harvest; The Road; The Bacchae of Euripides; Madmen and Specialists; Camwood on the Leaves; Jero's Metamorphosis; Death and the King's Horseman* and *Opera Wonyosi*.
14. Rosanna Carter, Lou Ferguson and Arlene Quiyou, Olivier Stephenson, William "Bunny Rugs" Clarke (who would later become lead singer for Third World) were some of the actors in the 1974 premier of *Lament for Rastafari*; Rosemary Stewart was the director.
15. Ed Bullins, see interview with Derek Walcott, note 2.
16. Charles H. Fuller, author of *A Soldier's Play* and the musical play *The Scotsboro Boys*.

INDEX